FROM **MODERN** PRODUCTION TO IMAGINED **PRIMITIVE**

FROM **MODERN PRODUCTION**

TO **IMAGINED PRIMITIVE**

The Social
World of Coffee
from Papua
New Guinea

PAIGE WEST

Duke University Press
Durham and London
2012

Duke University Press gratefully acknowledges the
support of Barnard College, which provided funds
toward the publication of this book.

Printed in the United States of America on acid-free
paper ∞

Designed by Heather Hensley

Typeset in Arno Pro by Keystone Typesetting, Inc.

Library of Congress Cataloging-in-Publication Data
appear on the last printed page of this book.

For J. C. Salyer

(with whom I hope to have coffee
every morning for the rest of my life)

CONTENTS

TABLES

ACKNOWLEDGMENTS

It is hard to decide when the research for this book really began. I have been thinking about coffee production in the Eastern Highlands Province of Papua New Guinea since I first arrived in Maimafu village as a graduate student in 1997. I initially went to Maimafu to study environmental conservation projects as a form of economic development, but it became quickly apparent that coffee production was the only economic development in Maimafu. In late 1998, I asked my friends Lucas Malewa and Philip Ine what I should study as a post-PhD project. They both said that it might be interesting to think about how coffee production, Christianity, and gold prospecting had changed socio-ecological life in their village. When I returned to Maimafu in April 2001, although my ultimate goal was to finish collecting data for my first book project, I began to collect some of the data presented in this book. Initially I wanted to write about coffee, gold, and souls as three commodities that have transformed social, economic, and ecological life in Maimafu. In the end that was too much, so I decided to focus on coffee.

I have returned to Maimafu specifically to conduct research on coffee production several times since that trip: in 2002, 2003, and 2005 during the North American academic breaks, during the fall term of 2004, and during the spring term of 2007. I've also conducted research for this book in Goroka, Lae, and Port Moresby (Papua New Guinea), Cairns, Brisbane, and Sydney

(Australia), London (England), Hamburg (Germany), and New York, Charlotte, and San Diego (United States) between 2002 and 2010.

After all the interviews, participant observation, archival work, and other forms of research that went into this book, it is really to Lucas and Philip that I owe the largest debt. At the time of the discussion I describe above, in the late 1990s, coffee was not a fashionable topic in anthropology. This has since changed drastically, and coffee has become a much discussed and often studied commodity in anthropology, sociology, and geography. I'm not sure that I would have focused on coffee production, distribution, and consumption for my second major research project in anthropology had Lucas and Philip not urged me to do so. The topic is extremely far-reaching spatially and disciplinarily. "Tracking globalization," to use Robert Foster's wonderful phrase, is hard work intellectually and physically. I hope that this book is close to what Lucas and Philip had in mind on that late afternoon in 1998 as we were sitting on a hill above one of Philip's father's coffee groves.

Along these same lines, I owe more than I can ever repay to Brian Greathead. I could not have conducted the research for this book without Brian's introductions to people in the global coffee industry or without his keen insights into the industry's history in Papua New Guinea. Brian opened his home and his deep knowledge of coffee to me, but more than that he allowed me to get to know his cheeky, sly, insightful, and deeply kind personality.

The Wenner-Gren Foundation for Anthropological Research funded the majority of the research that I present in this book. They have been incredibly supportive in this and other projects, and I thank them for all that support. Elizabeth Boylan, provost of Barnard College, and her office also provided research funds for this project. I could not have done this work without the provost's financial support and her willingness to allow me to accept faculty fellowships from the American Association of University Women and the American Council of Learned Societies that allowed me to have a yearlong leave from teaching in 2004–5.

In Goroka, Debra Wright and Andrew Mack provided me with an office, a place to lodge, wonderful colleagues, and exceptional students. I could not have carried out the research in Maimafu village without their logistical support or the research in Goroka without their help in arranging transportation and ensuring my safety. I also enjoyed tremendously the chance to spend time away from coffee-related work with friends and colleagues in Goroka. In particular I want to thank Anna Koki, Anakin, Kamaea, Miriam

Supuma, Banak Gamui, Leo Legra, Muse and Sandie Opiang, Michael Kigl, Jephet Kol, and Paul Igag. I would also like to acknowledge and thank all the guards at Pacific Estates in Goroka. These men are too numerous to name, but without their keen eyes and ears for spotting trouble in parts of Goroka, I would not have been able to move so easily around town on foot.

As always, Mal Smith's enthusiastic support of my research is much appreciated. Mal helped with this project in ways too numerous to enumerate, but it bears mentioning that one of his main ways of supporting research in the Eastern Highlands province, of which he was governor during the majority of my research for this book, was to encourage it and then to make sure that every possible avenue that he had any control over was open to the researcher. Any mention of the geography of the Highlands, the Highlands Highway, and the movement between villages, towns, and the coasts is based on what Mal taught me about the geography of the country.

The people of Maimafu village have put up with a nosey anthropologist for fifteen years now, and there are no words to express my gratitude to them for their support. I would especially like to thank Jonah and his parents, Semi and her mother, Little Daniel and his brilliant new wife, Bill and Tene Pone, as well as Ine, Robert, Sarau, Moyha, Daniel, Waymane, Betty, John Jerry, Naomi, Kusiomo, Kalasaga, Seahnabe, Karo, Wallis, Thomas, Hamasabi, Mybo, Kepsi, Anna, Tom, Carol, and Naison. I want to thank Kobe and Agua, who both passed away in 2006, for all the things they taught me about how to cultivate both plants and relationships, why the production of food is the production of life, and how coffee changes women's worlds.

I would also like to thank all of the men and woman that I interviewed in and around the "World Trade Center" coffee market on the backside of the main market in Goroka. Many of these people—who were all total strangers—spent valuable time with me and were patient with my somewhat long interviews. In addition, I want to thank all of the people at the various coffee factories, export companies, shipping and transport companies, and bulking companies in and around Goroka and Lae whom I spent time with and interviewed.

Many of the people in positions of leadership in the coffee industry in Papua New Guinea, England, Germany, and the United States have been incredibly supportive during my research. In particular I wish to thank Craig McConaghy. Craig has been beyond helpful in terms of connections with people in the Goroka coffee world and people working with New Guinea coffee in Hamburg, Sydney, Cairns, Brisbane, and London. He has also allowed me to test out ideas and arguments about the coffee world on him and has been generous in his comments, critiques, and suggestions. I would also like to thank Steve Teisl. I could never have carried out the United States portion of this research without his contacts, ideas, and enthusiasm for the project.

The access that members of the Goroka coffee community gave me during the research for this project was wonderful. People were not only happy to talk about their industry and spend time answering my endless questions, they were also incredibly kind. Each interview ended with suggestions for more people to interview and offers for help with other aspects of the project. I will never be able to express the gratitude I feel. Coffee industry participants in London, Hamburg, Sydney, Brisbane, Cairns, and San Diego were also very supportive of this project, and I thank them. In the global coffee world I would especially like to thank David Hannon, Amanda and Mick Hannon, John Fowke, Gerry Kapka, Ian and Lesley Matthews, Grant and April Jephcott, Nandu Namaiah, Terry Shelly, John and Cynthia Lehey, Jon Edwards, Col Williams, Jeff Lewis, Brian Owen, Henry Ame, Ricky Mitio, Bhan and Chandra Singh, Able Filiman, Sinake Giregire, Apare Goso, Arkipede Wamiri, Lucas Ambiyo, Huk Awute, Yerma Taylor, Fero Yasona, Pippa and Brendan Ellis, Brendan Moon, Lachlan Hoskins, Arthur Jones, Alex Scholton, Simon Wakefield, Mick Wheeler, Adrian Jones, Michael Lachner, Jorge Tiemeier, Jens Janecki, Andy Fawks, and Miriam Peters. The Coffee Industry Corporation in Goroka was very helpful and provided me with access to important economic and agricultural data.

Thomas Pierce, Patrick Gallagher, Scott Andrews, Jesse Hicks, Rebecca Feinberg, and Jordan Keenan helped me see Papua New Guinea through fresh eyes over the past few years, and I am extremely grateful to them all for their fascinating insights, their new perspectives, and their intrepid spirits.

While I was writing an early draft of this book I sat in on David Harvey's seminar "Reading Capital" at the City University of New York Graduate Center. I want to thank David for allowing me to sit in on the course. Kathy Creely, at the Melanesian Archive of the University of California, San Diego, helped tremendously with the archival research for this work, and the Friends of the Library funded a portion of my archival work. I thank them for that generosity. I also want to thank Nadia Abu El-Haj, Martine

Bellen, Andy Bickford, Aletta Biersack, James Carrier, Molly Doane, Robert Foster, Bruce Knauft, Brian Larkin, Shirley Lindenbaum, Beth Povinelli, G. S. Quid, and J. C. Salyer for their comments and suggestions on drafts of this book. Khi'a Fulton gave wonderful departmental assistance. Robbie Ethridge, Andrew Bickford, Trey Ollman, Ashley Parham, Lillian Martin, Michael Moore, John Aini, Fiona Weiba, Miriam Supuma, Deb Wright, Andy Mack, Paul Thomas and everyone at PSC, Debra Minkoff, and Silke Aisenbrey provided friendship and social support during the years it took to complete this book. As it neared completion Noah Aisenbrey Minkoff joined us in the world, and he makes that world better, just by his joyful presence.

Amanda Himmelstoss has worked as my research assistant for the past four years, and she has tirelessly fetched books and articles from the library, edited drafts of chapters, and listened to me as I have tried out arguments. For this, and for her constant reminders about the joys of youth and her hilarious observations about life, I thank her.

Colin Felsman worked as my intern during the editorial phase of writing and provided me with some of the most insightful comments, commentary, and critiques I have ever received. Florence Durney conducted several literature searches for me during the final year of writing, and I could not have completed the book without her help.

I wrote several chapters of this book when I was a resident at the Villa Serbelloni, the Rockefeller Foundation's study center in Bellagio, Italy. The foundation's generous fellowship allowed me to spend thirty days thinking and writing without the routine interruptions of life and labor in New York City. It also allowed me to meet and spend time with some of the most extraordinary academics and artists I have ever encountered. Pilar Palacia and the staff at the Villa Serbelloni also deserve special thanks.

I presented portions of this book at the Yale University Agrarian Studies Seminar in 2007, the Workshop on Environmental Politics at the University of California, Berkeley, in 2008, as a University Lecturer at the University of Wisconsin in 2009, and at the Columbia University School of Law in 2010. It was a privilege to be invited to take part in these events, and the book benefits from the careful readings and insightful comments from people at these four institutions.

Portions of this book appeared in the journals *Antipode* and *American Anthropologist*. I thank both journals for permission to reprint that material here. Unless otherwise stated, all photographs in this book are my own.

Valerie Millholland, my editor at Duke University Press, Miriam Angress, and Fred Kameny deserve special thanks for all that they have done to make writing, editing, and peer review a satisfying process. I also thank the anonymous reviewers for their insightful comments and their willingness to read multiple drafts of the book.

A note on the title of this book: In 1999, while I was writing my dissertation, I read a new book by Bruce Knauft, *From Primitive to Postcolonial in Melanesia and Anthropology,* one of the books to have most inspired my work as an anthropologist. In it Knauft traces the ways anthropology has worked in tandem with other forces to produce a particular view of Melanesia in general and Papua New Guinea specifically. He shows clearly that anthropological imaginings are at least to some extent at the roots of both the extraordinarily troubling images of the primitive and the more subtle images of profound otherness that endure even in the face of a fully postcolonial Melanesia, and perhaps even, Knauft argues, a postmodern, Melanesia. Yet in his analysis of these images and their history, he refuses to discount the real difference that exists in Melanesia. He affirms that the ways of life and living found there are distinct and have value. He manages to show, beautifully, that difference can exist alongside homogeneity and that anthropological analysis can be done in a way that is geared toward knowledge but not steeped in power. The title of this book is clearly a play on his title. I hope that I can contribute even a fraction of what Knauft has contributed to the discipline.

This book was written to the musical notes of New Order, Run DMC, and the Ahn Trio.

As always, J. C. Salyer, Pat West, Ellen Tom, and Daisy Henry deserve much of my gratitude. In addition to showing unyielding spousal support for this project, J. C. helped me work out some of the theoretical arguments about consumption, distribution, and production. This book is richer because of his brilliant theoretical mind and his nuanced readings of many of the texts I draw on for this work. My life is richer because of his ridiculous sense of humor and his ability to see beauty in this troubled world.

Pat's lived experience over the past ten years gave this book its focus on labor. Because of what she was put through as labor, she reminded me in important ways that powerful people for political reasons often work very hard to make labor invisible and that age and gender are constant points of discrimination in labor politics. She is, as always, my inspiration.

Ellen's friendship is a gift of such meaning and value that I cannot imagine how I might ever reciprocate. I could not have carried out any of my research in Maimafu without her, and I could not have begun to understand Gimi being-in-the-world without her keen anthropological mind.

Daisy, my grandmother, is a constant source of joy in my life, and I feel her in my heart and brain with every ethnographic word I write and with every joke I make.

My writing of this book has been bracketed by the deaths of three of the most important people in my life, John Clark Salyer III, Professor George E. B. Morren, and Bethshielah "Betsy" Tom-Jonah.

One of the first things that John and I talked about when I met him, after I was already married to his son, was coffee. He was a self-taught, late-in-life gourmet cook and champion buyer of unusual products. On my first visit to his house he purchased New Guinea coffee for me. Over the years morning coffee in his bright, sparse kitchen became a sort of meeting ground for two people who did not have anything in common except John's son, a love of coffee, and brash, opinionated personalities. He was the only father I have ever known, and every day I wish that I could have had more time with him.

I first met George Morren in the pages of his 1986 book, *The Miyanmin: Human Ecology in a Papua New Guinea Society.* I read it, along with Roy Rappaport's *Pigs for the Ancestors: Ritual in the Ecology of a New Guinea People,* when I was a senior psychology major at a tiny college in South Carolina. These books opened up the world of anthropology to me. George, when he accepted me as his graduate student in 1995, opened up the possibility of a life as an anthropologist. I will miss his practiced eye rolling, his humorous e-mails, his deep kindness, and his silly vests tremendously.

Betsy was born in Goroka in 1999 and spent the majority of her short life in Maimafu village. The last time I saw her was in 2005, when I dropped off a student in Maimafu and spent the day with Betsy's mother, Ellen. My last memory of Betsy is of her little, round face, as she excitedly told me about walking to the airstrip to meet me, and her sly grin as she got around to inquiring about what I had brought her from town. Betsy loved me, and she is the only child that has ever loved me in the way that only children can, unconditionally and with true, boundless joy. By calling me *Nano* (mother), the thing she called all her mother's sisters, she also brought me into the world in important ways. For Betsy I was not "fictive kin," because I was there from her earliest memories as her mother's sister, and not someone she had to find a place for in an already existing total system of kinship and obligation. If I sometimes paint an overwhelmingly beautiful picture of Maimafu in this book, or in other work, that picture should always be clouded by Betsy's death. She died of malaria because there is no health care in Maimafu and because her parents, although they grow coffee and make a small profit from it yearly, could not raise enough money to get her to the hospital in Goroka. I cannot believe that she is no longer in this world.

1 | THE WORLD OF COFFEE FROM PAPUA NEW GUINEA

One way that scholars have tried to understand the social effects of global capitalism has been by looking at the production, circulation, and consumption of commodities. Coffee is a commodity par excellence that has been uniquely important to Papua New Guinea and its citizens historically and currently, particularly in the Highlands Regions of the country.[1] Historically, coffee spread through capillary social networks and in many ways grafted onto and complemented existing Melanesian ideas of personhood and sociality. Today new neoliberal forms of capitalism have brought fair-trade, organic, and other coffee-certification schemes to Papua New Guinea—schemes which impose fully formed prescriptive regimes of governmentality at odds in many ways with Melanesian ways of seeing and being in the world. These same forms of capitalism have brought into being the specialty coffee market, a market in which coffee is valued, bought, and sold based on images of coffee producers and locations of production. This book uses coffee to understand *labor*, and the multiple forms it takes in our global economy, *value*, and the ways it is produced today with regard to both objects and human lives, *images*, and how specific ideas about nature and culture are made to adhere to objects, and the *politics* and *material effects* of the circulation of images of Papua New Guinea and the people whose labor brings Papua New Guinean coffee into being. With this, the book examines the world of coffee from Papua New Guinea, including its political ecology, social history, and social meaning, in order to contribute to anthropological discussions about circulation and neoliberalization. The book explores these issues ethnographically.[2]

Senses of Coffee

Coffee is a plant native to Ethiopia, which has, over the past two thousand years, become a commodity powerhouse producing physical spaces and human subjectivities on a global scale.[3] *Coffea*, the genus that encompasses the multiple species of coffee, is part of the enormous family *Rubiaceae*, which includes six hundred genera and about ten thousand species (Clifford and Wilson 1985; Wrigley 1988). Within the genus *Coffea* are ten species, two of which—*Coffea arabica* and *Coffea robusta*—have radically transformed ecologies and societies in the equatorial and subtropical parts of the world.[4] Today 25 million people in sixty countries produce 12 billion pounds of coffee a year, and each year coffee generates retail sales of over $70 billion, the vast majority produced in tropical countries and 75 percent of it imported by the United States, Europe, and Japan.[5] In the world market of commodities only petroleum has greater monetary value and is traded more frequently than coffee (Donald 2004).

Coffee grows on trees that thrive at altitudes between 1,800 and 3,600 feet in the subtropics and between 3,600 and 6,300 feet in the tropics (Illy and Viani 1995, 21). In these environments you can easily take a ripe, pulped, and fermented coffee bean, plant it, germinate it, and then propagate it as a coffee-tree seedling (Mitchell 1988, 46). You can then plant that seedling, once it reaches about 30 centimeters in height, in a field or a mixed-crop garden, and in three to four years your seedling, now a tree, will produce tiny white flowers. About thirty-five weeks after the flowers are pollinated your tree will be covered in ripe, red coffee "cherries" that are ready to be harvested.[6]

While there are some farms that use harvesting machines, the majority of coffee is harvested by hand, which allows farmers and pickers to go tree to tree and harvest only the ripest "cherry."[7] Pickers can also return to trees over and over again to make sure that every cherry is eventually harvested. Once the cherries are harvested they must be pulped, fermented, dried, processed, shipped, roasted, packaged, and marketed before they are consumed. Throughout this process the beans are bought and sold many times

Flowering coffee
plant

over and moved to numerous locations. With each relocation their economic and social value as well as their social and symbolic meaning changes.

Coffee moves around our planet. It is carried by farmers on their backs, in donkey-drawn wagons, and in wheelbarrows. It is loaded into trucks, cars, airplanes, boats, and ships. It moves down walking tracks through dense tropical forests and well-worn paths across deforested land. It travels on dirt and gravel roads, on regional highways, and on superhighways. It moves across our airways and shipping lanes. At every moment, every second of the day and night, there is coffee moving around our world. And it has moved like this for a very long time (Schivelbusch 1993; Wild 2005). Coffee has been at the commodity forefront of what is today described as "globalization" since the social, economic, and political processes and configurations that we name with that term began (Schivelbusch 1993).[8]

The smell of coffee is one of my first memories. When I was a child I spent a great deal of time at my grandparents' house in the rural mountains of northern Georgia. My grandfather's father built the farmhouse in 1882, and its old wooden walls allow for sound and smell to flow through it freely. As a child I slept in the room across the hall from the kitchen, and I remember waking up in the big, old bed, deep with quilts even during the hottest days of July, hearing my grandparents' voices and smelling my grandmother's coffee. I would lie in bed and let the sense of safe calmness wash over me before I sneaked into the kitchen. There my grandfather, eating a bowl of Kellogg's Corn Flakes, and my grandmother, drinking a cup of watery black instant Maxwell House coffee, would greet me.

Instant coffee—dried, crispy, diamond-like granules—was the staple coffee in most households from the end of the Second World War until the late 1980s. Between the late 1940s and the mid-1980s the global market for coffee was internationally regulated and dominated by large corporate roasters like Maxwell House and Procter and Gamble. These roasters produced what many coffee drinkers and coffee marketers today consider low-quality, homogeneous coffee, coffee that mirrored the Fordist industrial economy in which standardization and mass production were central goals (see Harvey 1990).

Today when I visit my grandmother, I bring the coffee. On most days she still drinks Maxwell House, but in the early mornings when I find her in the kitchen, I make a pot of what Roseberry (1996) calls "yuppie coffee," formally known as "specialty coffee." This kind of coffee gained entry into the global coffee market when it was deregulated in the late 1980s and when the International Coffee Agreement (ICA)—a global price stabilization agreement—fell apart in 1989. The term "specialty coffees" includes flavored coffees, "single-origin" coffees (e.g., Papua New Guinea coffee marketed as such and Jamaica Blue Mountain coffee), organic coffees, fair-trade coffees, and other seemingly socially responsible coffees that are usually brought to market by small coffee companies—roasters, distributors, and coffee shops. Specialty coffees are often marketed to communicate an evolution in our discerning palette, and their high prices convey their exclusivity. But in fact the availability of these diverse coffees reflects structural changes in the global economy. Their market is flexible, consumer-oriented, and specialized; we might think of them as post-Fordist coffees (Doane 2010; Harvey 1990).[9]

When I've recently returned from Papua New Guinea, the country where I have conducted anthropological research since 1997, I have brought

Arabicas Coffee, Goroka Coffee, or Kongo Coffee for my grandmother, brands that are produced, processed, packaged, and marketed locally in Papua New Guinea.[10] Arabicas Ltd. and Goroka Coffee Roasters are in the town of Goroka, the capital of the Eastern Highlands Province, and Kongo Coffee Ltd. is in Kundiawa, the capital of the Simbu Province. If I have not recently been to Papua New Guinea, I bring coffee from Coffee Connections, a Goroka-based company that exports to Vournas Coffee Trading, a small importing company in California that buys organic and fair-trade-certified coffees from around the world and sells them to roasters and distributors across the United States.

Among coffee experts, often called "cuppers" in the coffee business, Papua New Guinea coffee is variously described as "sweetly acidic with mild to medium body and fruity undertones," having "uniquely wild notes in the cup with a fruity endnote," "bright, clean, fruited," "rustic," "rich with good acidity and a rich chocolaty finish," "what Jamaica Blue Mountain used to taste like, primitive flavors," and "full-bodied with a thick texture and a smooth and soft aftertaste."[11] Papua New Guinea coffee, which is often described as one of the Indonesian coffees, is also discussed with other single-origin coffees. It is compared to coffees from Java and Sumatra because of similar "notes" in flavor and because of its shared Indonesian origin; to coffees from Jamaica's Blue Mountain region because of taste, and because seedlings planted in Papua New Guinea in the 1930s came from Jamaica; and to coffee grown in the mountains of Tanzania, because the flavor is derived from similar high-altitude, volcanic-soil cultivation.

My grandmother loves both the flavor and the packaging of New Guinea coffee; the Arabicas and Goroka coffee packages are the ones she likes the best. Arabicas Ltd. has a series of New Guinea Bird of Paradise paintings on its packaging. The bags are metallic blue, orange, or black, each with a different bird. The orange bag, the Paradiso Organic blend, has a Raggiana Bird of Paradise (*Paradisaea raggiana*) on it, the national symbol for the country of Papua New Guinea: it is depicted on the country's flag, and is the emblem of the Coffee Industry Corporation (CIC) of Papua New Guinea, the national agency for coffee. Birds of Paradise are also on the Goroka coffee packages, which are deep green, golden yellow, bright red, and sky blue, while a drawing of a man wearing face paint and a feathered headdress is on the white bag.[12]

The feathered and painted man on the white bag of "Goroka house-blended coffee" from Goroka Coffee Roasters is reminiscent of much of the

Cupping at Coffee Connections in Goroka

packaging on coffee that is marketed as New Guinea "single-origin" coffee.[13] New Guinea is known throughout the world for its cultural, linguistic, and biological diversity. According to the Ethnologue bibliography of world languages, Papua New Guinea has 841 living languages, while West Papua has 263.[14] This linguistic diversity, coupled with the unique and very recent history of exploration, colonization, and independence of Papua New Guinea, has lodged the place and its people in the consciousness of the rest of the world in compelling ways.[15] The entire island of New Guinea is often represented in popular media as a remote, Edenic paradise replete with undiscovered species of plants and animals and colorful, partially clothed natives, a beautiful and noble people balanced on a cliff between the savage, dangerously primitive aspects of humankind and a modernization which will destroy their pristine nature and culture.[16] The packaging and marketing of much Papua New Guinea single-origin and certified coffee draws on this imagery, as does much of the other marketing associated with coffee.

Arabicas Coffee, Goroka Coffee, and Coffee Connections all buy coffee from people in Maimafu village, a rural, Gimi-speaking village in the Lufa

District, on the border of the Eastern Highlands, Gulf, and Simbu provinces. I've spent over fifty months in Maimafu over the past sixteen years working as a cultural and environmental anthropologist, and much of the social and economic life that I have documented there revolves around coffee production. But not just rural villagers are connected to coffee production in Papua New Guinea. One of every three people in the country is connected to the coffee industry in some way, and between 300,000 and 400,000 households depend upon it as their only source of income.[17] People work as growers, workers in the processing factories and coffee transport industries, and businesspeople in the processing, transporting, and distributing industries. Thousands of people support the industry as security guards, cleaning women, clerical and accounting staff, and truck drivers. In the Eastern Highlands most other regional industry depends on coffee to keep the cash flowing: the secondhand clothing industry sees an increase in business during coffee season, the trade-stores see profits increase during the season, and the restaurants, shops, car dealerships, and other small businesses depend on the coffee season to make yearly profit margins.[18] In Goroka women in the craft and fresh vegetable markets say that their profits go up every coffee season. Many people in the country call coffee "the people's industry" because it directly links people throughout the country with each other socially and economically, and it links Papua New Guineans with other people across the globe.[19]

Between 86 and 89 percent of coffee grown in Papua New Guinea is "smallholder" coffee, grown by landowners who live in relatively rural settings with small family-owned and family-operated coffee gardens, and with little to no support from private or government agricultural extension.[20] Of all the coffee produced in Papua New Guinea, 95 percent is arabica coffee grown in the Highlands of the country. Among Gimi-speaking people, families run these small coffee businesses, which often serve as their only source of income.[21] During the coffee season men, women, and children work on coffee plots, and social life revolves around this seasonal agriculture. The season, which in Maimafu runs from late May to early October during the southwest monsoons, is the driest time of year in a place that is always hot, wet, and humid. During these months families pick their coffee. They begin in groves at the lower altitudes and move up the sides of the mountains as the coffee ripens. Maimafu is located in the high mountains and is made up of family group–based hamlets on fifteen ridge-tops that span a topographic range between 1,500 and 1,700 meters. Coffee groves have transformed the landscape in and around Maimafu village just as they have transformed landscapes across the Highlands.[22]

Families go to their coffee groves together, and everyone spends days picking the ripe, red cherries from the coffee trees. Women carry cherries back to the hamlet or to the closest source of running water—either streams or the village water system—and wash them. After washing, cherries are put into white coffee bags until the family has enough of the crop to begin the village-based wet processing. When a sufficient amount of coffee has been picked, the coffee is washed again and the red cherry (the pulp), which is held to the coffee beans with a thick, sticky-sweet substance, is taken off the beans. This can be done by hand or by using a hand-turned coffee-pulping machine.[23] The coffee is then placed in clean bags to ferment for twelve to twenty-four hours so that the sticky substance can be removed with a final washing. Once the water runs clean, the coffee beans are laid out in the sun to dry. Depending on the amount of rain that falls, the drying process may take a few or many days. Once the beans are dry the coffee (now called "parchment") is ready to be sold.[24] Unless these rural smallholders have a direct relationship with a coffee-buying company, they usually sell their coffee to intermediary buyers who visit villages and transport the coffee to Goroka.

Once the village-dry coffee is ready to be sold to buyers, women pack it in 60-kilogram bags and carry it to the village airstrip. In Maimafu this trip may be a ten-minute or one-hour walk, depending on the distance of a family's hamlet from the airstrip. After the coffee arrives at the airstrip it must be weighed by a buyer or by the village-aviation coordinator. The airfreight cost is calculated, and if the smallholders are selling to a buyer or a company with which they have a direct relationship, they receive the daily price of coffee in Goroka minus the freight cost.[25] On occasion growers take the coffee to Goroka themselves—this is rare but does happen when smallholders can get a better price in town than what is being offered to them by village-visiting buyers. Regardless of who takes the coffee to Goroka, all of this coffee is known as "airstrip coffee." When fuel prices rise, as they have done dramatically over the past several years, flying in and out of rural airstrips becomes more expensive, and since the cost of transportation is passed on to growers, coffee profits from airstrip coffee go down.

Whether purchased directly from coffee producers by a company or moved through an intermediary coffee buyer, once the coffee is in Goroka

Weighing airstrip coffee in Maimafu village

the parchment is usually dried a bit more and the waxy, white skin, the "silver skin," is removed. At this stage of development beans, until roasted, are referred to as "green bean." The green bean is either processed in Papua New Guinea (roasted and packaged for shipment to stores in Papua New Guinea and abroad) or sold for export to those who will then ship the beans through the international port in the Papua New Guinean city Lae, and then all over the world.

Locally owned coffee-producing factories and businesses and the processing and export subsidiaries of major global trading corporations like VOLCAFE and Neumann Kaffee Gruppe are found in Goroka. The coffee industry there consists of a rich mix of people from all over Papua New Guinea, Australia, Germany, India, England, and the United States. Many of the industry's expatriate leaders have long histories in Goroka, either through their parents' and grandparents' participation in the early coffee industry or through their own ties to the colonial history of the Highlands. And many of the industry's national leaders have equally involved family histories in the industry and its development.

For the past twenty years the total annual production of coffee in Papua New Guinea has hovered around one million bags.[26] Papua New Guinea produces only about 1 percent of the total amount of coffee worldwide. Nevertheless, the industry brings about $1.9 billion into the Papua New Guinea economy each year, thus accounting in the late 1990s and early 2000s for about 4 percent of total export revenue for the country. Given that the three main export commodities in Papua New Guinea are gold, crude oil, and copper, and that the other main agricultural commodities are timber and palm oil (which have slightly higher revenues than coffee), and that these commodities are owned and operated by the state and joint ventures between large multinational companies and the state (with minor revenue streams flowing down to landowners), coffee is the only export commodity owned and operated by the local people to be consumed both nationally and internationally.[27] Coffee connects people in Papua New Guinea with people all around the world along a "commodity ecumene," a "transcultural network of relationships linking producers, distributors, and consumers" (Appadurai 1986, 27).[28]

The CIC is the bureaucratic and administrative body that links the world of coffee in Papua New Guinea to the world of coffee that circulates globally. A private limited-guarantee company, it is made up of coffee growers, processors, and exporters, and the Departments of Agriculture and Livestock, Trade and Industry, and Treasury and Planning.[29] Its research and grower services division is charged with conducting research and training and providing extension services, its industry operations division with overseeing quality control, exports, levy collection, and the dissemination of economic studies and information concerning the industry. The CIC is supposed to regulate the formal relations between growers and the fifty-six coffee processors and seventeen coffee exporters countrywide, and attempts to regulate the informal relations between these growers and the independent coffee buyers, or "middlemen," who move between rural and urban areas, buying from growers and selling to processors. The CIC is meant to be the nexus—materially, monetarily, and ideologically—of rural and urban, of Papua New Guinea and elsewhere, of production, distribution, and consumption.

The world of Papua New Guinea coffee is multicultural, multiracial, multiethnic, multiclassed, and multisited. It is multicultural and multiracial in that its participants are from Papua New Guinea, Australia, the United Kingdom, India, the Philippines, South Korea, and the United States. It is multiethnic in that its national participants are from different regions (Highlanders, Coastals, and Sepiks) and provinces (such as Enga, Central, and Western). These verbal identifications mark both social style (Highlander versus Coastal) and province of origin (Enga Province versus Central Province). Within each of these categories people also identify self and other. For example, Highlanders may be from Goroka, Lufa, or Hagen, among other places, and each category carries with it specific ideas about behavior, values, and customs. And within these categories people identify themselves first by district (for example, the Eastern Highlands Province has eight districts: Daulo, Goroka, Henganofi, Kainantu, Lufa, Obura-Wonenara, Okapa, and Unggai-Bena), then by their sociolinguistic group.[30]

The industry is multiclassed in that its benefits and hardships are not distributed evenly among its participants, nor are its capital burdens (how much money one needs to take part in certain sectors of the industry like buying coffee or exporting coffee). Indeed, as an industry coffee has helped to create class in Papua New Guinea. Finally, the industry is multisited—people involved in it live in villages, towns, and cities, and the coffee they produce moves through places like Australia, Belgium, Denmark, England, Fiji, Finland, France, Germany, Hong Kong, Ireland, Italy, Japan, Malaysia, the Netherlands, New Caledonia, New Zealand, Portugal, Russia, Samoa, Scotland, Singapore, the Solomon Islands, South Africa, South Korea, Spain, Sweden, Tahiti, Taiwan, Tunisia, and the United States. The industry stretches around the globe and connects the political ecology of Papua New Guinea and Maimafu village with the rest of the world.

Through coffee production the people of Maimafu village, and other Papua New Guineans who live on the margins of government services, can access regional economies, connect with people in other places, and forge social identities as modern productive citizens. People who participate in its production often juxtapose an image of themselves as modern, developed, and educated with an image of a fabled Papua New Guinean of the past who was steeped in tradition, or *kastom* (Keesing 1989), myth, and underdevelopment. Coffee production is one means by which rural Papua New Guineans can imagine their relationships as extending out of their villages and connecting to people and places elsewhere. People in Maimafu are relationship seekers—always striving to enlarge their social worlds by connecting to people—and one way that they expand their world is through the connections that they imagine making to people who buy coffee, process coffee, sell coffee, and consume coffee.

In the town of Goroka, coffee also has multiple meanings. The coffee community in Goroka is a tight-knit one in which people often compete during their workdays and spend evenings and weekends together socializing. Papua New Guineans and expatriates run factories, own or manage export companies, work as executives and managers for large multinational interests, and hold other wage-earning positions that would be called white-collar jobs in the United States. For these people coffee is both an economic livelihood and the glue that holds their community and social world together. Their children attend school together; they play golf at the Goroka Golf Club; and they participate in the same civic societies, places such as the Rotary Club and the Goroka Chamber of Commerce. For these people coffee is a year-long business: even when the season is over there are machines to repair, paperwork to be completed, books to be balanced, and other work to be done.

Other coffee industry workers, such as the women who sort the parchment after drying, the men who run the machines in the factory, the office staff, the men and women who clean factories and offices, the security guards, and the drivers who transport the coffee, depend on the production of coffee for their economic livelihood. These people are for the most part enmeshed in village-based lives in their home hamlets and less dependent on the social network that characterizes coffee production in town. For many of them coffee is seasonal. During the busy part of the year they work in offices and factories, and during the off-season they have other jobs to make ends meet. Like my friends from Maimafu, many of them say that because of coffee production they are part of the modern economy and a global network of trade and relations. More often than not they, and the members of the executive coffee community, talk about coffee as it reflects on the nation of Papua New Guinea. For people in the Goroka coffee industry, coffee, as much as the Raggiana Bird of Paradise, both symbolizes and "materializes" the nation (Foster 2002).

When the coffee leaves Goroka it travels on trucks down the Highlands Highaway to Lae, the large international port on the northern coast of the country. There it passes through the hands and lives of people in the bulking industry, the men who fumigate agricultural exports, the men who work in the ports as drivers, guards, and other laborers, the women who work in the offices of bulking and shipping companies, and outside inspectors for the industry. Many of these people are middle-class Papua New

Guineans, like the members of the coffee industry in Goroka, and for them coffee is one part of their commerce-dependent lives. They see it as a vital link in the economy of their nation and they know that the shipping industry and all other industries associated with it depend on it. Coffee for them is not agriculture; it is commerce. And it is not their identity or social glue but rather a commodity that they help to move in order to make their living. Nevertheless, they very much see coffee as a symbol for the nation of Papua New Guinea.

On the journey from production to consumption, once Papua New Guinea coffee leaves the national port city of Lae it becomes commensurable with all other world coffee of a similar grade and quality. When this happens, once the coffee is transported over the rail of a ship, the symbolic messages that have been poured into the coffee by the people of Papua New Guinea are drained out of it. The coffee no longer means "we are a modern productive nation and part of a global commercial economy," as it does to people in the industry in Goroka and Lae, or "we are on the road to modernity and development," as it does to my friends in Maimafu, or any of the many other things that it means to Papua New Guineans.

Often the livelihoods of importers and roasters depend on having the commodity carry a different symbolic meaning from the one attributed to it by people living and working in Papua New Guinea. In order for Papua New Guinea coffee to have value in the contemporary global marketplace, it must carry a set of meanings that distinguish it from other coffees. That set of meanings is made up of the cupping descriptions that I mentioned earlier and a set of symbolic images of Papua New Guinea that marketers, distributors, roasters, and café owners infuse into the coffee. These businesses infuse a dual image onto the coffee. The first image of Papua New Guinea is exotic, primitive, dark, and dangerous, an Eden-like paradise with colorful natives. The second image of Papua New Guinea is one of poverty, decline, desperation, backwardness, sickness, corruption, and graft. These dueling yet intimately connected images are roasted onto the beans to distinguish them from other types of coffee beans that are traded in New York and then sold in New York, London, Hamburg, and Sydney. In some instances these images of cultural authenticity and poverty are then connected to a particular form of liberal politics. They are associated with the coffee beans through marketing and advertising, and consumers are told that by buying the coffee they will be able to preserve the valuable yet dying

Heading down the
Highlands Highway
from Goroka to Lae

Commensurable world coffees

Selling Papua
New Guinea

cultures of the natives who produce the coffee or help to ease the extreme
poverty of the coffee producers.

Labor and Value

My grandmother, who was 101 years old on her last birthday, is still quick-
witted and healthy, but no longer able to travel long distances from her
home. One of my greatest disappointments is that she will never see the
cities in which coffee from Papua New Guinea is served. I can imagine us
sitting in a tiny coffee shop in Covent Garden in London drinking cappuccino and eating sticky, sugary pastry, or enjoying a deep, rich espresso while
watching dancing couples at a wine festival in Hamburg as the evening
winds down, or sitting in a café in Cairns, Australia, watching swimmers
and sunbathers walk along the Esplanade. I can also imagine doing all these
things with some of my friends from Maimafu. I can picture sitting with my
friend Ellen in Cairns and discussing the entertaining fashion choices that

we see passing us by, with my friends Lucas and Philip in London while eating those same sticky pastries and laughing at some inside joke, or with Kobe, Ine, and Moyha in Hamburg discussing how Germans first brought coffee to Papua New Guinea in the 1800s. But like my grandmother, none of these people will ever visit those cities either, for although coffee connects people globally it does so in ways that are uneven. It does so in ways that both result from and lead to uneven development (see Smith 1991).

When sitting at a café, it's unusual to think about all the effort exerted to produce one cup of coffee. Let's consider the price that people are paid for their labor in coffee harvesting. When people harvest coffee they harvest enough to fill a bag weighing 60 kilograms (132 lbs.). One bag contains 198,000 cherries, or 396,000 coffee beans (since each cherry contains two beans). It takes 286 hours of labor to fill one bag with parchment (what results from the harvesting, washing, and drying of coffee in the village). This means that it takes approximately 2 hours and 10 minutes to harvest a pound of coffee (about 1,500 cherries, or 3,000 beans). One pound of coffee yields 40 6-ounce cups of coffee. So 130 minutes of labor produces 40 6-ounce cups of coffee. It thus takes about 3 minutes and 15 seconds of labor to harvest enough coffee to make one 6-ounce cup of coffee.

A one-pound bag of whole bean coffee from Starbucks under the name of Komodo Dragon Blend, a blend of Asia Pacific coffee beans with Papua New Guinea prominently mentioned on the label, costs $12.95. That pound of Komodo Dragon Blend yields forty cups at $0.32 a cup. If coffee producers were deriving all the money made from the coffee they produce, they would receive $12.95 per pound of coffee, or $12.95 per two hours and ten minutes of labor, or about $6 an hour. But of course coffee producers do not receive all of the profits from the coffee they grow.

If I choose randomly from among all the days when I recorded coffee prices in my field notes from Maimafu a day when coffee prices were low— 19 July 2003—I find that the price my friends got for coffee was $0.19 per pound of parchment. On 8 August 2006, a day with high international prices, growers got $0.59 per pound for parchment in Goroka. If we deduct the airfreight cost that day of about $0.26 per pound, the growers ended up with $0.33 per pound at the airstrip in Maimafu. For two hours and ten minutes of labor that equals an hourly wage of about $0.15. That statistic warrants repeating: *even when prices are high, coffee farmers in Maimafu make fifteen cents an hour for their labor.*

Growers in Maimafu received $0.33 for a pound of their coffee on 8 August, and yet one pound of origin marketed coffee—not organic or fair-trade-certified—costs $12.95 when purchased at a coffee shop in the United States. What adds $12.62 worth of value to that pound of coffee as it makes its way from Maimafu to New York, London, or Sydney? On that same day exporters in Goroka were paid between $1.00 and $1.41 per pound, depending upon the coffee's certification. If those exporters were working with fair-trade and organic-certified coffee, then they would have paid the grower $1.00 per pound of coffee if the coffee came from a location near a road (so no air transport costs) and received $1.41 when they sold it. The exporter would have had to pay all of the costs of getting the coffee from Goroka to the port in Lae out of that $1.41, after deducting $0.05 per pound as a payment to put back into the grower's cooperatives. Thus of the $12.95 paid for a pound of fair-trade or organic beans, only $1.41 stays in Papua New Guinea. The rest of that price, $11.54, goes somewhere else. That $11.54 is the value added to the coffee once it leaves Lae. And again, we have a statistic that warrants repeating: *For fair-trade and organic-certified coffee, only $1.41 of profit per pound stays in Papua New Guinea.*

The value created by the labor of my friends in Maimafu is added to the labor of other people along the commodity ecumene for coffee. The $12.62 of value added to the initial $0.33 represents all the nonagricultural productive aspects of the commodity. It includes the labor of people in Goroka and Lae and other places through which the coffee moves in Papua New Guinea. The $11.54 figure represents the labor of people after the coffee departs from the port at Lae. Yet a strange thing happens here. The labor that is expended in Papua New Guinea adds value to the parchment produced by people in Maimafu: it is the kind of socially necessary labor that we might think necessary to extract use value from a coffee bean—the labor that dries the beans in a factory dryer, skins them so that they are parchment ready to be roasted, and roasts them so that they make a tasty cup of coffee. But the labor that is expended after Lae is of another sort. The labor that is added after the fact is not used to make the commodity come into existence but to make another sort of thing, another sort of value, come into existence. Part of this value is the set of meanings and images that I discussed above. The infusing of coffee beans from Papua New Guinea with particular images and messages is also a form of labor. And people are willing to pay for this labor: they are even desirous of it. They seek it out by buying specialty coffees. Consumers are willing to pay more for coffee that has a particular story or a particular history. This process is the un-generification of commodities, the un-standardization, producing the opposite of the standardized mass-produced Fordist coffee that I remember from my childhood.

My grandmother still buys Maxwell House when she buys her own coffee. She buys it because it is inexpensive and consistent. Contemporary consumption of specialty coffee seeks to distinguish individual consumers from everyone else and similar coffees from each other. Coffee choice, like all commodity choice today, can be used to indicate important markers of status, knowledge, and politics. Through narratives that are seemingly about political ecology (the structural links between global processes and local social and ecological change) marketers convince well-meaning individuals that their everyday consumption choices can be "political" (Bryant and Goodman 2004). People who refuse to drink Starbucks coffee may think they are sending a message of opposition to large corporations that they imagine are putting mom-and-pop or individually owned establishments out of business. Those who always buy fair-trade coffee may be trying to send the message that they care about the plight of rural farmers in the tropics, and those who buy coffee certified by the Rainforest Alliance may be trying to make a statement about their commitment to environmental conservation. Additionally, consumers who buy a blend of Javanese, Sumatran, and Papua New Guinea coffees with a bit of East Timorese thrown in for a "note of wildness" may be attempting to show how developed their tastes are. Today, people often attempt to derive and express identity and politics through the coffee and other commodities that they buy and serve.

Circulations

Commodities and their circulation have been at the forefront of anthropological studies of materiality for quite some time now (see Miller 1995). While approaches to commodity circulation in anthropology are varied, they are all rooted in a series of debates about objects and their place in social life that began with Karl Marx's analysis of the commodity, its origin, and its power (Marx [1867] 1975). These debates have grown into a literature that serves as the backbone for the social analysis of objects, value, desire, image, and subjectivity (Baudrillard 1988; Benjamin 1968; Debord [1967] 1995; de Certeau 1984; Lee 1993; Lukács [1923] 1971; Mauss [1925] 1954; Storey 1993; Taussig 2000).[31]

Today anthropologists and others often use food as an entry point into the analysis of commodities and circulation. They trace the "trajectories" of food in order to understand global processes and to tell us something about social relationships between producers and consumers (Mintz and Du Bois 2002; Phillips 2006, 38). Some contemporary scholars argue that this work forms a new methodological approach to understanding social life and political economy, but anthropologists have been writing about agriculture (the social processes that bring plants and animals to life), culture (the social processes that make plants and animals edible), and political economy (the social processes that make some foods into valuable exchange items and commodities) since the beginnings of the discipline.[32]

The contemporary literature on food can be organized into several categories. First, there is the literature that follows food and its routes of circulation. Indeed, we could make quite a meal from the "follow the food" stories.[33] Another body of literature focuses on the social and economic relationships that move food and other commodities between particular sites along circulatory routes.[34] There is also literature that focuses on production and distribution processes.[35]

Much of this food-related literature fits into a larger category of literature that follows what we might call the commodity chain approach. In the earliest formulation of commodity chains as a heuristic device for understanding the global movements of objects, they were defined as "a network of labour and production processes whose end result is a finished commodity" (Hopkins and Wallerstein 1986, 159). In highlighting the links between production, distribution, and consumption, the global commodity chain approach "foregrounds vertical connections" (Leslie and Reimer 1999, 407). This means that there is a focus on the connections between consumer demand, product design, and the institutions that organize and control production and distribution. Sociologists and political scientists have most often taken this "vertical" approach and with it have provided valuable insights into the relations between different "sectors" along circulatory routes.

Leslie and Reimer locate space and place at the center of the analysis of commodity chains in their critique of this "vertical" approach. They advocate an analysis of how chains vary through time and space and how "commodity chains culminate in the production of space" (402). With this they call for a "horizontal" approach that focuses on distinct sites or places as nodes that tell us about the socio-spatial aspects of globalization.[36] They argue that this type of focus is essential for both understanding the material effects of commodity production and for the crafting of policy and politics (402). They highlight the importance of understanding "the particularity of individual nodes," and argue that without this spatial focus one cannot begin to understand social relations or answer questions about exploitation (404). Geographers have more often than not focused on "horizontal" analysis, giving us insightful readings of how space and place are produced, transformed, and destroyed and how certain sites, and their attendant raced, classed, and gendered social relations, come into and out of being.

Fine and Leopold, in work that highlights the semiotic components of circulation, argue that commodities are both materially and ideologically made in varying ways by different sectors along their way from production to consumption, and in varying ways at different sites of production and consumption (Fine and Leopold 1993, 28; see also Miller 1995). They also advocate understanding how the flows of specific commodities change over time, how systems of circulation are historically contingent. With this they push us past the separation of vertical and horizontal approaches. Barndt also argues that the routes taken today by foods in particular are neither simply vertical nor horizontal: they are infinitely complex, intertwined, and tangled (Barndt 2002). Similarly, with regard to coffee in particular, Brad Weiss argues that "the differing trajectories of coffee as a valued object demonstrate the difficulties of neatly distinguishing between producers and consumers and suggest that the connection between production and consumption is less a clear-cut sequence in economic practice than a multi-stranded and reflexive cultural process" (Weiss 1996a, 104).

This approach to commodities and their movement, which has highlighted political economy and an interest in discourse, power, and semiotics without fixating solely on spatial metaphors or ideas about the separation of sectors, is known as the commodity circuit approach (Cook and Crang 1996; Cook, Crang, and Thorpe 1998; Crang 1996; du Gay et al. 1997). This approach takes seriously the ways that both forms and meanings transform as commodities move, and it attempts to understand the social practices that lead to these transformations. Additionally, the approach emphasizes the nonlinear and non-closed nature of these systems. Things, ideas, and people move along circuits in both directions and come from all sorts of points outside the circuits themselves. Anthropological examinations of commodities that take this approach have also shown that "it can no longer be presumed that global forces like commoditization lead inevitably to the eradication of specific local meanings, no matter how ostensibly powerful and seductive commodity forms might appear" (Weiss 1996a, 103). With this they attend to how the seemingly particular and the seemingly universal intertwine in different ways at different sites and at different historic moments (Tsing 2004).

Almost all the literature about circulation and on food as commodity is interested in using the circulation of commodities to tell us something about globalization.[37] Coffee, as an agricultural commodity that tells us something about globalization, has received a great deal of attention from historians, geographers, and anthropologists for a very long time (see Hearst 1932; Hoy 1938; Jonasson 1933; Munger 1952; Van Dongen 1961). Scholars have used coffee to teach us about frontier politics, colonization, labor, and political ecology (Brannstrom 2001; Cambranes 1985; Holloway 1980), as a way to write national histories in Latin American countries so that we get a sense of the lived experiences of those histories (Palacio 1980), and as a window into how colonial practices produced space and laboring bodies in tandem (Duncan 2002).

More recently, scholars have used coffee and the coffee industry to examine the ways violence is enacted around the environment and the ways structural violence endures even after physical acts of violence have long ceased (Nevins 2003), the relationship between economic development and production diversification (Dorsey 1999), the links between biodiversity loss and modernization (Potvin et al. 2005), the value of ecosystem services (like bee pollination) for economic development (Olschewski et al. 2006), and the role of multi-cropping in agroecosystems on biodiversity rates (Gillison et al. 2004). Coffee is also a commodity that has brought anthropologists and other social scientists into sustained conversations with ecologists (Potvin et al. 2005, 11). Moreover, coffee has become one of the main commodities used to discuss voluntary regulation systems like fair-trade and organic certification, as well as other forms of ecological and social labeling (see Bacon, Mendez, Gliessman, et al. 2008; Bray, Sanchez, and Murphy 2002; Jaffee 2007; Larson 2003; Lyon and Moberg 2010; Ponte 2002a, 2002b; Raynolds 2000, 2002; Renard 1999).

As discussed earlier, many Papua New Guineans see coffee production as a means of development, and like other commodity production there it can be understood as a process that brings about social change (Biersack 1995, Gewertz and Errington 1996, Knauft 1993, 1999; LiPuma 2000; Robbins 1995; Sexton 1986a). Since coffee is a commodity that ties Papua New Guinea to a set of global markets, we can see it as an important site for examining globalization in terms of social change and tradition. Ethnography in Melanesia has demonstrated that culture change as the result of western penetration is a complex phenomenon, belying simplistic claims that western influence is a cultural solvent that erodes salient indigenous cultural features and "authenticity." While severe negative effects of such social and economic ruptures have been well documented (Gewertz and Errington 1999; Knauft 2002; Wardlow 2006), other accounts highlight the persistence of Melanesian social forms even in contexts that would seem to have caused massive social disruptions (Robbins 2004).

Introducing the neologism "developman," Marshall Sahlins posits one way to make sense of why certain introduced western concepts, technologies, and things are massively disruptive and others seem to be incorporated without disruption. To Sahlins "developman" describes "the indigenous way of coping with capitalism" (Sahlins 2005, 23) and how western commodities and technologies are put to use in traditional culture. It takes the form of people acquiring and exchanging objects for socially meaningful reasons such as expanding social relationships through exchange. Marilyn Strathern has made a similar point regarding Vanuatuans, who "turn European things to their own ends rather than seek to encompass European ends; in other words they Vanuatize things derived from the European world rather than Europeanize themselves" (Strathern 1988, 81). Because the "'wealth' consists in the kinds of things that organize the social totality, that create and ally clans and tribes," an increase in the supply of these objects does not bring a decline in value (Sahlins [1992] 2005, 29). That is to say, objects are valued so long as meaningful acts of exchanges can be enacted with them. This illustrates that even with the introduction of western commodities the value of an object inheres in the qualitative relationships that become embedded through the exchange rather than its quantitative value as a commodity. Strathern's description of the first European explorers who entered the interior of the Highlands in the 1930s shows a similar selectivity in how Europeans and their objects were incorporated into the existing social system (Strathern 1992). To the Europeans' surprise, the novel technology, such as metal and guns, that they thought would impress the Highlanders marked them as spirits with whom the Highlanders could establish no meaningful relationships. It was only when the Europeans revealed that they had large amounts of kina shell, which was used in numerous social exchanges such as bride price, that the Highlanders considered them social beings with whom one could enter into social relationships.

Thus the pertinent questions with respect to globalization and coffee production in Papua New Guinea are what sorts of changes have occurred as a result of the long history of coffee production in Papua New Guinea, and what sorts of changes are resulting from the new emphasis on fair-trade, organic, and single-origin marketing schemes. Rather than parallel-ing the capillary system through which coffee production spread and ex-panded and the vast network of social relationships that people cultivated through coffee, certification schemes bring with them fully formed pre-scriptive regimes of governmentality which were developed elsewhere and based on a value system separate from those of most Melanesians. While the proponents of these schemes intended to improve the lives of pro-ducers by promoting certain practices and restructuring the coffee trade, many of these changes are inconsistent with the way Melanesians have developed the coffee business over the many decades since coffee was introduced. These schemes also turn on images that marketers use to add value to coffee from Papua New Guinea in the global marketplace. These images do not reflect the lived experiences of people in Papua New Guinea. Additionally, they replicate neoliberal logics in ways that are ultimately detrimental to the social worlds and lives of the people growing coffee.

Anthropologists have examined the relationship between advertising, aesthetics, commodities, images, and fantasies and offered insights into how advertising and aesthetics produce consumer desires and consumer subjectivities (Buck-Morss 1992; Ivy 1995; Miller 1997). What this literature can help us do with regard to coffee is understand the process by which desire and fantasy become connected to politics. The contemporary adver-tising around specialty coffee intertwines coffee with images of poverty, native authenticity, nature, and Euro-American liberal ideas of progress. What sorts of desires does this advertising create, how are these desires enacted or made manifest, and how do they—if they do—feed back into the material lives of coffee producers?

Images can reflect reality, mask reality, mask the absence of reality, or have no connection to reality at all (Baudrillard 1988). Contemporary advertising is the point of intersection between capitalism, images, and semiotics (Goldman 1994, 183), and both packaging and marketing are the locus of the intense merging of people's commodity anticipation and desire with contemporary advertising (Willis 1991, 3). For many years advertising has circulated what Wolfgang Haug calls the "appearance of value" (1986, 16), while at the same time reifying anticipation and desire in ways that make them incapable of being satisfied through the actual use value of objects. We want and we want, and our wanting and desire are driven by advertising and packaging, which allow us to imagine new and wonderful worlds in which we are happy and fulfilled, yet when we get the object of our desire it seems somehow hollow and unfulfilling.

Today we take for granted the existence of a "social economy" of signs, symbols, representations, images, and fantasies that exist interlaced with the money economy (see Baudrillard 1981, 1983, 1993; Debord [1967] 1995). Commodities retain, of course, their material attributes, but their values and meanings are made through processes that may or may not have anything to do with their material nature, their use value, or the labor that went into their material production (Debord [1967] 1995; Haug 1986). When the abstract images associated with commodities begin to convey meanings that have nothing to do with the material aspects of commodities, Guy Debord ([1967] 1995, 63–65) argues that we have a social economy of "spectacle," an economy based on the exchange of signs, symbols, and images at least as much as it is based on the actual exchange of objects. In this spectacular economy, people come to rely on images instead of taking the time to learn about the commodities they are buying or the material relations that bring them the commodities. Abstract images become "real" for consumers in this economy, and these abstract images become things in and of themselves to be exchanged. The image promises more than the commodity can offer, and people trust the image more than the commodity.

But we are not simply blinded to the reality that all material and social products are made through human labor, and that systems of thought and value place some of the products over others in a hierarchical scale of value also produced by human labor—in addition, the reality has been completely displaced by fantasy (Taussig 2000, 250). These fantasies now guide our intellectual, our material, and our aesthetic relations with everything, including politics. It is not simply that the fetish as one of the "secrets of capital" conceals the truth (267). It becomes the truth, "it enters into the truth it conceals, making it impossible to separate the two, at least in the human social world" (267). Advertising is what transmits this truth and heightens exchange value, differentiates products, and creates desire for both the sign value and the commodity. And "advertising" is no longer exclusively packaging. It is now marketing, design, media events, and the creation of "hyper-commodities," or commodities whose sign value comes to spin off other products (Willis 1991, 2).

Today marketing is also about "feeling." The original meaning of "aesthetics" in Greek is "to perceive the world through bodily feeling"—a kind of pre-linguistic experience of the commodity that allows us to feel a perfect world or have nostalgia for something (even if we didn't really experience it). In this way commodities are also "anaesthetics" in the sense that they allow us to imagine a better life while at the same time blocking out the one we have (Buck-Morss 1992). With certified and single-origin coffees the images used to sell the products are also manipulated to make consumers feel as if they are also making other people's lives better through the act of buying. Every time a coffee marketer tells a story about a pristine native village on the edge of poverty that might have turned to logging or mining or one of the other ravages of modernity but that because of coffee certification, can happily grow coffee and live in primitive bliss for a little longer, it is attempting to make consumers feel as if their consumption makes people's lives better while at the same time making their own lives fuller. The appearance of value of coffee becomes this dreaming and imaging of better lives. With this, images of poverty and primitivity come to add value to the commodity.

The images used to add value to coffee, like all images in contemporary marketing, are part of a capitalism with an extraordinary velocity. Signs, symbols, and images turn over at an astounding rate today. Things that added value to a commodity yesterday might well detract from its value today. In fact, today "the incessant demands of commodity differentiation in the context of proliferating brands and product lines have made the rapid turnover of meaning in the form of decontextualized images as crucial as the turnover of material objects" (Goldman 1994, 184). In the contemporary marketplace there is a competition to "possess the preeminent sign value of the moment," and once that sign value is devalued because too many people possess it or use it or understand it, it is thrown by the wayside (184). This is, in fact, the planned obsolescence of the sign.

We know that capitalism needs to move the commodity form into ever-increasing zones of social life in order for it to flourish (Lukács 1971). One way this has happened historically has been through the usurpation of culture by capitalists who reinvented it as "the summation of individual commodity choices" (Baudrillard 1981, 1983, 1993; Goldman 1994, 185). We also know that one of the central inherent contractions in capitalism is that for it to flourish and realize profit it must forever increase production (Marx [1867] 1975). In the distant past increasing relative surplus value by making production more efficient might have done this. In the not-so-distant past outsourcing labor might have done this, by reducing the amount of profit that the capitalist had to spend to reproduce the labor force. Today capital breaks down the barriers to profit by continually increasing the desire for consumption. Capitalism today depends on a velocity of sign value, so that even if products don't change, their value can be increased by changing their appearance of value.

Today all commodities, including coffee, must be considered in light of flexible accumulation: "Flexible accumulation has been accompanied on the consumption side, therefore, by a much greater attention to quick-changing fashions and the mobilization of all the artifices of need inducement and cultural transformation that this implies. The relatively stable aesthetic of Fordist modernism has given way to all the ferment, instability, and fleeting qualities of a postmodernist aesthetic that celebrates difference, ephemerality, spectacle, fashion, and the commodification of cultural forms" (Harvey 1989, 156). The result is a push to accelerate the turnover time for commodities in terms of consumption and to a fixation on the production of spectacles and events and not the production of goods themselves (157). When the goal becomes the rapid turnover of capital and overcoming barriers to capital, and a commodity's meanings and values are tied to semiotics, there is also a rapid turnover of meanings, and the meanings, images, and values used to sell commodities can and will be thrown away once they no longer carry marketplace value. Once a meaning stops having value in the marketplace, the people who want to sell the object must immediately find new meaning to pour into the object or to wrap it in. Today images are used to sell coffee; one argument of this book is that the use of images to sell coffee is tied to neoliberalization.

Neoliberalization

Neoliberalism and neoliberalization are the contemporary terms used to denote ideologies, philosophies, policies, and practices based on economic liberalism and neoclassical economic theories, and in particular on a reduced role for the state, and increased role for the private sector, and market deregulation (see Friedman 1982; von Hayek 1960).[38] This philosophy and these policies have been circulated globally. In what follows I define what I mean by these terms because, as James Ferguson has recently argued, there is a "huge variation" in the ways they are used in contemporary scholarship (Ferguson 2010, 170). Neoliberalism assumes that governments, economies, and cultures are more efficient and productive, and that citizens more likely to have high standards of living, when the market self-regulates and goods and services are provided by private enterprise. In the political corollary to this economic school of thought individual liberty and freedom are hallowed and venerated (Harvey 2007, 24). The role of the state, in this philosophy, is to "maximize the independence" of people and corporations, and "markets" are thought to be intelligent and efficient (Castree 2010, 7–8). Left alone, markets will encourage competition, good companies will prevail, and individual consumers and producers will benefit.

Neoliberals propose privatizing and commodifying everything through the assigning of property rights; pursuing deregulation so that all private property and marketable things can be freely bought and sold; having the state withdraw from the realms of social and ecological life unless it is needed to enforce private property rights; commercializing services previously offered by the state; allowing NGOs and other non-state entities to step in where the state has withdrawn; and implementing policies and forms of government that make individuals feel compelled to do things that were formerly the job of the state. The neoliberal ideology has brought about a vast array of policies and programs intended to bring the virtual world created by the neoliberal philosophy into being (see Carrier 1998b).

Neoliberalization as a philosophical worldview as well as a set of policy-related discourses and practices has affected the world of coffee in two major ways. First, deregulation of the global coffee market that resulted in the collapse of the International Coffee Agreement in 1989 both opened the market to specialty coffee and created the structural conditions for the current "global coffee crisis" (see Doane 2010; Lyon and Moberg 2010). By opening the market to specialty coffee I mean that it created the conditions for both third-party certification schemes, like fair-trade and organic certification, intended to remedy the decline in growers' labor over the past three decades (Bacon, Mendez, Flores Gomez, et al. 2008; Jaffee 2007;). Additionally, by opening these markets it also created the space for the single-origin marketing of coffee, which draws on images of countries and cultures to add value to coffee (see Wilson 2010).

The second way that neoliberalization has affected the world of coffee is through the structural adjustment programs implemented in most coffee-growing countries beginning in the late 1950s. These programs, demanded of developing countries by the International Monetary Fund (IMF) and the World Bank in exchange for debt relief, new loans, and lower interest rates, were of a piece with neoliberal philosophy. Money would only be lent to countries that were willing to implement economic and political changes outlined by the IMF and the World Bank that were thought to open barriers to trade and strengthen the free market. These changes usually included privatizing state assets and all land, cutting state expenditures, loosening social and environmental regulations, refocusing economic attention on exports with a major emphasis on resource extraction, lifting export and import restrictions, devaluing currencies, creating domestic stock markets, removing state subsidies, removing price controls, increasing the rights of foreign investors, balancing state budgets, and fighting corruption.

In this book I provide an analysis of the circulation of coffee and images, in the context of neoliberalization and social change, and show how various forms of value, labor, and politics emerge along coffee's circulatory routes.[39] My ethnography is neither vertical nor horizontal; it is both. It is also multi-sited and multi-temporal, but it does not cover every institution of production and distribution evenly, nor does it cover each node of meaning making equally. In all of this I focus on the materiality of coffee, including its material effects on the landscape where it is grown and the people who grow it. I also focus on the material effects of its circulation, in terms of the growth of cities and the ways coffee shops change neighborhoods. In chapter 8 I also show the material effects of the images that are created as the coffee moves.

Throughout the book I discuss fair-trade and organic coffees, but these coffees are not my only focus. I also discuss single-origin-marketed coffee and coffee that has no third-party value added to it at all. Many scholars today examine the social and political aspects of third-party certification schemes like fair-trade and organic certification (see Bacon, Mendez, Gliessman, et al. 2008; Bray, Sanchez, and Murphy 2002; Bryant and Goodman 2004; Doane 2010; Jaffee 2007; Larson 2003; Lyon and Moberg 2010; Ponte 2002a, 2002b; Raynolds 2002a, 2002b, 2004; Renard 1999). These scholars carefully examine the relationship between neoliberalization and certification (Doane 2010; Jaffee 2007; Lyon and Moberg 2010; Moberg

2010), the ways images of indigenous authenticity are grafted onto certified commodities (Wilson 2010), and the representational practices of "Edenic myth-making" used to create a fiction whereby consumption can come to be seen as a political act (Bryant and Goodman 2004). I am not the first person to think about these things. However, this book combines an ethnographic analysis of all these issues—circulation, the power of images, neoliberalization, value, labor, politics, social change, political ecology, and coffee. In doing so it provides a rich and thick account of the lives that produce all the value in coffee, including the lives of growers, buyers, factory workers and owners, exporters, importers, roasters, marketers, and consumers. It does this by highlighting the social connections that coffee creates.

Throughout the following pages I show that in the Gimi-speaking world people make connections through reproduction, social reproduction, and genealogy. When Gimi enter into relationships with coffee-related actors and grow coffee, they expand their social and material world. They do this by growing coffee that will be ingested by others, thereby contributing to the actual production of person and personhood of the consumers, and by making kin and kinship relations out of buyers, traders, and others in the industry. Coffee makes the world bigger for Gimi. I also demonstrate that on the contrary, for consumers, coffee works to make the world smaller. They assume that with fair-trade and organic certification—which casts liberal politics like those of the consumer as the politics of everyone on the commodity circuit for coffee—everyone thinks as they do. They also, by literally buying into a troubling set of fantasy images of Papua New Guinea that are grafted onto the coffee through marketing, work to replicate dangerous ideas about indigenous people and poverty that have drastic material effects. The images that neoliberal coffee turns on assume a particular form of temporality. People like my Gimi friends are seen as living in a world similar to the past that all of humanity once shared. They are assumed to be moving toward the modern world. These images are in part the images of unilinear evolution, that old set of ideas from anthropology that assumed a global, uniform progression from primitive to modern.

What follows is also an ethnography of the creation of value along circulatory routes. I am concerned with the value that derives from the labor of people who produce, process, transport, market, and distribute coffee and the value that is attributed to people's ways of life. By "ways of life" I mean things like the socio-ecological practices thought of as "culture" when people think about my Gimi friends, the socio-spatial practices thought of as "culture" when people talk and write about my friends from Goroka, and the business practices in the coffee industry that people refer to with the shorthand term "being the middle man." Ethnographically, part of my goal with this book is to give the reader a sense of how these ways of life are both the real, day-to-day practices of people and how particular images of some people's ways of life are socially constructed by others. I also ask what happens when fantastic and fantasy-fueled images of Papua New Guinea come, because of the way that coffee is marketed, to signify Papua New Guinea in the global consciousness. And what happens when, because of the velocity of contemporary capitalism and flexible accumulation, these images are discarded by marketers? If they have come to represent the real for consumers and others and their value goes down in the marketplace, where does that leave the people in Papua New Guinea who have been branded with these fantastic images?

This book also embeds the analysis of coffee production, distribution, and circulation in political ecology. Political ecology is basically a sophisticated contemporary theory of accumulation by dispossession and the vast effects of this ongoing process (Blaikie and Brookfield 1987). Marx argued that "primitive accumulation" (which has also been translated as "original accumulation") has as its primary goal the privatization of land and means of production. This privatization yields a social situation in which some people must become workers who sell their labor to capitalists (the people who own the privatized land and means of production) for a wage, in order to live and reproduce self, family, and society. Also tied to this alienation of labor is the alienation of land and natural resources. All three commodities —land, labor, and natural resources—must be alienable for capital to continue to grow. Many scholars have read Marx's theory of primitive accumulation as a historical analysis that lays out what happened before capitalism and as an explanation of how capitalists originally gained wealth and resources, forcing the people who had been dispossessed of land and rights to enter into an unequal relationship with them based on the sale of labor. David Harvey, drawing heavily on Rosa Luxemburg, argues that Marx writes about a process that can be happening anywhere at any time; that he is not writing about a particular unilineal historical progression but that we can see his arguments about primitive accumulation in *Capital* as a case analysis of a more general principle. In fact, Harvey argues that to talk about "primitive" or "original" accumulation embeds the idea that this sort of accumulation is over and that we (and capital) have moved on. "Accumulation by dispossession" is another way of saying primitive accumulation or original accumulation without these temporal assumptions (see Harvey 2005, 2006a).

Political ecology takes this theory and asks why the people who are affected by accumulation by dispossession, who are dispossessed of labor, land, and natural resources, are then continually blamed for the ecological ravages (soil erosion, land degradation, deforestation, pollution, flooding, climate change) that result from this process. It also works to elucidate the connections between accumulation by dispossession, governmentality, the state, and semiotics (see Biersack 1999; Escobar 1999). By bringing together political ecology with the social analysis of a commodity, this book merges two important theoretical threads in contemporary anthropology. The environment is often thought of as translocal, as are the social, political, and economic relations associated with commodity chains. This book grounds the examination of commodity production, distribution, and consumption in the political ecology of the Highlands of Papua New Guinea. While political ecology has engaged development and commodity extraction (Peet and Watts 1996: Watts and McCarthy 1997), analyzed the destructive forces of capitalism and the state (Blaikie 1985; Blaikie and Brookfield 1987; Bryant and Bailey 1997), and used poststructural approaches to examine the cultural politics of environmental change (Escobar 1996; Peluso 1995; Rangan 1995; Rocheleau and Ross 1995) it has only just begun to systematically engage contemporary anthropological approaches to commodities and consumption (see Bryant and Goodman 2004; Doane 2010). Like much in the environmental realm, production and its social effects have been examined, but consumption has been left out of the analysis. This project engages both fields, consumption studies and political ecology, and locates these processes in a wider analysis of globalization. Finally, many scholars have shown that nature is now increasingly produced as a commodity and in the image of commodities (Castree 2005; Haraway 1997; Katz 1998; Smith 1991). By merging an examination of commodities as meaning bearers and social connectors across the commodity ecumene for coffee by examining how neoliberalization needs for nature to be a commodity, this book contributes to the social analysis of the production of nature.

Throughout the book I show that for rural villagers coffee allows access to the riches of globalization and lets them seek relationships with others (what they want and need to make self). I also show that for urban dwellers coffee materializes the nation in important ways (Foster 2002), but that the way it is sold dematerializes the nation insofar as it creates and reinforces two fantasies about Papua New Guinea's residents: that of the pristine primitive and that of the impoverished villagers. These fantasies intertwine to create the larger fantasy that poverty in Papua New Guinea is somehow the fault of the people there—that their primitivity disallows their movement up the scale of "development"—and this fantasy obscures the structural relations that actually give rise to poverty in the country. Poverty and primitivity are bonded together in the marketing of coffee today. I show that this is both a function of neoliberalization and one of the things that allow it to persist.

The world of coffee in Papua New Guinea has a long history, and since the industry's inception it has gone through many changes. People started growing coffee in what is now Papua New Guinea in the late 1890s. By 1901 Burns, Philp and Company, an Australian company, was exporting the coffee to Australia. The residents of Maimafu Village, and most other rural villages in the highlands of the country, began growing coffee in the late 1950s. By the early 1980s almost every household in the Highlands grew coffee for the international standardized and regulated coffee market. The coffee from Papua New Guinea was marketed internationally for its quality and taste and moved along networks that had been in existence since the colonial period. In this chapter I show the recent global political and economic changes that gave rise to today's specialty coffee industry, the marketing and advertising world that emerged around that industry, the ways that world works to create images of both Papua New Guinea and Papua New Guineans, and the new forms of networks that have been created to circulate Papua New Guinean coffee.

Consumer Production

The tall, blond man from Nebraska wears the clip-on microphone like a professional. He towers above us, the participants in his seminar on marketing at the Specialty Coffee Association of America's annual meeting, and smiles a radiant row of perfect white teeth. He breaks the ice by revving up the fairly caffeinated crowd when he says, "Okay. OKAY. We are here to sell coffee! YEAH." People in the audience cheer enthusiastically.

We are all (coffee-shop owners and an anthropologist who studies coffee consumption) here in this conference room in an attempt to understand why people buy specialty coffees. Our first task, before we begin any discussion of coffee, consumption, or anything, really, is to break into groups and come up with a list of the "essential qualities" (I know, too perfect for an anthropologist, right?) of our own "generation." I am put in the Generation X group. We were all born between 1964 and 1982, and although I momentarily hope that we will bond over our great love for the music of the Replacements, powerful memories of anti-apartheid protests and divestment campaigns, and our ability to quote long bits of the movie *Point Break*, we don't as a group seem to have much in common. So we get to our task and try to make a list of essentialisms. We have trouble because we don't seem to agree on any of them.

After a break, Mr. Nebraska smiles us back to our seats and we get started. People yell out the answers to his questions.

Mr. Nebraska (MN): "Okay, so you Silent Generation folks [those born between 1927 and 1944], give us your qualities."

"We are loyal and dependable," says one man in the front.

"We built and defended this country," says another who seems to be wearing a hat with a battleship's name on it.

MN: "Okay, now for the Baby Boomers [those born between 1945 and 1963], what do you have to contribute as a generation?"

"We are tenacious and idealistic," says a woman wearing a perky, little red suit.

"We are freethinkers!" shout several people at the same time.

MN: "What about the Xers?"

Several people from my seemingly stoic group now perk up and yell, "We are individuals," "We question authority," and "We are fast technology!"

MN: "Now, what about you Millennials? Hello, Millennials? Where are my Millennials?"

Two young guys shyly raise their hands. They appear to be just out of college and out of place in this older, business-suited crowd. One of them says, "We are *much* faster technology."

Everyone laughs. Then Mr. Nebraska begins his lecture.

For the next hour he talks about different American generations and how they hold the key to marketing. He begins with his analysis of the essential characteristics of each generation. "The Silent Generation" is "defined by World War II and the Korean War." They are hardworking-loyal-sacrificing-dedicated-conformist-never-questioning-authority-respectful-patient-delayed-gratification-duty-before-pleasure kinds of folks. Mr. Nebraska smiles broadly when he talks about these people, calling them "folks" at several points and mentioning his grandparents. Then he tells us that we won't talk about them anymore because as a generation they don't have any purchasing power in the retail world, so they are a waste of time for the seminar.

He then moves on to the Baby Boomers. They are "all about civil rights, Vietnam, and Woodstock" and they can be summed up as essentially full of "optimism," "team-oriented," dedicated to "personal growth" and "personal gratification." They work long hours and have a "hardcore" work ethic but a "youthful mindset" which they keep up with "health and fitness."

He says, "GUYS, come ON. There are some values going on here, right? VALUES." He says this meaningfully, pacing the stage and smiling at his own insight.

It turns out that my generation, Generation X, is defined by "Three-Mile Island," "the fall of the Berlin Wall," and "Rodney King," and that we are "liquid." We have "liquid value" and "a liquid mindset." We can "adjust to anything" because we are independent-individualist-selfish-latchkey kids who are "all about experience" and who have "no loyalty to anyone or anything." We are hard to work with because we have a "totally flat view of organization," which means we have "no respect for authority."

Finally, he moves on to the millennials, prefacing his discussion by saying, with no hint of insight into his role in the creation of this marketing fetish, "Isn't it just weird? It is just weird that generations are getting shorter. Isn't it?"

For Mr. Nebraska, millennials are defined by the Oklahoma City bombing, the Clinton–Lewinsky affair, 9/11, and the Columbine shootings. They want "achievement" but are "not driven." They value "globalism" but are "community focused" and think that by "looking inward" they can "change the world." They are also apparently "teetotalers" who "don't want drugs or alcohol."

When he is finished with his description of the millennials, Mr. Nebraska looks at us thoughtfully, pauses, and says meaningfully, "This, THIS, is at the very core of people, it is who they are."

Next we move on to how to market to the different generations. Mr. Nebraska says, "The logo, product, service and atmosphere, or CULTURE of a business" is "key" to making your "generational pitch." And he cautions the audience, "You want to listen to this, the cultures I'm talking about, they are in people's DNA."

Baby Boomers' DNA is apparently encoded with a deep and abiding desire for iconic logos that symbolize gratification, indulgence, and the "unyielding" defiance of age and aging. Their DNA forces them to desire lots of choices among products, quick and thoughtful professional services, and "upscale" consumer-comes-first "retail culture."

My "Generation X" "cultural DNA" makes me skeptical of logos and desirous of multiple, similar products with a unique story behind each of them and service that is "authentic," during which I can "make a connection" and "share a story." Culturally, I desire casual, flexible, liquid space where I can read the paper, check my e-mail, and chat with friends. I "can't abide" images of control.

Millennials are "encoded" with the desire for brands and logos. They "value the symbols of products" more than anything else "about the retail world." They want "global products" that are "political" and "environmentally friendly," things that allow them to "express" their "self-knowledge" and "politics." When buying services they want to "be coddled" and "made to feel important." They want to "see people who know, really know, how to work the equipment." And culturally, they desire and can find "a meaning-filled experience" during "retail time."

After the description of the generations, their "DNA," and the sort of "retail culture" that appeals to them, Mr. Nebraska begins to talk about specialty coffee and its emerging market. He focuses on the "stories" behind the coffee and the ways it can be made to appeal to different generations. The stories exist on two scales: that of the coffee shop and that of the coffee producer.

Mr. Nebraska's Baby Boomers, constructed against a social mirror of the 1960s (the civil rights movement, protests against the war in Vietnam) and the constrained, restrained rebellion of going to a music festival (Woodstock), who are said to be deeply desirous of validating their continued youth even in the face of their sixtieth birthdays and deeply connected to the idea that they have spent their lives working harder than others, can easily be sold specialty coffees and specialty coffee venues that appeal to their ideas of work and activism. He discusses their work ethic, how they "worked long hours themselves" when they were young and "understand" labor. Because of this, stories about coffee shops will appeal to the Boomers. He says that they "love Starbucks" because it started out as one shop and is now "the biggest and the best." They like a story of success that somewhere along the way meanders through a sense of helping "the downtrodden." If small coffee shops and roasters can tell a story of having "fought hard" for their market share and "made hard choices" along the way, the Boomers will flock to them. If people selling coffee can write stories about producers that appeal to the convictions they formed in the 1960s that rights must be defended and war ended, they can win consumers. He suggests that Boomers are more likely to buy coffee grown by people who live in a war-torn country ("Guatemala really appeals to their sense of postwar hardships"). Since they are health-conscious and "really wrote the first book on organics" they are particularly interested in organic-certified coffee, in that its story is one of a "more healthy" drink than regular coffee. He also argues that Boomers want the standardization of a chain retail outlet but the "feel" of an "upscale," personalized experience. This is why they especially like chains that are meant to feel like local coffee shops (e.g., Peets, Caribou, and Starbucks).

Since Generation X is defined by the depressing events of the Reagan era, and since we are "liquid," we are hard to sell to. We are "cynical" when it comes to retail and want "diverse venues" for standard consumer products. We don't want the same experience over and over again (the aforementioned chain coffee shops). We want a coffee shop that has an authentic story that we can connect with. We like alternative venues that might have been begun as anti-establishment shops. We like the "Seattle connection" to be articulated in the shop stories. We want to know the story of the shop and the stories of the people who work there. We also want stories behind each of the products, all similar but marketed to us as "unique." We like the idea of authenticity when it comes to the people who grow the coffee. And we like the idea of experiencing some aspect of their lives by drinking the coffee. We want to connect to the authenticity of others in some way, and that way can easily be through buying a particular product. We also like the idea of supporting people whose story shows that they are "bucking" the establishment in some way.

The people that Mr. Nebraska called millennials are for him the "driving force" behind the "globalism" that is emerging in the specialty coffee market. While Boomers and Generation Xers appreciate certain aspects of the

Coffee growers from the Eastern Highlands at the SCAA

stories behind origin-marketed, fair-trade, and organic coffees, it is the millennials who "thrive" on these stories. "They want to change the world and they know that they can do it through coffee." They also "know that the politics of their parents are not their politics" and that their politics "can change the world one village at a time." They are much less concerned with the shop and its story and much more with the ways coffee can connect them with "people all over the world" and allow them to "participate in" the grower's struggles. They define self through their consumption, seeing themselves as politically active through their connection with "these stories about growers and the environment."

The marketing seminar is wrapped up by Mr. Nebraska with a long discussion about how each generation wants a particular story about the products that it buys. He talks about the process of creating a story for a business and how coffee works to "sell itself in today's market universe" because of the stories of growers that can be associated with it. He is passionate about the reality that he has just laid out for us—he repeatedly talks about how the "DNA" of the consumer is set along generational lines and how these generations want to "know and experience" stories about their coffee.

Producer Production

The following blog entry, entitled, "Papua New Guinea—Back to the Future," is one example of how coffees from Papua New Guinea are given a story by marketers and roasters and how that story is conveyed to consumers. It was written by an employee of Dean's Beans and placed on the company's website—a form of media with increasing power both in terms of number of consumers reached and the reach of what is inspired by the media.[1] The company is a small, extremely successful specialty coffee-roasting company in Massachusetts that specializes in organic and fair trade–certified coffee. It sells only certified specialty organic and fair-trade coffees and associates each of its coffees with certain origins. The Dean's Beans employee who visited the Eastern and Western Highlands of Papua New Guinea in 2005 writes:

> Chiseled warriors in Bird of Paradise headdresses and spears, impassable mountain roads, stunning vistas, abundant gardens of coffee and vegetables. Papua–New Guinea is the final frontier of dreams, of images from the pre-colonial past. Yet here I am, the first American anyone can remember coming into these Highlands, many say the first white guy. I have dreamed of this land since I was a child, looking at National Geographic (yeah, those photos!), reading about its wildness in my Golden Book Encyclopedia.
>
> There are no roads connecting the capital, Port Moresby, with the rest of this island, which is the size of New England. We have to fly to the interior, and I am glued to the window of the small plane, knowing that below me are anacondas and pythons, tree kangaroos and Birds of Paradise, wild rivers and still uncontacted tribes.
>
> There is also coffee, introduced to the Highlands only in the 1950's from rootstock taken from the famed Jamaican Blue Mountains. Coffee is the only cash crop in the Highlands. The people grow all of their own food, using the coffee money to buy cooking oil, sugar, used clothes and other necessaries. They depulp the cherries by hand using round rocks. This is the only place in the world where coffee is depulped this way. It is a family affair, and I visit with several families singing and depulping by the river. After sun drying the beans, the villagers have to carry the sixty pound sacks on their backs for up to twenty miles, over mountains, through rivers via rocky paths.

Historically, they would sell their beans to a number of middlemen who wait by the only road, giving the farmers pennies for their labor. But we are here to change that. We are here to work with several farmer associations to create legally recognized cooperatives, and to create more direct trade relationships that should increase the farmer's income fourfold, as well as increase sales.

As I am the first coffee buyer to come into this area, the farmers organize a Coffee Cultural Show. I thought that meant a few dancing and singing groups, a feast and a gift exchange. Wrong! As we rolled into a distant village after three hours over rivers, boulders, mudpits and bridges that shook beneath the land rover, we were greeted by ten thousand people! It was the largest gathering ever seen in these parts. Traditional warrior societies, women's clans, singing groups, hunters and every possible combination of feathers, noses pierced with tusks, and painted bodies festooned with coffee branches and berries greeted us riotously. I was hoisted into the air and carried almost a mile by joyful men, while the women called a welcoming chant. There were speeches by every village's elders, by coffee farmers and of course by me.

For two days the festivities roared on, segued together by an all-night discussion around a fire about coffee techniques, trade justice, the role of women and every imaginable subject for people who have never met an American or a Fair Trader. Wild pigs were cooked on hot stones in pits, covered with banana leaves. Huge plates of yams (they laughed when I told them about research which links yam consumption to twin births—and they have a lot of twins there!). Of course, we brewed up lots of Dean's Beans Papuan coffee (Ring of Fire). It was the first time these farmers had ever had their own coffee, and they loved the taste almost as much as they loved seeing their own tribal names on the coffee bags, tee-shirts and hats I had made for the visit. As we passed through the Highlands, we had to stop at each tribal boundary for permission to enter the territory.

Considering that there are over eight hundred tribes in PNG, we were crossing boundaries every ten miles or so. At each boundary we were greeted by warriors in full dress, with welcoming chants and speeches, and invited to feast and speak. Needless to say, it took a long time to get a short distance, but we were well fed and made hundreds of new friends every day.

Back in the capital, we went on the radio (four million listeners nightly, as there is no electricity in the villages, only battery powered radios) and talked about making strong cooperatives and quality coffee to insure vibrant communities. Our meeting with the Prime Minister didn't happen, so we spent a day on an island of fishermen and their families, cooking the bounty of the sea and playing with the kids. My kinda day. Papua–New Guinea. A lifelong dream come true. It was a profound honor to be able to go as an emissary of peace and positive social change. If you ever get to go, DO IT! You can be assured of a warm welcome and a great cup of coffee. Just tell them you're a friend of mine.[2]

This blog entry is a good example of what Mr. Nebraska suggested that roasters, importers, and marketers do to create a story for specialty coffees.[3] It is representative of many of the narratives one finds today about specialty coffee from Papua New Guinea. You can see this same system of representation of images in a form of visual marketing on Youtube. In one video the man who wrote the blog entry above provides commentary over a set of images that portray the poverty and primitivism he discursively produces above.[4]

The narratives created by Mr. Nebraska and the Dean's Beans employee are what Bryant and Goodman (2004, 344) have called "political ecology narratives." These marketing narratives engage a set of representational practices that seem to show clear connections between "alternative forms of consumption in the North" and social and environmental justice in the South (345). However, they show a fictitious version of political ecology. In addition, they craft producers and consumers in ways that are equally fictitious. These moments, the moment of consumer production, the moment of producer production, and the moment of fictitious political ecology, would not be possible were it not for the neoliberal changes in the global economy that have taken place over the past fifty years. Nor would they be possible without the growth of the specialty coffee industry.

Specialty Coffee

In the late 1980s the popular media in the United States began to carry stories about the relationship between coffee production and environmental sustainability, and by the mid-1990s "sustainable" coffee production was being directly linked to "saving" tropical rainforests ("The Greening of Giving" 1993; Hull 1999; Pennypacker 1997). Throughout the late 1990s and during the early 2000s this trend continued, with an almost exponential growth in the number of stories linking coffee to the environment.[5] Today the coffee-related popular narrative around the world encompasses not only an environmental message but also a message about how growing particular kinds of coffee can help rural peoples pursue small-scale economic development in ways that allow them access to their fair share of the global circulation of cash, without destroying the natural environments in which many of them live (Alsever 2006; Pascual 2006). In addition, the purchasing of coffee and other kinds of commodities that have been cast as embedding "ecological, social, and/or place-based values" into market transactions has come to be thought of as a potential "form of resistance" to globalization that individual consumers can practice (Guthman 2007, 456; see also Bryant and Goodman 2004). The kinds of coffee that are linked to environmental and social sustainability, economic justice, and resistance are known as specialty coffees. These coffees include single-origin-marketed coffee, organic coffee, fair-trade coffee, flavored coffee, bird-friendly coffee, and other coffees that are seemingly socially responsible. These new types of coffee differ markedly from coffees of the past in a number of significant ways.

From the 1940s to the 1990s corporate roasters like Maxwell House dominated the international market for coffee, to the total exclusion of small companies (Roseberry 1996). In the United States, while coffee consumption was at first a practice favored by the elite, by the beginning of the twentieth century it was a drink accessible to all—consumed in both working-class and elite homes (Jimenez 1995). In 1864 Jabez Burns had invented an inexpensive roasting machine, and small roasting companies emerged across the northeastern United States (Pendergrast 1999, 55–57). These small companies grew, and by the 1890s there was a thriving coffee industry in the Northeast. During the first three decades of the 1900s a true national market for coffee emerged, and the process standardizing quality, taste, and production began (Jimenez 1995; Roseberry 1996).

The Second World War was a "boon for the coffee industry" worldwide (Pendergrast 1999, 222). This was in part because the United States army began to requisition about 140,000 bags of coffee a month to serve to the troops, and in part because the war precipitated notable shifts in the supply chain for coffee. To supply troops with vast quantities of coffee the government, rather than buy from many small roasters, contracted with Maxwell House and a few other factories for coffee to be produced specifically for the military. In 1942, to assure that there was enough coffee for its contracted factories, the War Production Board took control over all coffee entering the United States market and began to regulate and ration the commodity (Pendergrast 1999, 222). In practice this regulation meant that coffee was rationed for civilians. The result, perhaps predictable in hindsight, was that both civilians and the coffee industry panicked. Although the rationing policy ended in July 1943, the perception of coffee as a limited and luxury good had been firmly planted in the minds of consumers (Pendergrast 1999, 223). Hence, the war simultaneously created an enhanced desire for coffee among civilians and soldiers and pumped money into the major coffee manufacturers. After the war these manufacturers embarked on expensive and expansive advertising campaigns to keep coffee in people's heads as an item that played an important role in their daily life. This influx of cash into the industry, and into the pockets of big companies like Maxwell House, allowed for continued standardization and set the stage for a "trend toward coffee of the lowest common denominator" (Roseberry 1996, 765).

In 1963 the International Coffee Organization (ICO) was formed. This body was charged with regulating the industry globally and meant to enforce the International Coffee Agreement (ICA) of 1962. The ICA set production quotas based on a combination of global supply and demand trends and predictions for future crops. It was justified by the argument that the coffee market had long suffered from vacillations between oversupply, and thus low prices, and undersupply, with high prices. The ICA was meant to stabilize the market and the industry so that the producing countries in Latin America, Africa, and Asia would not suffer the social, economic, and political consequences of sudden falls in prices. The first ICA, in 1962, was followed by a second agreement in 1968 that created a system whereby coffee produced in excess of the quota of any country was barred from the market or withheld from circulation. Additionally, the ICO played a role in promoting coffee consumption and increasing demand, so that extra coffee being withheld from the market would eventually find consumers. The original quota system collapsed in 1973 but was renegotiated in 1975 after a frost in Brazil destroyed the largest coffee crop in the world. Ratified in 1983, the new agreement negotiated a flexible quota system.

From the conclusion of the Second World War through the 1950s, coffee consumption in the United States remained relatively flat, with little fluctuation in the levels of coffee that were bought and sold (Roseberry 1996,

765). Between 1962 and 1980, however, coffee consumption declined radically in the United States (Roseberry 1996, 765; see also Pendergrast 1999, chapter 16). During this period of decline fewer people were becoming coffee drinkers, and those who were regular coffee drinkers were cutting back. Even more troubling for the coffee marketing industry was the inconvenient fact that coffee drinking was "skewed toward an older set," most of whom had become hooked on coffee during the war (Roseberry 1996, 765). Companies were struggling to bring young people into the market.

As coffee consumption gradually declined in the United States, the ICO and its member countries were having trouble meeting their agreed-upon production and consumption quotas. As a result, big companies began pushing for less government intervention into the market. These companies were not the coffee companies of the 1940s and 1950s but rather gigantic agro-industrial groups like the Philip Morris Corporation, which had slowly grown into leviathan-like entities that held extraordinary power to influence governments and international treaty making. In 1989 the ICA broke down altogether when negotiations over quotas forced the ICO to recognize that it would not be able to reach a new agreement by the time the agreement of 1983 was set to expire. Scholars track this breakdown to a combination of various factors, including the renegotiation of production quota allocations globally, lobbying by the agro-industrial companies, which sought more freedom to buy extra-quota coffee at prices lower than those set by the ICA, and the inability of both consuming and producing countries to control the movement of extra-quota coffee (Muradian and Pelupessy 2005). This breakdown resulted in a crisis in the financial structures that move the global coffee supply and prompted a price collapse. The late 1990s and early 2000s saw some of the lowest prices for coffee ever seen, a deregulation of the market that allowed gigantic companies to move their capital rapidly and with no regulation, the movement of new producers (like Vietnam) into the market with no controls on their production at all, and a flooding of the market with low-quality coffee from Vietnam and higher-quality coffee from Brazil (which had always resented the quota system because of historic overproduction in the country). Some economists argue that "from the standpoint of economic efficiency, the crisis is an adaptation period that would lead to a more efficient allocation of resources, as a result of increased competition and the removal of market distortions, particularly those exerted by national coffee boards. Indeed, the post-ICA situation has led to better price transmission between exporters and producers, which is an indication of large efficiency" (Muradian and Pelupessy 2005, 2029). Yet so-called price transmission has not been improved for everyone along the global circuit of coffee movement. Today coffee growers make less money for their coffee while coffee consumers pay more for theirs.

Throughout the 1990s, after deregulation, the conditions of the global coffee market became "oligopolistic," with a few groups (Kraft Jacobs–Suchard, Philip Morris, Nestlé, the Sara Lee multiproduct group, and Procter and Gamble) dominating the market. For example, Kraft Jacobs–Suchard owns Kraft, General Foods, Jacobs, and Suchard, and through these food giants and their coffee brands (Maxwell, Jacques Vabre, Carte Noire, Cafés Grand-Mère, Samaiza, Hag, On-ko), controls 32 percent of the global coffee market. (Renard 1999, 34). As of 2000 in the United States "73 per cent of the market" was "in the hands of the top three: Kraft General Food (31 per cent), Folgers Coffee (24 per cent), and Nestlé (18 per cent)," while in European countries like Germany, Italy, Belgium, and France 77 percent of the market was controlled by five companies (Renard 1999, 34). This "modern capitalist" form of food production, the global agro-food system, is known to be both ecologically and socially destructive (see Raynolds 2000; Renard 1999). Over the past thirty years it has developed in such a way as to capture and hold profits at the top of its vertical chains of integration (e.g., in the form of CEO salaries, shareholder profits, and capital for multinational expansion) while distributing fewer and fewer profits to the very bottom (e.g., to agricultural laborers; see Jaffee 2007).

During the deregulation of the coffee industry that resulted in the conditions described above, the ICA was cast as a set of regulations unfriendly to business, and as it was phased out, the coffee industry was affected by privatization, corporate attempts to minimize labor costs, state attempts to reduce public spending on social welfare, and the retreat of the state from the support and regulation of public life in general. Since the breakdown of the ICA in 1989—when quota and control provisions were suspended and the verification of stocks as well as certain provisions related to labor and production were suspended—there have been negotiations and new agreements. Yet none of these agreements have had quotas, control provisions, stock verification, environmental controls, or any provisions related to labor. At just about the same time as the decline of the ICA, the World Bank was implementing its first Structural Adjustment Loan Project in Papua New Guinea. The project began in June 1990 and closed in June 1992, and while the majority—62 percent—of the $50 million in project funds went to reforming the public administration, law, and justice sectors, 14 percent went to industry and trade reforms (Easterly 2000; Elek 1991). This is not unusual, because during the 1980s and 1990s, under pressure from the World Bank and the IMF, most coffee-producing countries underwent comprehensive market deregulation under the rubric of neoliberalization (see chapter 1).[6]

Neoliberalization's connection to coffee begins with the Structural Adjustment Programs encouraged and imposed by the IMF and the World Bank since the 1950s. More broadly, Castree has argued that all "neoliberal ideas may well have 'gone global' from the mid-1980s courtesy of the USA and its influence at the World Bank and the IMF" (Castree 2010, 13). These programs promoted growth-oriented, outward-focused economies, an expanded role for the private sector in providing state-like services and driving national growth, the removal of barriers perceived to hinder the flow of international capital, a diminished role for the state in economic regulation and the provision of services, and the deregulation of domestic labor markets (Harvey 2006a).

While solidifying control of the market by huge companies, the neoliberalization of coffee production and consumption through the retreat of the state has the odd effect of opening spaces for other industry actors in the market (Bacon 2004, 499). The dissolution of the ICA created a gap that allowed small companies to enter the global coffee market. With direct access to producers and consumers, small-scale coffee roasters, traders, and sellers of coffee-related objects flourished in this newly deregulated market.

Another aspect of this phase of neoliberalization, broadly speaking, was that governance that had once been the purview of the state became the purview of NGOs: so-called civil society groups like churches, development agencies, and other international bodies and organizations. These actors moved into various structural positions concerned with the environment, economic development, and human rights—areas thought of today as directly connected to coffee production—that had been previously filled by state agencies. Additionally, in the past decade numerous voluntary regulatory systems have emerged within the coffee industry. These voluntary systems are meant to help govern the movement of coffee and lend some form of governance to the entire structure of the commodity chain (Muradian and Pelupessy 2005, 2030).

As mentioned above, with changes in the structure of the global market for coffee the wholesale prices of coffee and thus the prices paid to producers have fallen drastically (Bacon 2004; Ponte 2002a; Ponte 2002b). Some scholars and activists argue that the sharp decline in prices paid to farmers between 1999 and 2004 (with a global thirty-year low in 2001) galvanized NGOs, development organizations, well-meaning companies, and well-meaning consumers to expand the market for socially responsible coffees that bring more money to producers and contribute to environmental sustainability by creating voluntary systems of regulation (Bacon 2004; Bacon, Mendez, Flores Gomez, et al. 2008; Moberg and Lyon 2010, 4). They also argue that the trend toward socially responsible coffee is tied to increased consumer knowledge about the plight of poor farmers and a heightened awareness of "quality, taste, health, and environment" (Bacon 2004, 497).[7] According to these scholars, pressure from consumers resulted in the growth of the specialty market and the development of the Specialty Coffee Association of America (SCAA), an industry group made up of roasters, traders, and sellers that promotes specialty coffees in North America. Activists and scholars who argue that these coffees can redress inequality do so because they believe that production and distribution monitoring through certification and labeling can work to protect conditions of production, land use, labor relations, and the environment, thus countering some of the ravages of neoliberalization (Guthman 2007). Labeling is the practice by which certification standards are expressed visibly on the packaging of commodities. For example, products identified as "fair trade–certified," "organic," "free-range," or "vegetarian" are all "labeled."

In contrast to those who view specialty coffee as a corrective to neoliberal changes, others see these coffees, the conditions of their production, and their market as brought about by deregulation and neoliberalization (Doane 2010; Roseberry 1996). Roseberry argues that as the market structure changed with the demise of the ICO, small-scale coffee-producing companies, distributors, and roasters began to "envision a segmented market rather than a mass market," and that as they imagined this market, the advertising agencies working for them attempted to create new consumers (Roseberry 1996, 765).[8] People who had previously not been coffee drinkers were targeted through the creation of stories and images designed to appeal to them along generational, political, and class lines. Certain types of specialty coffee were marketed to appeal to people's ideas about their own refined tastes and their unique position as a certain type of consumer, while others were marketed to appeal to people with particular political

Rainforest Alliance coffee at the SCAA

beliefs. Marketers wanted coffee consumption to be seen as a way to distinguish oneself in terms of class and to express one's political ideas. To this end they worked to create consumers' desire right along with the growth of the new specialty industry. As with other commodities, marketers worked to produce the demand first and then present products that would fill people's sense of need, like a "key in a lock" (Haug 1986, 93). As these specialty markets developed they came to resemble what has been called a "post-Fordist" regime (Harvey 1989); they were flexible and supposedly consumer-oriented and consumer-driven, two of the hallmarks of neoliberalized markets.

Voluntary Regulatory Systems

The global commodity circuit or ecumene for coffee is a set of networks that connect the labor of some people to the purchasing power and consumption habits of others. Under the ICA these social relations of production and consumption were regulated by international agreements between national coffee boards and governments. Now that these agreements no longer regulate the circuit, other forms of regulation have emerged. Some economists argue that "an essential property" of any commodity circuit or "chain" is "its governance structure, which determines to a considerable extent how resources and gains are allocated and flow within the chain" (Muradian and Pelupessy 2005, 2030). These governance structures regulate the flow of information, production activities, and entrance into the commodity circuit. Without a government-organized governance structure, the most powerful entities in the commodity circuit fill the void of governance and begin to exert control over the entire circuit. Governance structures determine "the distribution of income and margins between different segments of the chain" (Muradian and Pelupessy 2005, 2030). When national marketing boards had a say in the governance structure of the global commodity circuit for coffee, there was often a "guaranteed" "survival income" for growers and a large portion of the retail value of coffee making its way to "agents in producing countries" (Muradian and Pelupessy 2005, 2031).

Today, without those mandatory governance controls, a large number of voluntary regulatory systems have emerged in the world of coffee. These systems are supposedly meant to "set quality, social or environmental standards, and typically involve a larger degree of traceability, and monitoring along different agents of the commodity chain" (Muradian and Pelupessy 2005, 2032; see also Blowfield 1999; Goodman 2004; Ponte 2002b; Raynolds 2000). Gereffi, Garcia-Johnson, and Sasser (2001) and Muradian and Pelupessy (2005) identify the following forms of voluntary regulation within the coffee industry: first-party systems, such as the self-generated ethical guidelines of Starbucks; second-party systems, which include things like the Sustainable Agriculture Platform and are meant to offer guidelines for numerous food commodities for social and ecological sustainability; third-party systems, such as fair-trade, organic, shade-grown, and Utz Kapeh certifications, all created by parties that entered into the coffee world after the deregulation of the market and that set voluntary standards meant to increase income for growers and market knowledge for consumers; and fourth-party systems, under which multiple parties come together to develop sustainability goals for the industry.

Because they are the most important (or pertinent or influential or disruptive?) mechanisms for the coffee industry today, this chapter focuses on third-party voluntary regulation systems. Third-party certification initially brought groups with a particular political agenda or ideology into the role of governance. The stated goals were to bring information about the product and its conditions of production to consumers so that they could make informed choices about the products they were buying. In a sense the consumer could cast a ballot for particular social or ecological goods by buying particular kinds of coffee. For example, if consumers felt ethically connected to the issue of environmental sustainability, they might vote for it by buying organic-certified coffee. Alternatively, they might vote for fair labor practices by buying fair trade-certified coffee. These third-party regulatory systems have even been characterized as "alternative" economic projects (Fridell 2003, 4), projects that will begin to alter the global economy in ways that make it more socially and ecologically equitable. Voluntary regulation systems were initially meant to "re-embed" global agriculture—a set of commodity circuits that have become "ecologically and socially destructive"—in a set of equitable and sustainable social relationships (Raynolds 2000, 297).

One primary goal of most third-party systems is to reconnect commodities, their producers, and their locations of origin in the minds of consumers. Guthman (2004, 235) has called this a "politics of re-location" and argues that while activists see this process as working to de-fethishize food commodities, it is doubtful that food labeling, one of the major actions taken by third-party certifiers, will be "able to do this work in a substantive manner" (Guthman 2004, 235). Guthman shows that the current paradigm for consuming correctly, or ethically, has seen a conflation between civil protest or political action and consumer choice; that people read a label and assume that it enacts their politics. As someone who has traced the organic movement from a truly political movement in the 1960s to an industry-led movement today—characterized by the hollowing out of regulatory codes that govern organic labeling by state and national governments so that large corporations can get into the organics market—she views the movement as decreasingly about politics and civil protest and increasingly about large producers wanting to outcompete small producers. For large producers, organic labeling is seen as a highly effective way to accomplish this goal (336). With regard to coffee specifically, Molly Doane (2010, 230) argues that "rather than shed light on the ongoing challenges faced by producers and the solutions they have fashioned, fair trade practice highlights the power of persona choice and agency of consumers." With this, third-party certification schemes, like fair trade, may actually "refetishize" coffee rather than "defetishize" it, by hiding the social relations of production of the fair-trade system.

Today ethical labels embed a perception of increased value in commodities that allows producers to increase their rents. Consumers pay higher prices for products with these labels because they assume that the products meet food safety, quality, and ethical standards. They also assume that they learn something about the people who produce the commodity along the way. As labeling has been hollowed out by large producers, however, this is no longer true in all instances. And as large producers have entered the game, small producers have found it more difficult to obtain raw materials and consequently have been forced to raise their prices. This means that ethical consumption is now a class-related act (Guthman 2004, 336), a lifestyle choice that marks status. By the same token it means that poor people do not have access to the truly organic products that they did in the past. The process of regulation of labels has not solved the issues of commodity fetishes at all; rather, organic labeling "creates its own fictions and erasures in order to fill the gap between physical use value and signification" (244).

Like Guthman, Blowfield analyzes third-party regulation systems in terms of labeling initiatives but also adds to the analysis "enterprise initiatives" (Blowfield 1999, 756). With enterprise initiatives, companies develop "codes of practice" to help them implement ethical standards (157). Power relations are implicit in these initiatives, because the (often southern) international labor that is meant to be socially protected by these codes of practice or even economically benefit from them is almost never consulted when they are formulated. In fact, depending on what is easiest for them, businesses can put in or take out whatever they like in their "codes of practice." Hence codes of practice often fail to take into account the whole social and economic impact of production. Usually they are targeted at the production site itself and not at other sites along the global commodity chains that may have unfair social or economic impacts. Moreover, these codes of practice, at the time when Blowfield was writing, rarely combined social and environmental factors.

While Blowfield argues that labeling initiatives suffer from the same problems as enterprise initiatives, they are better equipped to adapt to the realities of global commodity flows and relations of production. Blowfield contends that through social and environmental auditing, labeling initiatives can begin to have an effect on sustainability, accountability, and the like (1999). The grading by labels is based on either "performance methods" or "procedural methods." Blowfield argues that both methods have weaknesses: "Performance approaches . . . have the advantage of setting clear standards that observers can understand, but are often criticized for being too static, and for encouraging performance to be measured on a pass-fail basis. Procedural approaches are more dynamic and many value progress towards a goal rather than simply its achievement. However, exclusively procedural schemes can allow organizations to set goals that are too low, and may be too complicated and reliant on a paper trial to be implemented by small producers" (1999, 764). In the end what matters most is participation from the global South, as implicitly all of Blowfield's paper is about North-South relations: "Without greater participation from developing countries, and particularly a shift in decision making from the North to the South, ethical trade will at best be paternalistic and at worst harmful to those it is intended to benefit" (767).

Some scholars have examined labeling initiatives specifically focused on ecological outcomes and environmental conservation. Bray, Sanchez, and Murphy examine the history and successes of "shade-grown" and "bird-friendly" coffees in Mexico (Bray, Sanchez, and Murphy 2002). If ecologically focused producers join cooperatives or are already connected to networks of growers (e.g., the vast Catholic church network in some Latin American countries), they are able to increase profits, for several reasons: larger quantities of coffee for sale attract buyers; the growers are able to share certification costs and the costs of adopting certain forms of production technology, to pool labor at the more labor-intensive times of the season, and to draw on the strengths of some cooperative members (e.g., marketing expertise or education); and NGOs tend to work with larger networks rather than small groups (Bray, Sanchez, and Murphy 2002). But these ecologically minded initiatives, like most enterprise and labeling initiatives, focus only on production.

Fair-trade certification was meant to counter some of the problems with ethical consumption in the early 1990s that focused only on production. By contrast, "unlike other certifications . . . Fair Trade is unique in that it covers both trade and production conditions" (Raynolds 2002, 5). Fair trade has a history that has been told elsewhere. It began on the continent and then moved quickly to the UK, the United States, and Japan, focusing on coffee and tea as its biggest sectors. Most producers who are regulated by fair-trade standards reside in the global South. Raynolds critically analyzed how fair trade worked, when it worked, and what its successes were in the late 1990s and early 2000s with coffee production in Latin and South America. She concluded that producers did well with fair trade when strong organizational links already existed within producer groups, when there were good links between producers and the outside markets, when there was a higher level of education or knowledge of markets among producers, and when the bio-physical conditions for productions were favorable (e.g., good soil fertility, good elevation for certain crops, and stable long-term land tenure regimes). Raynolds was unable, however, to adequately assess the poverty alleviation claims tied to fair-trade certification. Though some farmers make more money under fair trade, others do not. Though some networks distribute profits equally and move profits to the farmer end of the chain, others do not. More recently scholars have found that fair trade means different things to different people (see Lyon and Moberg 2010). In some places there is high demand for fair-trade items, meaning that some people are willing to pay a higher premium for certified commodities (Smith 2010). The certification of bananas in St. Lucia has meant that some growers earn more money and have more satisfying lives as producers (Moberg 2010). Banana certification has also positively benefited women, since they are the growers who most often take part in certification (Moberg 2010). This situation can be contrasted with that surrounding coffee certification in Guatemala, where male growers are benefiting more than female growers as members of cooperatives (Lyon 2010). Indeed, across Mexico and Central America the benefits of certification are mixed (Bacon, Mendez, Flores Gomez, et al. 2008).

To understand voluntary regulatory systems and certification standards in general, and to show how certification has changed global markets, Conroy (2001) examined the Rainforest Stewardship Council and fair-trade certification. Through this comparative work Conroy demonstrates how labeling certification, which has been championed by NGOs and consumers, has become a powerful ideology that affects markets and has captured the imagination of international firms. He shows how pressure from NGOs and consumers works in light of the importance that contemporary companies attach to their "brands," as well as how these companies are perceived in the globalizing market. Today, Conroy argues, when NGOs and consumer groups threaten companies with protests, most will comply in some ways with their demands. Today labeling initiatives are advantageous for both NGOs and large companies (Conroy 2001). For companies, labels increase their brands' value and reduce their vulnerability to adverse publicity and political action, while at the same time making consumers feel as if the companies are willingly opening themselves to external auditing

(Conroy 2001, 12). The result is increased consumer trust for the companies, which in turn benefits the brand. For NGOs labeling works to bring multiple forms of advocacy under one rubric (e.g., human rights, the environment, children's rights), makes it easier to hold large companies accountable, seemingly creates standards that are based on the interests of "stakeholders" and therefore have some potential for being successfully imposed, and allows for the easy identification of industry leaders who can be the targets of political pressure from the NGOs (Conroy 2001, 13). Conroy argues that "in an increasingly privatized world, with restrictions on what the global trading system will allow local and national governments to legislate, these movements may be the only alternative to the competitive downgrading of social and environmental practices by firms worldwide" (18).

Some scholars have written about the potential for integrating several forms of voluntary third-party regulation. Browne et al. (2000) explore the link between ethical trade, the organic movement, and the fair-trade movement to assess the potential for a timely integration of all three. They argue that while the social good that might ensue is substantial, integrating all three forms of auditing would potentially make goods prohibitively expensive for prospective consumers. Browne et al. (2000) show that most consumers in the late 1990s bought organic products primarily because of health concerns—more specifically health concerns for themselves, not concerns for producers nor for the global environment. As long as they would not need to pay higher prices for the products they desired, these consumers would have been willing to buy products certified or labeled as ethical or fair trade. Their research also shows that in the late 1990s the large companies marketing organic products and the large supermarket chains selling them were against the full integration of standards because they feared this very consequence. They conclude, "Ethical trading does not prioritize environmental issues, but nor can it ignore them. The dialogue linking organic to ethical is therefore asymmetrical: the organic movement is positively seeking links but the ethical lobby has less commitment to organics" (Browne et al. 2000, 87).

While there has been this vast work done on third-party certifications, almost no one has carefully examined the images that go along with single-origin marketing, even though the same structural changes that allowed for, or forced, the certification movement also opened the space for this form of marketing. Patrick Wilson's work (2010) on how the marketing of fair-trade crafts creates conditions for indigenous authenticity is one exception. Wilson shows how fair-trade-marketed crafts rely on two representational strategies: reinforcing the authenticity of the objects by linking them to seemingly authentic natives, and "sanitizing" the social and economic lives of producers by framing them with "idyllic rural backdrops" (177). The aim is to show consumers what will be lost if they do not, through their individual actions, buy these products. These representational strategies "reproduce central commonsense Western assumptions of indigeneity" that draw on images of harmony between nature and culture, images of "cultural purity," ideas about community and its place of primacy in indigenous lives, and ideas about strong traditions (178). This crafting of indigeneity "narrows the range of economic activities that would fall under the rubric of acceptable indigeneities, thereby constraining the range of potential economic outlets that would be supported by fair trade for indigenous producers" (192). It effectively forces indigenous peoples into particular forms of production, whether they want to be there or not.

Embedded Social Relations?

Whether one thinks that the market for specialty coffees emerged because of consumers' desires to redress global inequities generated by neoliberalization through consumption choices, or because of the desires of businesses to find new consumers for their products, we can see that the market for specialty coffee attempts to merge seemingly disparate strands of consumer life: economic choice, political action, and identity production. Economic choice (what people buy, when they buy it, where they buy it, and why they buy it) is wedded to political action (both the ideas and practices that people associate with their politics and the sense of communities-of-sentiment that goes along with politics and political affinity), and the two then contribute to identity production (how people come to be in the world and see themselves in the world and in relation to others, especially in terms of identities based in social and environmental equity). At first glance, the contemporary specialty-coffee market seems to be countering the very process that Karl Polanyi called "disembedding" (Guthman 2007; Jaffee 2007).

In writing about the economy as a "process" in general and the emergence of the modern market as a system of organization specifically, Polanyi argues that the economy "is embedded and enmeshed in institutions, economic and noneconomic. The inclusion of the noneconomic is vital.

For religion or government may be as important for the structure and functioning of the economy as monetary institutions or the availability of tools and machines themselves that lighten the toil of labour" (Polanyi 1958, 127). As Polanyi traces how and when markets gain radical importance over other aspects of social life, he shows how the process of "disembedding" has taken place. Disembedding, as Polanyi saw it, occurred when economic activities, like buying coffee, became increasingly removed from the social relationships in which they had historically occurred and when the objects circulating in the economy came to be seen as fetishes seen as emerging in and of themselves and not from labor. In his discussion of disembedding, Polanyi shows how economic transactions increasingly became abstracted from social relations. Disembedding allowed for the disarticulation of economic choice, political action, social relationships, and identity production through abstraction, and in this way made the market less a web of social bonds and relations and more a clean and sharp set of economic transactions.

At first glance specialty coffees, again regardless of whether we imagine them as resulting from consumer desire or from market manipulation, seem to re-embed coffee into a web of social relationships. Well-meaning consumers are connected to well-meaning producers by well-meaning coffee industry businesses. A veritable love fest of learning about each other, supporting each other, and contributing to environmental sustainability while still taking part in the global market seems to have emerged. Conversely, it is my argument that these specialty coffees are first and foremost neoliberal coffees: coffees that have a place in the market because of structural changes in the global economy, changes that in addition to many other things target individuals as the seat of economic rights and responsibilities. In targeting them the purveyors of specialty coffee both produce and draw on the fantasy filled worlds of Mr. Nebraska and Dean's Beans. These worlds are full of virtual producers and virtual consumers.

Mr. Nebraska works to both create "virtual consumers" for his audience and to imbue them with particular sets of values.[9] James Carrier and Daniel Miller have built on Polyani's previously discussed notion of abstraction to propose a new set of theories about how we might think about contemporary social relationships in general and people's roles as consumers more specifically (Carrier and Miller 1998). They call this set of theories "virtualism." Carrier defines virtualism as the attempt to make the world around us look like and conform to an abstract model of it (Carrier

1998b, 2). He uses the concept to criticize thinking and policies in economics, a field in which there is a common tendency to abstract human decision making from its complex social context, and to build models of the world and its workings that cannot take into account the full range or complexity of people's daily social activities, practices, and lives. This much is normal for modelers. But these abstractions become virtualism when the real world is expected to transform itself in accordance with the models: "Perceiving a virtual reality becomes virtualism when people take this virtual reality to be not just a parsimonious description of what is really happening, but prescriptive of what the world ought to be; when, that is, they seek to make the world conform to their virtual vision. Virtualism, thus, operates at both the conceptual and practical levels, for it is a practical effort to make the world conform to the structures of the conceptual" (Carrier 1998b, 2).

Miller (1998b) argues that we can see this virtualism at work in the production of the contemporary consumer in economic discourses. He sees the creation of a "virtual consumer," or the image of a person who wants and desires and buys certain things, according to models of consumer behavior based on aggregate figures used in economic modeling. The world of retail then comes to resemble the world in this economistically modeled world—storeowners and shopkeepers alter the physical space of their businesses and the social actions of their business in attempts to catch part of the market of this virtual consumer. Eventually, if we follow Miller's argument, because the physical world has come to look like the virtual world, the consumer's actual behavior comes to mirror the virtual behavior, and the virtual consumers become real.

Mr. Nebraska creates virtual consumers and then lays out the process by which the physical world should and will come to reflect the wants, desires, and values of this consumer. He takes generational stereotypes and casts them as immutable biophysical characteristics that work to guide tastes, desires, politics, and economic choices. He also argues that the evaluative processes that consumers use to make choices are based in these immutable generational characteristics. But "generations" as objects and entities are a production of contemporary public culture; they are social artifacts. As artifacts they give demographers, journalists, and marketers a way of describing social and economic trends by age group without attending to race or class. In her analysis of the social creation of "Generation X," Sherry B. Ortner (1998) shows that the idea of "generations" began as a way of categorizing people as they bought homes and competed for jobs, promotions, and places in universities and colleges. In the past, generations were used to predict and talk about "identity through work: jobs, money, and careers" (Ortner 1998, 421). Today Mr. Nebraska relies on "generational marketing" to construct his virtual consumers, and to set the stage for telling stories about producers and production that draw on the assumed values of these virtual consumers. It is therefore a fictional, virtual consumer and her values that guide how coffee production is to be told as a marketing narrative.

How is coffee production in Papua New Guinea turned into a story that consumers can "thrive" on? How does it become a story that makes people "want to change the world" or feel as if they learn something special about the world and themselves through its consumption? And how are stories told that will reconnect consumers' choice of coffee to politics in a way that fosters social relationships between producers and consumers and allows consumers to feel good about themselves? This is where companies like Dean's Beans enter the equation.

Dean's Beans focuses not only on commerce but also on "people-centered development," defined by the company as "an approach to international development that focuses on the real needs of local communities for the necessities of life (clean water, health care, income generation) that are often disrupted by conventional development assistance."[10] The company's website contrasts this form of development with "conventional development," which includes, "military aid, large dams, free trade zones and export economies that bring lots of money to the contractors and aid organizations, but often result in massive deforestation, resettlement of communities, introduction of pollutants and diseases." And the website states that the company is "committed to small, meaningful projects that the community actually wants, and that are sustainable over time without our continued involvement." It specifically links organic and fair trade–certified coffee with the company's critique of "conventional development," stating repeatedly that specialty coffees help growers to get their fair share of profit and contribute to the ecological health of the planet. Dean's Beans is therefore positioning itself as a company that attempts to redress the social and environmental inequity generated by neoliberalization. While this commitment to countering the evils of neoliberalization is noble, the way the company presents images of and ideas about Papua New Guinea reveals a global vision that has been produced by an imaginary progression from "stone age" to "civilized" and people without history, a vision which actually fuels neoliberalization.

Natural Stone Age Natives Marching toward Modernity

Over five hundred articles in the popular media are accessible through the search engine Lexis Nexis by means of the search terms "New Guinea" and "Stone Age." This image of New Guinea and its inhabitants—the inhabitants of both West Papua and Papua New Guinea—as somehow located close to or directly linked to something called the "Stone Age" is deeply embedded in the fantasy lives of Europeans, Americans, and Australians. In previous writings concerned with natural scientists working in Papua New Guinea, I have argued that anthropology, mass media, and individual fantasies of exotic nature and culture work to draw people to Papua New Guinea as researchers, activists, and tourists (West 2006, 160–63). Many visitors to Papua New Guinea fantasize about and desire "authentic" natives who live in an "authentic" and "untouched" nature. They want these natives to confrom to the stereotypes of "indigenous," "native," and "tribal" peoples that they have been exposed to through undergraduate anthropology classes, television programs, magazines, and movies. When the real residents of Papua New Guinea do not fit these stereotypes, they are considered not only less authentic but also less deserving of the rights to their traditional lands and livelihood strategies (West 2006, 167).

In previous work (West 2006, 2001) I have argued that through a series of comparative measures and visual tests based on these fantasy formations, conservation-minded people, both European-descended and elite Papua New Guinean, ideologically produce rural forest dwelling Papua New Guineans as either "authentic" or "inauthentic." For example, rural landholders who participate in the cash economy are seen as less authentic than rural landholders who do not have access to the cash economy; if people have houses made of "traditional" materials they are seen as more authentic than people who have houses made of store-bought materials; and if people attend missionary-inspired churches they are assumed to be less authentic than those who do not. After rural people are measured and understood through this process, they are accorded rights and responsibilities according to a set of rhetorical devices that locate them on a scale that assumes a linear progression from indigeneity to modernity.

The rhetorical devices used include discourses of parental relations that liken rural peoples to "children" who must be helped to understand the modern world by well-meaning outsiders, and discourses of threat and danger that characterize rural peoples who are not "indigenous enough" as overpopulating, tree-cutting, over-harvesting resource users. The assumed linear progression locates authentic indigeneity as a prior condition for modernization and fixes authentic relations with the biophysical world directly to indigeneity. According to conservation activists, as people are moved from indigenous to modern, either by forces beyond human control like capitalism and globalization or by their own desire to "modernize," they lose the ability to relate to their surroundings in ways that are appropriate for conservation. Yet much conservation intervention often attempts to "teach" rural peoples how to take part in the modern world so that they will not have to rely on their biophysical surroundings for their livelihoods and therefore will not destroy "nature."

Flora Lu Holt examines how conservation, in part because of the images discussed above, works to enforce a kind of subsistence primitivism on Huaorani communities in Ecuadorian Amazon (2005, 203). She argues that contemporary environmental protectionists have located indigenous peoples in an impossible position that she calls a Catch-22, in which "the cultural conditions deemed compatible with biodiversity conservation (i.e., low densities, limited technology, and subsistence production) are precisely those under which a common property theoretical framework would not predict conservationist practices to emerge. Conservation awareness arises when people exert pressure on resources and recognize the potential for overexploitation, conditions concurrent with population growth, adoption of Western technologies, and market production" (2005, 201). Ironically, in contemporary conservation western ways of seeing and being in the environment are implied to be both the problem and the solution.

In a discussion of a candlelight vigil for indigenous peoples on a college campus on "Indigenous People's Day," Liisa Malkki (1997, 59) raises the question of why indigenous peoples are often conflated with, and even seen as, an environmental issue: "fusing the faraway people with their forests . . . may have the effect of subtly animalizing while it spiritualizes. Like the wildlife, the indigenous are an object of inquiry and imagination not only for the anthropologist but also for the naturalist, the environmentalist, and the tourist." Malkki asks, "Are people 'rooted' in their native soil somehow more natural, their rights somehow more sacred, than those of other exploited and oppressed people? And, one wonders, if an 'indigenous Person' wanted to move away to a city, would her or his candle be extinguished?"

(59). This conflation of people and nature performs a double move, creating indigenous people as both heroes (defenders of the forests) and animals (residents of natural spaces who are only considered in that context). It also contributes to a politics that Malkki calls "magical naturalism" (Malkki 1997, 60). This politics spatially incarcerates the rooted, natural, loving, gentle natives by juxtaposing them with rootless, mobile, restless civilization.

In a reading of the popular and scholarly examinations of instances where "natives" do move and give up their "rootedness," Malkki shows that they are pathologized. Refugees, exiles, migrants, displaced persons—they are all seen as having the potential to suffer from a moral breakdown, to become apathetic, restless, or reckless terrorists, criminals, or untrustworthy persons who have lost their moral bearings. Instead of showing the structural constraints that make displacement "a shattering experience" for some, the literature on native movements and displacement locates pathology within the bodies of the natives (1997, 64). Historically, anthropology has contributed to the process whereby "culture" was territorialized and some people were ideologically tied to places: "Natives are not only persons who are from certain places, and belong to those places, but they are also those who are somehow incarcerated, or confined, in those places" (Appadurai 1988, 37).

These fantasies that locate groups of people on a scale from indigenous to modern are apparent not only in the worlds of environmental conservation and social activism but also in contemporary tourism. Rupert Stasch (2006), writing about primitivist tourism coming to the lands of Korowai peoples of West Papua, Indonesia (tourism that is meant to expose western people to primitive peoples), argues that "the models of 'primitive,' 'Stone Age,' or 'indigenous' humanity that tourists expect Korowai to fit are fantasy-formations acquired and elaborated in tourists' own cultural homes through mass media, through anthropology, through people's own imagining of alternatives to their home cultural lives, and in some cases through prior histories of encounter with people they find to match the stereotypy" (Stasch 2006, 1).

The tourists to whom Stasch refers focus on "violence, relation to nature, material technology, racial phenotype, and type of polity" in their assessments of Korowai's location on a scale from "stone age" to "modern" (2). There is an analogous assumption of a liner progression from indigeneity to modernity. Stasch's tourists see the indigenous side of the scale as primi-

Selling Papua New Guinea at the SCAA

Etau in coffee garden, Maimafu village

tive, and for them the primitive is equated with war, hunting, headhunting, and cannibalism.[11] Tourists also fantasize about their "primitives" as living in "intimate as well as dangerous" contact with the natural world (3). Their vision is similar to the conservation-related ones. The touristic primitive is also "uncontacted" or only "contacted slightly," and for Stasch's tourists this notion of "isolation" encompasses all the other attributes that he examines (4). The tourists whom Stasch worked with saw themselves as "metonymic extrusions of civilization and global history" (4) and as the bringers of the very thing from which their "primitives" were isolated. And these tourists want to catch people on the cusp of change, just as ecologists and other scientists want to catch ecosystems on the cusp of change.

More recently Stasch has tracked these ideas about Korowai across the popular media and back in time (Stasch 2011). He shows how the figure of the primitive endures and circulates globally, and he connects the images used to describe Korowai lives to historic travel writing and its role in "colonial or neo-colonial cognitive and political ends" (1). Stasch examines seven recent popular magazine articles, five newspaper stories, one book chapter, and one blog to argue that stories about Korowai rely on iconicity that he tracks in three ways. Stasch uses Bakhtin's notion of the "chronotope" to describe three scales of spatio-temporal understanding that are displayed in primitivist travel writing. Bakhtin argued that a chronotope is "the intrinsic connectedness of temporal and spatial relationships that are artistically expressed in literature" (1981, 84). Writers create worlds that reflect the spatio-temporal reality of their own worlds, or at least of how they experience their worlds.

For Stasch, in primitivist travel writing the first world created is the "narrated chronotope," or the narrated sequence of the writer's interactions with seemingly primitive peoples; the second is the "chronotope of textual performance," or the set of material, ideological, and linguistic relations between the writer and the reader; and the third is the "mythic chronotope," or the "mythic relation between contrasting primitive and civilized humans" (2011, 3). This final chronotope maps a spatiotemporal scale that mirrors notions of unilinear evolution and forms a set of ingrained ideas and images concerned with the relationship between modern media consumers, like tourists, and people who are considered by that first group to be "primitive" (6–9). So-called primitive people, who according to these travel writers are the people found on the island of New Guinea, are lost, childlike, Stone Age, cannibal savages who are losing their culture on their way to modernity, living in an ever-shrinking world on a last frontier which is a hell-on-earth jungle on the edge of humanity. The narrators, on the other hand, are intrepid, thoughtful adventurers, latter-day Michael Rockefellers primed for the discovery of untouched nature and culture who, like the tourists they inspire, can cross chronotopes. Stasch tracks these chronotopes, and the images they rely on, produce, and reinforce, in fourteen recent texts, arguing that the repetitive nature of the cronotopes makes the genre persuasive, and that its persuasiveness drives tourism.

Stasch's work complements David Lipset's argument about the agential nature of Bakhtin's original idea (Lipset 2011, 21; see also 1997, 2004, and 2007). Lipset argues that in addition to being a "category or unit of analysis" that orders events in time and space, a chronotope also engenders agency (Lipset 2011, 21). He goes on to argue that in Papua New Guinea, and by extension in other localities where modern institutions may not have the hold that they have in the global North, cases may arise where rival chronotopes give rise to "rival chronotopic claims about human agency in time and space" (21). These rival claims about agency then drive particular kinds of actions and the unfolding of events in a particular sequence in particular places. Lipset shows us that these chronotopic fantasies result in action, that they have physical effects on the world.

These chronotopic fantasies are grafted onto coffee from Papua New Guinea by the likes of Mr. Nebraska, Dean's Beans, and other people and organizations engaged in specialty marketing. The images and fantasies discussed above also endure in, and are perpetuated by, coffee marketing and certification, through the physical and ideological layout of coffee shops across the world, through the discursive production of "middlemen" who are out to rob authentic natives of their income, and in the rhetoric about saving the lifestyles of indigenous peoples living in "stone age" conditions through the helping hand of capitalism (even though it is capital's evils that are forcing the inevitable march toward modernity).

Using images of native peoples to sell commodities is nothing new, nor is the knowledge that western consumers "respond positively" to images of natives in ways that may well aid the political, social, and environmental causes of the natives (Conklin and Graham 1995, 102; Pigliasco 2010). The worry is that "the external market that bestows symbolic value may also take it away, particularly if the conditions of its legitimacy fail to be met" (Conklin and Graham 2005, 706). Recently John and Jean Comaroff have compelled us to think about a whole host of contemporary events and phenomena showing that there are new articulations, or what they call a "triangulation" of market forces, identity politics, and cultural practices (Comaroff and Comaroff 2009, 20). One of these articulations is the rapid rise of locally generated commodifications of culture. Papua New Guineans are rarely in control of the images used to sell the coffee they produce. It is much more the case that the commodification of the coffee results in the production of images of ethnicity (see Comaroff and Comaroff 2009, 67). It is the politics of these images that I am concerned with.

The Politics of Neoliberal Consumer and Producer Production

Two questions related to coffee grow out of all this work: How are the commercial possibilities for coffee in the United States and other northern nations tied to particular narratives about indigenous peoples, savagery, pristine nature and culture, and development in places like Papua New Guinea (Bryant and Goodman 2004)? And what are the material effects of these narratives on the people portrayed by them?

The coffee growers constructed by the Dean's Beans narrative seem to possess the same values as the virtual consumers for which the narrative was constructed. These growers seem to want to maintain tradition and maintain benign ecological relations with their forests. But at the same time they seem to wish to become incorporated more fully into the market economy as it is represented by Dean's Beans and its emissaries for coffee-based sustainability. They want to understand modernity but not lose their souls to it; they are ecologically noble savages who are fallen from grace but deeply want to maintain the ecological stability of their pristine forested lands. As the work of Holt, Malkki, and Stasch shows us, these images penetrate deeply into the Euro-American psyche and are a reflection of Euro-American fantasies about indigenous peoples.

When businesses tell stories like this one about virtual producers, they also want consumers to see natives as poor, third-world agricultural laborers who value and contribute to the ecological sustainability of the earth, while at the same time making just enough money to maintain their coffee-producing ways of life without wanting to gain access to all the things that consumers have, including the feeling of having the right to overconsume the world's resources. They want to provide consumers with an aura of social responsibility, political action, exotic locality, environmental sustainability, and social status through a capitalist marketing version of a Geertzian "being there" narrative. The idea is to market meaningfulness without actually going all the way down the road of consumer education. Coffee companies like Dean's Beans add value to their products by going halfway, by creating virtual producers and hoping that their narratives appeal to the virtual consumers who have been made for them by the likes of Mr. Nebraska.

This process makes consumers who do not enact real politics. The marketers recommend that retailers create a particular narrative, and retailers create stories which coffee drinkers consume. Not only do they reproduce troubling stereotypical images, they occlude the real history and political economic position of the real producers and both the social benefits and consequences of coffee production. Under the regulatory system in place from the end of the Second World War to the 1980s, the coffee industry in Papua New Guinea had a stable market. There was a place—set and standard—for the coffee grown there, and growers could expect a certain price for their coffee. Today, with a deregulated coffee market, Papua New Guinea coffee has to compete in a different way. This has caused a particular sort of marketing—marketing that rests on images of nature and culture in Papua New Guinea that may or may not be offensive, racist, and inaccurate. These images now create a location within the global market for the coffee. My argument is that these images have bled into coffee from other sites and are bleeding out of coffee, with real political and economic consequences.

Narratives like the one presented by Dean's Beans also attempt to repackage poverty as uniqueness and primitivism as a form of scarcity. Scarce things have value, and by producing a fantasy of Papua New Guinea's coffee industry as primitive and of primitivism as scarce, this narrative adds value to the coffee at the expense of people from Papua New Guinea by turning them into virtual producers.[12] The virtual producers created by Dean's Beans are poor farmers yearning for a benevolent and right-thinking American businessman to come in and create economic equality through the softer side of capitalism. They are also crafted as if the coffee industry in Papua New Guinea had no history and as if the rural smallholders who grow coffee there were the only people whose lives depended on coffee production.

By fixing these images and fantasies onto the people who grow coffee in Papua New Guinea and the places where it is grown, these agents of neoliberalization work to erase history and society. By erasing history and society and replacing it with fantasy, they set the stage for dispossession.

Elsewhere, following Scott (1998) and Errington and Gewertz (2001), I have argued that images of authentic nature and culture in Papua New Guinea generally, and of Gimi specifically, simplify and generify culture (West 2005b; West and Carrier 2004). Fantasy-fueled images come to reshape the desires of ecologists and tourists (the two groups I have written about previously) and both Gimi peoples and the natural environment "come to be recognizable only to the extent that they fit the generic categories" (West and Carrier 2004, 491). The lives of Gimi are then affected by these fantasies in material ways. To understand the material ways in which the images and fantasies produced by, perpetuated by, and created by the coffee industry affect people's lives, it is necessary to understand the industry both historically and ethnographically. The next five chapters of this book lay out the industry in those terms. Understanding how these images diverge from the lives of the people who make up the world of coffee from Papua New Guinea also helps to answer the question that people always ask me about certified coffees. People ask if, after all my time spent studying the coffee industry in Papua New Guinea, I think that they should buy certified coffees. This book is an attempt to answer that question.

3 | HISTORIC COFFEE

The island of New Guinea has a long and complicated history of colonization, independence, and nationalism.[1] Coffee is an important part of that history.[2] Because this book is about the lives affected by coffee today, I will not cover the colonial period extensively. In this chapter I provide a brief summary of the history of the coffee industry in the Highlands of Papua New Guinea and describe some of the events, policies, practices, and personalities that are directly connected to the story that I tell in the rest of the book. This summary places the current industry and its socio-ecological effects in a wider historic and political-economic context. It is also meant to begin a discussion of Goroka and its place in the coffee industry. Finally, it is meant to show the historical development of the routes by which coffee travels today. Here I refer to the physical routes (e.g., roads and air), the social routes (e.g., the relationships between national businesspeople and expatriates), and the ideological routes (e.g., the international documents discussed at the end of the chapter). I begin with a discussion of the Highlands Highway, one artery of movement that connects rural coffee growers with the larger coffee market. I then move rapidly through German and British colonial coffee and coffee production during the world wars before proceeding to a discussion of the movement of the colonial government and coffee production into the rural parts of the Highlands after the Second World War. I focus on the social worlds of rural growers and Australian planters and the ways their lives were touched by colonial policy and practice. I then cover coffee production and government policy in the 1960s and 1970s and discuss early documents focused on international and national "development" that directed the policies and practices of Papua New Guinea in the 1970s and 1980s. I conclude the chapter with a discussion of the 1980s and early 1990s and the ways the fall of the ICO, structural adjustment programs, and the decline of one major coffee export company affected Papua New Guinea.

The Highlands Highway

There is a hole in the tropical foliage on the fence surrounding the old plantation mechanic's house where I sometimes stay when I am in Goroka. In the mornings I peer through the hole and watch the people walk down the Highlands Highway toward Goroka Town. They come from Asaro and points north, from villages that are off the main road by many miles or only a few feet. These people walk to town to take part in social, economic, and political life. Before dawn women walk by and ride by in the back of trucks and on buses, carrying bags of garden-grown food. They bring carrots, sweet potatoes, cabbage, tomatoes, papayas, avocados, and other vegetables to sell in the main market in Goroka. At first light women and men walk and ride by with white bags of coffee weighing 60 kilograms. Some have one bag from their own garden, while others have truckloads brought in from their village. These women and men may stop at one of the coffee-buying stands at the five-mile market before they get to Goroka, or at one of the factories along the way. If they do not get the price they want at one of these venues, they will go all the way to the World Trade Center coffee market on the backside of the main Goroka market. As these smallholders walk by, huge eighteen-wheel trucks filled with coffee rumble by as well. The trucks are on their way from other parts of the Highlands with coffee that will be processed in Goroka. They race by on squealing wheels with nearly bald tires at breakneck speeds, forcing people, pigs, and goats into ditches in their diesel-dusty wake. After the trucks pass, the pedestrians dust themselves off and continue their long walks into town. In addition to carrying produce and coffee to market, people go into Goroka for banking business, to shop at trade-stores and the market, to attend school, to work, and to socialize.

Through the hole in the fence one can also see the mountain ranges circling the Goroka Valley, their high peeks reaching into the deep, foggy sky. Almost every morning a dense fog rests on the mountains, and it breaks slowly as the day heats up. In 1930 Michael "Mick" Leahy and Michael Dwyer were the first Europeans to see the valley as they walked the Dunantina trail.[3] In the 1940s Mick's brother James "Jim" Leahy was the first person to establish a coffee plantation in the Highlands, and he would certainly have spent time at the plantation house that once stood behind this mechanic's home, modest by European standards. The house is surrounded on three sides by coffee gardens and on the fourth side by a coffee-drying factory, the oldest in the Highlands. The machines hum and whir in the tin building, running almost twenty-four hours a day, every day, during the coffee season.

This former plantation is one of many along the Highlands Highway as it snakes out of Goroka Town toward Hagen, the capital of the Western Highlands Province. The highway, which was built to link the coffee-rich Highlands with the coast, begins in Lae and winds through the Markham Valley. A branch darts off through the Ramu Valley and ends in Madang, the capital of Madang Province. Another branch climbs up through the Kassam Pass into the Eastern Highlands through the Arona Valley. The road goes through Goroka and then climbs again through the Daulo Pass into the Simbu Province, through Kundiawa.[4] It makes its way from Kundiawa through Waghi Valley in the Western Highlands Province and passes through Mount Hagen. From the Western Highlands it branches again, with one leg going up to the Southern Highlands through its capital Mendi before ending in Tari. The other leg goes through Enga Province and its capital Wabag, finally ending in Porgera. The highway is the life link for commerce in the country and an engineering and public works wonder. Moving from the coast up across the high spine of the country through passes at 1,500 meters into the Eastern Highlands and 2,479 meters out of the province, it is a bit of a miracle.

One of the highway's early architects, George Greathead, was a colonial patrol officer who in 1949 became the district officer of what was then called the Central Highlands District when Jim Taylor, the Australian official who had first set up an administration post in the Highlands in 1932, retired.[5] Greathead joined the New Guinea administration in 1933 as a cadet patrol officer and in 1935 helped to "pacify" the Simbu Valley. Beginning in 1938 Greathead was the patrol officer at Hagen, one of the far outposts of the administration. He served the war years in the Australian New Guinea Administrative Unit, surviving the Japanese invasion of Rabaul by escaping on foot, walking over two hundred miles across New Britain, taking canoes and locally owned boats along the coast and across the sea, and ending up on Samarai island.[6] After the war he was moved to the coast, where he was made district commissioner at Wewak and in 1949 was posted to Goroka.[7] During his time in Hagen, Greathead worked, with little support from the administration, to stem the warfare that he understood to be endemic in the area. He directed the Hagen police camp and used general labor around the government station and on road-building crews as a punishment for crimes committed. Men who assaulted others, trespassed, and stole things were remanded to his custody and detained at the station. While there, they worked.

The Highlands Highway was built in part with this detained labor. After a series of minor incidents and then the death of an important man near Hagen in 1939, Greathead wrote, "In all, 76 of the 218 arrested were detained on road construction work for various terms compatible with the seriousness of the part each played in the disturbances." But the people who lived along the highway's route also built it: "The construction of the great arterial highway of which Hagen boasts today were got under way (during his time at Hagen), each group constructed roads surveyed through its own territory." The "great arterial highway" of which Greathead boasts was not the highway of today, which only opened to unrestricted traffic in 1966. During Greathead's time the Highlands relied on aircraft to move in the colonial settlers' necessities and move out the commodities that they, and the indigenous inhabitants of the Highlands, grew (see Hawksley 2007).

Today the coffee factory behind the old plantation mechanic's house is leased by a small company that dries coffee for many of the national export companies and sells a bit of its own coffee to exporters. During all the times that I stayed there in the early to mid-2000s Brian Greathead, George's son, ran the factory. The plantation itself, started by Jim Taylor when he retired, is now owned by the original landowners—the descendants of the people who leased the land to Taylor all those years ago—and worked by them today. On many days during the height of the coffee season, when Brian ran this factory, it worked every minute that he was awake. It seems as if there is always something going wrong in coffee. Some days a bridge may be impassable on the highway between Hagen and Goroka, a problem that slows work and then, once the bridge is repaired, makes it impossible to do all of the day's work in twenty-four hours. On other days the company may have a problem with the people whom they depend on for their coffee. For example, the growers might want an advance payment for coffee they will bring later even though they already owe the man who runs the company thousands of kilos of coffee as a result of previous advances. Occasional power outages, air traffic stoppages, impassable roads to coffee-growing areas, and the like may affect the little company's work. On other days things run smoothly at this factory, which has been in production since the colonial period.

Coffee's Beginnings

The island of New Guinea was cut in half by the expansion of European powers in the nineteenth century. In 1928 the Dutch took control of the western half of the island and held it until 1963, when it was given to Indonesia by the United Nations. In 1884 the Germans claimed the northern quarter of the island of New Guinea and the islands to the north, and the British claimed the southern quarter of the eastern half of New Guinea. The Germans held their territory until 1914, when war broke out. In 1919 the German territory was given to Australia for administration by the League of Nations to accompany the former British territory that had been transferred to it in 1906. The northern quarter of the Australian territory was given the colonial name Mandated Territory of New Guinea in 1921, when Australia began non-wartime administration, while the southern quarter was administered under the name Papua. The two quarters were administered separately until 1942, when the Japanese invaded and the civil administration of both quarters was suspended, and then brought together under the Australian New Guinea Administrative Unit (ANGAU). This unit existed until 1946, when Australia reinstated a civil administration and combined the two areas as the Territory of Papua and New Guinea. Australia served as the colonial power in the territory until national independence on 16 September 1975. Today the independent nation-state of Papua New Guinea is a member of the British Commonwealth.

Coffee is mentioned in colonial documents from both British New Guinea and German New Guinea in 1889 (Sinclair 1995, 8, 23). But it was in German New Guinea that coffee cultivation seems to have first become entrenched. The Neu Guinea Compagnie maintained several plantations in the 1880s, and by 1889 a company had been formed in Hamburg to buy the coffee from the German colony (Sinclair 1995, 24). In 1897 the Australian company Burns, Philp and Company established a plantation in the mountains behind Port Moresby, and by 1901, the same year the six British colonies on the Australian continent became federated and part of the British Commonwealth, it was exporting coffee to Australia (Sinclair 1995, 11).

In Papua the colonial government established a Department of Agriculture in 1907, having passed the Native Regulation Act in 1894 (Sinclair 1995, 14). This act compelled Papuans to plant trees deemed economically useful by the colonial government. This, coupled with the Native Taxation Ordinance and the Native Plantations Ordinance in 1918, created a compelled labor pool for the plantations. The first act forced villagers to pay a tax to the colonial government and the second relieved them of that tax if they provided their labor to lands which, with the same act, the government turned into plantations (14). These acts and events inextricably tied local people—"natives" in the language of the colonial powers—to the development of the coffee industry.

The years between the world wars were successful for the coffee sector in both the Mandated Territory and Papua. This success was in part due to the passing of the Customs Tariff (Papua and New Guinea Preference) Act in 1926 by Australia. The act mandated that agricultural products, which did not compete with products grown in Australia, were to be allowed into Australia duty-free (Cartledge 1978; Sinclair 1995, 15). Between 1918 and 1939 production slowly increased on both the Australian-owned and government-run plantations and on what were called "Native" plantations in the Mandated Territory of New Guinea and in Papua. A Department of Agriculture had been established in 1921 and 1922 in the Mandated Territory of New Guinea, and by 1928 its director, George Hugh Murray, began to focus on coffee as a key crop for commercial trade (Cartledge 1978, 6).

In 1926 prospectors at Edie Creek near Wau, in what is now the Morobe Province, discovered gold, and by 1927 an airstrip had been built in Wau and commercial traffic began between Lae and Wau (Bradley 2008). This served as the beginning of the air transport industry in the country, and in 1928, now that Wau was accessible by air, the Department of Agriculture decided to establish an agricultural experiment station there (Cartledge 1978, 6; Sinclair 1995, 32). Between 1929 and 1931 the station became increasingly focused on coffee as a viable commercial crop that could anchor an agricultural economy (Sinclair 1995, 32–35). In 1931 the station was sold to a German expatriate, but the Department of Agriculture continued to push the idea of both coffee plantations and the growing of coffee by the so-called natives. By 1937 about 621 hectares of land were in coffee production in the Mandated Territory (Sinclair 1995, 36). There the strategy for production was to create settler colonial plantations, while in Papua it was to create "Native" or "Village" plantations. The opening of the Highlands and the unification of the two territories after the Second World War would combine these two strategies.

In the mid-1930s, while the plantations were growing near Wau, the Department of Agriculture began to consider the plantation potential of the newly opened Highlands. In 1935 the director began to remark publicly that the Upper Ramu Mountains would be perfect for coffee cultivation once roads were built, and in 1937 a research station was established in the Aiyura Valley near the Upper Ramu police post (an area now known as Kainantu). By 1940 the Aiyura Station produced 64 tons of arabica coffee a year and had begun to distribute seeds and seedlings to local people across the Highlands (Bourke 1986, 101; Sinclair 1995, 55; see also MacWilliam 2009).

Even with these advancements the modern agricultural development of the Highlands did not take off until after the Second World War. Between first contact, the establishment of the station at Aiyura, and the end of the war, the Highlands fell off the radar of the Australian administration. Australia was preoccupied with the war between 1942 and 1945 and could devote few resources to patrolling the Highlands.[8] In January 1942 the Japanese bombed Rabaul, and they invaded on 21 February. Japan quickly defeated the New Guinea and Australian forces and took control of the entire Bismarck Archipelago, the Admirality Islands, Bougainville, and the coastal and subcoastal regions of the Morobe, Madang, and Sepik districts (Gailey 2004). In May of the same year the Japanese forces moved toward Port Moresby and were met by Australian and American naval forces. In the ensuing Battle of the Coral Sea Japanese forces were turned back, but the battle continued on the mainland with the Kokoda Track campaign between July 1942 and January 1943.

While the Lowlands were part of the war, the Highlands seemed safe until 1943, when the Japanese bombed Goroka, Asaroka, and Bena and a Japanese patrol was spotted near Bena (Sinclair 1995, 59). The first Goroka airstrip had been established in 1939 as an emergency landing site.[9] The second Goroka airstrip was built in 1941, near what is now the Goroka Teachers College. It was bombed in May 1943 (Sinclair 1939, 60–61).[10] The third and final airstrip, six hundred feet long and still functioning as the airport today, was built in a matter of days in June 1943 by American engineers with the labor of local people. Clearly, during the war the administration's efforts were not on coffee, but much of the infrastructure developed during the war, for example the airstrip and a road between Aiyura and Goroka, began to make Goroka the regional center that it became after the war ended.

Pacification and Legibility across the Highlands

In the Territory of Papua and New Guinea after the war the Australian administration focused on the development of tea, cocoa, and coffee production for commercial purposes (Cartledge 1978, 15). The goal was to make the economy of the territory complement the economy of Australia. The territory, with Europeans and "natives" working together, would provide commodities not already produced in Australia, and this scheme would strengthen both economies while proving beneficial to "native" welfare (15). Although the Australian administration wanted to preserve land rights for the indigenous peoples, it was also believed that some land had to be alienated to create plantations (15). To alienate land for the production of valuable high-altitude-grown coffee, and implement the policies necessary for development of an agricultural industry, the Highlands had to be "pacified" and made "legible" (Scott 1998).

Before "pacification," which began in the pre-war period but was the main focus of the administration after the war, the Highlands were in a constant state of recovery from local wars, negotiations to avoid local wars, and wars. These battles, often called "tribal fights," were the way Highlanders conducted social business. In 1947 the Australian government began to organize and conduct patrols, establish outposts of government in rural areas, build roads, centralize government, control and punish, establish health clinics, facilitate the creation of mission-run schools, encourage a money economy, create waged labor possibilities for highland men, establish notions of property, and distribute and encourage the production of cash crops like peanuts, passion fruit, and coffee. Charles Hawksley argues that "the colonial state created for itself a key role in the production, distribution, and exchange of commodities, and the colonial 'trade-off' permitted administrative control over previously autonomous populations in exchange for the general promise of something called 'development'" (Hawksley 2005, 3). One of the conditions for this tradeoff was pacification.

Before the Australian demarcation the Highlands were not considered a region, since those living in the area were not involved in regional social and political interactions. As in many other parts of the country, spaces of social life were transformed through shifting power relations between colonial officers and local actors. For example, "Maimafu Village" was the colonial demarcation of fifteen distinct ridge-top hamlets, or settlements. This demarcation, or production of space and place, was imposed on the area during pacification by three patrol officers sent out in 1950 by George Greathead, then a district administrator, to map and visit the unmapped and unvisited area south and west of the Kratke Range and south of Mount Michael. Maimafu was named by the patrol officer McArthur on 21 January 1953 as part of this scheme to make the Highlands legible to the colonial officials and thus make them possible sites of pacification (McArthur 1953, 5).

In the 1950s, when the first mention of Maimafu was recorded in colonial patrol reports, it was not a village at all. Family-based settlements existed on adjacent ridge-tops, in a shifting landscape of social and political alliance and warfare. Alliances ebbed and flowed over time. When McArthur named the area Maimafu he was probably standing at the southern end of Wayoarabirai, a location from which one can see all the ridge-top settlements that are now considered Maimafu. He most likely asked someone where he was, and was told Maimafu. McArthur noted this in his patrol report, and the entire place became, for the administration, an administrative area united under that place name. The administration, through subsequent patrols, the allocation of health services, and a tendency to treat the area as if it were a real, cohesive place, produced Maimafu and made the category and place name take hold.

Maimafu is a small-scale example of what happened in the rest of the Highlands. Before the administration's movements into the Highlands, those who lived there were not highly mobile. Geographic, linguistic, and political barriers existed and were constantly being negotiated, fought over, and renegotiated. People did not get along with members of other linguistic groups, or even with other extended families within their own linguistic group. Linguistic groups made alliances with other linguistic groups, just as families made alliances with other families. And these conflicts and alliances were always open to change.[11]

With the administrative creation of villages, census divisions, districts, and regional centers, and with pacification, troubles associated with warfare, interclan conflict, and intraclan conflict were meant to take a backseat to "development." Village courts were established to resolve conflict, and in some instances they worked. People brought claims to the courts, worked them out, and then abided by the decision of the magistrate or patrol officer. But in other instances people used local traditional sociopolitical means of conflict resolution. For the most part this meant that immediate resolutions were agreed on but solutions were not made to last. All settlements were open to renegotiation in the future.

In the early days of the administration, officers who had spent time in the field or worked in patrol posts in rural areas understood that much of men's time was spent on the social aspects of alliance, warfare, and negotiation. They understood that with pacification a set of social interactions would be missing from their lives, and that they would thus have time on their hands. By 1952 Greathead was advocating government support for "native" coffee plantations to fill what he thought of as the void created by pacification (Downs 1986, 222). He and others who had been in the country before pacification felt that coffee would provide a link between the Highlands and the Australian economy, and keep men busy.[12] For men like Greathead coffee was in some ways part of a civilizing mission. It was seen as a way to combat what was perceived of as a negative side-effect of leisure (fighting) and to turn it into a productive (and corrective) enterprise.

The Eastern Highlands administrative unit came into existence in September 1951, when the Central Highlands District, which had been created in 1947 but was too large to be administered from already existing patrol and administrative posts, was split into the Western, Southern, and Eastern districts (Hawksley 2005, 5; also Central Highlands District 1947–48, 2).[13] The Eastern Highlands were administered through three posts, one at Bena Bena (later moved to Goroka), one at Kainantu, and one at Kundiawa. Experienced colonial officials like Greathead were brought to the district for the hard work of final exploration, contact, and pacification.

During the war Jim Taylor had been the district officer for ANGAU at Ramu, and Jim Leahy had been a farm manager at Aiyura and spent the war expanding plantings in the rural villages. As part of his job Taylor had been involved in conferences in which plans for postwar development were being decided, and he believed that coffee plantations were the direction to go for economic and social development (Sinclair 1995, 62). This wartime extension was successful, and patrols to rural areas near Kainantu, Aiyura, Bena, and Goroka in the late 1940s showed that many villages had planted coffee groves before the war and that there were high-yielding trees when the war ended (Bourke 1986, 101; Sinclair 1995, 64).

As discussed at the beginning of this chapter, Greathead and others had begun the work of road building during their early administration days. However, it was really in the period between 1952 and 1957 that road building became a focus of the Highlands administrators. District Commissioner Ian Downs linked existing roads that had been built in various districts between the Markham Valley, Kainantu, Goroka, and Hagen (Downs 1986; Hawksley 2005, 8). The roads facilitated the movement of people and commodities around the Highlands. Administration patrol officers could more easily cover their districts, agricultural extension agents could more easily visit rural areas, and doctors could go to rural villages and patrol posts instead of having villagers make long treks to the hospital in Goroka.

After the war ended, in 1946 the only whites in the Central Highlands were administration officers and missionaries, many of whom had fled during the war but were slowly returning. By the middle of 1947 thirty-one administrators, together with twenty family members, seventy missionaries, forty men, and a handful of wives and children, lived in the Central Highlands (Sinclair 1995, 68). Settlement began to increase in late 1947 because of an influx of gold prospectors and missionaries. Coffee, gold, and the promise of native souls to be saved drove the white settlement of the Highlands.

In 1947 the administration introduced cash into the social lives of Highlanders. Before these interracial transactions, which whites understood to be economic and which the indigenous residents of the Goroka Valley and the rest of the Highlands saw as exchanges, were made up of material items that were both useful and that gave prestige to their owners. These items were things like steel axes, salt, tobacco, cloth, machetes, shovels, and beads (Finney 1973, 23–25).[14] The introduction of the cash economy altered this by changing local markers of prestige and status. Socially, people in the Highlands amassed and distributed wealth, and through that process of amassing and distributing they gained prestige. The sociopolitical organization of family-based groups, which are called "clans" in the literature and by Highlanders today, and the sociopolitical relations between groups, are based on prestige. Material items are of course meaningful in themselves, but it is through the exchange of these items that people come into being as persons, and it is only in the social relations of exchange that people have identities (see Strathern 1988). Exchanges are both between individuals and, in more ceremonial settings, between families, clans, and language groups.[15]

When money was first introduced into the Highlands people did not want it (Finney 1973, 40). They wanted goods that they had grown accustomed to and that they found useful. The Highlands administration, through Jim Taylor, the district officer at the time, did not want to introduce cash to the Highlanders, because there was nowhere to spend it and because people did not understand its value (37–41). The larger administrative body based in Port Moresby forced the introduction of money, and one of the main ways that it was introduced was through paid agricultural labor.

Throughout this period the administration encouraged the growth of agricultural labor in two main ways. First, it instituted the Highlands Labour Scheme in 1950. This instrument of administration set up a structure under which the government paid for men from the Highlands to gain waged labor on coastal plantations on the New Guinea Islands and the northern coast of the island near Madang. It introduced men to both plantation labor and the cash economy. Second, from 1947 to 1950 the administration encouraged the gardening of local and European vegetables for markets across the other districts of Papua and New Guinea, and between 1952 and 1957 it promoted cash crops for the international market (Hawksley 2005, 17–18). Coffee was one of the crops hotly promoted during this second period of market gardening promotion.

Settler Colonialism in the Highlands

In 1936 the administration had placed a ban on new white settlement in the Central Highlands. In May 1952 that restriction was lifted (Finney 1973, 45; Hawksley 2005, 9; Sinclair 1995, 96). With the lifting of the ban settler colonials arrived in the Eastern Highlands in greater numbers than ever before. The lifting of the ban also forced a formalization of land transfer policy. Before 1952 all a planter had to do was find a landowner willing to sell a plot of land, and the two would approach the administration and say that they had reached a fair agreement. With this, the land would become the property of the settler. Before the lifting of the ban in 1952 several Australians who were former administrative officials had also settled in the Eastern Highlands by squatting on land and then making informal agreements with locals (Downs 1980, 178; Hawksley 2005, 10). Indeed Jim Taylor had already settled near Goroka, and Greathead retired and settled near Goroka in early 1952.

With the lifting of the ban "a flood of applicants" petitioned to settle in the Highlands (Downs 1980). The men who had already settled in and around Goroka were displeased by the great interest shown in the area by the outside world and potential planters. Jim Leahy wanted to protect his growing empire, and Greathead worried about land shortages among the indigenous people. Ian Downs, who was then the district administrator, was resolutely against uncontrolled land alienation from the beginning, but he was not against settlement. Indeed he wanted to promote settlement so that "his" district would outperform others (Sinclair 1995, 152). Charles Hawksley (2005, 10) argues that "Downs sought to control both the number and the type of European settlers. Those whom he regarded as profiteers, absentee landlords and freebooters were quickly rebuffed or not granted land" (10). Downs's monitoring of settlers led to the evolution of "an active settler class" in the Eastern Highlands "with the promise of an expanding coffee industry," causing the Eastern Highlands to be "seen in government circles in Papua New Guinea and Australia as an exemplar of what could be achieved with careful planning, dedicated staff and limited funding" (10).[16]

But even with the opposition to uncontrolled settlement, there was a land rush. After lifting the ban the Australian government began to publicize the "opening" of Papua and New Guinea (Downs 1980; Sinclair 1995, 103). In 1953 the government issued a press release about the success of coffee plantations in the territory, stating that there was land available and suitable for both arabica and robusta cultivation (Sinclair 1995, 103). There were newspaper articles published in Australia calling New Guinea a "miracle" and likening it to "Shangri-La" (103). Between 1952 and 1954 about 3,550 acres of indigenous land were alienated, and fifty new white settlers moved to the Eastern Highlands (Finney 1973, 45; Sinclair 1995, 106).

In some ways Downs handpicked the men and women who had settled in Goroka early on.[17] Paul Hasluck, from 1951 to 1963 the minister for territories (the senior Australian government official in the territory), worried that Downs's overzealous approach to deciding who was allowed to settle and who was not would cause major problems in the Highlands (1976). He noted that Europeans were creating "planter enclaves" for themselves, and that they were happy to leave the indigenous people behind in the coffee boom. He also worried about the potential for a land shortage among indigenous people (Hasluck 1976; see also Finney 1968, 3–4). In Australia critics of the territory administration were vocal in print, and in public, about the threat of rapid alienation in the country, and the possibility that an influx of European settlers could lead to an uprising of the indigenous people like the one that had recently occurred in Kenya (Finney 1973, 46).

In October 1953 the administration placed a freeze on land allocation while it worked out a new policy, and in October 1954 the new policy was announced. In the old policy prospective planters had gone to Downs with a possible site for a plantation. Before meeting with Downs they had negotiated with the family of the group that would be selling the land. Initial negotiations would include gifts of goods to the landholders, money exchanges, and promises by settlers to help locals with everything from instruction on how to use equipment to advice on maintaining friendships with other whites to suggestions for developing other lands. If Downs felt that the match was a good one, he would approve the lease of the land and the settler would hold it for ninety-nine years. Hasluck's new policy was meant to avoid negotiations that were initiated by settlers, not by the administration. The goal was to put the choice of lands into the hands of the administration, so that it could assure that land alienation would not disrupt the lives of the indigenous people too drastically (Finney 1973, 47). Under the new policy the Lands Department would decide on land that was "surplus to the future as well as the present needs of the group" and offer it for alienation (47). With this policy virtually all the land in Goroka was made off-limits based on population projections for a ninety-nine-year period. There was bitter opposition to the new policy, even on the part of J. Leahy, Taylor, and Greathead, people who had wanted to control settlements (Sinclair 1995, 154). When it became clear that no amount of opposition would change Hasluck's new policy, people got on with the business of running their own plantations. In the end they benefited from the alienation stoppage, because they, along with thousands of indigenous planters, now controlled the territory's crop production.

In and around Goroka the indigenous inhabitants had begun to make extraordinary profits from the coffee industry. They had already been growing coffee before 1952, but during the late 1950s and early 1960s the indigenous production system boomed (MacWilliam 2008). By 1970 there were at least 45,000 native coffee growers in the Eastern Highlands alone (Stewart 1992). What emerges during this period is a complicated social mosaic that is based on race, class, gender, status politics, intra-ethnic politics, and inter-ethnic politics.[18] Many of the white planters and administration officials (who were to become planters in many instances) saw themselves as reformers who were creating employment opportunities for the indigenous peoples, creating markets for their garden-grown produce, encouraging their social and economic development through the encouragement of their participation in growing coffee, and teaching them how to understand and take part in the money economy (Finney 1973, 49; Sinclair 1995; and personal communication from numerous present-day coffee industry participants who were in country during this time).[19] The term used to describe the coffee economy in Goroka and distinguish it from systems of interaction between the indigenous and settlers in other parts of the territory was "partnership" (Finney 1973, 49). The settlers discussed their relations with the indigenous people as "nontraditional," and the residents of Goroka wanted settlers to live on their lands or adjacent to their lands, so they worked to find people who were willing to lease their lands (49).

Ben Finney, in ethnographic work that began in 1967 with Goroka's indigenous farmers and business leaders, describes the four primary reasons why the residents of the Highlands were so willing to lease their lands to white settlers (1973, 50–56). First, Highlanders were experiencing a boom in their traditional exchange system because of European trade goods and the influx of cash in 1957, which quickly entered into prosperous systems of exchange. They were "optimistic" about the benefits of association and "anxious" to further relationships so as to continue to benefit (50). Second, indigenous people wanted money, and there were few opportunities to earn it. People living outside what was becoming Goroka Town proper were not benefiting from the cash-earning opportunities in town. By encouraging whites to settle on lands further out of town, Highlanders would gain access to cash and trade-store goods. They might also learn from the planters how to gain access to these items so that eventually the whites would not be needed. Third, although indigenous Gorokans knew where money and goods came from (land sales, produce sales, labor, trade), Highlanders believed that whites had a secret formula for obtaining goods (50). Fourth, because whites desired land but knew nothing of the history of the land, people could lease to them plots and sections of their territory that had traditionally been deemed useless or been the subject of inter- or intra-clan disputes (51).

Finney argues that the minor settler land rush in the 1950s was two-sided —whites wanted land for planting, and indigenous landholders wanted whites for the reasons outlined above (1973, 50). Each group had a set of expectations that arose from social interactions surrounding land and coffee. Finney concludes that whites did quite well during the land rush. About thirty men were able to get leases for plantations, and many of these plantations, in part because of the cheap labor pool in Goroka, became prosperous and profitable. For Gorokans the outcomes, according to Finney, are more complicated and less resoundingly successful.

Once money was transferred to Gorokans for land, the money was then distributed to the entire social network of kinship and obligation. This meant that even if a group got a large sum for the lease of their land, once the money flowed through chains of obligation and exchange the regular Gorokan on the street, so to speak, only made a tiny profit (Finney 1973, 52). Once the lands were transferred and the plantations were being built, Gorokans expected to be privileged in terms of waged labor. They were for a while, but when conflicts arose over wages, attendance at work, and other issues, planters began to gravitate toward hiring day laborers from Chimbu and other areas of the Highlands. Women from Goroka gained employment as laborers during the harvest, but men from Goroka, who were not plantation owners, were relegated to making money from vegetable sales to the plantations.

Throughout the early years of the coffee economy Highlanders thought that they were entering into one sort of social relationship with the settlers, while the settlers thought they were entering into another. The settlers saw the relationships as one-time transactions, while the Highlanders saw each transaction as building upon the previous one and setting the stage for future transactions. The Highlanders, as will be discussed extensively in chapter 4, see all personhood as resulting from exchange. Each exchange, for them, works to indissolubly bind the people taking part in it and form lifelong pathways for social relationships. For the whites, exchanges were seen as market-based transactions and nothing more.[20]

Finney shows that even though disappointed with the outcome of many of their interactions with whites, Gorokans felt that they gained something valuable from the whites who settled on their lands. At the same time, the white planters and settlers knew that they could not meet their market contracts without the coffee grown by the locals (1973, 54). The demand for coffee had outstripped the supply that could be produced by the white settlers, and Highlanders were meeting the excess demands with their own coffee. In addition, the white settlers owned the means of processing the coffee for sale, so they made money off local production by charging for processing. The white settlers needed the indigenous coffee, and the locals needed the market access granted by the whites, as well as the processing facilities owned and operated by whites.

Industry Growth in the 1950s, 1960s, and 1970s

In the mid- to late 1950s Goroka and its indigenous and white coffee planters experienced economic growth that was unheard of throughout the rest of the country. The government was invested in agricultural extension work, in part to meet the needs of the industry and in part to provide labor for men who had been recently pacified. However, the administration was not prepared for the verve with which people in the Highlands took to planting coffee (Finney 1973, 65). Indeed, by the late 1950s the demand for seedlings and extension support around Goroka and in rural areas of the Eastern Highlands was so great that the extension officers could not meet the need. They were out of seedlings, and their offices were strapped for officers and money (66). The government's willingness to invest in coffee agriculture changed when the territory had trouble selling the crop in 1958 (Cartledge 1978, 29). The territory's administrators began to wonder about New Guinea's role in the world coffee market. By early 1959 they were also worrying about the reliance on one crop by so many people and about the possibility that local growers were flooding the coffee market and depressing the price for New Guinea coffee (28; Finney 1973, 66).

In January 1959 a conference was held in Goroka to discuss the market for the coffee grown in the territory (Cartledge 1978, 29). The conference reaffirmed the connection between production in New Guinea and consumption in Australia, the need for a uniform grading system for New Guinea coffee, and the need for increased marketing for the coffee from New Guinea (30; Sinclair 1995, 234). But even with the conference, as 1959 wore on the government became increasingly worried about the extent of indigenous plantings. By the end of the year the administration placed a ban on further planting and production, and in 1961 the ban was made permanent and the government began to focus extension services on other cash crops (Finney 1973, 66; Temu 1991, 16).

The formation of the New Guinea Coffee Agents Association, through which most coffee from the territory was sold between 1959 and 1964, and the creation of the coffee industry marketing board by 1963, were outcomes of the Goroka conference (Sinclair 1995, 241). Another result of the conference was that coffee companies began to consider exporting to markets other than Australia. In the 1950s several large Australian companies trading in and from the territory focused on coffee exports. Burns, Philp (NG) Ltd, W. R. Carpenter and Company, Colyer Watson (NG) Ltd, and New Guinea Company Ltd were a few. All these companies began to develop markets outside Australia after the ban went into effect.

The initial ban in 1959 on new plantings and extension was also due in part to the entry by Australia and New Guinea, as a single coffee consumption and production unit, into the International Coffee Agreement (ICA; Finney 1973, 67). The territory now had to manage the production of what it had the right to sell on the world market at the prices set up and upheld by the agreement. At the time New Guinea still produced less than Australia consumed, but the agreement required that Australia take steps to slow production in New Guinea and attempt to reduce the expansion of indigenous production (Finney 1973, 67). Yet by the time this ban went into effect in full in the 1960s, the indigenous people were making such significant amounts of cash from their production that stopping the growth of the industry proved very difficult (67–70).

There was also a major change in transport in the early 1960s that affected the industry. During the years after the Second World War coffee exporters and merchants in the territory benefited from the growth of the Civil Aviation Authority and the stability of charges for carrying freight, which had not increased since 1953. Because of this it was economically feasible for small companies to work in the territory and fly coffee out of rural areas (remember, the Highlands Highway was not fully operational until 1966). In February 1961 it was announced that airfreight costs would increase by about 20 percent (Sinclair 1995, 236). Growers in the Highlands and companies that relied on inexpensive airfreight were thrown into an uproar (236; and personal communication from various informants in Goroka). There was a public debate about the increase and about other new operating standards proposed at the same time for the planes used to move freight into and out of the Highlands. These new standards limited load weights and forced the lengthening of airstrips in rural villages. Even with the debates and the outcry, the restrictions stood and were enforced after 1961. This made it much more expensive to move coffee, and many of the small companies working in coffee moved out of the industry.

Another significant event was the ratification of the first International Coffee Agreement (ICA) in 1962. The ratification, came on the heels of a report by the Australian tariff board recommending that raw coffee from the territory should continue to be granted duty-free entry into Australia and that the duty for coffee from elsewhere should be increased. The ICA, as discussed in chapter 2, began with meetings in 1958 intended to formulate an international consensus about the world production of coffee. The agreement culminated with the ratification of a set of export quotas, export limits, and penalties for countries that did not follow the letter of the agreement. Australia, and by extension its colony, signed the five-year agreement. For the territory this meant that in addition to the exports to Australia, it could export 100,000 sixty-kilo bags of coffee to other countries (Sinclair 1995, 240). The tradeoff was that the territory had to agree to stop land alienation for the plantation sector and to stop agricultural extension that was focused on increasing acreage of coffee among local landowners (240).

In 1959 the New Guinea Coffee Agents' Association was formed, an industry association made up of the various export companies mentioned above. These companies were dominated by Australian businesspeople and former settlers who had effectively centralized the trading of coffee into the hands of a very few firms (Cartledge 1978, 71; MacWilliam 1993, 48). This centralization made the Australian government nervous and by 1963 forced the creation of the Coffee Marketing Board, or CBM (MacWilliam 1993, 48; Sinclair 1995, 241), charged with "policing exports" so that the terms of the ICA were met and defending the prices paid to smallholder producers (MacWilliam 1993, 48). The board, which was meant to stabilize the industry and protect everyone in it, actually had the effect of increasing the dominance of a few export companies.

After a series of complicated mergers and takeovers involving the export companies mentioned above, the Australian and New Guinea Coffee Company Marketing Proprietary Limited (ANGCO) was formed in 1964. The company amassed power and influence in the territory and developed markets for coffee overseas. This amassing of power worked to drive most of the other export companies out of the country. But for growers, the late 1960s and first few years of the 1970s were extremely profitable. Coffee prices had been stabilized by the ICA, the market for coffee in Australia was strong, and coffee grown in New Guinea was developing a reputation internationally for quality and taste. The early managers of ANGCO worked to create an image for New Guinea coffee as high-altitude arabica with a volcanic soil–grown acidic taste similar to that of coffee from other high-altitude regions—"high acidity in the cup" and a "rich," "nutty" flavor. The reputation of the coffee was also based on the men who sold it. ANGCO had relations with all the major trade houses in Europe and Australia dating back to the early colonial period.

In short, indigenous and white growers were making good money, as were the exporters, from coffee that was being sold because of its ecological background and the reputations of the "coffee men" associated with it. In 1973 things began to change. During the 1973–74 growing year prices began to fall internationally because of a boom year in Brazil, which hit at the same time that white planters in the territory were becoming nervous about the coming independence of Papua and New Guinea. The prospect of independence for the territory did not sit well with many of the Europeans in the country, and from June 1972 to June 1975 the white population in the territory fell from 51,076 to 38,442 (May 1981, 24).[21]

By 1973 the territory had self-rule and by 1975 independence. Some saw the country's independence as directly connected to the coffee industry. A Papua New Guinean government official who has been in government and coffee for many years told me that he believes "independence was built on coffee. In 1974 coffee was our biggest export, we were getting rich off of it, no, Australians were getting rich off of it. After independence the Australians started going home and we got the plantations back from them but the government forgot about coffee. They stopped extension, they stopped caring about it and all they cared about was mining" (interview, Goroka, 2004). Another long-time government employee, one who has worked in Eastern Highlands government since independence, said: "Coffee is one of the things that forces us to act like a nation. It is the only thing that makes us work across ethnicity. We have to interact cross culturally: Highlanders work with Coastals and they work with Engans and they work with Sepiks. . . . Working in coffee, that made us a nation" (interview, Goroka, 2004). In a different interview the same man said: "Development? Coffee is the only development that the Highlands has today and it is the only development that we have ever had. It brings development, brings the roads, the industry. And it is how people induce development. I would even say it has faces . . . Its faces are cash, education, politics, medicine, air travel, roads . . . and it has transformed our culture. . . . The rhythm of the season is now the rhythm of life in the Highlands. Its cycle is our cycle of life" (interview, Goroka, 2005).

Coffee is one of the most volatile crops or commodities. Inclement weather, including frost, drought, and excess heat, can drastically alter the crop. The weather in Brazil, the world's biggest producer of coffee, is particularly important for international coffee prices. Right after independence, when white planters in the Highlands were growing increasingly nervous and beginning to sell their plantations to ANGCO and to Highland businessmen, there was a drought in Brazil. Those who had plantations in Papua New Guinea at the time made more money than they ever thought they would, and the people who left the industry because of the fears of independence lost out enormously.

In addition to lands sales motivated by fear, from 1974 to 1980 the Plantation Redistribution Scheme took effect, altering landholdings for whites. On the Gazelle Peninsula in the years leading to self-rule and independence, there had been a push for plantation redistribution and land reform. There was a land shortage on the peninsula, and the idea behind the scheme was to give white-owned plantations to people who had no land of their own (Sinclair 1995, 350; see Walter 1980, 1981).[22] The scheme used government money to buy white-owned plantations and redistribute them to local groups, but it was not supported with money to help local owners keep the plantations in production for profit.[23]

Many whites in the country are still bitter about the Plantation Redistribution Scheme. One man said to me in August 2001, "Somare handed over the most productive and beautiful plantations in the country to a bunch of *Kanakas* who knew nothing about real agriculture. They could grow sweet potatoes and that was about it, and they were going to run plantations?" This bitterness seeps into discussions about why production went down in the plantation sector after redistribution, and many whites blame natives for an inability to manage cash and a lack of desire to "make a better life for themselves."[24] Others have suggested that the decline in production was caused by a lack of extension services and of support from banks to black-owned plantations for replanting and other purposes, and by various structural factors (Walter 1980, 6). Another, longer-term explanation for the decline in production is that the scheme contributed to a "differentiation of Papua New Guinea society": landowners who were already wealthy could benefit in areas like the coffee-rich Highlands where there was no land shortage, while other people could not benefit (7). This inequity would have caused infighting and jealousy in many places and perhaps led to the declines.

At a conference entitled "What to Do about Plantations" held in 1979, anthropologists gave various other possible social reasons for the decline in production: tempering of the initial desire for the prestige of owning a plantation by the day-to-day workings of sociality in villages (sorcery, family obligations outweighing financial considerations); labor problems caused by the clash between hiring by locals and social obligations; a lack of government infrastructure (road maintenance, extension services, loan facilitation); and the lack of benefits accruing to villages when one of their own buys a plantation and their only chance to benefit is from hard labor (Walter 1980, 10–13).

After the redistribution of lands, the majority of white-owned plantations eventually ended up in the hands of national groups—family groups, cooperatives, and businessmen—while some found themselves owned by ANGCO and other companies with white directors. Even with these changes, some whites who had been in the country before independence stayed on in capacities other than that of plantation owner. Many went to work for ANGCO, and today the vast majority of white expatriates working in the coffee industry have had ties to the company, now defunct.

Coffee as Territory Development

With the founding and chartering of the United Nations in 1945 came a worldwide push for colonial powers to "develop" trust territories (Cartledge 1978, 15). Throughout the postwar colonial period in what is now Papua New Guinea there were reports, papers, and books published about the territory's development potential. Each report weighed the economic costs and benefits of particular development strategies and advocated one over the other. In 1963 an economic mission from the World Bank visiting the territory suggested that agricultural development would bring the highest returns (IBRD 1965, 35–37; see also Errington and Gewertz 2004, 48). Given the potentially productive and easily accessible land in the territory, agriculture could serve as a means for development even with the "unfortunate tendency of the indigene. . . . to cling to the past, to traditions, to special beliefs that oppose the unknown" (IBRD 1965, 37, also quoted in Errington and Gewertz 2004, 48). This could be countered "through education and vocational training" provided by expatriates (Errington and Gewertz 2004, 48).

A report from 1967 by the Territory of Papua and New Guinea states: "Economic development comes about when a country makes increasingly greater and more effective use of its resources. Its most important elements are increased production of goods and services and greater and more varied employment for the people of the country. It leads to rising standards of living, including increased health, education and other services, as well as more material goods such as food and clothing. Economic development also increases the stock of capital equipment—roads, bridges, houses and countless other items—and thereby capacity for further and more diversified development in the future" (Territory of Papua and New Guinea 1967, 1). The document goes on to provide a "progress report" on the development and development potential of the territory (2). On the second page it is stated that "problems arise from the tradition of communal land ownership which tends to work against personal initiative and investment in cash cropping. A gradual changeover to individual ownership is in progress in some areas taking account of increasing awareness of commercial possibilities. An acceleration of this process in certain areas could be advantageous." The report then discusses exports and imports for the territory, gross territory expenditure and gross domestic capital formation, the investments made by Australia, the budget of the administration, growth rates in the monetary sector, and the like. It also makes mention of how "important" the "increasing participation of the indigenous people in the cash economy" has been for the economy (Territory of Papua and New Guinea 1967, 4). What emerges from the report is a vision of the administration's imaginary of the territory as a white Australian economy supplemented by the participation of the indigenous peoples. This vision is supported by the International Bank for Reconstruction and Development, the institution that was to become the World Bank.

The second section of the report, "Future Development: General Proposals and Programmes," calls for expanded production in the private sector, "achieving the highest possible degree of indigenous participation in the economy" so that exports can increase and imports decline, more private savings and finance development, more private investment from overseas, a more skilled workforce, marketing of territory products overseas, and government policies to further the goals of development (Territory of Papua and New Guinea 1967, 6). Below this list of "requirements" for development is a mention of a request from the Australian government in 1963 to the International Bank for Reconstruction and Development to send a mission to the territory and review its "economic potential," so as to make recommendations that will allow the government to "expand and stimulate the economy and thereby raise the standard of living of the people" (6).

In 1968, after the World Bank report, the territory's administration re-leased *Programmes and Policies for the Economic Development of Papua New Guinea*, a document meant to show its acceptance of most of the bank's suggestions (Errington and Gewertz 2004, 49). The one difference was the report's insistence that indigenous people be allowed to participate in all development. This insistence was designed to acknowledge the "impend-ing" self-government and independence. The racism embedded in the bank reports was not reflected in the ones issued by the territory, if only because of the knowledge in country of the coming changes and the inevi-tability that indigenous peoples would play a role in the future of the country.

In the Highlands, according to a previously released bank document, the indigenous people were "a Primitive, Stone Age folk, virtually cut off by precipitous mountains from the rest of mankind" (IBRD 1965, 75). These "primitive" people, who had "an unusually efficient type of subsistence farming," lived in "small villages" with "land-use rights to well-defined surrounding areas," where their gardens were "operated by families or individuals" (75). They grew sweet potato, taro, and sugarcane, and con-sumed pork "at organized sing-sings," "festive occasions" that were "pecu-liar" to them (75). Although "primitive," these Highlanders had one major success story: coffee. The administration was lauded for "stimulating na-tive interest in the crop" and for providing extension services and super-vising harvesting and processing (101). The "large number of native fami-lies" who "obtained a cash income from coffee production after only eight years of planned extension effort" were part of a "phenomenal develop-ment considering the short time these people have had contact with the outside world" (101–2). This success "argues well for the future economic development of natural resources of the Highlands by indigenes" (102).

Unfortunately, even with this success there were "very real limitations" to the development of the coffee industry in the territory (102). These limitations included limits on expansion and growth of the industry due to marketing problems, low levels of coffee consumption in Australia, prob-lems with moving the crop to existing Australian importers, and limits on exports to countries other than Australia imposed by the ICA agreement. According to the bank, the ICA limited growth of the industry and the mission saw the limiting of growth as an impediment to development. In general the report argues that there are major "weaknesses" in the development potential of the industry, both on "European Estates" and in the "Indigenous Sector" (104–5).

The "European Estates," a gloss for the white-owned plantations, were too small to "justify the large capital outlay involved in modern equipment" and thus weak (IBRD 1965, 104). Although some had encouraged cooperatives with other plantation-owning whites and "native growers," which was a possible "way of making more efficient use of capital," it was not enough (104). The white owners needed to do more outreach to include indigenous producers in cooperative ventures and needed to "develop partnerships," because it was "essential for the future welfare of the Territory that indigenous people become not only competent in production and processing but also familiar with the economic and technical aspects of processing and marketing upon which a high-quality, high-price, viable industry depends" (104). Their involvement would help to develop the economy, "produce native entrepreneurs," and "improve the social and economic status of such people" (104). Another weakness of the plantation sector was the lack of training of indigenous people on the plantations. The report suggests that on all the plantations visited, skilled labor was done by whites and indigenous people were confined to the lowest levels of unskilled labor, never learning how to manage the more complicated aspects of plantation production (105).

But according to the report, the "indigenous sector" also had weaknesses. The major problem was that "a large proportion of the native acreage under coffee occurs in tiny scattered units which are not only sub-economic in structure, but are also costly and difficult to aid through extension and supervision" (105). This pattern was due to the "original problem," which was that landownership was not vested in individuals (105). The solution was "the evolution of a positive land-use / tenure policy which is development and production oriented" (105). The administration was also encouraged to step up efforts to "increase the efficiency of indigenous growers" through the development of "central processing units with the basic objectives of improving quality of the product and increasing their cash returns" (105).

By 1967 the administration was openly stating that there were no plans to expand the coffee industry, even though 60 percent of the territory's coffee exports were produced by indigenous people (Territory of Papua and New Guinea 1967, 12). Coffee production was in fact growing without extension, so much so that the IBRD projected that by 1973–74 production would reach 20,000 tons, with revenues of $16 million (13). In the same report palm oil production, beef cattle production, commercial fishing, forestry product exports, and mining are seen as having great potential for developing the territory. Most of these industries had not yet shown significant commercial viability, and none had yet shown themselves to have economic benefits for indigenous peoples, but all were seen as having the potential for economic growth and development of the territory.

"Investing in Papua and New Guinea," published by the Australia Department of External Territories, was an attempt to bring external investors into the territory (Department of External Territories, Australia, 1968). It covered the social aspects of investing (what the people are like, the languages, the political system, the system of education), the infrastructural aspects of investing (power, water, transport, shipping, ports, roads, medical services), the economic structures for investing (taxes and tariffs, banking, the national economy), labor supply and demand, and export and import opportunities, and provided an outline for establishing a business in the territory. In terms of export production development it stated that the IBRD had "suggested a development program aimed at doubling total existing plantations of coconuts, cocoa and rubber by 1973–1974 and increasing cattle numbers to 300,000 in the same period" and that the administration "envisaged a tripling of forestry production from 800 million log super feet cut in 1962–63 to a level of 300 million log super feet cut annually by the end of 1968–69" (Department of External Territories, Australia, 1968, 21). It went on to say that the "Australian Government accepted the Mission's proposed development programme as a working basis for future planning in the Territory, conscious of the fact that substantial investment from overseas to supplement investment by expatriate settlers and by local farmers would be necessary to achieve the targets" (21). The investment guide suggested coconuts, rubber, cocoa, oil palm, tea, pyrethrum (a natural insecticide made from chrysanthemums), forestry, and minerals as possible investment opportunities for readers (21–27). Coffee was mentioned only in terms of the "secondary industry" that already existed around it (drying factories; 29).

The bank and the administration wanted to encourage export industries that were not localized. By the 1960s the indigenous planters of coffee in the Highlands had fully localized coffee production. They had turned it into what I think of as a subsistence export industry, by which I mean an industry in which people invested enough labor to make a profit that would meet their day-to-day monetary needs, with little to no desire on the part of the majority of rural landholders to amass capital and reinvest it in the industry, other industries, or large goods and services. While Finney shows that the indigenous "businessmen" in the coffee industry reinvested in their businesses, the majority of very rural growers, the people who were the backbone of the industry, did not. The coffee industry was molded to fit the lives of Highlanders. But according to the bank and other assessors of development, that fit between cash-generating industry and local social lives and needs did not do enough to put money into the pockets of expatriates and foreign investors.

In 1972, as the territory was preparing for self-government and as Michael Somare, leader of the Papua and New Guinea Union Party (Pangu Pati) and member of the House of Assembly, who would become the first prime minister, was forming a political platform that advocated increased localized economic development, the United Nations Development Program and the Australian government sponsored another study known as the Faber Report (Errington and Gewertz 2004, 50). While earlier reports advocated development of industry that directly benefited foreigners and foreign investors, the Faber Report advocated development that benefited the indigenous inhabitants of the country and the government so that it could develop infrastructure, which would also benefit the indigenous inhabitants (Errington and Gewertz 2004, 50).

The Faber Report was embraced by Somare, other indigenous politicians associated with the Pangu Pati, and the Australian government, while at the same time it was shunned by the in-country colonial officials (Errington and Gewertz 2004, 50–51). The Australian government was trying to "disentangle" itself from the territory and get out quickly (269 n. 7), and this report allowed the government to advocate independence with the aim of putting less Australian government money into the land and its development. Somare and his party used the Faber Report to inform their writing of the "Eight Aims," the document that became the basis for the independent government of Papua New Guinea (50).

The Faber Report emphasized several changes that needed to be put into place in order for the territory to develop in a way that benefited indigenous people and the soon-to-be new nation-state: "(i) increased indigenous control of the economy and indigenisation of many forms of economic activity (including the public service); (ii) increases in opportunities for employment, especially income-generating self-employment; (iii) emphasis on 'projects and policies that will directly increase the incomes of PNG nationals, and of the poorest sections amongst PNG nationals'; (iv) greater emphasis on rural development, including food production and the development of urban-centres in the countryside; and (v) a progressive reduction in dependence on aid and, ultimately, foreign capital" (May 1996). These recommendations were translated into the Eight Aims:

1. a rapid increase in the proportion of the economy under the control of Papua New Guinean individuals and groups and in the proportion of personal and property income that goes to Papua New Guineans;
2. more equal distribution of economic benefits, including movement toward equalisation of incomes amongst people and toward equalisation of services amongst different areas of the country;
3. decentralisation of economic activity, planning and government spending, with emphasis on agricultural development, village industry, better internal trade, and more spending channelled to local and area bodies;
4. an emphasis on small scale artisan, service and business activity, relying where possible on typical Papua New Guinean forms of business activity;
5. a more self-reliant economy, less dependent for its needs on imported goods and services and better able to meet the needs of its people through local production;
6. an increasing capacity for meeting government spending needs from locally raised revenue;
7. a rapid increase in the equal and active participation of women in all forms of economic and social activity;
8. government control and involvement in those sectors of the economy where control is necessary to achieve the desired kind of development.

Privatization of the Industry

With independence and the Eight Aims in Papua New Guinea we see the beginnings of the "ascendancy of an indigenous class of capital" (MacWilliam 1993, 482). The push for privatization that was happening internationally, having been given steam by the United States and the United

Kingdom, was also happening for slightly different ideological reasons in the new nation. In Australia, the United States, and the United Kingdom, the late 1970s and early 1980s saw the selling-off of state enterprises and the retreat of the state from social services and the maintenance of public works. In Papua New Guinea these same years saw wealthy Papua New Guineans advocating the privatization of institutions that had been run by the colonial administration, along with the simultaneous nationalization of some public works enterprises. With this seemingly contradictory set of goals, the new nation of Papua New Guinea privatized things like the Coffee Industry Board (which became the Coffee Industry Corporation) and nationalized things like Air Niugini (see MacWilliam 1993). Even as indigenous businessmen were seeking the privatization of colonially owned enterprises and the nationalization of internationally owned enterprises, the goal of the international community was the privatization of all state enterprises and, for Papua New Guinea, the development of a business climate that was welcoming to external capital from large multinational firms.

The politics of the privatization of the Coffee Industry Board, along with politically driven changes about who could export coffee from Papua New Guinea, eventually gave rise to the coffee industry that we see today. The current industry has very few exporters: gigantic international firms dominate the export market. All the privatizations associated with coffee in Papua New Guinea coincided with the decline in international prices for coffee beginning in the 1980s.

The "Global Coffee Crisis," Structural Adjustments, and the Demise of ANGCO

The International Coffee Agreement (ICA) broke down in 1989. As discussed in chapter 2, the breakdown was directly tied to the policy discourses and practices of neoliberalization.[25] At about the same time Vietnam, a country that had not produced much coffee historically, emerged rapidly as a major coffee producer. The country flooded the market with its coffee when there was already global overproduction. This, combined with the new deregulated market, drove the price of coffee down sharply. The enormous reduction in prices, coupled with the deregulation that had caused the price depression in the first place, resulted in two seemingly contradictory trends. First, major companies were able to control even more of the global market (see Ponte 2002a). Second, small roasters and importers were able to slip into the market for the first time (see Roseberry 1996).

At the exact same time, the major source of state revenue in Papua New Guinea, the Panguna mine, was shut down, and revenue from it ceased overnight. The Panguna mine, the largest open-cut mine in the world, was on the island of Bougainville, an island that while part of Papua New Guinea is in the Solomon Islands archipelago, and operated by Bougainville Copper Ltd, an Australian company dominated by two major shareholders: Rio Tinto (holding 53.6 percent) and the state of Papua New Guinea (holding 19.1 percent). There had been unrest associated with the mine in Bougainville since the Australian colonial period. An independence movement took root there in the early 1960s, but through a series of mediations with the men who would bring Papua New Guinea to independence, the political leaders in Bougainville agreed to become part of the new nation if allowed a great deal of autonomy. In the end the leaders of the Papuan parliament did not uphold their end of the bargain, and talks between them and the Bougainville leaders fell apart in early 1975. They declared independence as the Republic of North Solomons in September of that year (fourteen days before Papua New Guinea declared independence), but the United Nations refused to recognize them, and the Solomon Islands, which were preparing for their own independence (granted in 1978) refused to unite with them. By 1976 the leaders realized that they would have to be a part of Papua New Guinea. They advocated for autonomy within the nation and were granted it on paper, but the massive revenues from the mine were not evenly distributed. People in Bougainville did not benefit from the mine in the ways they had demanded. In 1987 resistance leaders, through the Bougainville Revolutionary Army, began violently resisting the mine, and by 1989 it ended operations completely. By 1990 all the foreign investors had pulled out and the revenues that had been flowing to the nation of Papua New Guinea ceased.[26]

During the first ten years of the mine's operation after independence about 48 percent of Papua New Guinea's export earnings had come from the Bougainville mine. This valuable export economy allowed the country to have a "hard kina policy" that kept the national currency's value on par with the U.S. dollar. After the breakdown of the relationship between Papua New Guinea and Bougainville, the prime minister devalued the Kina and the economy of the country went into a tailspin. While there were other high-yielding mines, especially the Ok Tedi and Porgera mines, the loss of income from Bougainville put the government in a bad position. Because of advice it had taken from the International Monetary Fund and the World

Bank before independence, as discussed at the end of chapter 3, the country had put its efforts into expanding the mining sector, and between 1972 and 1989 over 50 percent of Papua New Guinea's exports came from mining (this is compared to the second-highest earner, coffee, at 15 percent).

What this means is that in 1989 all the price supports for coffee internationally that allowed growers in Papua New Guinea and elsewhere to make a living wage for their labor fell apart at the same moment that the government of Papua New Guinea stopped putting any money into infrastructure. The roads, school system, and hospitals began to decline. Simultaneously, the World Bank and the International Monetary Fund began to agitate for the country to undergo structural adjustment reforms (Kavanamur et al. 2004, 4). These calls for reform grew, and by 1990 the country adopted its first structural adjustment program. There have been three periods of structural reform periods in the country, in 1990–92, 1994–97, and 1999–2004 (2004; see also Elek 1991).[27] The economic reforms implemented affected rates of wages and employment, the budget process, the financial sector, the privatization of government-owned industry and public-private partnerships, land reform, and the forestry sector, while the political reforms decreased the size of the public service sector and reshaped the provincial government system, the voting system, and the political party system (Kavanamur et al. 2004).

While all of this was happening, the largest coffee company in the country was falling apart. According to one long-time ANGCO employee: "The ANGCO story is pretty simple, really. Leading up to August 2000 ANGCO had invested over 25 million Kina in both coffee and cocoa plantation development. For various reasons, the main one being a civil war on Bougainville and lawlessness in the Highlands, the company was virtually forced to walk away from all of these investments. The company's banking facilities were called up by the bank at a time when trading conditions were difficult. Although the level of trading debt was high it had been higher in previous years, and the company had survived. It apparently suited the bank at that time to call in the facilities, and receivers were appointed in August 2000. ANGCO traded for another year in receivership, but the penalty interest rates were too great and the company was dismantled and the assets sold off in September 2001" (September 2010). Another long-time employee said: "ANGCO got new managers in the late 1980s and they got greedy. They took the liquidity that we needed to stay solvent in the coffee world and saw opportunity for investment in other sectors. They didn't understand the necessity of liquidity for the coffee market and they saw all this cash in the bank and invested it in things that we had no business getting into. Then the bank, because of the economic crisis in the country after Bougainville, called in the notes. [The new managers] had invested all our capital and then borrowed even more money" (August 2009). ANGCO ceased to exist in 2001. Until the new management strategy was put in place it had been continuing its long-standing relationships with rural growers, and growers could depend on ANGCO to buy their coffee at a fair price. This was not the case with other companies that moved into the market when ANGCO moved out.

Writing about the effects of several structural adjustment programs happening simultaneously, Kavanamur et al. observed:

> Despite reform efforts, the country continues to record negative growth in GDP per person and has Human Development Indicators (HDIs) that are amongst the lowest in the world. With a population 5.2 million people (up by 36 percent since the last census in 1990) and a growth rate of 3.1 percent compared to 2.7 percent in the last decade, the Asian Development Bank (ADB) declared that over a third of the population now live in absolute poverty (ADB 2001). The country's average income fell by almost 75 percent from a high of $1,300 in 1994 to $744 in the new millennium as the economy entered a non-transitory period of recession (*The National*, 24 September 2001). The country's rural infrastructure has collapsed and macroeconomic management has produced unsustainable results with inflation oscillating between 9–21 percent within short-time ranges coupled with a public debt ratio of over 80 percent of GDP. (2004, 2)[28]

Globally, structural adjustment programs have made the poorest of the poor even poorer (see Abouharb and Cingranelli 2007; Babb 2005; Easterly 2007; George 1990). They have also resulted in drastic changes to people's social, moral, material, and ideological lives (see Comaroff and Comaroff 1999). This is most certainly the case in Papua New Guinea, and it is the context of the contemporary coffee industry there.

In this chapter I describe the lives of some of the people who grow coffee in Papua New Guinea and show how coffee has worked to produce space, place, and subjectivity for Gimi-speaking peoples. The chapter begins with an introduction to the rural parts of the Eastern Highlands Province, highlighting the visual aspects of place. I then describe the ecology of coffee in the Highlands and the ways it is cultivated in rural Papua New Guinea. Next I discuss Gimi subjectivity in the past and present, to show the fundamental changes to Gimi personhood that result from the ways their lives have intertwined with coffee production. After discussing personhood in general I juxtapose the cultivation of sweet potatoes (a staple crop for Gimi) and coffee, in order to highlight the difference between social reproduction through cultivation and cultivation as labor. I also discuss how Gimi understand value and see coffee as a marker of modernity.

Pastor Les

Les Anderson had a swagger, one providing no hint of his position as a Seventh-Day Adventist missionary. Sometimes, after he landed his plane in Maimafu village, I would sit at the top of the airstrip and watch him. That is part of what we anthropologists do; we observe, we listen, and we participate. Pastor Les understood this, but he thought it was funny. After he had finished his business with those who gathered around his airplane he would hike up the airstrip, looking like a cross between John Wayne and a back-country rescuer at Yellowstone National Park, smiling at me as he approached. "You collecting data?," he would ask as he laughed at the absurdity of my waged labor and probably my visage—cowboy-hatted, soaked in sunscreen, pale, pale, pale there in the middle of the tropics, several pens clipped onto my John Smoltz Atlanta Braves baseball T-shirt. It was certainly not a picture that anyone would or should take seriously, and not one that I can easily imagine myself striking today. There are moments in our lives as anthropologists when we are intensely public in how we participate and observe, yet that are intensely private in that we rarely talk about the things we observe in the field with our colleagues, friends, family, or students. But let's return to Les Anderson: After laughing at me, Les would sit down and we would talk about life, about work, and about God. On a couple of occasions after our discussions he would say, "You know, I have to come back here later today and I have to save room in the plane for some coffee going to Goroka. Do you want to fly with me?"

What a question to ask someone. "Do you want to fly with me?" Kabe, a Gimi sorcerer, says that to fly in a plane in New Guinea is as close to becoming a bird as I will ever experience. And Kabe would know: he has shifted and transformed between human and avian in ways that are not open to me. In the past Gimi peoples believed that nothing ever began or ended. They believed that all matter was here from the beginning of time, and through social and environmental relations it changed form for all eternity. Men's souls became birds and bird's souls became men—all the time. There was an exchange between people and the forest and between the past and the present that was central to social, ecological, and spiritual life. Kabe is sure that this is the way of the soul today, but his children are not. His children are all Seventh-Day Adventist. They believe that when you die, your body becomes part of the dust from which it came, but that depending on how you spent your time here on earth, your soul goes to either heaven or hell. Pastor Les Anderson baptized all of Kabe's children.

But let's consider flying in New Guinea. You soar against a backdrop of high mountains, green forests, and wide, winding rivers. On a clear afternoon you can see forever. You see tree-covered landscapes punctuated by villages with tiny airstrips, coffee groves, and gardens. You skim by waterfalls dripping or pouring, depending on the wetness or dryness of the season, down craggy mountains with trees growing out of them at seemingly impossible angles. You fly through the valleys, weaving between steep ridges, and sometimes when you crest a ridge, just barely making it over the top because of the weight of the plane full of coffee and people, the valley that stretches before you feels otherworldly. It feels as if you are the first to see it, as if you have just discovered it, and it is exhilarating.

In the 1840s Joseph B. Jukes wrote about the voyage of the HMS *Fly*: "I know of no part of the world, the exploration of which is so flattering to the imagination, so likely to be fruitful in interesting results, whether to the naturalist, the ethnologist, or the geographer, and altogether so well calculated to gratify the enlightened curiosity of an adventurous explorer, as the interior of New Guinea! The very mention of being taken into the interior of New Guinea sounds like being allowed to visit some of the enchanted regions of the *Arabian Nights*, so dim an atmosphere of obscurity rests at present on the wonders it probably conceals" (Jukes 1847, 291). Jukes wrote in a romantic haze of orientalism and imperialism, but the pull of the imagination and of the fantasy that he felt is very much alive today. *"The wonders it probably conceals."* Expatriates in New Guinea, especially working-class men and women from northern Queensland in Australia, have a saying about the people that come to New Guinea. They say that they are "misfits, missionaries and mercenaries." Some, like miners and people in the coffee industry for whom the wonders concealed by New Guinea are its natural resources, dream of the riches they will acquire when these resources are extracted, exported, processed, and marketed abroad. Others, like missionaries, dream of the wondrous wealth of native souls concealed by New Guinea. They imagine that these souls are in need, that they are souls crying out for Jesus.

Before Pastor Les and other Seventh-Day Adventist pilots fly, they pray. They ask you to close your eyes and pray with them before you put your life in their hands. Les Anderson had capable hands. He was a mission pilot for twenty-five years, having begun his work in Ethiopia and flown the emperor Haile Selassie in 1974 during its revolution. He was a great pilot and a devout and successful missionary. He flew the first plane ever to land in Sogo, a village near Karamui, the Simbu province regional center some two days' walk from Maimafu. In an article about the experience in the *Adventist Review* (14 October 1999) he wrote, "They mobbed the plane after we had landed and, whooping with joy, carried us shoulder-high around it. We told them how we hoped to teach them about God. We could sense their need."[1]

Mission Aviation Fellowship loading coffee in Maimafu village

On 3 May 2002 at 3:52 p.m. Les Anderson died in a plane crash in Papua New Guinea. His wife Mary Lane told me afterward that the two had spent their last Sabbath in Maimafu with Kabe's children, celebrating the completion of a small church near the airstrip. Les was buried in Papua New Guinea, and from his hillside gravesite you can see the landscape over which he so loved to fly. He was fifty-eight when he died, and he and Mary Lane were planning on retiring and going home to California only a few weeks later, on 10 June. They had just bought some land and were going to build a house and live quietly. Mary Lane told me that Les was looking forward to reading some anthropology about Papua New Guinea in his retirement. He was especially interested in how Christianity had altered traditional belief systems. But he also wanted to learn more about the socio-ecology of the coffee that he had spent so many years flying out of places like Maimafu.

Coffee Ecology

When you fly into Maimafu from Goroka, it is as though you are flying from a peopled landscape to a pristine, untouched, and uncultivated landscape. At least that is what it seems like the first few times you fly into the place. You take off and fly to the southwest over west Goroka town and its warehouse stores, neighborhoods, sports complex, and museum. Farther south you fly over the Goroka Golf Club and a power plant. As you turn westward toward Simbu Province and begin to ascend toward Mount Elimbari, you fly over dusty roads and mountains that were deforested long ago. When you cross over the mountain ranges and out of the Goroka Valley, you see a stark line of forest begin. The landscape outside of the Goroka Valley, south of Elimbari, is shockingly green, with tiny villages peeking out from high ridge-tops. It is breathtakingly beautiful. The first few times you feel as if you are seeing mile upon mile of rich, uninhabited forest. However, as you get to know the landscape, you begin to see where the forest is interspersed with gardens and coffee groves.

The island of New Guinea sits directly below the equator. At 786,000 square kilometers it takes up less than half of 1 percent of the earth's surface, but it contains about 10 percent of the total species on the planet. Many of these species are endemic, found only on New Guinea. There are over 200,000 species of insects, 20,000 of plants, 725 of birds, 400 of amphibians, 455 of butterflies, and 200 of mammals. Gimi territory, unlike most of the rural Eastern Highlands today, has an extremely high degree of biological diversity, even by New Guinea standards. Although species lists are incomplete for the area, biological surveys conducted by the Papua New Guinea Institute of Biological Research reveal 286 species of birds (100 of these endemic), 84 of mammals (20 endemic), 71 of frogs (5 of these occurring nowhere on the planet besides the slopes of Crater Mountain), 28 of lizards, and 17 of snakes. In forest test plots botanists have found 228 species of trees per hectare. In addition, 5 major vegetation types and 7 major terrain types have been identified on Gimi-held lands.

Scholars often discuss three events when they describe ecological changes on the island of New Guinea in terms of human impacts (see Filer 2010). These are thought of as the three major transitions which have worked to produce space, alter ecologies, and transform human habits on the island. The first event was the invention of agriculture, which according to mounting evidence may have occurred as early as ten thousand years ago and has been followed ever since by a series of transformations on the island through agricultural practices (see Denham, Golson, and Hughes 2003). The second event was the large-scale peopling of the island; although the subject has been hotly debated, there is evidence that there were two distinct migrations of people to the island (Austronesian-language speakers and non-Austronesian-language speakers), one ancient and the other approximately four thousand years ago (see Filer 2010 for a review of this literature). The third event was a set of drastic changes in landscapes and societies resulting from the introduction of sweet potatoes to the island.

Scholars have failed to adequately address the ecological changes produced by coffee agriculture in the Highlands of Papua New Guinea. Coffee has radically transformed both society and ecology over the past sixty years. Indeed, coffee cultivation has transformed much of the tropical mountainous regions near the equator worldwide. Coffee is best grown at the boundary of tropical and temperate ecotones (Donald 2004). In the tropics it is typically grown in lower- and middle-elevation forests in biologically diverse regions on the fringe or edge of forests, or at biogeographically and ecologically significant elevations where tropical and temperate forest types overlap (Moguel and Toldeo 2004; Philpott and Dietsch 2003; Ricketts 2004). Coffee is grown several ways globally, but the two most important methods in Papua New Guinea are shade-growing and sun-growing, with each method having different effects on local ecosystems.

Shade-grown coffee is preferable from a conservation point of view since it can support more biological diversity in the groves than sun-grown coffee can (Donald 2004; Rappole, King, and Vega Rivera 2003; Roberts, Cooper, and Petit 2000). Shaded coffee groves seem to serve as corridors between fragmented tropical forests and thus preserve biodiversity by providing a road for mammals and a flight path for birds (Pineda et al. 2005).[2] However, sun-grown coffee is more popular with growers, both because it is more profitable (Donald 2004; Rappole, King, and Vega Rivera 2003), and because coffee leaf rust, a pathogenic leaf fungus that destroys coffee crops, is easier to control in sun-grown systems (Donald 2004). *Coffea arabica*, the species grown in the highlands of Papua New Guinea and in most other higher-altitude tropical areas, is autogamous—capable of fruiting without cross-pollination (Ricketts 2004). Yet field studies in Costa Rica have shown that coffee yields decrease between 15 and 50 percent without bee visitation, and that bee visitation to coffee groves increases in proximity to forests (Ricketts 2004; see also Donald 2004; Roubik 2002). This may mean that because of pollination, coffee grown near standing forests is more profitable than coffee grown away from them (Ricketts 2004). In addition, the species richness and abundance of bees affects pollination, with rich bee diversity leading to higher coffee yields (Klein et al. 2003). The process seems to go both ways—rich bee diversity means more coffee, and shade-grown coffee leads to bee species diversity and abundance. It has also been argued that the more tree cover a shade-grown-coffee garden has, the higher its yields (Donald 2004); however, recent studies have shown that tree cover may not affect yields as much as shrub cover within the gardens (Soto-Pinto et al. 2000).

In Latin America shaded coffee gardens grown by small-scale, community-based growers are important repositories for tree, epiphyte, mammal, bird, reptile, amphibian, and arthropod diversity (Moguel and Toldeo 2004). They are especially important for epiphytes (Hietz 2005). In other parts of the Neotropics the forest-like conditions of shade-grown coffee gardens have been shown to clearly foster ant diversity (Roberts, Cooper, and Petit 2000). Ant diversity, in turn, may foster a greater diversity of birds. However, some studies show that while areas with organic, polygeneric shade-grown coffee have the largest number of species of ants, the rapid intensification of all coffee agriculture causes a loss in diversity (Armbrecht, Rivera, and Perfecto 2005). In a comparison between tropical mountain cloud forests and shaded coffee groves, a recent study shows that frogs were more abundant in forests, beetles more abundant in coffee groves, and bats equally abundant in both systems (Pineda et al. 2005). All agricultural production changes landscapes and alters forests, yet while some scientists have argued that the cultivation of shade-grown coffee promotes forest destruction, other types of agriculture are much more harmful (Philpott and Dietsch 2003). In fact, there is some evidence that when located in heavily deforested areas, shade-grown plots protect the remaining biodiversity (Perfecto et al. 1996).

It is often the combination of shade-grown coffee groves and an additional type of biodiversity that fosters other biodiversities. For example, in Coaptepec, Vera Cruz, Mexico, experiments show that shade-grown plantations with epiphytes have a higher diversity and abundance of bird species than shade-grown plantations with epiphytes removed (Cruz-Angon and Greenberg 2005). The removal of the epiphytes resulted in a decline in nesting sites and materials, fewer foraging opportunities, and changes to microclimates. In Mexico coffee plantations with traditional polycultures are better suited to epiphyte diversity than other plantations are (Hietz 2005). In terms of soils, nitrogen is cycled more conservatively in shade-grown groves than in sun-grown ones, and it is leached less in shaded areas, yet it is more available in sun-grown areas (Babbar and Zak 1994).

What all of this tells us is that coffee cultivation can have some environmental benefits if practiced in particular ways. However, the claims often made by the marketers of contemporary specialty coffees about the tremendous ecological benefits derived from cultivating certain types of coffee are not borne out by the science. These claims also often fail to acknowledge the ecological practices that indigenous peoples were undertaking far before third-party certification schemes entered into their lives. There are numerous examples of this from Papua New Guinea.

In the highlands of Papua New Guinea many indigenous soil fertility maintenance techniques are practiced (Bourke 1997, 1).[3] Instead of moving on to unused land after a garden has been harvested, people use the same gardens repeatedly, thereby intensifying their horticulture and creating a need for management techniques such as composting, rotations of leguminous crops with root crops, human-made barriers to reduce erosion, mulching, animal manure fertilizing, and terrace construction, which maintain soil quality and fertility (1). One of the most important techniques is fallow species management with tree planting. Numerous minor tree species are used in this practice, but the main species in the highlands is *Casuarina oligodon* (7; Bourke 1989).[4]

Casuarina oligodon is a multipurpose tree species, which provides timber for construction, fencing, and firewood. Villagers in Papua New Guinea plant it to reduce erosion and increase soil fertility, and to provide shade for arabica coffee groves (Bourke 1997, 7). Across the highlands people plant Casuarina seedlings, coffee seedlings, annual food crops, and banana plants at the same time (7). As the Casuarina and coffee mature, the annuals provide initial shade, and when they are harvested the banana plants provide shade. As the grove matures, the Casuarina grow faster and higher than the coffee trees and eventually provide the needed shade (7). Studies show that the soil in groves dedicated to Casuarina and coffee cultivation have higher levels of nitrogen and carbon than groves under coffee cultivation alone (8). Since the mid-1960s people in the Eastern Highlands have been planting the trees with the purpose of shading their coffee groves (6). This management technique is extremely important given the large number of people who grow coffee in the Highlands and the vast amount of land under cultivation.

Coffee Is the Bones of the Highlands:
Production in Rural Papua New Guinea Today

In Papua New Guinea almost 400,000 households grow coffee, with 30 percent of those households in the Eastern Highlands Province. Most of that coffee is grown in rural villages, such as Maimafu village. Located in the Lufa District of the Eastern Highlands Province, Maimafu is a Unavisa-Gimi-speaking village with approximately seven hundred residents, and is made up of fifteen small, family-group-organized hamlets.[5] Maimafu's hamlets are organized around a 442-meter airstrip that sits at about 4,600 feet in elevation. It has the steepest slope of any airstrip in Papua New Guinea.[6] The ridge-top settlements that make up Maimafu are Motai, Tulai, Aeyahaepi, Abigarima, Kolatai, Harontai, Lasoabei, Kuseri, Atobatai, Bayabei, Iyahaetai, Wayoarabirai, Kalopayahaetai, Halabaebitai, and Biabitai, with the airstrip located at Biabitai. People from numerous extended family groups, often called "clans" in the literature and by people in Papua New Guinean government and industry, live along these ridge-tops. The extended family groups are patrilineal. Among Gimi-speakers, clans have enduring historic, social, and cosmological relations with particular tracts of land, and men gain access to land for houses, gardens, and hunting through negotiations with their male kinsmen. A woman works on land held by her father's clan until she is married, and then on land owned by her husband's clan. Women are the horticulturalists in Gimi society, a society that was historically based on subsistence horticulture, pig husbandry, and hunting. Today in Maimafu, people depend on subsistence horticulture, hunting, and imported meat. This is because the majority of Maimafu's residents are Seventh-Day Adventists and do not consume pork.

Australian colonial patrol reports concerned with Gimi-speaking areas offered sporadic accounts of coffee production in the early 1960s.[7] By the mid-1960s coffee had been introduced as a cash crop in most Gimi villages, and by the mid-1970s it had taken off as a system of production. Gimi men, like their Fore neighbors, had taken part in the Highlands Labor Scheme and left their villages during the late 1960s and early 1970s to work on coffee plantations around the Highlands, as well as plantations in coastal areas (Lindenbaum 2002, 67 n. 5). However, coffee production at home had come to the people of Maimafu through rural agricultural extension and traditional networks of exchange. One man recounts how coffee first came from the west through the Eastern Highlands:

> An old man came from Lufa through Gwausa to this place (Maimafu), I don't remember when but I was already a man and had been to Rabaul to work on the copra plantations. I had money and he said that if I bought plants from him, they were coffee seedlings, that I could grow coffee and make money here and never have to go work on the coast again. The man spoke our language and he made a picture with words saying that coffee could become our new pigs. That we could grow it and make money from it and then use that money for things that we used pigs for. At the time I was getting ready to marry and the idea of having lots of money meant to me that I could someday have lots of wives!

Another man recalls how coffee came through what is now Simbu:

> I bought the first seedlings with bird feathers, the tails of tree kangaroos, and the skins of cuscus. After I bought it the old man told me that a Didiman (an agricultural extension agent) would come and help us someday and sell us more seedlings. He was telling the truth about that but not about the coffee. The Didiman came soon afterwards and gave everyone else coffee seedlings. He said that the government was providing them for free so that we would have a way to make money. In those days when the Didiman came he would explain to us that when we grew coffee we would make money and that then we could buy things from stores in Goroka.

In Maimafu, as in other sites in the Highlands, coffee cultivation took root, and today every family in Maimafu has a coffee grove. Their coffee is a mix of shade-grown and sun-grown, with the majority of it shade-grown.

Since the mid-1990s people in Maimafu have been involved in the national Wildlife Management Area—the Crater Mountain Wildlife Management Area, which subsumes their traditional land holdings. Over the years the residents of Maimafu have worked with the Research and Conservation Foundation of Papua New Guinea (RCF), a nongovernmental organization in Goroka, on projects to increase their cash income, like ecotourism, handicraft production, and biological diversity education with training to become guides and parabiologists. Even with these conservation-as-development efforts, coffee production is still the most significant source of

Kobe Falau, Maimafu village

income and in fact the only source of income for most people.[8] People in Maimafu use the cash they derive from coffee production for various needs. They use cash to meet social obligations by paying bride prices, head payments, and school fees. Additionally, they use it to buy commodities like rice, cooking oil, soap, secondhand clothing, and other household needs. Finally, they use cash for socio-financial needs associated with church.[9]

Despite the important economic role that coffee plays in their lives, people in Maimafu do not drink coffee. They do not like it. It is thought of as bitter and tasting rather like soil. They do, however, understand that people elsewhere drink it, and they talk about how others "overseas" drink their coffee. They think about how far away they are from the people who drink their coffee, but they see themselves as connected to them. They discuss what people who drink coffee must think when they see photographs of them working in their gardens (gardens which are tidy and modern), processing the coffee (with modern and efficient hand-cranked machines for skinning the coffee), and loading the coffee on airplanes (which are modern, if not particularly efficient). Coffee is seen as their link to cash and the root of their claims to modernity. In addition to being the link between Gimi and their vision of modernity, coffee brings into being coffee-specific sorts of Gimi persons, coffee-specific social relations, and coffee-specific knowledges. Indeed, coffee has changed the Gimi world in particular ways. To understand these changes, one must understand larger issues of gender, knowledge, power, and change in Melanesia.

Gender, Knowledge, Power, and Change in Melanesia

In Melanesian societies the divisions between the sexes are highly differentiated. Within these societies division of production and cultural knowledge is gendered, as is the allocation of responsibility for certain aspects of material and social reproduction (Tuzin 1997; Weiner 1992). The result is that the totality of cultural knowledge never rests with a single individual within society but is distributed along gendered, age, and possibly ranked categories. Because social practice is intertwined with mythological significance that is both explanatory and prescriptive, these gendered divisions are not limited to production of material goods but are the basis by which the cosmological domain of a given culture is formed. The gendered division of material and cultural production is reinforced by taboos on practice and the gendered allocation of stories, myths, and esoteric knowledge. As a result, no one person has access to the entirety of the cultural repertoire, and cultural knowledge and power are thus indeterminate and sublime. Members of one sex are aware that members of the other possess important and powerful cultural knowledges but are unaware of the nature or boundaries of these knowledges. Thus aspects of cultural power are simultaneously revealed to exist while their specifics remain hidden. This can be seen in the common story that an important aspect of men's power or esoteric knowledge was stolen from women in the mythic past, which acknowledges that men have information denied to women while recognizing women as generative of knowledge and power. The most significant result is that the culture as a whole appears to any given individual as a total social system of indeterminate, and thus potentially limitless, powers to control and explain experience.

The corollary to this is that the loss of these gendered divisions does not affect just the individuals involved or one sex but can result in the culture as a whole losing its transcendent characteristics and its ability to inscribe meaning onto the world. For instance, Tuzin recounts how the advent of a Christian revivalist movement among the people with whom he worked ultimately led to the revealing and undermining of the men's cult (*tambaran*) and its secret practices and stories. As a result,

Agua, Maimafu village, Papua New Guinea

certain ceremonial activities were halted or lost cultural significance and daily activities were "converted from meaningful endeavor[s] into unredeemed drudgery" (Tuzin 1997, 34). The lacuna left in the social order by the end of the tambaran also led to negative social effects such as loss of control over children by parents and increased domestic violence by frustrated men.

Because social and cultural significance is not limited to ceremonial practices but rather infuses daily practices, these effects can also result from altering other aspects of life such as production practices just as much as they can from spiritual missionizing. The changes that have historically been brought about by the introduction of coffee production for a market and the contemporary changes being brought by advocates of fair-trade, organic, and other specialty coffees alter these relationships, with ramifications for the producers' society and culture. This is because in the context of Melanesian exchange systems, social relationships and social meaning remain within objects and between the givers and receivers. Production, exchange, and consumption take place within existing social relationships, maintain those relationships, and generate new social relationships. To understand how seemingly mundane daily practices are inextricable from cultural and social reproduction one must understand the nature of Melanesian personhood.

Melanesian Personhood and Capitalism

In *The Gender of the Gift* (1988) Strathern argues that identities in Melanesia embody the relationships that exist by virtue of acts of exchange. Thus personhood and identity are tied to social relationships and the maintenance of social exchange relationships. As a corollary, any given construction of a person's identity is a fluid one based on the social transactions in which she is engaged, or, as Strathern puts it, there is a "partibility of persons under the regime of a gift economy" and "persons do not have to strive for singular identities" (1988, 162). Strathern's point is not that the concept of individuals is nonexistent in Melanesia; rather, she argues, "Melanesian persons are as dividually as they are individually conceived" (13), and one misses the point by focusing on the relationship of individuals to society when what is salient to Melanesians is the relationships by which one is brought into being and sustained. By this account the body is not the site of the individual but a "*microcosm of relations*," and "if the body is composed of relations, if it shows the imprint of past encounters, then the relations are not in a state of stasis. Awareness of them implies that they must be attended to" (131). With specific reference to material objects of these exchanges, "persons simply do not have alienable items, that is, property, at their disposal; they can only dispose of items by enchaining themselves in relations with others. . . . Enchainment is a condition of all relations based on gift" (161). Melanesian personhood is the embodiment of all the gift exchanges that brought it into bring and sustained it, and that embodiment is enchained to all the relationships from which those exchanges flowed. These enchainments require further reciprocal action, such that the dividual selves are remade based on all the actions of the other actors in the relationships. Just as these selves embody relationships, the objects exchanged both precipitate and embody these relationships and elicit particular actions. This view of personhood creates different kinds of bodies and different kinds of selves and necessarily means that Melanesians engaged in exchange have a vastly different relationship to the things exchanged than would individuals residing in a capitalist, market-based society. Strathern argues that human labor and the relationships of production and exchange appear as things in a western, commodity-based economic system, but in a gift system objects maintain their appearance as related to the people who made and gave them. In the exchange context, social relationships and social meaning remain within objects and between the givers and receivers. This is in stark contrast to the alienable nature of western commodities.

While the distinction that Strathern makes between gift and commodity societies is certainly drawn starkly (see Appadurai 1986; Carrier 1995, 1998c; LiPuma 2000), her point is to highlight the taken-for-grantedness of bourgeoisie notions of self and individualism and to demonstrate that in Melanesia at least, alternative notions of self and personhood persist. Melanesians have had over a century of contact, interaction, and exchange with Europeans and the capitalist economic system. Many Melanesians have had waged labor positions and most have experience producing cash crops. Given this familiarity with, and enmeshment in, the capitalist system, it would be naïve to insist that *all* economic activity takes place in the context of social exchange relationships. That is not to deny, however, that such socially and culturally generative exchange occur within *many* economic contexts. An examination of the introduction of coffee production, its development into "the people's business," and the ways coffee production is undertaken today shows that it is very much controlled by and generative of the kinds of social relationships that go into creating Melanesian persons, society, and culture.

Gimi Personhood

To understand the way coffee production relates to Gimi subjectivities, one must first understand how Gimi personhood is constituted and the roles that agricultural and horticultural practices play in that process. Gimi personhood is attained through transactive relationships between living people, mutual recognition between people and other species, and exchanges between living people, ancestors, and other species (see West 2005b).[10] So at its base, it is relational in nature. It is also composite, in that Gimi conceive of themselves and others as made from substances, objects, and exchanges.[11] And to some extent, today Gimi personhood has elements of individuality, insofar as individual achievement and self-assertion are valued along with relationships and transactions (see Keck 2005, 71).

When Gimi conceptualize and interact with what we might refer to as other species (and what biologists might refer to as biological diversity and agronomists as agri-diversity), they are taking part in dialectical, transactive relationships that produce them as persons, plants and animals as active agents, and forests as living social arenas. These relationships are entered into on three levels—among people, between people and ancestors, and between people, plants, and animals—and they are what create Gimi subjectivity and produce the Gimi physical surroundings.[12] The generative relations that produce Gimi and Gimi-space unfold on five levels, through (1) the movements of *auna* (life forces) and *kore* (spirits); (2) the hunting of animals by men and their consumption by all; (3) actions that make forests into property; (4) social relations between people, spirits, and animals and between people and plants; and (5) women's reproductive labor with regard to plants, pigs (for Gimi who are not Seventh-Day Adventist), and people. Gimi being-in-the-world is dialectically connected to animal being-in-the-world and plant being-in-the-world, and it is through this mutual recognition that the Gimi socioecological world is created (see West 2005b).

For Gimi, since everything is the physical incarnation of their ancestors' life force, everything is a "gift" from the forest (Gillison 1980, 1993).[13] People and forests will always be—and have always been—in a constant transactive relationship, making and remaking each other over time. Gimi believe that people are made up of flesh, which is made by their social relations and transactions with the living, and auna, which is made by their social relations and transactions with the dead. Auna can be translated as "soul," "power," "vital spirit," "familiar spirit," and "life-force" (see Gillison 1993, 365; Glick 1963, 201) and described as "Invisible animating aspect of a person, ghost (*kore*), animal, or plant manifested in breath, voice, pulse, heart beat, etc., and in the capacity for growth, and present in all body exuviae (urine, feces, sweat, tears, hair, blood, etc.) and discarded scraps of food or tobacco" (Gillison 1993, 365). When a person dies, the auna leaves the body and the person's hamlet. This can take several days, and during this time the auna can be quite dangerous, because it can cause sickness and even death of the living (122). When a man's auna leaves his body for good, it migrates to his clan's ancestral hunting grounds. If a woman dies when she is unmarried, her auna goes to her father's clan's grounds; if she is married, it goes to that of her husband. Once there, the auna slowly turns into kore ("ghost," "spirit," "ancestor," and "wild") and lodges in plants, animals, streams, mountains, birds, and other bits of the forest (122). Women and their spirits are cold, low, and close to the ground, and they infuse the things that slither and move along the forest floors. Men and their spirits are lofty and high, so they soar through the forests as birds and as wind. As auna dissipates, it lodges everywhere. The life-force of a person becomes the forest, the "wild" parts of the forest filled with and "animated by" the kore of deceased Gimi (199). In the past, when a man died his relatives took his bones to his ancestor's lands so that they could "enrich his clan forest, giving rise to new life forms in the way semen engenders life in a woman's body" (101).

Gimi also believe that auna can leave the live body of a sleeping person and fly through the forests and village at night. At times this life-force can lodge itself in the bodies of birds, tree kangaroos, possums, and other animals (108). These nighttime adventures of the auna manifest themselves as dreams, and they are intimately tied to Gimi ideas about conception. When a woman first comes to her husband, she still has her father's clan's life-force inside of her. During her waking hours she is forced to drink water from rivers that flow on her husband's land, so that his ancestors can drive out her father's clan's life-force (Gillison 1980, 163). Thereafter, as she dreams, her auna leaves her body and goes to her husband's clan's forests. In these nighttime journeys the animals in which the woman's auna chooses to lodge itself reveal the gender of the child she will have: if she dreams about a frog, fish, or ground-dwelling animal, she will conceive and bear a female child; if she dreams about birds, she will conceive and bear a male. The animal in the dream is "the ancestral incarnation of the fetus" (Gillison 1993, 208).

In death the auna of a man becomes kore and then returns to the forests from which it came. The auna was merely the form that kore took while the person was living, but it always was, and always will be, the kore that animates the forests. That same kore merges with a woman's auna when it travels at night to her husband's clan's forests, allowing her to conceive his child (Gillison 1980, 160).

The human life-force, plants, and animals are intimately tied. When a person dies, the auna "clings to its body" and must be helped along toward the wooded lands of the person's clan (Gillison 1993, 122). People must sing to a corpse, sit with it, and wail in their sorrow so that it does not cling to the body or hamlet forever. But slowly, "over time, auna penetrates the deep forests and is gradually transformed entirely into kore, taking up residence in giant trees, high mountain caves, and every kind of wildlife" (and this includes plants, not just animals; Gillison 1993, 122). Once the auna goes to the forests and begins to infuse itself into wildlife, it becomes part of not only the forest but also the never-ending cycle of Gimi mythology. This constant transactive cycle happens to all people, plants, and animals, but the forests and the transactions that enliven it are most often discussed in terms of male patrilines and male aspects of socio-ecological regeneration.

Mihi *(Sweet Potato, Ipomoea batatas), or the Girl-from-Ipomoea*

Women come into being in the world and bring the world into being through their relations with the domestic (*kora*) things in their family's gardens and around their hamlets.[14] Their repetitive loving labor of child caring, pig rearing, and tending gardens is deeply productive, and the cultivation of gardens is a particularly feminine way of bringing objects, people, and places into being. Through rules of patrilineal inheritance, family leaders, men who have been called Big Men in the anthropological literature, decide where a man and his wife (or wives) will have access to garden land.[15] Men carefully divide land and monitor women's gardening labor, because if they did not, women might work "haphazardly," so that men could not identify the plants cultivated by their wives, and plants would not be able to identify their mothers (Gillison 1993, 42).

Once a man has cleared land for a garden, women from his family cultivate that land. The man, his wife, and his parents will be forbidden to eat the first crop from his wife's labor. Her early productive labor will go to feed his patrilineage. He, his wife, and his parents will eat the plants cultivated by his sisters and other women whom he allowed into the new plot.[16] This exchange of women's labor through the consumption of cultigens, such as sweet potatoes, ensures that wives become part of a man's family— her labor literally makes his family, she becomes infused into their bodies, and they literally make her, the plants they grow turning into her over the years that she consumes them.

Women have intimate relations with plants, and these relations are in some senses "magical" (Gillison 1993, 167). They sing and chant to them (*anobak*),[17] flattering them and stroking them into maturity with their songs. When women sing to sweet potato plants they "extol" their potential for growth, use intimate names for them, and merge their auna with the auna of the plant (168). A woman's song, combined with the nurturing care that she gives her plants and the intimate relations she has with them, works to merge her life-force with their life-force. Indeed all of her songs use the first-person dual form of the verb "we two," showing linguistically that she and the plant are one (168; McBride and McBride 1973, 21).

While women's songs are powerful, their incantations are even more so (Gillison 1993, 170). New sweet potatoes are sewn from the cuttings of vines grown in established gardens. While a woman cuts the vines she chants to them about highly reproductive animals like megapodes (ground-dwelling birds that have many eggs). She chants to them about her husband's clan and the features of its lands: the waterfalls, mountains, and rich animal and plant life there. When women plant the sweet potato cuttings they also chant to them, urging the cuttings to become enormous and to proliferate. The efficacy of the incantations is tied to this speaking of the clan's land and the animals that live there. The incantations are particularly effective when a woman mentions the birds of paradise that live there and the sounds they make.[18] Gillison argues that some of the chants are also meant to teach women how to be proper Gimi (1993, 171). She says: "During the recitations of 'food talk' and planting instructions older women give to a bride on the eve of her departure, they tell her that she will make gardens 'out of yourself.' 'You cannot be lazy!' they warn. 'The sweet potatoes and pigs you rear come out of you . . . when you care for something, it is your own self you produce'" (172).

These incantations, as they become more and more powerful, slip out of Gimi language and into patterned rhythmic sounds that hold no conventional meaning. They "cannot be translated or explained" and are "inexpressible in any other form," as they become "a private language, binding speaker and object by giving voice to the uniqueness of their attachment" (172). This language "conjures a closed world like the one inside (the gardener's) body," a place where the auna of the plant and the auna of the woman can become one (172). Women's relations with sweet potatoes are just as intimate as the relations with their unborn children. They communicate with them in similar ways, through these songs and powerful incantations. The maturation of sweet potatoes, which are grown in earthen mounds, parallels the gestation of a fetus inside a woman's own mound of a stomach.[19]

The first sweet potato came from the forest, from *kore maha* (wild land and ancestor land). In one Gimi story a man died and his children buried him. That night one of his daughters (his son's wife) dreamed of her father's grave. In the dream a vine was growing from the grave that she had never seen before. When she woke up the next morning she and her co-wives went to investigate and found that there was a unique and unknown plant growing from the center of the grave. They nurtured the vine, and

Betty Philip with a day's work in the gardens

once it was mature they cut bits of it and replanted it all around their village. The first sweet potatoes came from this vine.[20]

This first sweet potato was animated by the kore of a dead man, by his ghost. Life cannot come from nothing; it must come from a transaction with Gimi. Nonhuman life cannot come from the living at first; it must come from the dead, from the ancestors. But once brought into the world it can then exchange with the living: the auna of the Gimi and the auna of the nonhuman species can merge. Sweet potatoes and other cultivated plants are the worldly manifestations of the merging of the auna of two beings. They exist in-the-world only because of these transactive relations.

Kaffe (*Coffee*)

Among people in Maimafu, when a couple marries, the man's father and his father's brothers allocate certain lands to him for coffee cultivation.[21] This process is similar to that for all garden land allocation. Once married, the man's new wife will procure coffee seedlings from her new mother-in law, her sisters-in-law, and on occasion other women in her husband's extended family.[22] After the new bride has obtained seedlings, she will nurture them, in old tin cans or in makeshift greenhouses made of recycled rice bags and plastic tarps, until the garden plot has been prepared and the seedlings are hearty enough to survive. Women do not sing to their coffee seedlings. They may sing in their presence, to other cultivars, but they do not sing directly to them. And a woman would never quietly recite an incantation to the coffee seedlings. Kobe told me: "Coffee seedlings are strong without me. They are from somewhere else, Australia at first, I think, they don't need me as much as sweet potato and taro. They grow tall and straight without my words" (October 2004). Kobe's words tell us that women do not merge their auna with coffee plants and because of this, although coffee plants are of course the fruit of their labor, they are not the physical manifestation of the undying bond between past and present that is embodied in sweet potatoes and therefore do not bring Gimi into the world in the same ways as other cultigens. They do not make Gimi bodies and subjectivities that are fully and totally connected to ancestors and to future offspring. Thus they interrupt the constant transactive cycle that is the Gimi world.

Today one of the first tasks for a married couple is to clear and plant their new coffee garden, or, if they were given part of an existing garden by one of the man's father's brothers, they go to it and determine what work needs to be done. Marriage has always been considered productive, as mentioned above in the discussion of the sweet potato. The first act together between husband and wife used to be sharing bits of pig from a bamboo cooking vessel. This act of consumption, coupled with drinking water from streams that run on the husband's family's lands, helped to make the woman part of her husband's family. Kobe explained: "Before, to seal a marriage a man and a woman would get a bamboo in their new home from the man's family. It was filled with finely sliced banana and the greasy meat from a pig. They would split the bamboo together, jointly, and they would each eat from one end. When they met in the middle, when they finished, they no longer had to be shy around each other, they could talk face to face" (June 2003).

Now people talk about that first act of working in the coffee garden as the seminal moment in sealing a marriage. The production of a commodity now defines the marital bond and the way that a woman becomes part of the husband's clan; it is no longer the act of partaking in the clan's pigs and bananas and thereby taking in, consuming, the past and his past family. Also, since no Gimi consume the coffee beans, the system of taboo mentioned above regarding sweet potato cultivation does not exist with coffee. Coffee's planting and then use (as it has no use value for Gimi) do not work to make a woman part of her husband's family in the same way as sweet potato cultivation does. Additionally, with sweet potato the (re)productive capacity was female. Now, men take part in (re)productive capacity through coffee production.

Today almost all new garden plots around Maimafu village are created in sites where there is secondary or tertiary growth. Women and men work to clear this growth, with men cutting the large trees and women clearing the brush and cutting the smaller shrubs. Afterwards, the garden area is burned to clear the final forest refuse and prepare the ground for planting. People tend to leave a few large trees inside and on the edges of plots that are to become coffee groves, because they understand that shade helps coffee grow. They also, as discussed above, plant specific tree species to shade their gardens. Women plant their seedlings in the new plots and work throughout the year to weed the young plants. In fact, women do all the labor associated with coffee between the clearing of the garden (during which, as mentioned above, men fell large trees) and the harvest.

In rural coffee groves in the Eastern Highlands, coffee trees are usually between fourteen and twenty-four feet tall. In other parts of the world, and on plantations in Papua New Guinea, people prune their trees, keeping them shorter for ease in picking and because pruning increases productivity. In Maimafu very few people prune their trees. The trees have dark green leaves, with a rather waxy or shiny sheen, and they bear small, delicate white flowers right before they begin to produce tiny clusters of green buds which mature into deep, rich red cherries. Once the cherries are almost crimson-purple they are ready to be harvested. In Maimafu, because of the high altitude, trees fruit only once a year, and it takes about six months for the cherries to mature on the tree. A tree raised from a seedling flowers after four or five years and can be productive for up to twenty years. Once a tree stops producing cherries it is cut down completely, and a new tree is allowed to regenerate by sprouting from the stump.

When the coffee begins to ripen around the beginning of June, men take an interest in their coffee groves again after leaving to their wives the work of clearing brush and weeding throughout the rest of the year. When a man thinks that he has enough cherry on the branch to begin the harvest, he and his entire family go to the lowest-altitude grove of trees that he possesses and begin to harvest the coffee. The amount of coffee that any man has in

Coffee-growing family, Maimafu village

production varies widely. For example, among the eleven men in the Somo extended family (or "clan"), one man has 200 yielding trees, while another has 2,500 trees in production. The former is a young man who was only married seven years ago, while the latter is a very old man with two wives who has been growing coffee since the 1970s. Another example is that of three brothers who are quite close in age. Thomo has 649 trees, Nato has 100, and Samo has 3,408. As the eldest, Samo inherited his father's coffee groves; in addition, his wife is a miraculous gardener, known throughout the village as one of the hardest-working women in a place where all women work hard. Thomo has worked as a "para-biologist" with biological researchers who have been visiting Maimafu for some years now, so he has other ways to make money and depends less on coffee income than his brother does. Nato is a lay minister who has little time for anything besides church. This clearly shows that while small-scale coffee production is a central feature of life in Maimafu, it is not a total social fact or the only occupation or defining role for everyone. What the data illustrate is that coffee production is much more complex at the local level, that it depends on personal choices and people's other obligations.

Many of the coffee groves held by people from Maimafu are quite close to the village hamlets. When coffee-harvest time arrives, families go to their gardens together. People hand-harvest the coffee and then prepare it, using the wet method of processing. The woman pours cherries into its top and then, as the man turns the crank, pours water in with the cherries. The turning cherries are forced off the beans, and the slimy beans drop out of the machine. Once the pulp has been removed the berries are placed into clean bags and allowed to ferment. They must be fermented so that the sticky substance on the parchment can be washed off. The fermentation process takes between twelve and twenty-four hours. Once fermented, the coffee is washed over and over again until the water runs perfectly clear. It is then placed in the sun to dry, and when drying is complete what is left are dry, silver-skin-covered beans called parchment. This parchment is placed in bags and left to wait until a coffee buyer comes to the village, or until a plane lands in the village, allowing a village man to take it to market in Goroka.

Coffee harvesting is most often done in single-family groups, meaning that a man, his wife, and their children harvest all their coffee. But on occasion people share labor between single-family groups. This sharing is not always patrilineally organized—and it makes coffee harvesting different from almost every other labor-sharing activity in Maimafu. For example, Lukas, his wife Sara, and their two young daughters go each year to the hamlet of Sara's father, where they live for a few weeks while they help Sara's brother Jonah, his wife Ellen, and their children harvest coffee. Then Jonah's family returns the labor in Lukas's gardens. During the time they are together they work as well as socialize. Sara says, "I miss my mother and my brothers so much, and this is the only time that I get to stay with them; to really see my mother." Ellen also enjoys this time and feels as if her labor is less stretched because of these arrangements. She says, "Even though you do the work twice, in two sets of gardens, it seems somehow like less work." Even with these women's talk of interesting labor configurations, all village-level coffee production is an extremely time-consuming kind of labor (see table 1).

In Gimi villages where coffee production is high, women have a difficult time doing all the labor necessary to tend food crops and coffee groves (see also Finch 1992; Sexton 1986a). There has always been a disproportionate burden put on Gimi women in terms of horticultural labor. Men, while helping to clear new gardens of the secondary and tertiary growth and helping to build fences around the gardens, historically were needed to

TABLE 1 Low-end estimates of labor associated with harvesting of one pound of coffee, 2004–2007

Walk to garden (carrying tools, food, water, and children)	30 minutes
Climb tree	5 minutes
Pick one cherry (two beans)	5 seconds
Pick 1,500 cherries (1 lb., or 0.45 kilogram)	2 hours 5 minutes
Pick 198,000 cherries (one bag: 132 lbs., or 60 kilograms)	275 hours
Carry coffee to water for washing	40 minutes
Wash coffee (once as cherry, once when pulped, several times after fermenting)	2 hours
Store coffee in bags	10 minutes
Pulp coffee with hand-cranked hulling machine and bag for fermentation process	3 hours
Unpack and spread coffee on tarp for drying (twice)	1 hour 20 minutes
Pack and store coffee (twice)	40 minutes
Various other drying labors (turning mats in sun, shooing away chickens, dogs, children, and captive cassowaries)	1 hour
Carry coffee between village and washing to village airstrip in 60-kilogram bags	1 hour 50 minutes
Total	286 hours for 132 lbs., or 60 kilograms (2 hours 10 minutes for 1 pound of coffee)

Source: Data generated by author based on average of fifty time-allocation measures for fifty families.

conduct social business in the village. They oversaw inter- and intra-clan related disputes, compensation claims, sorcery and magic cases and claims, and much of the village-wide ritual business.

The women of Maimafu today, because of coffee production, often discuss the burden which horticulture places on women's labor. Their discussions are more than simple complaints about men and their failures to contribute to social and horticultural reproduction.[23] In these discussions women talk about the need to weigh the time and returns they get from garden work against the time and returns they get from coffee-grove work. They muse about labor-saving techniques like multigenerational and multilineage weeding parties, at which women from several lineages weed each other's groves in rotation so that the work can be done more quickly and efficiently. They discuss the state of women's health in the face of these labor burdens. For example, most women agree that the number of miscarriages is steadily on the rise in Maimafu. While men attribute this to the increase in sorcery in the Lufa District (which in turn is due to jealousy over a proposed mine on the border of the Eastern Highlands, Gulf, and Chimbu provinces), women correlate miscarriage and overwork. Additionally, women often discuss how spending so much time working in coffee groves and on coffee processing is affecting them in terms of socially reproductive practices, such as making net string bags, visiting sisters and mothers, and going to church.

Plants as Objects, People, and Personhood

The Gimi world is produced through social relationships between organisms. These organisms can be people, ancestors, spirits, animals, and plants. The social relations are not neutral and economic; they are familial and poetic. In societies based on gift exchange, like Gimi society, people's identity, personhood, and capacities are defined through social relationships with others and the sources that went into making them (Strathern 1988, 131). Personhood is at the confluence of relationships encompassing certain knowledges, social capacities, and practices that can only be expressed and utilized with reference to others. Since people are constantly entering into new social relationships, they are always making and remaking identity (128). For Gimi these generative transactions include transactions with cultigens such as the sweet potato.

When Gimi think about and interact with the forests, there is a constant dialectical relation between organism and environment which is directly connected to how Gimi "make" themselves and others through transactive relationships (Strathern 1988) and through the sort of "mutual recognition" that creates subjectivity (Robbins 2003, 10). This mutual recognition takes place on four levels: (1) between individuals, (2) between people and their ancestors, (3) between people and animals (West 2005b), and

(4) between people and cultivated plants meant for human consumption. This recognition brings the world into being: with no Gimi there is no tree kangaroo or sweet potato, and with no tree kangaroo or sweet potato there is no Gimi. Ancestral spirits enliven Gimi forests, but it is in part the mutual recognition between Gimi hunters and hunted animals that creates subjects, produces space, and lies at the heart of Gimi politics of forests. When it comes to horticulture, women and their songs and incantations bring the plants into the world, and the social relation between woman and cultivar creates subjectivity, produces space, and lies at the heart of Gimi politics of reproduction.

This transactional being-in-the-world, in which subjectivity is constantly being produced, is the way that Gimi see "self" and "other"—whether that other is a person, an ancestor's spirit, a tree kangaroo, or a sweet potato. Gimi are in existence in relation to their forests and gardens, and their forests and gardens are in existence in relation to Gimi; there is no Gimi without forest and garden and no forest and garden without Gimi. This being-in-the-world as a generative transactional relationship takes place on five levels for Gimi: (1) through the movements and transactions of their auna (life force) and kore (spirit) during conception, in dreams, and after death; (2) through the hunting and eating of animals; (3) through the meaningful human action that transforms forests into clan property; (4) through relations between humans, animals, and spirits that literally created the Gimi universe and that are retold through a concert of male and female myths; and (5) through reproductive horticultural labor.

The cultivation of coffee, which as I have stated is sold, never consumed, and never exchanged by Gimi, is fundamentally different from other forms of cultivation. Women do not merge their auna with the seedlings or with the plants as they mature. They do not sing to them or chant to them. They are not part of Gimi coming-into-being, and while their coming-into-being is guided by Gimi women, it is not brought forth from Gimi bodies in the same way that other cultigens are.

Sweet potatoes have meaning and also have what westerners and western-educated Papua New Guineans would call "value," because they are literally part of Gimi. They are the momentary physical manifestation of Gimi living and dead, and Mihi (sweet potato) living and dead. They are the melding of human and plant that is part of the forever transaction that makes the Gimi world come into being. They are in the moment at which they become an object, when they are no longer a process of nurturing and loving and chanting and singing, when they are no longer in the process of coming into the world by merging with the auna of their "mother," an object that has meaning and value because of its relation with the past and its potential to be eaten and become Gimi again in this way.

Coffee, in contrast, has no meaning or "value" in the Gimi sense. It does not work to bring Gimi into-the-world. The "valuable" thing about coffee beans to Gimi is the social exchanges and transactions that go into its production. It is the shared labor of families and the social life connected to that labor—the exchanges of time between families, the exchanges of food between women when they are resting during harvest, the exchanges between little children playing in the gardens while their families work, the water brought to a garden by a twelve-year-old girl and given to her uncle who will consume her bride price, the tiny snake caught by a five-year-old boy and given to his older male cousin.

The coffee beans themselves have commodity value for Gimi. They are considered "money in the bank"; indeed coffee beans are totally commensurable with money for Gimi. But in and of themselves they are not valuable in the Gimi sense in the way that sweet potatoes are. They are not part of the same sort of transactive relationship. For Gimi sweet potatoes and other cultigens are part of Gimi past, present, and future. Coffee, on the other hand, is not part of this cycle of transaction; it is only the present and the future. Sweet potatoes connect Gimi with other Gimi cross-temporally. Coffee instead connects Gimi with other people and places which are decidedly not Gimi, and which are all in the present and future.

But coffee is also one of the elements of Gimi life that are working to slowly change how Gimi come to be in-the-world as persons. Coffee production, like Christianity, waged labor, and commodity consumption, refocuses Gimi toward individuality instead of collectivity (see Foster 2002; Robbins 2004), and this transformation is one of the hallmarks of modernity (LiPuma 2000). So Gimi see their production of coffee as placing them within wider systems of relationships and exchanges. These relationships and exchanges mean that they are part of the modern global economy. Ironically, at the same time coffee production refocuses Gimi's notions of personhood away from collectivity and transaction and toward being individualized, self-possessed persons. These social relations that both widen the Gimi social world and work to produce Gimi who may, in the future, need a less wide social world can be clearly seen in Gimi relationships with the rural coffee buyers who come to Maimafu on airplanes.

Because people do not draw a bright line between daily practice and cosmological significance, imposing an economic regime that assumes individual producers who alienate the products of their labor to individual consumers alters the cosmological view of what it means to be a person, and does so just as radically as a religious mission's undermining of ritual beliefs and practices does. This means that attempts to rationalize production and commodity labor necessarily alter the way people see their place in the world. For this reason, the ways that fair-trade and single-origin-coffee schemes exert their influence can be seen as neoliberal projects which impose the strictures of a liberal moral economy and value system on producers in Papua New Guinea.

5 | RELATIONAL COFFEE

This chapter is concerned with the routes, machines, and people that connect Maimafu, Goroka, and the rest of the world, and the social relations that emerge along these paths. It is also concerned with structural changes beginning in the 1980s, both global and national, that resulted in the state of the Papua New Guinean coffee industry today. I begin with a discussion of the mechanism by which the coffee moves: airplanes and various missionary-run air services. I then provide an ethnographic description of one of the people glossed as "middlemen" by the specialty coffee industry and his social connections with people in Maimafu. I show that in Papua New Guinea the social and material labor of so-called middlemen is crucial for the movement of coffee, and that they, like the rural growers highlighted by contemporary coffee marketing, make lives and selves out of this labor. I then move to a description of the fragile, but crucial, social relations between villagers and coffee buyers and exporters, and discuss issues of trust, secrecy, and knowledge. I describe three national processes that changed the face of the coffee world in Papua New Guinea in the 1990s. Next I examine the recent fixation on coffee certification in Papua New Guinea, showing that people in the industry have mixed feelings about the claims of certification advocates. I also describe the current state of third-party certification in Maimafu and compare the fantasies that growers have about certification to the fantasies that urban coffee industry workers have about it. I conclude the chapter with another ethnographic description of the social relationship of coffee.

Stuck in Maimafu: Rural to Urban Transport

In 2002, the last year for which there are reliable numbers, the residents of Maimafu sold 74,044 kilograms (163,239 pounds) of coffee harvested from 223,375 coffee trees owned by 193 growers.[1] All the coffee grown in Maimafu, a place that is a three-day walk from the nearest road, is flown out to Goroka by small mission-owned planes—like the ones that Pastor Les Anderson flew. The coffee price that villagers receive is the daily countrywide price, less the cost of fuel to fly it out of Maimafu. Thus for coffee growers in Maimafu, the village airstrip and the airplanes that use it are a vital, if expensive, part of their coffee businesses.

In 1982, with initial financial support from the Seventh-Day Adventist Church, the residents of Maimafu began building their airstrip. And in 1991, after a man from Maimafu was elected to provincial government, the airstrip was completed with funds provided by the government. The first plane landed in 1992. Most people directly relate their desire to undertake the backbreaking work of this construction to their experience of carrying coffee bags to the closest road to meet buyers and get the coffee to market.[2] Seventh-Day Adventist Aviation (SDAA) and Mission Aviation Fellowship (MAF), the two mission aviation companies that serve most of the Highlands of Papua New Guinea, use the airstrip.

From 1992 until around 2003 the airstrip was the center of modern community life in Maimafu. During that period there were regular flights from Maimafu to Goroka, and from other regional village airstrips to and from Maimafu. The network of airstrips served as a conduit for goods, services, and people. Most importantly, it was the way people got their coffee to market in a timely manner. Since mid-March 2003 the price of aviation gas has steadily risen. This has drastically decreased service to the rural areas.

Mission Aviation Fellowship is a not-for-profit Christian air services organization. It operates about 140 airplanes in 31 countries and employs between 1,000 and 1,100 people each year.[3] The organization has branch administrative offices in Canada, the United States, South Africa, Europe, and Australia, and it is from these offices that the "in-country" offices are managed. So, for example, the Papua New Guinea office is managed through the Australian branch of the organization, which also manages the offices in Arnhem Land, Aceh, and Cambodia (Mission Aviation Fellowship 2005, 1).[4] The primary mission, according to the employees of the organization, is to provide a link for roadless rural communities and communities that have been cut off from roads because of natural disaster, infrastructure breakdown, or war, and to provide "vital life-giving services" such as medical care. The fellowship's secondary mission is to provide transportation for mission workers like pastors, Bible translators, missionaries of other sorts, and other church-related workers. In addition, it has become the airline link between urban areas and roadless rural places for people of all sorts (local people needing to travel for business, education and nonemergency medical care, anthropologists, ecologists, development workers, teachers, tourists, government officials, gold miners, and others). Finally, the organization transports goods between urban areas and rural communities and agricultural products from rural areas to urban markets.

When employees of the Mission Aviation Fellowship are asked about the mission of the organization, they often direct people to their webpage.[5] The "purpose" of the organization is "to share God's love through aviation and technology," and the "vision" is "that isolated people will be physically and spiritually transformed in Christ's name." The webpage also lists the "core values" of the organization, including "Christ-like behavior" in work and relationships, "respect" and "compassion" for those in need, sensitivity to "cultural differences," "integrity, professionalism, safety and competence in all areas," and a belief that all work "should honor and glorify Christ."

While Mission Aviation Fellowship is a not-for-profit organization, almost none of its services are free. The organization uses profits from the transportation of people not working with the mission to heavily subsidize the mission workers, the medical evacuations, and the transport of medical-related items, such as medicines and equipment.[6] On the MAF webpage it is stated that "each year MAF (in Papua New Guinea) is able to subsidize fares for over 6,000 church and mission staff and transport hundreds of tonnes of 'church' freight (building supplies etc) great distances in Papua New Guinea. Churches with commitments to health service programs also benefit from MAF flights."

The other main source of transport to and from Maimafu is Adventist Aviation Services, a legal entity of the Papua New Guinea Seventh-Day Adventists Union Mission.[7] According to its webpage, "Adventist World Aviation exists to provide aviation and communications support to those serving the physical, mental, and spiritual needs of the forgotten peoples of

Mission Aviation Fellowship in Goroka

the earth."[8] The Papua New Guinea branch, because of the "financial constraints" of the larger mission, developed a system of operation, like the Mission Aviation Fellowship, under which commercial flying and paying customers subsidize the mission-related work of the airline. The organization provides transport for nonmission passengers, agricultural products, and goods purchased in towns in bulk and then sold in rural areas. Several of the pilots who have worked with Adventist Aviation Services in Papua New Guinea have maintained long-term relationships with Maimafu village. Without Mission Aviation Fellowship and Seventh-Day Adventists Aviation, people living in the rural areas of the country would have no way to get their coffee to market.

During interviews with me, several of the mission pilots expressed a deep ambivalence with regard to flying coffee. Referring to the fact that Seventh-Day Adventists are not supposed to ingest any form of stimulant, one of the SDAA pilots said: "We have to go back to churches in the United States and tell them what we do. And what we do, in addition to all the normal mission stuff, is fly coffee. You try and explain that to a congregation who does not drink coffee or anything with caffeine in it and they react by questioning what you do. It gets frustrating" (12 September 2004). The pilot went on to say that since he feels criticized whenever he tells congregations in the United States about what he does, he begins to question the activity but then returns to Papua New Guinea and sees that coffee is rural people's only link to cash and development.

The flip side is that without the revenues from flying coffee, SDAA and MAF would have trouble meeting their operating costs and thus doing all the other flying they do in PNG. On one level these missions are among the middlemen in the specialty coffee industry literature. They make a profit off the growers and their labor, which allows them to provide free transportation for people with life-threatening conditions and transportation for "flying doctors." In Maimafu I have seen fourteen lives saved by these free flights to emergency medical care.[9] I have also been in the village when the flying doctors arrive and watched them provide a wide range of medical services. Given that there is no healthcare at all in the village, these services are crucial. With this said, the revenue from Maimafu coffee growers also goes to support the mission-related activities of both MAF and the SDA church. This means that the labor of people from the village is going to support religious causes they may or may not believe in.

Today air service to Maimafu is at times less than regular. In 1998, during the coffee season, it was not unusual for there to be daily flights in and out of Maimafu. For example, on 4 May 1998 1,000 kilograms of coffee were flown from Maimafu to Goroka. In 2004 during the coffee season, it was not unusual for a weeklong period to pass without a single airplane visit to Maimafu. In October 2004, for example, a coffee buyer from Goroka was stuck in Maimafu for three weeks.

The day that the coffee buyer was set to arrive from Goroka, everyone was excited. A group of men came to the house I stay in when I am in Maimafu, the house next door to the shed where the village shortwave radio is housed, and called out to the Mission Aviation Fellowship office at 7 a.m. They wanted to know exactly what time the buyer would arrive. People waited excitedly for the plane, sitting around the airstrip, men playing cards and women weaving net string bags called *bilum*, everyone talking about the coffee price in Goroka. People wondered what the buyer would be offering. They wondered if the price had gone up since yesterday (the prices are set daily and people hear talk about them on the radio at night) and if the plane would come back today and get the buyer, or if he would spend the night in Maimafu. They wondered if the buyer would give a good price or if the price of gas had gone up again, thus cutting into profits.

People in Maimafu keep abreast of the daily price for two globally traded commodities—coffee and gas—through communications on the radio. There is a constant flow between Maimafu and Goroka. There is both a material flow—coffee, people, and trade-store items—and a flow of information and gossip through the village radio network. The radio brings information about the daily price of coffee and about when buyers will come to Maimafu. It takes people's trade-store orders to relatives in Goroka and brings messages from family in other villages or towns. The radio provides information about when airplanes will land, gets word out when there is a medical emergency, and brings information about children living in other places who are attending school. It allows people to work out business deals, make plans to go to training courses in other villages, and go to church-related revivals and meetings. It is the main form of communication between Maimafu and any other place.

When Atticks, the coffee buyer, arrived, my first reaction was, "Wow!" He sauntered off the plane, sunglasses on—posh by New Guinea village standards—wearing a rugby shirt, with a Goroka-town swagger. He oozed urban. Atticks was about thirty years old, from a village right outside Goroka. He was one of the ten regional coffee buyers working for Thomas, a man from Goroka who has a large coffee-buying business that many would call a middleman business. Thomas sends young men like Atticks out to rural villages, and they buy coffee and bring it back to him.[10] He then sells it to factories in Goroka. His profit is in the margin between what the growers will accept as payment per kilo of village-processed coffee and what the factory owners will pay for it.

Thomas's business model is simple. He provides what he calls a "service" to rural landowners. Having been in the coffee world in Goroka for many years, first as a casual laborer at a large, now-defunct coffee company, then as a steady seasonal employee in one of the factories run by the same company, and now, since 1998, as a business owner, he knows not only the way the industry works but also most of the people who run factories in and around Goroka. Thomas has cultivated social relations with the people who run factories. He sells to four of the major processors in Goroka and has a good reputation with them because he delivers coffee when he says he will. When his cash reserves are low he is able to borrow money from the factories to buy the village coffee that he will then return to the factories.

Discussing flying
and airplanes in
Maimafu village

Most of the factories in Goroka get their coffee from a number of sources. They have open hours when landowners with access to cars and trucks and coffee buyers like Thomas can bring coffee directly to the factory door. Factory owners have arrangements with villages or village leaders and coffee buyers according to which they are promised a certain amount of coffee at a certain time and their partners deliver that coffee. They also have some trucks of their own with which their drivers can go and get coffee from the World Trade Center market, the Five-Mile market, and other, smaller coffee-trading venues around Goroka. Some of these trucks go to rural villages that are served by roads and buy the coffee grown there. None of the factories have direct access to airstrip coffee with their own airplanes. Some of them have relations with rural villages enabling them to radio out on the mission radio network and make a deal to send a chartered airplane in to pick up coffee. Finally, they have relations with people like Thomas, who go and get the airstrip coffee.

Thomas and all the young men who work for him are from the Gahuka ethnic group, the largest ethno-linguistic group in the Eastern Highlands Province. They all live up the Highlands Highway from the Five-Mile market in villages within walking distance of Goroka. Thomas estimates that his business provides much of the financial support for at least one hundred people through direct payment for labor, as in the case of his coffee buyers, through casual work for which he pays his kinspeople during the season, and through the filtering of money from his wages and his workers' wages through village-wide social networks. Atticks, the young man who usually buys the coffee in Maimafu for Thomas, supports his wife, his two young children, and his elderly father.

When Atticks arrived in Maimafu he was businesslike. He got people organized and started weighing coffee bags immediately. On the day he arrived there were about twenty families there waiting for him, with about three hundred bags of coffee. The price for parchment that day was 3 Kina per kilo in Goroka. The price that people in Maimafu got that day was 1.75 Kina per kilo—this is the price from Goroka minus the freight charges and minus the fee that Atticks charged for the service he was providing. That is about $0.60 per kilo. All was going well: Atticks was handing out money, weighing coffee, and storing it in huts built especially for the purpose. Then it started to rain. For the next three weeks it rained day and night, night and day, and was so cloudy that you could not see from one ridge-top to the next. This meant that no airplanes could fly into the village. Atticks was stuck in Maimafu.

For the first week or so he had a good time. He went on walks around the village to interesting places, such as bat caves and high-mountain lakes that are perfectly round, ate delicious food prepared for him by the clan that he stayed with (all visitors are treated with an unusual amount of hospitality, but Atticks was treated even better because he was the social node in a relationship between the residents of Maimafu and Thomas, someone with whom they had worked for years), played some extremely fun and funny water-soaked rugby matches on the ever increasingly soaked airstrip, and stayed up late into the night hearing stories of tradition—ones with ghosts and sprits and sorcery. During the second week the boundaries of the village were beginning to wear on him. He was getting bored, increasing the frequency of his radio calls to Goroka, increasing the amount of time he would spend with my student, an American there for two months, and increasing the amount of time he would stay late into the night at my house. By the third week Atticks was basically living with us, talking about music and sports with my student, asking me about my work, offering to help me write about coffee, and calling Goroka on the radio six or seven times a day.

Atticks confided in me that at first it had been fun to play village, that he had grown up in a rather urban village (one on a road, with power, TVs, schools, organized sports, access to stores, access to Goroka whenever he wanted) and that what he liked best about his job was going to rural places and pretending to be a "real villager." He said, "They live simply here. They are not developed and they don't mind it. They just live and eat and play, there aren't any worries of the modern world." He talked about how lucky Papua New Guinea was to have "traditional villages" and "modern places" like Goroka and Port Moresby. But, he said, "I could never live in a place like this. I could never live in underdeveloped circumstances."

As the days wore on, Atticks also expressed to me his dismay with the quality of the coffee he had purchased in Maimafu. He began to articulate some of the standard critiques of growers and their practices that one hears among the coffee-buying and coffee-processing community in Goroka. Finally, the airplane came to collect Atticks and the coffee he had purchased. He was thrilled to go home and told me he was happy not to be stranded in Maimafu.

About a year later, when I ran into Atticks in Goroka, he had fond memories of his visit to Maimafu. I met him and his wife on the sidewalk in front of a store in downtown Goroka, and he introduced me as "his village and America sister." I was in Goroka with my friend Sam, a resident of Maimafu, who has his own story of being stuck away from home and encountering the sorts of social entanglements that one finds in towns. Atticks told us that since his visit to Maimafu, numerous men and boys from the village had come to visit him in Goroka and that he had housed them, fed them, helped a few of them with a bit of cash for their time in town, and basically fulfilled the social role that he expected to have after establishing a relationship with people by staying in their village. In mid-2010, while I was in Papua New Guinea working on another project, I received a phone call from one of the young men who had played rugby with Atticks and spent a great deal of time with him in Maimafu. He told me that he was finishing the tenth grade in Goroka and that every weekend he went to Atticks's house compound and spent the weekend with his

Mobile coffee buyers just arriving home to Goroka from rural villages

family. He said he was deeply homesick for Maimafu and his family, but that Atticks's family helped to fill the void.

Growers, Buyers, and Exporters: A Fragile Social Matrix

Each link in the social path that coffee takes from production to export is fragile. The link between rural growers, coffee buyers, and factory owners in Goroka is complex. At times it is a set of transactions and exchanges that are distinctly Melanesian, like the relationships discussed above between Atticks and the young man from Maimafu. At times, however, the relationship is subject to criticism from all sides and marked by a great deal of mistrust. These times of fragility are also distinctly Melanesian. Growers do not fully trust buyers and factory owners. Buyers and factory owners think that growers do not understand how to properly grow and process their coffee, and that they and the industry suffers because growers refuse to reinvest their profits in the industry by buying equipment, fertilizer, and tools for pruning and other husbandry practices. Growers, buyers, and factory owners all criticize the government for shortchanging the industry by failing to maintain infrastructure (like roads and agricultural extension) and for doing little to bring down the outrageously high price of aviation fuel. The government, through government workers and elected officials, distrusts the people working in the coffee industry in Goroka. Government officials express constant anger because they perceive that the industry elites refuse to keep their profits in Papua New Guinea but rather spend them in Australia.

One of the arguments that many growers in Maimafu make with regard to coffee buyers and coffee-industry workers in Goroka is that they make money off growers in an inequitable way. People say that they "don't do any work but still reap the benefits of our work." The growers tell stories about going to the office of an export company or the home of someone who buys coffee and seeing signs of material wealth. They say, "I went to his factory and he had two brand new cars," or "the office is full of new computers and new telephones." They also argue that other people—people from other ethnic groups—are "taking jobs away from us" when they go to Goroka and meet the people working in the factory offices.

Growers from Maimafu who visit Goroka fail to understand the social relations of the nonagricultural labor that goes into coffee. If they notice security guards, cleaning women, office staff, and other often-invisible labor, they say they do not understand why "those people" should have the jobs that they do. They think that since the company is dealing in their coffee the staff should all be from Maimafu. But more often than not, they rarely even see this labor, as it is completely invisible to them. When asked, "But don't you think that people who live around Goroka need jobs too? Don't you think they have the same sorts of money needs that you do?," people from Maimafu overwhelmingly state that they are not interested in other people's needs. They concede that other people need money but believe that they and their families need it and deserve it more. They say things like, "X coffee company made its name using our coffee, so we should work in the offices, not people whose coffee is rubbish."

Here people draw on some set scripts about national and regional identity. Take the example of a casual wage laborer who sweeps the floor at a factory right outside Goroka. When I toured the factory with friends from the Uya family from Maimafu and we discussed this position, they argued that someone from Uya should have the job, and if not Uya, then someone from Maimafu. If not someone from Maimafu, then someone from Mengeno or Herowana or Ubaigubi, three villages near Maimafu where people speak similar subdialects of the Gimi language and to which Maimafu has thick marriage and exchange-related ties. If not someone from these villages, then someone from Gwasa, Gona, or one of the other Gimi-speaking villages in the Lufa District. If not someone from Lufa, then someone from the Eastern Highlands. But not, under any circumstances, someone from Simbu, where the man that spurred this conservation happened to be from.

What growers do not understand is that the coffee buyers and factories are dealing with hundreds and hundreds of growers and thousands and thousands of pounds of coffee. The factories and exporters make a profit (in the years that they do make a profit) because of the huge volumes that they move and because they blend airstrip and village coffee with plantation-grown coffee. Without the blending that coffee buyers and factories undertake, the coffee grown in villages would have no value on the market. According to factory owners in Goroka, village-processed coffee is too wet, and much of it has been stored improperly at airstrips waiting for planes, causing it to develop a musty smell and taste. The factories both dry the coffee correctly, so that the beans have a low enough moisture content to be of export quality, and mix the musty coffee with properly processed green bean from well-run plantations so that it can be sold. One factory owner says, "No one would buy their coffee in a million years if it wasn't for us." Yet the people of Maimafu wholeheartedly believe that they grow the best and most valuable coffee in Papua New Guinea and that people (coffee buyers, factory owners, exporters, people living in Goroka) buy their coffee at unfair prices and then blend it with their own inferior coffee to increase the value of their coffee. They believe that they "lift" bad coffee by blending it with coffee grown in Maimafu.

Since air service has deteriorated in the rural areas in Papua New Guinea, growers increasingly have to store their processed coffee for long periods while they wait for airplanes. Also, growers hold onto their processed coffee in anticipation of prices going up. In the rural areas where airstrip coffee is grown there is not a workable banking system. But in rural Papua New Guinea coffee—the physical commodity itself—can be used as currency. Coffee is traded on the international market in U.S. dollars. The value of every bean is figured in dollars. Thus by holding on to coffee until the price of the commodity meets their idea of "a good price," growers can convert the beans (which are really dollars) into Kina, which they can then use for their financial needs. So the smallholder farmer is holding his savings in U.S. dollars and carrying a hedge. This is particularly true with well-processed coffee at the parchment stage. It can also be held until money is needed for weddings, school fees, and other social obligations.

For people who process their coffee perfectly this hedging is a smart strategy, but for those who do not it is a problem. When coffee develops a musty smell and flavor it becomes unsuitable for consumption on its own and therefore not worth the money that coffee buyers and factories pay for it. The coffee can only be used in Y grade blends that fetch a very low price on the open market. Growers in Maimafu have been told that this is unacceptable, but they refuse to believe that their coffee is ever bad.

There is some truth to the claim that coffee from Papua New Guinea is used to "lift" other world coffees to make an average cup of coffee. According to professional coffee "cuppers," the coffee grown in the Highlands has very good acidity and a robust flavor that holds up in blends with less tasty coffee.[11] What this means in practice is that the coffee can be mixed with coffee from Brazil, coffee that is often flat and bland, and that the blend can then be sold for a higher price than the Brazilian alone would have garnered.

But according to people in the industry in Goroka, this miscibility of Highlands coffee has nothing to do with the labor invested in the coffee on the part of growers, but everything to do with the ecology of the coffee: where it is grown in terms of altitude and soil. Indeed, one factory owner in Goroka expresses one of the general sentiments about growers' husbandry, labor, and place in the industry: "In the rural areas there is almost no husbandry at all. They just keep growing more and more and expect more and more money. Well the industry does not work that way. Everyone needs to learn to reinvest in this industry. The growers, who throw their money away on worthless things from China, the exporters who do not reinvest in extension, and the government who does not invest in us at all. The growers complain all the time that they don't get enough money but they are not willing to do anything at all except sit out there and watch their coffee grow" (4 September 2004). Another factory owner has a less critical view of growers: "Growers don't understand things. They don't understand about moisture content, about over-fermentation, about that musty flavor coffee gets when it has been in bags too long. It is a lack of knowledge that causes them to complain all the time" (24 September 2004).

This idea of a lack of knowledge about the coffee on the part of growers was expressed to me by almost everyone I interviewed in the coffee industry in Goroka. According to a longtime coffee processor, coffee cherry should be pulped and bagged to ferment the same day it is picked. If it is not processed on the same day, "the sugar and the tannic acid in the cherry begin to affect the taste of the coffee beans." Most rural growers do not process the coffee the same day they pick it. They pick the cherry and store it until they have harvested their entire crop, or until they have enough to garner access to one of the hand-cranked pulping machines in the village. By this time, according to this coffee processor, the taste of the bean has most likely been affected:

> After growers have harvested their crop they pulp it and put it in bags to ferment. This process allows the mucous-like substance on the beans, an enzyme rich coating, to breakdown and disarticulate itself from the beans. After fermenting the beans are washed. Growers often allow their beans to ferment for numerous days when the optimal time is 24 hours to 48 hours maximum.
>
> Washing the coffee after fermentation is also an issue. For the process of fermentation to end, one must thoroughly wash the beans, removing all of the slimy, enzyme-rich mucous. If it is not all washed away the beans continue to ferment. In rural villages running water may well be an issue. The farther you have to walk and the farther you have to carry your coffee, the less likely you are to thoroughly rinse it.
>
> Another issue is the ripeness of the cherry when it is picked. When a cherry is dark purple-red it is ready to be harvested, not before and not after. Before, the beans have not developed the rich acidic flavor that Papua New Guinea coffee is prized for and they are likely to have more impurities; after, and the beans are likely to be too acidic in flavor. Many growers pick all the coffee at once—they go to harvest their groves and pick it all off the tree—ripe, semi-ripe, overripe, and green.
>
> There is also an aesthetic aspect to coffee harvesting. The riper the cherry, the heavier and better looking the bean. It is hard for us to move light ugly beans. . . . But growers don't understand any of this. (Goroka, 15 September 2004)

One member of the industry who runs a factory does his own "out-reach" with growers and argues that about 75 percent of the cherry he processes fetches a premium price because of this outreach. He sends men who work for him out to the rural areas served by roads near Goroka each year and has them "remind" growers about ripeness and processing. He argues that this works, and that for the most part people in these villages bring him better coffee: "I am just one guy and I don't have that many resources. Imagine if the government actually put any effort into coffee extension here, what sort of crop we could have! Imagine if they taught growers about the coffee market and they really understood about quality control!" (Goroka, 22 September 2004).

Growers do have particular ways of dealing with and understanding the market for coffee and the returns they get from selling their coffee. When money is short because of low coffee prices, instead of trying to increase the value of their coffee crop through husbandry people in Maimafu just plant more coffee. People do not see value in the beans—in their "quality" or "shape" or in how they are processed. If one wants more money, one simply plants more coffee, harvests more coffee, and then makes more money. Another way people from Maimafu try to derive more income from coffee is by attempting to strengthen their social relationships with coffee buyers and factory owners in Goroka. They assume that the thicker and stronger these bonds are, the more money they will make. Finally, they attempt to exploit new ways of reaching better markets. This has especially been the case since the mid-1990s, when the prices paid to growers began to fall globally and the infrastructure for moving coffee began to decline in Papua New Guinea.

The "White Horse" and the Hope for a Better Coffee Future

One way to add value to coffee according to some people in the wider global industry and in the national industry, and thus make it worth people's time again, is to have it certified as organic or fair trade. In Papua New Guinea it costs fifteen thousand Kina to engage an organic and fair-trade certification team to come from Australia and inspect coffee groves. This price does not include the transportation and lodging while the team is in the country. In 2005 there were 2,604 farmers registered as organic and fair trade in the Purosa and Maimafu-Mengeno areas of the Eastern Highlands. They are all registered through the company Coffee Connections, from which they receive financial support. In Purosa people are organized into a growers' cooperative (the Highlands Organic Agriculture Cooperative Society), which works in conjunction with Coffee Connections. The cooperative is made up of multiple extended family groups ("clans") and run by a board of local directors from each clan that represent their extended family's interests in decision making. With the current agreement Coffee Connections provides the yearly financial support for certification and reinspection as well as the infrastructural support needed to get the coffee to market. For example, after a particularly wet, rainy season the company hired road graders to go to the Purosa area and repair damaged roads. In return for the services provided, the collective agrees to work exclusively with Coffee Connections and to have a small part of its coffee income deducted so that Coffee Connections is reimbursed for the certification costs. The social ideology of cooperatives is an external imposition as much as other forms of western ideology, in that it reorganizes social relations in ways that do not fit with traditional society. That the extended family groups at Purosa can work together in a cooperative is striking.

Historically, Highlands social organization turned on alliances between extended family groups that were tenuous and ephemeral. Individuals had primary social responsibility to their immediate family and then to their extended patriline. Families had connections as trade partners, exchangers of women, and fighting allies. These connections were constantly under review and mediation, and while some of them may have lasted for long periods, most were fragile. Today this is less true of alliances for warfare and protection, but people still have primary allegiance to their family, and the typical conflicts of village life often become points of contention in extended family groups. Asking people to organize into village-wide or regional cooperatives and then manage these cooperatives collectively is asking more than most people can do. The historical social matrix was one in which jealousy, suspicion, and gossip worked to keep level the status of each extended family group. Since in business the jealousy, suspicion, and gossip attach to cash income, people often cannot practice trust and cooperation. But when cooperatives work, as they have done in Purosa, people make more money from their coffee.

In Maimafu people do not get along. The extended family groups cannot work together, and although their coffee was certified in 2004 and 2005, this occurred mostly because of the generosity of one of the principals at Coffee Connections, who was a Kiap in the Lufa District in the 1970s and had a soft spot for Maimafu. Today this certification has lapsed. In fact, even after the support that Coffee Connections showed for the coffee producers of Maimafu in the mid-2000s, the growers there became suspicious of the company when an outsider from Okapa married into the village (this is unusual because marriage is exogamous for women in the Highlands) and began to spread rumors that Coffee Connections was making an enormous profit from the coffee from Maimafu. A group of the growers there, not knowing the process of certification or anything about export laws and regulations, decided to organize into a new cooperative

Coffee Connections office in Goroka

encompassing three of the families from Maimafu and to export the coffee themselves. The actions of these three families, one of them the family of the woman who married the man from Okapa, forced Coffee Connections out of Maimafu.

In Maimafu there is a constant, nagging worry that someone somewhere is making money off something that rightfully belongs to people from Maimafu. The few tourists who visit Maiamfu are always harassed for "compensation" when they take photographs. People argue that "all the tourists take the pictures of our things and sell them for big money overseas." The villagers have long conversations late at night about whether a postcard of a tree kangaroo that someone saw in Port Moresby was made from a picture taken on their land. They have debates about whether I, having worked there for many years and having taken thousands of photographs, have "become rich and famous" by selling the images. When a group of students from the university in Goroka came to Maimafu to conduct a "genealogy mapping exercise" as part of a course, people debated whether the students had "sold the family trees" to mining companies and the government. And finally, every research or infrastructural development grant ever received by the conservation organizations that have worked in

Maimafu for numerous years is said to be income made off the land and labor of people from Maimafu, and it is thought that the money should directly accrue to Maimafu's residents (West 2006).

With coffee, this unyielding and exhausting suspicion is expressed in several ways. First, as discussed above, many people in Maimafu think that all coffee companies across the globe use their coffee, which is "perfect," "the best coffee," "better than every other coffee," to blend with "bad," "disgusting," or "rotten" coffee so as to raise the value of the poor coffee. They think they are constantly being underpaid for their coffee, because it is better than all other coffee. Second, some people from Maimafu believe that buyers and exporters lie to them about how much they sell the coffee for. Third, most people believe that they are intentionally kept in the dark about how coffee is sold, so that they cannot have access to the markets themselves and sell their coffee to people "overseas," thus gaining the profits that they believe are being stolen by the exporters.

Since about 2003 these suspicions and fears have been coupled with a kind of discursive frenzy over coffee certification in the country. This frenzy was initially generated by newspaper articles that had statements like the following: "PNG coffee will soon become an instant hit with coffee drinkers as scientists continue their study into antioxidants contained in this 'green gold.' A coffee tasting competition currently underway in Goroka, Eastern Highlands Province, may come up with the conclusion that PNG made coffee was organically grown and coffee drinkers had the opportunities to drink the best coffee in the world" (*Post Courier*, 28 September 2005). Companies like Dean's Beans and Café Pacifica, which made visits to Papua New Guinea beginning in the early 2000s, also bolstered this frenzy. Representatives of several of these companies went on national radio and talked about certification, arguing that by working with them and bypassing the middlemen, growers would increase their profits markedly.

Since this boom in national discussions about certified coffees, people in rural areas have begun to imagine, even more than usual, that exporters are taking advantage of them. Rural growers argue that they grow "organic" coffee, by which they mean coffee that has not been grown with pesticides and is therefore much more valuable than any other coffee. They argue this while not understanding that "organic" is a form of third-party certification and not a descriptive term. This media-induced boom in discussion of certified coffees has given rise to high hopes and expectations, but among businesspeople in Goroka the possibility of organic and fair-trade certification is hotly debated.

This debate is exemplified by two comments: the first was made by the governor of the Eastern Highlands Province during a small focus group in June 2003: "I think we can get the whole province certified and then the whole country. This should be the primary goal of the coffee industry here. Organic certification means that the rural people make more money for their labor. This should be the priority." The governor's pronouncement was met with the following response from a man who had been in the coffee industry in the country since 1968: "These people can't do organic. They don't have it in them. They won't do the work necessary to produce a decent product much less the kinds of accounting you have to do to meet certification requirements." During that same focus group another long-time coffee industry participant who was a grower before he became an executive said: "Everyone goes out to the rural areas and brings hope to people. And you can't help it. You go out there and you are the only person who has been out there, you are the only one they see, no one else goes out there and they begin to hope that you can help them. And you want to help them but this national obsession with organic coffee has made it harder. You tell them that it is not a miracle, that it takes work, but they don't believe you. You tell them that you will try and help and the next thing you know there are thirty people in your office accusing you of selling their coffee—which is not certified at all—as organic and keeping the profit yourself."

Other long-time industry participants have similar worries: "You have to think about the different buyers for this — Papua New Guinean — coffee carefully. Most of it goes to the blenders — Nestlé, Kraft, and Folgers — but some of the most interesting is the boutique — Starbucks, and others — and that does raise a better price for all of us, but the fixation on organic coffee and fair-trade certification in the country may be raising expectations in ways that are problematic. Not everyone can get the best price for his coffee and not all coffee here, or even the majority of it, is boutique quality."

Another long-term industry person said: "There are these two new concepts in coffee that have been put out on the international marketplace — and the marketplace of ideas — by Starbucks. They are 'traceability' and 'sustainability' and they are the cornerstone of the so-called socially conscious consumption movement. The idea is that there are ways, with a commodity like coffee, to trace the beans themselves from grower to cup and that with that you can make sure that the grower is getting a fair wage for their labor. The sustainability aspect is that there are multiple sorts of sustainability—ecological, economic, and social . . . all of which can be monitored and made fair. I am really passionate about Starbucks. . . . They are the best things to happen for the growers in years. That they build schools and hospitals and the like."

This view is not held by everyone in the industry. In the words of one coffee executive in Papua New Guinea: "Specialty coffee? What makes the coffee special? Is it the fact that a half-naked person grew it what makes it special? The whole idea of this special coffee is raising unnatural expectations in the country. The newspapers and the Coffee Industry Cooperation are to blame for this. You have to have corporate owner groups for certification and that is fucking impossible in this country. And Starbucks is a joke. First, and most, the coffee is terrible. They buy beautiful beans and then roast them to death. But your question, about specialty coffee. Starbucks uses the image of village coffee in their marketing but they are buying plantation. There is nothing village about their coffee and it may be certified, but the plantation owner is making a better profit, not some poor villager. Certification is a lie."

Certification is not always a lie. Companies like Coffee Connections bring their growers certification and through this certification a higher profit. But Coffee Connections is one of the few companies in the country that have actually maintained certification over an extended period, and it has only maintained this certification in the Purosa Valley area.

The cooperative at Purosa is a legally registered entity under the Co-operative Societies Act of 1985. About 2,600 people in the cooperative live in 32 villages and support about 12,000 extended family members with their coffee business. Coffee is the only cash crop and the only source of development in the valley. The process of creating the cooperative took over two years and was achieved, in part, because of one charismatic leader from the community. This man is also one of the principal owners of Coffee Connections. He began his life in coffee working at ANGCO and has an insider's perspective on the industry. The other principal in the company is an Australian man who has worked in coffee his entire life. This cooperative works for several reasons. First, the community knows and trusts both owners of the company—the national owner because he is from their community and the expatriate owner because they have known him for over three decades. He began visiting the community before the plantation redistribution scheme, when the coffee fields in the area were owned by ANGCO. He worked with these growers in the past and stayed with them even as they regained ownership of their land and began to sell their own coffee. In other words, these two men have real, longstanding, enduring social relationships with the people of the Purosa Valley.

Coffee Connections sells its coffee to six companies. All six have deep connections to the history of the coffee industry in Papua New Guinea. People who either lived in Papua New Guinea or worked internationally with ANGCO manage four of the companies. This means that the two principals at Coffee Connections have known these men for roughly thirty years. These are, again, real, longstanding, enduring social relationships.

The Purosa Valley is close enough to Goroka and the offices and factory of Coffee Connections for growers to visit the company when they have questions or concerns. Coffee Connections employs people from many areas, but the vast majority are from the Purosa Valley. These workers have met all the international buyers from the six companies who buy and sell their coffee. Many of these companies have sent employees from their international offices to Papua New Guinea to visit the factory and visit the cooperative. This means that the social relations of production at every single step from grower to importer are transparent. If a grower from Purosa wants to understand where her coffee goes, she simply talks to someone who works at Coffee Connections, who can tell her a story about one of the buyers who came to visit. These are meaningful connections as far as Melanesians are concerned. The other meaningful aspect of the connections between the company and the cooperative is that the principals of the company understand that by working with the growers they have entered into a never-ending cycle of exchange relationships. Both principals expressed this to me repeatedly in interviews. They understand that when a grower comes to talk to them about coffee and ends up talking about the decline of the road from Purosa to Goroka, he wants them to do something about it. More than that, he wants them to fix it and expects that they will.

The story of Coffee Connections is a success story that happens to have certified coffees as its product. But it is a success story because of the social connections on which it is built. These connections were in place and were linking people across the planet long before the coffee was ever certified. There are other wonderful stories of successful coffee companies in Papua New Guinea that have nothing to do with certification. For example Kongo

Coffee, another small company, is owned and operated by one man who began the company by working exclusively with people from his language group. He slowly expanded through social networks that already existed. People from other language groups began coming to him after they saw their kin (people to whom they were related by marriage) receiving higher prices for their coffee than they were. The company provides extensive agricultural extension to the growers, teaching people how to prune trees, care for aging trees (and thus get a better crop from them), and process coffee in villages so as not to get the moldy and musty flavors discussed above. With this work it has increased the profit that its growers get from the coffee. In fact, the company has made the coffee from Elimbari some of the most sought-after coffee in the country. It has marketed this coffee both internationally and nationally, capturing the growing market for good coffee in Papua New Guinea.

From Village to Town

One night in August 2003, as I sat on the edge of a mountain watching the sunset with Sam, Jonah, and my husband, we began a conversation about the difference between Maimafu and New York City. Jonah asked me, "What would you be doing at home if you were there now?"

Jonah's question led to a long conversation about things to do in cities. Jonah and Sam, like all the other residents of Maimafu, know that I live in New York. Here are some of the things that they associate with the city: big airplanes, big buildings, big airplanes flying into big buildings, subways, schools, and a whole host of my friends and family that they have seen in photographs. After quite a bit of discussion about New York we turned to Goroka, the urban center closest physically and imaginatively to Maimafu. Sam, sly smile in place, said, "Now, I can tell you a story about Goroka."

One day during coffee season Otis, "resident coordinator" for the Research and Conservation Foundation of Papua New Guinea (RCF), the conservation organization that has an office in Maimafu, visited Sam at his house. Sam remembered that Otis had seemed more distracted than usual. Otis, like all the other field officers employed by the RCF, is from an urban center and often finds it difficult to live in a rural place away from his friends and his family. In one of my own interviews with him, Otis has said, "Oh, there is nothing to do. It is boring. It is all work and work and village arguments and then sleep. No fun for me." He freely extols, to anyone who will listen, the virtues of Goroka, his hometown. He spins tales about the marketplace there, the goings-on in Peace Park, the outdoor dining area at the Bird of Paradise Hotel, and many other urban spaces.

On the day that Sam recounted for us in his story, Otis was particularly agitated. He had spoken on the radio maintained by the RCF to one of his cousins, which had made him want to "go out" of the village on the next plane. Radio calls are moments of fantasy and image creation for the rural residents of Maimafu. Many residents have never been to Goroka; it exists only in the radio calls and in the stories that people bring home. Most of the people who have been to Goroka are men and boys, with the exception of some women who have attended school or mission-related workshops there and some women who are from more urban-linked villages or areas. For the residents of Maimafu who have not visited a town or city, the image of Goroka made through these calls is fantastic—there are stores and airplanes and cars and big buildings and people from all over the country and the world.

On the day Sam's story begins, Otis had received news that his cousin and several of their friends would be going to a new bar near the World Trade Center coffee market that weekend. His cousin had been in the Goroka office of RCF, heard Otis on the radio, and mentioned the new bar. Otis was feeling restless anyway, and that, combined with the news of the bar, made him want to go to Goroka. In order for Otis to get time off from work, he needed a reason to go to town. Sam and coffee seasons provided that reason. That day a coffee buyer from Goroka was finishing his work in Maimafu. He had bought a significant amount of coffee, and SDA aviation would be flying in to pick up his coffee while he walked to Mengeno, a village some two hours from Maimafu. The plane would come several times that day and several times the next.

Otis called Sam and suggested that they go to Goroka together. Otis suggested that Sam might want to let people in Maimafu know that there was a plane going and that Sam could take their coffee cash into town for them and purchase the trade-store items they needed. If Sam did this, Otis told him, he would buy Sam's ticket. This arrangement gave Otis an excuse to "go out" of the village: Sam, whom Otis described to his superiors as a naïve villager, was going out with a great deal of village money and would need Otis's help in Goroka.

Otis flew to Goroka on the next plane. The next day, after collecting the village coffee money, Sam flew to Goroka. He took only the clothes on his back and over 5,000 Kina (about $1,800) in coffee cash. He had been given elaborate shopping lists from his family and others in Maimafu and was expected to serve as their personal shopper while in Goroka.

Sam arrived in Goroka and went straight to Otis's house. When he got there Otis and his cousins were already in full swing. They had been drinking and were more than ready to go to the new bar. They gathered their money and went around to several of their friends' houses to pick up more bar-goers. About an hour later they arrived at the bar. Sam recalls that the bar sold only two things: South Pacific Lager (SP) and a "giant" concoction of several different liqueurs that was billed as "homemade beer." This "homemade beer" cost 12 Kina per drink.

Otis bought the first round of drinks, an SP for everyone except for himself and Sam, for whom he bought the homemade beer. Sam drank the "beer" and realized about halfway through that he needed to do something to safeguard the money that he had brought from Maimafu. He had been wary of leaving it at Otis's house, so he still had it in his trouser pockets. He finished his beer and went to the bathroom. There he took all the money, except 100 Kina of his own money, and stuffed it in his underpants and his shoes, then returned to the bar. He and Otis drank, and drank, and drank. Sam told us that although he rarely drinks too much, this time was different. The "beer" was delicious and he was having a wonderful time.

At some point in the evening a woman approached Sam and asked him to dance. He obliged and spent about an hour or so dancing with her and talking to her. Sam is about 5 feet 9 inches tall, played rugby in Goroka on a league team, speaks excellent English, has a wonderful, offbeat sense of humor, and is extremely attractive. He is also incredibly charming. While this wins him friends and admirers in Goroka, it causes problems for him in Maimafu. There is lots of gossip about Sam, and he is constantly contending with jealousy over him or one of his wives. He is married to two women from Maimafu and one from Okapa.

So Sam and the woman in the bar danced and drank and had a wonderful time. After a while she suggested that he might want to go home with her. He declined, telling her that he was married, not once but three times, so had to take extra care when it came to extramarital dalliances. She agreed that three wives was quite a lot and said her goodbyes. Sam returned to the table. By this point, Sam says, "I was very drunk." But he also says that even intoxicated, he knew that the woman he had been dancing with was a *pamuk*, or prostitute, and that she was trying to lure him to her house.

Upon returning to the table Sam decided to have another drink. He reached into his trouser pockets, expecting to find the 5,000 Kina he had brought with him from Goroka. He had forgotten that earlier he had had the presence of mind to hide the money from himself. At this point he panicked. He remembered the woman dancing with him, dancing close to him and rubbing against him with her hands, and he concluded that she must have picked his pockets. Believing that the money was gone, he pulled Otis aside and told him what had happened. Sam and Otis went to the woman, who was still at the bar, and confronted her. She protested that she most certainly did not steal the money, that they were stupid village boys, and that if they wanted to accuse someone or fight with someone she could call her brothers. As she was yelling, a crowd of people formed, most of them friends and relatives of the young woman. Sam says he expected that he and Otis would be killed. Sam began to back down, but Otis, who by now could barely stand up, threw himself across the bar's doorway and slurred that no one was allowed out or in until they found Sam's money.

Luckily, Sam convinced Otis that there was nothing they could do and that they had better just go home. So Otis and Sam left the bar and returned to Otis's house, both of them passing out minutes after they got home. Sam said, "I was so drunk I didn't even take my shoes off."

Early the next morning Sam woke up with an overpowering desire to urinate. He did not want to disturb Otis and his cousins, who were still asleep, so he walked out the back door of the house. Sam says, "I reached in and pulled hundreds of Kina out of my fly. All of a sudden I remembered what I had done. I pulled my trousers down and then my shorts and the money fell out all over the yard!"

After Sam told the story and we all laughed for what seemed like hours, Jonah went home, and my husband went down to our house to do some work. Sam and I stayed on, talking into the twilight. I asked him what he would have done if he had really lost 5,000 Kina of village coffee money in Goroka. He sat quietly for a while and then told me that if that had really happened he would have had to stay in Goroka and get a job working for a coffee factory to pay back the money, or else be "stuck in Goroka forever." He said he thought he could secure a position with one of the many coffee buyers he knows or with one of the export companies that exports the coffee grown by him and his family. He assumed that the social bonds and relationships that he had been forging over the course of his coffee-growing life had bound these people to him in particular ways, and that these bonds would benefit him if he were ever stranded.

6 | NATIONAL COFFEE

In this chapter I describe the spaces and lives that the coffee from Maimafu village intertwines with, produces, and is produced by as it moves from village to town. I begin with a description of Goroka, the coffee center for processing and exporting, and the spatial and social node that connects rural growers to the rest of the world. I then describe some of the lives of the people in the vast coffee industry in Goroka. My descriptions are taken from over a decade of conducting research in Goroka for this and other projects. While they are not the thick, rich descriptions of Gimi being-in-the-world that I presented in chapter 5, they are portraits of some of the lives made by and that make coffee in Papua New Guinea. I also describe some of the social institutions in Goroka where these people go to socialize, to give the reader a sense of the pace and content of the multicultural world of coffee. I then move to a more technical presentation of the statistics on coffee processing and export, and describe in detail how coffee is processed at factories. I also show some of the social worlds that emerge on the factory floor and how the factories affect the lives of a range of people in Goroka. I then ask questions about the role of race, class, and nationality in the industry, with a specific focus on how various members of the industry see themselves, others, and the nation-state of Papua New Guinea.

More briefly, I describe the journeys of the people who move coffee from Goroka to the international port of Lae. I do not do

Lae justice ethnographically. While Goroka feels like a second home to me, after having worked there so long and developed ties to various communities there, Lae feels like a large, alienating city. I discuss the process of distribution and statistics on coffee exporting, and describe the port and what happens there. The human element that I write about when I focus on Maimafu and Goroka is lacking in my descriptions of Lae. While there, I stayed in hotels and conducted one-to-two-hour interviews with people. I also toured warehouses and offices. By contrast, in Goroka, after years of knowing people in the industry, I went to their homes for meals, stayed in their spare bedrooms, played golf with them, moved freely around their factories, babysat their children, drank many South Pacific Lager beers with them, and became a part of their social world.

Port Moresby to Goroka

The flight from Brisbane to Port Moresby is exhausting, not because it is long—indeed it is much shorter than the flight from New York to Los Angeles to Brisbane—but because I'm already tired from other flights. For me it is the "almost there" flight, the one that's ripe with anticipation. Papua New Guineans take this flight. In the United States I almost never see people from Papua New Guinea. But in the airport in Brisbane, the minute I round the corner to the flight gate, there are Papua New Guineans everywhere.

Every year when I arrive in Port Moresby I dash off the plane as quickly as possible, desperate to get near the front of the immigration line. Though perhaps not the longest, this is the slowest line on the planet. The anticipation of almost being in Goroka, combined with the anxiety about baggage (thirteen thousand miles from New York to Port Moresby is a long way for a backpack to travel), makes the line seem endless. Before I leave the international terminal I usually stop to call a friend in Port Moresby who meets me for a drink between my flights. Immediately one of the airport security guards comes up to me to ask in English if I need help. The liminal feeling of being in transit subsides and I stare blankly at him, and then rapidly I become the person I always want to be—open, friendly, willing to take the time to talk to strangers—the person I can never find back home in New York City. I tell him that I don't need help, but we strike up a conversation anyway. Two other guards join us, and we have a conversation about where I'm from, where I'm going, who I am, why I am in Papua New Guinea, and if I know one of the guard's cousins who works in Goroka. My reserved, New Yorker façade slips away and I am standing there, grinning stupidly, laughing with these familiar strangers.

After my phone call I make my way out of the international terminal. In the domestic terminal I go to the line at the Air Niugini desk and am reminded of the impossibility of the orderly queue in Papua New Guinea. I stand behind one man and then another man immediately steps in front of me. In New York I would not put up with this. Here I just push myself in between the first man and the newcomer and begin talking to the newcomer (he is from Hagen, he is trying to get home, and his brother was supposed to have booked him a ticket). I get to the window and the woman at the counter finds my booking, prints my boarding pass, and tells me to have a good flight.

The flight from Port Moresby to Goroka is breathtaking. From Port Moresby we fly west along the coast until Kerema, then take a sharp turn to the north and over the gulf province up to the highlands. Flying over the area where the land meets the brilliant blue sea, you can see the coral reefs from the air. Once the plane turns north, the rivers and streams pour down the country into the ocean. After about thirty minutes of flight, the foothills that lead to the Highlands come into view. Then the deep valleys and high mountains come into view and before long we've flown down the Goroka Valley and are preparing to land in Goroka.[1]

On the day I'm thinking of now, I disembarked from the plane, cushioned by the cool, late-afternoon Highlands air, and saw hundreds of people who had come to the airport to watch the plane land. Whenever an Air Niugini flight lands in Goroka a crowd gathers to watch it. They are people on their way home from a day of work, a day of shopping, a day of conducting business. They stop to watch the plane land and its passengers arrive.

This sort of gathering is a social event at which friends visit and exchange information about business, family, church, and other aspects of life, and at which social bonds are solidified. A woman who has been to market sees her sister's son and gives him peanuts. A man who has been to the bank sees his sister's daughter and gives her one Kina to buy a soda or some savory snacks. The use of public space—the parking lot at Air Niugini and the park on the northern end of the airport—as social space is something that many expatriates in Goroka find unsettling. But the area surrounding the Goroka airfield has been social space as long as anyone from Goroka can remember.

In 1950, when the anthropologist Kenneth Read arrived in Humeleveka,

Waiting for the airplane at the Goroka airport

as Goroka was then known, Dudley Young-Whitford, George Greathead's assistant district officer, met him at the airstrip and explained that the Gahuka people occupied the land from Humeleveka and the Asaro Valley (Read 1965, 13). At that time Humeleveka was becoming Goroka. Read writes of his first impressions of the area, expressing his disappointment in this process:

> It was apparent that I had arrived at a time when the life of the valley was changing rapidly, fulfilling the expectations of every past visitor to these high and temperate regions. New Bungalows, replicas of the boxy home-steads on Australian farms, each sensibly and unimaginatively placed in what could be a suburban square of lawn, were rising near the airstrip where I landed. Eventually they replaced the decorative but insubstantial house of the native materials that stood so unobtrusively among the trees of Humeleveka. The neat streets of a settlement were marked out in surveyor's pegs, and the town plan in the District Office properly stipu-lated the sections for future residential and commercial development. It was an idiom I disliked even on its home ground; here it seemed com-pletely misplaced, so insensitively imposed upon alien elements that

even the flamboyant crotons, crouching like plumed warriors against the neutral background of the tall kunai grass, were reduced to stiff and brassy vulgarity in the rectangular beds and borders. (1965, 13)

The managed and legible colonial world desired by Greathead and his staff was coming into being (Scott 1998). This world was one of orderly and regularized spaces in which orderly and regularized natives moved quickly from place to place, never congregating and presenting a sense of unrest.

A little over fifty years later, on the day I'm remembering, I collect my bags, pass the security checkpoint, and exit into the parking lot, looking for the driver who will pick me up and give me a ride to the Greathead Road and Pacific Estates, the upper-middle-class neighborhood where my friends Deb and Andy live and where I'm staying. Inevitably, on this day as on all others when I have arrived in Goroka, I see someone I know from Maimafu. It is always a man or teenage boy who is in town to sell coffee or go to school. We greet each other loudly in the dialect of the Gimi language spoken in Maimafu, Unavisa-Gimi, and hug rambunctiously if it is an older man or shake hands and do a finger-snap ending to the shake if it is a teenage boy or young man. This draws the attention of much of the crowd. Strangers say, "White woman, say something in *tok ples* [local language] again." Or they whisper, "She must be a missionary," since many New Tribes missionaries come in and out of Goroka and many speak indigenous languages. My Maimafu friends and I catch up a little, and I promise to find them the next day in town. Then I spot Joseph, the driver who is always sent to collect me.

Social Lives in Goroka

Joseph was born in 1957 near Goroka—in a village right on the outskirts of town. He went to school in Goroka, and after finishing primary school at an Australian-run school he moved around the country, working in Lae and on the islands at coconut plantations, spending time in Port Moresby, "seeing a bit of the world," as he puts it. When he returned to Goroka the settler colonial plantation system was breaking down, local people were taking over coffee production, and ANGCO, what was to become the largest, most powerful coffee company in the Pacific, was in its infancy. Since Joseph had a degree from an Australian-run school, he could be "trained" by ANGCO to do various jobs. He decided to take a training course to become a driver. He says, "I did not want to work in the fields, I had done that. I did not want to work in the factory, that was too much time inside, so driving was for me."

Joseph describes his youthful wanderlust poetically. He talks about seeing the ocean for the first time, seeing the planes fly into the international airport in Port Moresby, seeing the huge ships docking in Lae, and meeting people from all over the country. He talks about the richness of his country—the plantations, the gold mines, the people, how he has seen the world through his travels in Papua New Guinea and his work for ANGCO: "For ANGCO I drove everyone. I met men and their wives from Australia, Germany, England, France, Switzerland, Japan, Indonesia, America, Brazil, Mexico, India, the whole world. I was here, but making friends, meeting people, I was part of their lives so I know their places."

While working for ANGCO Joseph raised a family. He married a woman from Goroka town, built a house, sent her to school so she could finish her primary-school education, had three sons and a daughter, and then sent them all to school. "I had an education, but it was not a good one. When I finished I could not be a businessman. For that you need secondary school and university. So that was what I wanted. . . . for my children to go to school." During a different interview he recalled, "I look back on how my parents lived, that village life, and I did not want that for myself or my children. I wanted them to know development. I wanted them to know the world." Joseph's children have done well for themselves—two of them (one boy and one girl) earned bachelor's degrees from the university in Port Moresby. They both have very good jobs in the coffee industry, one as a manager and one as an accountant. Another son finished high school and works at a shop in Goroka. Although the last son never finished school, he still has a good job as a rural coffee buyer.

For Joseph and his family, coffee makes them middle class. They see their lives as radically different from "village lives." Joseph's daughter, Mary, and I had several long discussions about her parents, her dreams for her own children, and how the world of coffee intersects with her life. She almost can't find the words to talk about her parents: "What they did. They were both villagers. You have worked in a village, you know what that means. What they had to overcome." She says that coffee is what runs the entire economy of the highlands. Her job shows her how much money comes in and goes out of her company, but, she says, "we are such a small player." She discusses how her father worked on "the edge of the industry," but she and her husband (a manager at a major coffee factory in town) and

their children are "in the middle of it." Their friends are middle-class coffee people—her husband sometimes even plays golf at the Goroka Golf
Club, the hub of the Goroka coffee elite, and a holdover from the white-
dominated colonial and plantation economy. "Coffee means that we have a
life," she says. Mary has big dreams for her children. She expects them to
complete high school and to go on to the University of Papua New Guinea.
She hopes that after that they can somehow get jobs "overseas" for a while.
Mary sees her and her husband's roles in the coffee industry as the foundation of a bright future for her children.

On the afternoon that I described a few pages ago, Joseph took me to my
friend's house, and after I showered and unpacked my backpack, I went to
meet other friends at the Goroka Golf Club. There was a golf tournament
going on that weekend, and the night before was the opening barbeque for
it. As my friend and I drove to the golf club I remembered how dark it got
there—with no streetlights and only a few homes lit up brightly—and that
people walked in the middle of the road at night. I always found it mildly
terrifying to drive at night. The roads are a mix of dirt, stone, and asphalt,
washed out from recent rains and from coffee-laden trucks traveling between villages and the town. Although the lights on the trucks dimly
illuminate the road, because the driver must maintain a certain speed to
make it over the potholes, we seemed to fly down the dangerous road,
barely missing people who were walking in it and across it. All in all, driving
conditions are terrifying. On this night, after laughing at my white knuckles
as I clung to the dash, after what seemed like thousands of bumps, my
friend reminded me that the road between town and the golf club was the
best road in town.

The Goroka Golf Club, founded in 1959, is in some ways a window to a
different time. The first president was Ian Downs, and the club is a holdover from a sort of golden age for expatriates; a sense of colonial nostalgia
that gets going among them as the beers begin to flow. Among the old-
timers, people who have been in Goroka since before independence, there
is a feeling that the glory days of expatriate life are over and that since the
early 1980s it has been all downhill. In talking with two friends in the coffee
industry, both of whom have been members of the club for years, I learned
that membership has dwindled over the past ten years and that there has
also been a decline in the kinds of activities the club sponsors. While it used
to draw over 150 participants from all over the country, this weekend the
tournament has fewer than 50. In the past, people from Goroka came to

watch, and members of other golf clubs from Lae, Port Moresby, Hagen, Madang, and other areas came to participate. Now, with steep airfares, highways that are dangerous or impassable, and a declining number of expatriates who think of Papua New Guinea as their home and not a transit stop on the way to a better life elsewhere, the expatriate participation in this and other activities has decreased. But today participation is more indigenous. More than ever before, there are more Papua New Guinean members of the golf club, and most of those members work in the coffee processing and export industry.[2]

Coffee Processing

As of March 2005 there were sixty coffee processors in Papua New Guinea, with nineteen of them in Goroka and most of the rest in Mt. Hagen (fifteen), Kainantu (six), Lae (five), and Banz–Western Highlands (four). There was one each in Kerowagi Kundiawa, Simbu, Bulolo, Menyamia, Morobe, Wabag, Enga, Boroko, Central, Wewak, and East Sepik. There were five manufacturers, two in Goroka, two in Mt. Hagen, and one in Kundiawa. And there were nineteen exporters, with five in Goroka, five in Mt. Hagen, three in Lae, and one each in Wau, Morobe, Kundiawa, Minz, Western Highlands, and Banz (Coffee Industry Corporation 2005, 24–27).

In 2004 the export market was controlled by Papua New Guinea Coffee Exports (24 percent), New Guinea Highlands Coffee Export (20 percent), and Niugini Coffee Tea and Spice (12 percent).[3] Other major exporters were Kongo Coffee (10 percent), Nama (9 percent), Monpi (8 percent), Pacific Trading Company (6 percent), and Kundu (5 percent), with others exporting 6 percent. Papua New Guinea Coffee Exports and New Guinea Highlands Coffee Export are located in Goroka, as is the coffee arm of Niugini Coffee Tea and Spice. Kongo is up the Highlands Highway, right across the border of the Eastern Highlands Province in Chimbu, and both Nama and Monpi have offices in Goroka and Hagen.

Of the coffee exported in 2004 from Papua New Guinea, 57 percent was Y1 grade, 17 percent was premium smallholder, 1 percent was organic, 5 percent was Y3 grade, 7 percent was A grade, 13 percent was X grade, and less than 1 percent was Y2 and robusta (Coffee Industry Corporation 2005, 15).[4] Of the A grade 52 percent went to the United States, with 11 percent going to Australia, 10.6 percent to Germany, and 6.5 percent to Japan. Other countries that imported Papua New Guinea A grade were Sweden, Belgium, France, the UK, Hong Kong, Italy, New Zealand, Singapore, Fiji, the

Netherlands, Tahiti, Taiwan, and the French territory of New Caledonia. Germany bought the majority of Y2 (88.9 percent), Y1 (72.3 percent), X (39.7 percent), and Y3 (39.2 percent). The rest of these low grades went to the United States, Japan, Australia, Ireland, Sweden, South Korea, Belgium, Denmark, France, the UK, Hong Kong, Italy, Malaysia, New Zealand, Finland, Singapore, New Caledonia, the Netherlands, Russia, Spain, Taiwan, and Western Samoa.

Australia (44 percent), Japan (27 percent), and Germany (9.9 percent) bought the majority of the premium smallholder coffee, with the rest going to the United States, South Korea, Hong Kong, South Africa, Malaysia, New Zealand, Finland, Portugal, Singapore, and Tunisia. Most of the organic coffee was bought by the United States (35 percent) and Germany (33.9 percent), most of the fair-trade coffee by Belgium (69 percent) and the United States (31 percent). Other organic buyers were Australia, the UK, and New Zealand.

Most New Guinea robusta went to New Caledonia (50 percent) and Australia (45.2 percent), with tiny percentages going to New Zealand (about 1 percent) and Tahiti (4 percent; Coffee Industry Corporation 2005, 16–17). Roasted and ground coffee from Papua New Guinea was exported to Australia (62 percent), the Netherlands (17 percent), New Zealand (12 percent), Fiji (7 percent), and the Solomon Islands (2 percent), with about 75 tonnes (1,257 bags of green bean) being consumed domestically in Papua New Guinea (Coffee Industry Corporation 2005, 19).

Growers in Papua New Guinea receive less than growers of similar coffees elsewhere in the world (Tanzania, Kenya, and Guatemala, for example), and since 1988 they have received less than the average world price (Coffee Industry Corporation 2005, 20; see table 2). This is due to production gains and reductions in production costs in the major producing countries, and what is called "increased competition and market efficiency as a result of market liberalization in competitor arabica producing countries" (20).

Once a coffee bean has been harvested and village-processed, its life becomes more complicated. First, as discussed in chapter 5, the coffee leaves the village on an airplane and the seller (the villager) pays for transporting the coffee from the village to the Goroka airport. Once the coffee arrives at the Goroka airport the buyer (the factory owner, processor, or exporter) bears the cost of transportation from the airport to the factory. If the coffee leaves a village in a truck, then the buyer bears all costs

TABLE 2 Prices paid to coffee growers by country, in U.S. cents per pound

	1999	2000	2001	2002	2003	2004
Papua New Guinea	69.62	50.56	35.70	31.07	31.79	40.70
World average	76.08	72.30	50.40	69.55	59.43	54.80
Papua New Guinea as proportion of world average	91.5%	69.9%	70.8%	44.7%	53.5%	74.3%
Tanzania	67.30	63.82	35.07	23.67	25.09	—
Kenya	88.04	62.68	74.84	62.77	46.67	—
Colombia	88.41	72.77	55.62	53.32	46.53	63.19
Guatemala	81.98	71.77	50.60	48.26	50.96	79.24

Source: Coffee Industry Corporation 2005, 20–21.

of transportation from the seller's premises to the factory. At the factory the coffee is processed. It must be dried completely, and since much village coffee is too wet for processing, most factories have huge mechanical drying vats into which the village coffee is poured and dried. After drying the coffee is hulled, polished, air-cleaned, sorted, and bagged. The hulling, polishing, and air cleaning are done by machines. The coffee is then sorted by hand by women, and bagged by a combination of machinery and hand bagging. The coffee is then classified as export-quality green bean.

During the peak of the season at one of the coffee mills, located about twenty minutes outside Goroka, the factory processes 130,000 tons of coffee a day and pays out 500,000 Kina a day (about $160,000). This factory works directly with the people whom the man who runs it refers to as "the grassroots." By this he means that he purchases the majority of his coffee from smallholders and not from coffee buyers or at the coffee market in Goroka. The factory is on the stretch of the Highlands Highway that leads out of Goroka toward Lae and Madang. When I last visited the factory in 2005, the first thing I noticed was the strange beauty of its square steel façade. Set against the backdrop of the valley walls rising to the south and west, it is the largest factory in the Eastern Highlands Province. The man who runs it, a mixed-race descendant of a white settler and a Papua New Guinean woman, is very well-known. He has a big, generous laugh and a deep, soft accent that he picked up in Australia, where he went to boarding school from an early age, and loves his factory and his work.

Coffee factory
in Goroka

This man, who began building his factory twenty years ago, grew up on a coffee plantation near Hagen. During each break from boarding school he would return home to work with his father on the plantation, learning every aspect of the industry from agriculture to processing to exporting. After taking a postgraduate course in fitting and engineering, he built the factory with his "own hands" and continues to run it even though it is now owned by VOLCAFE.[5] He says, "I don't do this to make money for any multinational company, although I work for one. I do it to make a better price for the grassroots, for the people living out there in villages who depend on coffee."

Each day, when people bring their coffee beans to the factory, they are offered one of three possible prices for them. The growers give burlap sacks filled with beans to the men working in the factory, and the workers take a handful of beans out to judge the moisture content of the beans. By holding the bags, workers then decide if they can weigh the beans in the bags to

Coffee factory worker in Goroka

determine a price or if they will have to empty the bags to remove rocks and other weighty materials before weighing.[6] On 22 September 2004 at the factory door this factory paid growers 2.55 Kina per kilo if the beans had 11 to 15 percent moisture, 2.50 Kina for 15 to 20 percent moisture, and 2.34 Kina for 20 to 25 percent moisture, and refused to buy beans with more than a 25 percent moisture content. The moisture content is important because it indicates how much more labor must go into the beans before the hulling and polishing process. This factory is both a wet and dry factory: it buys both parchment (the coffee beans dried in villages that only need to be dried a bit more, hulled, and polished to turn them into "green beans") for dry processing and cherry (the fruit directly from the coffee trees) for wet processing.

Cherry is a bit harder for people in rural places to sell than parchment because of the road and public works problems in Papua New Guinea (remember that most villagers process their cherry into parchment in the villages). However, everyone makes more money if the cherry can be processed by a factory, because cherry that is picked, washed, dried, and processed the same day is always more valuable than cherry that has been slowly processed in village settings over several days or weeks. The same-day process meets "industry standards" for moisture content, bean aesthetics, and fermentation. The factory discussed above gives about 50 percent more in price for cherry because when it is processed to meet industry standards the factory can get about 75 percent more for the coffee, which it can sell as a premium smallholder grade of coffee bean. The factory manager discussed above is committed to "investing time and energy" into the wet factory "because that is where the money is at."

In all the factories in and around Goroka there are numerous industry-mandated checks for quality and defects. Before the unripe cherry goes in for pulping, the machinery in the factory sorts it, separates the heavy beans from the ones with flaws before fermenting, and grades the coffee in-factory so that only the most nearly perfect beans are sent to the premium area. Finally, women hand-remove the impure or ugly beans before they go into bags.

Coffee is priced based on the number of defects per kilo of a particular grade. A buyer pulls out one kilo of coffee per bag to check for defects when he is buying. That kilo represents the rest of the coffee in the lot. Though there is a market for all the coffee, the higher the grade and the fewer the defects, the better the price. Premium coffee is expected to have zero defects per kilo. The process of achieving aesthetic perfection is performed by groups of women who do the work of hand sorting. At most factories the sorting is done by thirty to fifty women sitting on the ground, who take the "impure" or "bad" or "ugly" beans out of the mix.

These women laugh and socialize while sorting the beans, mocking the men who run the machinery, discussing family or town gossip and business. They build social bonds between different lineages, ethno-linguistic groups, districts, and regions. At one factory on the northern side of Goroka, the women working the sorting tables represent six lineages and four clans in the ethno-linguistic group that owns the land on which the factory is located. They all have their own coffee groves and with their husbands work as smallholders themselves. Still, the sorting jobs add to their income in important ways. These women and their families have the same cash needs as all village-based Highlands families (bride price, school fees, church tithing, clothing), and in addition they must buy food. The volume of coffee production around Goroka and the density of the population mean that people do not have the seemingly unlimited access to land that people living in the more rural parts of the Eastern Highlands have. There is not enough land in town for everyone to have extensive gardens, so these

Sorting coffee
in Goroka

women supplement what garden food they can produce with town food and food purchased at the fresh vegetable market in Goroka.

Socially, the women working at factories interact with women from different lineages and clans with whom they might not get the chance to interact under other circumstances. Of the twenty women I interviewed at a factory north of Goroka, eight were sisters. These sisters, once married out of their father's clans and into their husband's clans, are expected to form social bonds with their husband's female relatives (his mother, his brother's wives, his unmarried sisters, and his young nieces). During their labor time at the coffee factory they reconnect with each other. Two sisters, whom I will call Sara and Mary, are about one year apart in age and were very close growing up. They married men from two rival clans and are not allowed to interact in or around their village. Their position of labor at the factory affords them time together.

At one of the factories within the town limits of Goroka, the women who work the sorting tables are from seven ethno-linguistic groups and five districts within the Eastern Highlands (Goroka, Henganofi, Lufa, Okapa, and Unggai-Bena). All of them live in town, in urban neighborhoods without extensive gardens. For them, labor at the sorting tables is not a supplement to their subsistence: it is their subsistence. In a focus group with eight of these women we discussed the possible labor opportunities for women who had no formal schooling or only a few years of primary school, and all agreed that the sorting tables were the best employment to which they had access. The only other possible waged labor positions are in stores and offices in Goroka town. None of the women in the focus group are literate, so these are not options for them.

The multiethnic male labor force in the factories mirrors the multiethnic labor of the women. At all the factories in and around Goroka, both the year-round and the seasonal factory floor workforces are composed of men from multiple ethno-linguistic groups and provinces. These men unload coffee from trucks, move it into and out of the machinery for pulping, drying, and hulling, bag the processed coffee for shipment, and load the bags onto trucks. Their labor is a mixture of skilled and unskilled, with men who have machinery experience making significantly more income than men with no machinery experience. For the most part the labor in the factories is seasonal. When coffee begins to trickle in during the beginning of the harvest season the factory managers and owners send word out to the communities surrounding them that the harvest is picking up, and men and women who have worked at the factory in previous seasons arrive at the factory door seeking work.

Factory managers and owners make staffing decisions based on experiences with individual workers and assumptions about ethnicity. Many managers in and around Goroka give preference to men from the Goroka, Henganofi, Lufa, Okapa, and Unggai-Bena districts of the Eastern Highlands and tend to avoid men from other provinces. They are particularly wary of hiring men from Chimbu and Hagen because of the reputation that these localities have for violence. They also shy away from hiring migrants from the coastal areas of the country because of assumptions that coastal peoples are less willing to work long and hard hours. Once a factory has been initially staffed with the seasonal labor, there is still a great deal of hiring because of the rapid turnover of workers. Some men work for the entire season, but many simply work to make enough money to meet some social need, and when that cash requirement is met they stop coming to work.

Women from
several clans
sorting coffee
together

Experienced factory worker sewing coffee bags in Goroka

The factories also employ year-round factory staff that run and maintain the machinery, and office staff that work on accounts and other financial matters. These employees are from equally diverse backgrounds, but there is little turnover in these jobs, which are considered middle-class. They pay well and often include benefits, such as access to superannuation, insurance, and other additions to the standard fortnightly pay packages. The security guards, who guard the buildings at night and who control access to the compounds during the day, make up another set of factory employees. Once again, these are multiethnic groups of local men, all with long ties to coffee. For the most part, their families have grown it and worked in the industry for as long as anyone can remember. In fact, many of these men and women I have discussed above are from the ethnic groups that once, so long ago, worked on the plantations run by white settlers.

Race and Coffee

Jim Leahy, Jim Taylor, and George Greathead formed the Highlands Farmers and Settlers' Association in 1953 in Goroka (Sinclair 1995, 137). All European planters were invited to join, and the association quickly spread from Goroka to Hagen and Wau. The association was meant to serve and protect the interests of settlers and farmers, according to Ian Downs, who upon his retirement from administrative service became the president of the association. Downs wrote a charter that stressed several operating beliefs of the membership (*Highlands Quarterly Bulletin* 1960b, 6; Sinclair 1995, 137). Although today's white residents of Goroka, many of whom have familial connections to these settlers, insist that the association was a kind of professional organization for both indigenous people and whites, Downs's charter stresses the "moral obligation" of settlers to provide Highlanders with skills and services that would lead to economic development but also protect their "traditional customs" "until such time as they themselves by natural processes of development desire to make changes which will better adjust them to their contact with Western civilization" (*Highlands Quarterly Bulletin* 1960b, 6). The charter also opposed laws that institutionalized race-based discrimination (by which they meant discrimination against whites) and deplored "any weakness by those in authority to enforce the laws and regulations of the country upon the indigenous inhabitants" (6). Downs asserts that even though the settlers were "sincere" in their "desires to see the highland people advance and progress without restraint," they also vowed to "oppose with all means . . . any attempt to obstruct" their "economic and social status in the community" (6). The association was powerful and influential from the 1950s through independence.[7]

The association began publishing the *Highlands Quarterly Bulletin* in January 1960. The *Bulletin*, which adopted the masthead slogan, "We Are Here To Stay" in January 1962, provides insight into the politics and day-to-day lives of the settler colonists. In the pages of the *Bulletin* a fantasy settler emerges alongside fantasy "natives." The fantasy settler is male, primarily invested in coffee but willing to diversify into chickens and pigs, and interested in all agricultural production in the country. He is socially and economically conservative, a "gentleman" who respects white women and loves his children. He enjoys a bit of "grog" and sport but is aware that "natives" should not be allowed to be seduced by either. He is interested in local politics, as they affect coffee, and territory politics, as they affect land use, wages, and self-rule or independence. He is respectful of native politics, land ownership, and custom as long as they do not get in the way of the native's doing for himself by contributing to the coffee-based economy or the settler's various economic goals. He is skeptical of the natives' ability to govern themselves without his advice and guidance. He is interested in international politics as they relate to coffee prices, so he is particularly interested in production in Brazil and Kenya and consumption in the United States, Europe, and Australia, especially as they relate to international trade and war. He is worried about the effect that the war in Vietnam will have on him, afraid of Indonesia, and terrified of China.

The fantasy settler's wife, who emerges in the *Bulletin* starting in 1969, is a married woman who is referred to as a "girl." She spends her time cooking (even using "native" foods to make KauKau pudding!—August 1971) and taking care of children. She likes to clean, using ingenious combinations of local things, since the tried-and-true products she might find in Australia are not available in the territory ("to remove dark film from the inside of aluminum saucepans, cook an acid food like rhubarb or tomatoes"—October 1969). The settler's wife worries about tropical problems like prickly heat and that ever-present threat of "tummy wog" (June 1971). Perhaps most importantly, she and the other "girls" like to make innovative liquor drinks to serve at social functions.

The first two fantasy natives who emerge from the *Bulletin* are both male: the "partner" and the "scoundrel." The partner works with the white settler in partnership and never asks about issues of social equity, such as wages, land alienation, the lack of training of rural people as skilled labor, or anything else that might make the settler uncomfortable. This native is happily content to work for a wage on the settler's farm. If this native is successful he may become a member, after 1959, of the association. If he is, he runs his business exactly like the white planters and emulates them in dress, social behavior, and work schedule. However, the fantasy native never oversteps his role to think that he is one of them. The partner knows his place in society and never challenges it.

The scoundrel drinks too much, throws beer bottles all over Goroka, is interested in politics and political processes like self-government and independence, wants to understand the economics of the industry, supports the administration, and wears a suit. This native fails to understand that he is not ready to run his country or even the coffee industry, and that it is only with the benevolent partnership and guidance of the settler that he will develop. He is dangerous, not so much physically but morally. He is always hovering around other natives waiting to turn them from benign partners into scoundrels. As natives are easily swayed, it is up to the planters to make sure that their partners do not fall into social relations with scoundrels.

In my reading of the *Bulletin* the only mention of New Guinea women was a statement in a labor story from 1969 that it was illegal to hire a woman day laborer with a contract—contracts covered only the labor of men. The female native emerges pictorially. She is bare-breasted, very young, looking away from the camera, wrapped in traditional necklaces and skirts, and in a coffee garden (see April 1962, January 1960, July 1960, October 1969, October 1965, July 1965, April 1965). There is no discussion of the fantasy female native: she is simply there, waiting for the viewers' gaze and harvesting coffee.

These imaginary natives and settlers that emerge from the *Bulletin*, along with this sensibility of partnership without equity, are one vision of the colonial coffee world in the Territory of Papua and New Guinea. The images created in the *Bulletin* are the ones held dear by many expatriate residents in and around Goroka today.

The first real conversation I had about race and the coffee industry in Papua New Guinea was with the man who runs the first factory I discussed in this chapter. As I mentioned earlier, this man is of mixed race, the son of an Irish Australian and a woman from Hagen. As a child he remembers being sent by his father to spend a few weeks a year with his mother's father, a Big Man who spent much of his time on ritual business associated with

Highlands Quarterly Bulletin (January 1960). Photo by Kathy Creely. Courtesy of University of California, San Diego, Library, Melanesia Archive.

his lineage: "I spent time with him and in the *hausman* [men's house] and became a part of the culture." Then he added, "but then I went to Australia and I felt part of the culture there also." I asked if he had felt the radical difference between the two cultures that he was part of when he was a child and he said that he had. Then I asked if he felt any racial tension within the coffee industry today and he said that he did not, that the racial tensions he felt today were more connected to interactions that he witnessed between Papua New Guineans and "those academic types." This tension between "coffee people" and other elites is illustrated by some events that occurred in 2004.

One day, after a long series of interviews with coffee industry workers and executives in Goroka, I left the office of a man who had just spent two hours with me and, over the years, seven hours being taped for my research on coffee. I went back to the house where I was staying in Goroka. Also staying in the house were several volunteers and several biologists, all of them whites of European descent. I suggested that we go to the Aero Club, one of the clubs that many people in the coffee industry attend in the evenings, because I had been invited by my informant friend earlier that day, and I was met with, "Ugh, too expat-y and cliquey," "they are a bunch of racists," and "too many of those coffee assholes." The counter-suggestion for an evening out was dinner and drinks at the Bird of Paradise Hotel. I was overruled, so we went to "the Bird."[8]

We arrived at the hotel around 7:30 p.m., right as the streets in Goroka were beginning to clear of foot traffic. By early evening most people who live outside the city limits but who come into town for business, labor, shopping, and pleasure have left town for the day. The majority of people in and around Goroka do not own cars, so they must walk or take public (but privately owned) buses, called PMVs, to and from their home villages and hamlets to the center of town. We disembarked from our SUV and paraded upstairs to the bistro restaurant at the hotel. We were met by two large tables of expatriates, whites who work as volunteers, teachers, and researchers in and around Goroka. The only nonwhite faces in the crowd were scientists who arrived with us. They were able to come because we had swung by the offices of the Wildlife Conservation Society to pick up several Papua New Guinean scientists who work there. This white crowd was somehow less offensive to my housemates—thoughtful people who mean well, do good work in Papua New Guinea, and think of themselves as equality-minded—than the coffee-related crowd, erroneously assumed to be uniformly expatriate and white, at the Aero Club.

Whiteness as "inherently problematic" has been the topic of much scholarship in the past twenty years (Spark 2005, 214). Critical race theorists have destabilized the idea that whiteness is a blank, normative, unmarked state. And activists and politicians in many postcolonial settings, including Papua New Guinea, have been quick to grab on to arguments about whiteness as a "source of unnamed and unmarked power, terror and domination" (214). In Papua New Guinea whiteness as a social category has to be disassembled according to practice, history, and economics (see Bashkow 2006). All whiteness is a marked category, coding power and privilege for Papua New Guineans, but how power and privilege are understood and how people react to them are based on social factors that are more complicated than they may at first seem.

Ira Bashkow has recently argued that for the Orokaiva (the people he works with in Papua New Guinea) "modernity and race are understood in terms of each other," and that the Orokaiva construct "whitemen" through their experiences of modernity and development while at the same time understanding both modernity and development as "personified" by their own constructions of whiteness (2006, 9). His work shows quite clearly the process by which race is constructed by rural Papua New Guineans; far from consistently demonizing or canonizing whites, the people he works with see "whitemen are morally ambiguous figures which are evaluated differently depending on people's purposes in the context of speaking" (13). This is markedly different from the way some whites are portrayed by other whites in the literature on race in the country.

Some argue that historically, people in the coffee industry in Goroka—whites, that is—belonged to a privileged class of expatriates who should be regarded with some level of disdain (Manuell 2003; Spark 2005). Indeed, Naomi Manuell goes so far as to call them "coffee barons," "the town's elite," and "social hyenas" (Manuell 2003, 185, 187), as she carefully constructs her own family's story in Goroka in 1978 as that of a hippie-like journey of social and self-discovery. Manuell works to disentangle multiple sorts of expatriate experience in Goroka by creating one category for people in "the Goroka establishment" (coffee people and those who belonged to the Goroka Golf Club and the Goroka Horse Club) and another category for people like her parents who were drifting through life "back home" (people who did things like work for the Commonwealth Scientific and Industrial Research Organisation, or CSIRO, as teachers and who had a "shared love of the locally grown pot"; 185). She and her family regarded those in the first category as working-class Australians who were in the country simply to make money and exploit the "Stone Age" highlanders (186), while those in the second category are portrayed as sympathetic, well-meaning, gentle travelers who just happen to also be white. She also portrays Goroka as the Papua New Guinea version of "some dreary Australian country town" that was, because of its tropical nature, always on the brink of being swallowed by its "strange and colorful core" (187).

Throughout Manuell's essay, she works to distance herself and her family from what she sees as the racist ways of the Goroka establishment: having black servants, calling blacks "locals," making openly racist statements, and relying on a battery of well-worn anecdotes "so grotesque and frightening" that the young Manuell "never felt entirely at ease" in Goroka (Manuell 2003, 186). She marks the first colonial settlers as possessing "the souls of dumb, greedy farm boys" and as bringing "bagfuls of tat to barter and build up coffee plantations across the mountains" (186–87).

Manuell leaves unexamined several important markers of race and class privilege in her own family's story in Goroka. She narrates her disdain for "those coffee kids" at her school, which was "every bit as parochial as the clubs the kids' parents clung to for safety," and which she eventually ceased to attend, her mother letting her quit school until they "got back to Australia" (187–88). She mocks the secondhand jeans and T-shirts worn by her father's students at the University of Goroka, whom she called "complete fashion victims" interested only in color, "the louder the better" because "modern Papua New Guinea was still all about decoration." And she describes her mother's "friendship" with an elderly woman from Goroka who spoke no English and no Melanesian Pidgin. She said that the old woman and her mother "had some sort of affinity," that the woman "let Mum try her betel nut once and, in return, Mum brought her inside and rolled her a spliff," finally giving her "some marijuana seeds, hoping she'd plant them," and enjoying the thought that "she'd quietly undermined the PNG economy with the gesture" (190).

Manuell seems unaware of several markers of social and economic privilege: dropping out of school, not for lack of money or because there is no school in the area (as was true for most people in Papua New Guinea then and remains true today) but because one's parents find the other parents not to their liking; and buying new garments rather than castoff used clothing from the United States and Australia. She seems equally unmindful of the raced interactions of giving a drug to a person who does not understand anything you are saying. Her work casts some whites as exploitative racists who are making money off poor Highlanders, and others as their benign opponents.

While Manuell's portrayal is troubling, her instinct to disentangle the idea of "expatriates" in Goroka is an interesting pursuit. In a more scholarly vein, Ceridwen Spark takes recent comments about expelling all whites from Papua New Guinea by Luther Wenge, governor of the Morobe Province of Papua New Guinea, and uses them as a point of entry into a similar project (2005). She attempts to disentangle the sorts of "whiteness" that existed in Papua New Guinea when she was a child growing up in the Eastern Highlands. There is some personal identity work that takes place in Spark's paper, for example this statement: "Despite my youth, I deemed the ensconcement of these families in the town's white enclaves as question-able, not least because it seemed to involve a hiding away from PNG while making quick money from the country's burgeoning industries, including coffee" (2005, 215). For the most part, however, Spark focuses on an analy-sis of the meaningful cross-cultural interactions and engagements that introduced Papua New Guineans to social and racial "others" during the 1950s, 1960s, and 1970s, and the ways these interactions created other worlds of the modern for them (214–15). Spark makes a distinction be-tween the people whom both she and Manuell portray as coffee people and a group of people that she said were "often bearded and sometimes long-socked, [who] tended to speak good Pidgin and to know a bit about the many PNG peoples and cultures they had encountered" (215). These peo-ple were researchers, and Spark saw them as allowing her to show that "whiteness in PNG is neither monolithic, nor inherently destructive or problematic" (215). She attempts to show, in the face of "the current cli-mate of anxiety about whiteness" in Papua New Guinea, "that white ex-patriates have had variable—not merely negative—impacts in PNG" (215).

This splitting, representing, and casting others as racist postcolonial ex-ploiters while casting oneself and one's mates as well-meaning do-gooders is alive and well in modern-day Goroka. It is often still the coffee-related families who bear the brunt of the critique.[9] But the coffee community is vastly more complicated now, because it is not a white community. There are numerous white expatriates who are part of the community, but of all the industries in Goroka it is the most racially mixed at the levels of management and elite status. Of the thirty-five in-depth life history inter-views that I conducted in Goroka between 2002 and 2005 among people in what would be considered the coffee-economy elite, fifteen of the inter-viewees were white, three were Indian, two were the children of one white and one Papua New Guinean parent, one was from the Philippines, and the remaining fourteen were Papua New Guinean.

Expatriates and Industry Elites

Fredrick Errington and Deborah Gewertz describe three genres of litera-ture that contend with the lives of expatriates of European origin in Papua New Guinea (2004, 116). The first focuses on the individual lives of "magis-trates, prospectors, educators, missionaries, and other colonial types" are usually meant to be humorous, flattering portraits of the hardy characters who made New Guinea their home away from home (116). The second genre, which is vaguely quantitative, focuses on testing hypotheses and understanding "the troubling aspects of cultural contact" (116). The final genre is one in which the author analyzes texts concerned with and written during the colonial period. Errington and Gewertz contend that with a few important exceptions, there is a lack of anthropological literature which provides rich descriptions of expatriate lives and contextualizes them ethnographically (116, 275 n. 7). They argue that this lack of anthropological writing about expatriates and the "thinness" of the accounts that do exist "indicate something about both the conventions of anthropologists and the conventions of expatriates" (116). It is worth quoting them at length, to understand their argument and how I wish to complicate it: "Certainly, most anthropologists who journey to Papua New Guinea, themselves often white and at least middle class, come to study people assumed to be substantially different from themselves. Why, after all, go to such a 'remote' place to study those you can readily find at home, those you thereby feel you already know? Correspondingly, expatriates assume that the job of anthropologists is to study natives, not expatriates. This assumption, moreover, rests on pervasive understandings about who is appropriately studied by whom, who is scrutinized by whom, who is represented by whom, and who is gazed upon and objectified by whom" (117). Errington and Gewertz go on to note that anthropologists often form relationships with and rely on "well-established" expatriates for logistical help in the country (117). These social relations are defined, according to Errington and Gewertz, as friendships and take on a private or off-the-record character. Both parties would be uncomfortable with having the anthropologists write about the encounters. Moreover, anthropologists might be extremely wary of writing about often-powerful actors who can read their work and "take legal action for violation of privacy or for misrepresentation" (117).

I wish to complicate these observations on several levels. First, the things that one studies in Papua New Guinea today are often very different from the things that people who worked there in the past studied. I know of few scholars of Melanesia today who go to Papua New Guinea to "study" a particular ethno-linguistic group. Rather, they go to study contemporary anthropological problems as they are manifest in Papua New Guinea. Thus topics that would have been seen as non-anthropological in the past, such as environmental conservation, mines, prisons, and the military, are being studied. And the social worlds that encompass these topics are made up of rural and urban Papua New Guineans, expatriates of European origin, and additional expatriates of many different origins. I would contend that anyone who studies one of these contemporary topics and does not write about the expatriates involved is presenting only a part of the picture. This does not mean that people are no longer undertaking studies of social institutions that are uniquely Papua New Guinean or the ways that Papua New Guineas understand and make their worlds. But even these studies show how the intersections of indigenous sociality and expatriate sociality work to make worlds as well.

Second, contemporary expatriates are highly aware that academics critique their presence in Papua New Guinea, their motivation for being there, and the economic benefits they derive from being there. My previous experience in the country, when I was conducting research on the social relations between Gimi, expatriate biologists and conservationists, and national biologists and environmental activists taught me that it takes years for expatriates to trust my motivations, to believe that my wanting to understand their lives is not based in any desire to judge them but rather in a desire to understand the social worlds of which they are a part. My experience working with people in the coffee industry has been similar. The research that I conducted for this book with expatriates took place over several years. Initially, while I was accepted as another expatriate and as a welcome addition to venues like the Goroka Aero Club and the Goroka Golf Club, people were suspicious when I began to question them about their business dealings. It was only through my relationships with several gatekeepers in the Goroka coffee community that I began to schedule interviews with expatriate industry elites, or with national industry elites for that matter.

Many of my conversations and interviews with expatriates—and here I remind the reader that the term covers people of European descent as well as people of South Asian and Asian descent—led to long off-the-record conversations about how I was planning to represent them in my work. People were highly sensitive to issues of race and class, within the industry specifically and within the country more generally, and yet worked to demonstrate to me that their critiques of local people (growers, laborers, guards, and others) had nothing to do with race and everything to do with attitudes and approaches to work and specific infrastructural problems in the country. The very fact that these critiques were always voiced to me, after being prefaced by discussions of how they are not racially motivated, is telling.

Expatriates spend a great deal of time and energy critiquing aspects of their lives in Papua New Guinea. The critiques fall into four categories: critiques of public works and the government, of local social life and culture, and of law and order, and critiques that juxtapose the past and the present. In the following pages I describe several expatriates who are involved in the industry, and through my descriptions I illustrate the four categories of critique. I hope to show that these critiques are always combined with moments of valorization, which almost always have to do with the social networks that are possible in Papua New Guinea and the joys of raising a family there.

Madu Namdu is from a region in northern India called Assam, one of the largest tea-growing regions in the world. He worked there, managing a tea plantation, as well as in Darjeeling and Nilgiri, the two other major tea-growing regions in India, before coming to Papua New Guinea. He and his young wife were too socially isolated by plantation life in India and felt that in their youth and early marriage they wanted to experience some of the rest of the world. So Madu found a job in Papua New Guinea, thinking that he and his wife would have "a big adventure" and then return home to India. He said to me on a Wednesday in September 2004, "We couldn't leave this place now!"

Madu, as the manager of one of the large export companies in the country, sees Papua New Guinea and Papua New Guinean coffee growers through the lens of India, India's colonial history, and the poverty that he saw in Mumbai and other urban areas in his home country. He critiques Papua New Guinea for its failed and failing infrastructure and the government's inability to maintain it. This is a critique that one hears constantly in the coffee community. The industry depends on being able to move the commodity from grower to processor to distributor to consumer, and in Papua New Guinea the government's lack of attention to roads and rural airstrips makes transportation a constant worry. Madu filters his critique through his view of colonization: "People here have made a quantum leap from stone axes to computers in sixty years. It is not like India where you had the British, who were good, and by that I mean effective, colonizers." He goes on to discuss the links that he sees between the failures of Australian colonization and the contemporary failings of the government: "The British set up a system, an infrastructure, that could be used when they left. And they had people who went to India to live their whole lives, who went there as a part of their commitment to the idea of empire and not simply as a way to make cash. Australians came here simply to make a profit. So Papua New Guinea was never fully colonized, in that Australians never thought that they would live out their lives here and by extension have to depend on the roads and airports and hospitals they built long term."[10]

Madu's critique of the roads and other transport-related infrastructure resonates with all the interviews that I conducted with expatriates. The infrastructure critiques ranged from thoughtful and provocative, like Madu's, to outright racist, like the one from an Australian working for one of the security companies that provides security for the coffee industry, who told me that "Pacific Islanders" were "incapable" of maintaining roads and airstrips because they were "genetically inferior when it comes to intelligence" and did not understand the importance of public works and transportation infrastructure. The majority of critiques, though, focused on the lack of government funding for keeping roads and airstrips maintained.

In addition to Madu's critiques of Papua New Guinea, which he compared to India, he compared the "need" that he saw in the two countries: "People need three things. They need food, clothing, and shelter. Here, people have that. They own land so they are never hungry and never homeless. The poverty that I see when I go back to India now . . . that is . . . that is because of the lack of land. Because people can't feed themselves." He stated this again in another way in a different interview: "The weakness of smallholder production is that there is no quality control. The strength is that there is no paid labor and people have other means of making ends meet. At the end of the day if prices are low, they can all feed themselves, they don't have to buy their food; they can grow it." He went on to passionately discuss the benefits of land ownership and the starkness that he now saw in what he called the "deep poverty" in India: "I can't imagine living there now and seeing people who don't have enough to eat." But his musings about the "gentle" nature of life in Papua New Guinea were tempered by his notion that because people had access to "food, clothing, and shelter" they were "not really willing to work hard enough." "People will work to get better prestige, food, and a tin roof, but when things get hard they don't innovate, they just go back to bush products and village life. They are blessed, and with that blessing, cursed. They will never get ahead because they have enough to live." Madu's critiques of infrastructure overlap with the next set of expatriate-generated critiques—those that address local social life and culture.

Bruce Matton was born and spent his childhood and early adolescence in Goroka. His father was in the coffee business in Papua New Guinea, and although he loved the industry, he and his wife did not want to send Bruce and his siblings to boarding school in Australia, so they left the country when Bruce was about ten years old. He attended school there, and after school he studied hotel management and worked for a time in Australia, but he missed Papua New Guinea in general and Goroka specifically, so he moved back and began working in coffee. Bruce saw the industry as an opportunity to utilize many of the skills he had learned in management school and to work with his hands, one of the things that he loves but found hard to do "down south." Today he runs a dry factory in Goroka.

Bruce is fluent in Melanesian Pidgin and extremely knowledgeable about local social issues, customs, and traditions. And it was after talking to Bruce about how he sees other expatriates in the country that I began to categorize many of their critiques of life in Papua New Guinea as "critiques of local social life and custom": "What gets me is when people come here and live here for ten years and work here and never get to know anyone from here. And then they spend hours complaining about how people here do things. They complain about things like compensation payments but they don't understand the role that compensation plays here." He went on to offer a critical reading of the importance of compensation to the maintenance of local social relations: people must demand compensation to maintain their social status and place, but in the coffee industry the constant demands for compensation for various things force buyers and factories to curtail business relations with certain groups and individuals. Bruce argued that these social pressures put local people in a precarious position: they must maintain their social obligations, even when they fully understand that maintaining them will negatively affect their relations with expatriates and local elites that manage and own coffee companies.

Bruce insightfully critiqued the expatriates who constantly complain about how local people use the money they earn from their coffee production: "It drives me crazy that the people we buy from never have any money. You know, you pay someone hundreds of Kina one day and then the next day you see them in town and they are broke and asking you for money. But then when people who don't understand how things work here complain about it, that drives me crazy too." Here he went on to discuss the social needs that people have for cash and how these needs do not mirror the ways that cash is utilized by many business people: "In a normal businessperson's mind, when they make a profit, they invest that profit back into their business. Here, people put that profit into their village or family. They invest there and not in growing their business."

Bruce's critique resonates with the work of Peter Fitzpatrick (1980) on the articulation of capitalism with noneconomic capital in Papua New Guinea. Fitzpatrick argues that the social economy subsidizes the capitalist economy, in that the constant investment of cash in the social economy solidifies social connections that support people when the capitalist economy falters or when work and wages become scarce. Social reproduction through the investment of cash in things like bride price, head payments, compensation payments, and other social obligations strengthens the social networks that protect people and allow the capitalist economy in Papua New Guinea to remain highly flexible. This is crucial with an agricultural crop like coffee that is affected by unpredictable factors like in-country climate (a delay in the dry season by a month in Papua New Guinea means that exporters cannot meet contracts and importers turn to other countries to fill them, forcing down the price of coffee in Papua New Guinea), global climate (frosts in Brazil make coffee from Papua New Guinea more valuable in the global marketplace and thus raise the price that growers get in Papua New Guinea), and geopolitical forces (social unrest and violence in Kenya force buyers to turn to Papua New Guinea to meet orders, again forcing up the price of coffee). There is a great deal of uncertainty in the coffee market which is borne by businesspeople who need to have enormous reserves of capital so that when the price of coffee drops they can pay the growers, and so that they can meet orders made in other parts of the world; they must also have social networks that they can fall back on when the price of coffee drops.

Bruce's insights into the importance of maintaining social networks do not temper his critique of some aspects of social network investment. He stated that "there are legitimate claims for things like your truck hitting a pig or someone getting hurt at work but there are hundreds of illegitimate claims, people who just want money for nothing. And it is exhausting trying to manage it all." He went on to say: "I'm hesitant to send trucks out to some areas to get coffee because of the threat of compensation claims. It is just too much. And it hurts the majority of people out in the areas. Mostly they won't make the claims, but it is just a few bad guys who make you not want to do business out there." He described how this affects the international side of businesses: "And then you have to explain to international backers why you are sitting there waiting for coffee to come to you when you know that there are two tons of it out in some village somewhere. And they just think you are cheap or stupid."

Dorian Hempsted, a more recent expatriate migrant to Papua New Guinea, filtered Bruce's critiques of local social life and culture through his experiences of living and working in Africa. Dorian is "fourth-generation African on both sides," his ancestors having come from England to Zimbabwe (Rhodesia at the time). He critiqued local social practices among growers and what he calls "expatriate culture." Dorian found the lack of in-country reinvestment on the part of expatriates particularly troubling: "All over Africa you see people putting their profits back into the places they live. Here, everyone puts all the profit into something in Australia. They buy real estate there, a house at least. Then they spend all their time thinking about how they will get to leave New Guinea soon and go live there. They don't treat it like home here."[11] "If you watch how people spend their money here, you see it. Clothing is one example. They wait till they go on leave to Australia to buy clothes because they say that there is nothing decent here in the stores. But there is nothing decent here in the stores because they don't demand it. If they created a market for it, shops would stock it and then people from Goroka would be able to buy nice things also. And having some nice clothing makes people feel good. Don't people from Goroka deserve that?"

Dorian's other critique of investment is about business investment: "So many of the people here from Australia and elsewhere see themselves as not permanent also—that they are only passing through—they are all always about to leave and they don't seem to think of this as 'home'—this is one of the weird things about the work here—because they all do live here and they all are rather permanent." Further, "because people don't think of it as 'home' they only make short-term investments in their businesses. They want to be able to get their money out fast. They invest a little and don't see a huge return instantly and then they blame it on Papua New Guinea and not on the fact that they are not patient." Dorian's critique of investment strategies was also leveled against local people: "But people from villages and Goroka are just as bad. They spend all their money on a combination of beer and brideprice. They don't buy bricks and concrete to build houses that will endure. I mean fly-wire for windows also. Why can't people just spend some money on fly-wire? You go to these villages and there are flies and mosquitoes in the houses and buying fly-wire is dead easy . . . And people here see copper as permanent and buy that, but why not build a proper house out of concrete or brick to go along with the copper roof? I'll tell you why, because then they couldn't waste the money on beer and Twisties and compensation."[12]

Dorian, like other expatriates, is frustrated with the degree to which local people continued to maintain social obligations before taking part in the sort of economic transactions and investments that he saw as proper and important. But unlike others who attributed this tendency to a lack in the character of Papua New Guineans, Dorian associated it with a particular, forward-looking notion of "development" linked to colonial history: "Papua New Guinea is like the most postmodern state in the world. Stone age to computer age in seventy-five years. A place like India or Rhodesia had two hundred years of colonial investment and Papua New Guinea had significantly less than that—really only from about the 1930s to 1975—so forty-five years, and yet people expect the country to be 'modern' and 'developed' through the Western view of 'developed' and 'modern.' . . . So we expect people to use money the way we would, to invest it in their businesses but there is no history of that here. There has only been a short time for them to model us, to emulate us." Dorian connected his critique of social investments to his critique of land tenure: "And that is a blessing and a curse. They maintain their families and that is good but they don't put money into business. It is the same as land tenure. It is a blessing and a curse. For the coffee industry to grow, land must be turned into a commodity, but this is culturally difficult—no, it is impossible here. And so the culture here, which protects people in terms of them having land to grow food, makes it difficult for the industry to advance, so there is less money than there might be otherwise."

Ed Johnson works for a coffee exporter in Goroka that is part of the global VOLCAFE Group, a large multinational company with holdings in every coffee-producing nation. Ed was born in Australia, but when he was a child he came with his family to live in the Eastern Highlands. His parents were teachers, and they settled in the Asaro Valley to the north of Goroka in the mid-1960s. Ed left the country when he was of boarding school age (around thirteen years old). He attended boarding school and university in Australia and then became a primary-school teacher in Australia. After working for several years he became disillusioned, because the men whom he worked with seemed to have very dull lives. Although he has respect for them, he saw that they had been "doing the same thing for twenty or thirty years, almost living by rote," and he decided to give up teaching for a while to travel and figure out what to do with his life. He traveled throughout the 1970s and returned to Australia in 1981. At the time he was related by marriage to a man who had worked in the Papua New Guinea coffee industry since the colonial period and was offered a job running a hotel in Lae. He took the job, thinking that he would be there for a couple of years at the most. He has never left. Ed has loved living in Papua New Guinea. He says things like, "The bonds you make here are special," that he and his wife have raised "amazing" children, children who seem "different" from their friends' children back in Australia.

But for Ed, the increasing law-and-order problems in the country are his main complaint. His critiques are interesting because they, like many of the other critiques discussed above, amount to critiques of Papua New Guineans and expatriates. In conversations about law and order in the country, Ed recounts stories from the early 1980s, when "this place was safer than Australia." He talks about how safe he felt with his children growing up in Goroka, in a small town where there was little violence, no drugs, no gangs, and none of the other social ills that he perceives in Australian towns and cities. He said that his family was "lucky" to get to Papua New Guinea when it did and that now, "I wouldn't bring a child up here." He juxtaposes the past to the situation today in Goroka:

> You have people from everywhere, from Hagen and Chimbu mostly, who come here because they have relatives here or because they don't have access to land where they live or because of the coffee industry and the idea that they can get jobs, but they don't work so they don't have any money and we have crime now. . . . I've never had a problem, in large part, I think, because I've always been fair to people. I've never done bad business, I've never gotten involved in local disputes, I've never raised my voice. But also because I respect people. I see expatriates driving around in their vehicles at top speed throwing dust up all over the road, and almost running people down, expecting them to get out of the way. I've never been like that. And I think that it is those expatriates that have to worry about the violence here. There can be random violence anywhere, but I think people here target people that they think of as disrespectful.

Ravi and Anu Savarti also juxtapose the past with the present in their critiques of life and labor in Papua New Guinea. Ravi and Anu moved to the country in 1975 from Rajasthan, India. Ravi was twenty-six and Anu nineteen and they had just been wed, through an arranged marriage. Anu said, "Now I laugh about it, but then, I had never seen him. Never met him. We married and then we moved across the world to Papua New Guinea!" Before the marriage Ravi had worked on several tea and coffee plantations and wanted to continue to do plantation work, but not in India: "In India if you work on plantations, you have to send your children to boarding school because the plantations are so isolated, and I didn't want to live without my family." He was given an offer in Papua New Guinea that was "too good to bypass," so his family relocated to the Highlands.

On the day that I conducted my final interview with Ravi and Anu, they were preparing to move to Jodhpur for retirement. They love Papua New Guinea and, like Ed, feel that one of the "true joys" of the country was the situation in which they raised their children. They discussed how much they enjoyed the close-knit community of Papua New Guinea: "You know everyone, black, white, Asian, everyone. And everyone has children and all the children are friends and you are friends with the other parents." They went on to talk about the "kind" of children they felt they had raised: "Our children are colorblind. They can get along with anyone and they see people for who they are, not what color they are or how wealthy their families are." But today seems quite different from how they were when their children were growing up: "Now, all of our children are away. They are at university or living abroad. And for parents here now it is different. You have to watch your children. Things are unsafe now, and when our children were young things were safe. They could play outside, ride their bikes, they could be children. But now life is more restricted because of the decline in law and order. We wouldn't have children here now."

Angella and Shannon are best friends and on numerous occasions during my research in Goroka I spent very pleasant afternoons having lunch with them. Both their husbands work in the coffee industry and both have strong opinions about social life and the benefits of living and raising a family in Goroka. Like Ravi and Anu Savarti, they think that one of the major benefits to living in Goroka is that it makes you "a much more open person." Angella, who was born in South Africa, said: "Because of how I've lived, I have no loyalty about nationality or race and living here makes sense to me. It makes you a more open person and it means you raise your kids that way. They live in a multiracial society and one where they have to look past class. My children play with the maid's children and with Shannon's children and they treat them the same."

On the day that Angella said this I pushed her by asking about an incident that had occurred the night before. I had been riding to the Goroka Golf Club with an Australian friend who is a longtime Goroka resident. As we passed a village along the road he said, "I don't know how they live like that. Why can't they make a better life for themselves?" I expressed to Angella my distress on hearing him say this. I stated that I couldn't really believe he had said it because it seemed to me to show such a lack of understanding of the economic disparity among Goroka's residents, as well as a lack of understanding about social life and organization among local people. I then told her how interesting it was to me that she had unselfconsciously mentioned her "maid" in her previous statement. Angella thought about this for a minute, but before she could speak Shannon said: "Well, some people here are more like us than others. I'm not afraid to say that. And I don't think it is racist. People that live in villages, the people that grow the coffee that my husband buys, they are not like us. They don't have the same. . . . I don't know. They don't have the same . . ." At that point Angella chimed in: "They don't have the same background or the same goals and challenges and pastimes. I see your point about _____ and the comment he made on the way to the club, but I don't think it is racist. I think that he sees town life and Goroka town as the way people should live; as what they should aspire to. I don't think they have to aspire to it, but like Shannon said, I don't have much in common with a mom who works in her garden all day or a person who lives fifty kilometers deep in the forests. It doesn't mean I think less of them but I do think of them as different." Shannon replied: "The bonds you make here that cross boundaries are deep. You make a network that has people in it that would do anything for you and you would do anything for them. I'll give you an example. You know _____, right? And you know about his son, the one that has _____. Well, he needs to take this special medication now and his doctor from home won't give them a prescription for it unless there is someone here to administer it to him. All of us, every women married to the coffee industry, has been on the phone all over the country this week trying to find someone qualified to administer the medication. And those poor people who have so much to endure because of [their son's] illness, well their burden is lightened."

At this Angella said: "And all these women are different ages, and those bonds, across ages, you wouldn't have in Australia. I am thirty-seven, Shannon is thirty, and Dona is fifty-one, and we are best friends. Where else could you get that?" Shannon added that she felt as if Goroka's coffee society allowed her to "be friends with men, where at home, people are isolated based on sex." She continued: "I see my sister and she has other women she is friends with, other moms, but she doesn't know any of her husband's friends. Here men and women are a team—you have to be because it's hard here, so you are a unit. And you have friends that are like that also." They both cautioned me that other cities in Papua New Guinea were not, in their opinion, similar to Goroka. Shannon said: "But Lae and Moresby are different. There you have fly-in, fly-out people and more short-term people. People who work for mining companies or for AusAid and other organizations. They are just here to make money, not to raise a family and have a community."

They also both talked about how although the coffee industry in Goroka was small and highly competitive, people got along and depended on each other. Angella noted: "The competition between the buyers and factories is really intense and really good for the local people, because it means that they get more money for their coffee, a better price." But according to Shannon, "Even with this competition people here seem to get along for the most part. It is sort of like boarding school, you have to depend on each other and get along and give a hand when someone else needs it, even if they are in direct competition with you in business. . . . And you know the fact is that lots of people in the industry grew up here, their parents know each other, that it is the Melanesian way, that it is a very, very small community and that it is so isolated so if you need a hand, or advice, who else are you going to ask?" As the conversation turned to "the Melanesian way" Shannon concluded with the following: "In this business, in this place, you can't just be 'middlemen,' you become family. And you hate it at first because of the obligation, but then you see all the good people out there and you know that you can help, and you see the hope . . . And don't forget that it is different here, in Goroka, than it is everywhere else in the country. Goroka is still a wonderful place to live. It's not like Madang or Moresby or Lae."

On the Road Again: From Production to Distribution

"Patrick Faden sounds like an Irish name."

"I am Irish. . . . Black Irish"

Patrick Faden has a booming laugh, and its echo drifted across the dining room at the Bird of Paradise Hotel, where I interviewed him. I tell him that

I really did expect an Irish guy, and he just laughs again. For about two years Patrick has been working for a transport company that drives from Hagen to Goroka to Lae. He trucks food up the highway from the port, and coffee down the highway to the port, in trucks that are legally meant to carry 25 tons but that almost always carry at least 30.

Patrick began his work life as a teacher, receiving his teaching degree from the University of Papua New Guinea in the 1970s. After graduation he moved back to Goroka, where he was born, and slowly moved up through the school system before eventually becoming a high-ranking government official in the Eastern Highlands Province. In 2003 he retired and decided to work for a trucking company. He makes about 1,600 Kina (about $570) every two weeks, driving about six trips during that time. A trip from Goroka to Lae earns him about 120 Kina, while Hagen to Lae earns about 250 Kina. Patrick is squarely middle-class, with a small house in Queenslander style in Goroka town, a gracious and charming wife, three children who are teachers, and a number of school-aged grandchildren who attend private schools in Goroka.

I met with Patrick to talk about transportation and the coffee industry, and to see if I could ride with him from Goroka to Lae, to literally accompany the beans grown in Maimafu village, processed by Coffee Connections, and headed to Vournas Coffee Trading in California. Patrick said that although it would be interesting to have me along for the ride, he thought it would be dangerous. He was about 80 percent sure we would not have a problem, but "What if the road is bad or the truck breaks down? Then I have you out there on the highway and that is not safe for you." I pressed him a bit and he said, "No, and you should not be going to Lae anyway."

Everyone in Goroka made a point of telling me how dangerous Lae was. Muse and Sandie, two colleagues and friends, were so concerned that Muse called his brothers to tell them to put the word out on the street that I was to be protected and to tell them to expect my phone call in case of emergency. He then made me promise that I would allow them to escort me everywhere I went in Lae. None of this was particularly comforting, especially when I arrived in Lae and realized that my contact in the shipping industry who was supposed to pick me up from the airport was nowhere to be seen.

My flight from Goroka had been almost empty—apart from me the only passengers were a man from somewhere in the Highlands (Hagen would be my guess), who looked to be in his mid-forties; a young man from

Goroka (we talked); a woman from Hagen (we talked); and an expatriate named John. I know John's name because he came to my rescue in the Lae airport after the flight. John saw that I was alone and insisted on waiting—holding his driver—until he saw that I was safely with someone who was meant to meet me. That never happened.

When you land at Nadzab at the Lae airport, about a thirty-minute drive from the town, the heat bursts through the door of the plane the second they open it. The word "oppressive" does not begin to describe the conditions. The air is thick and wet, so tropical that it is heavy on your skin as you walk across the tarmac toward the terminal. The area around the airport is practically deserted. Aside from about a dozen men and boys watching the planes land, there is no one. No crowds of people watching and talking, no children running and playing as they wait for their parents, no bustling town bus traffic, absolutely nothing like the Goroka airport.

John and I waited and waited for my ride but he never came (it turns out that he got "held up in a meeting" and figured that I would "find my way to town somehow"), so John gave me a lift into town and to the hotel. The experience was deeply unsettling. It had been a while since I had felt totally alone in Papua New Guinea. My contact in Lae was an expatriate I had met in Goroka through coffee people, and he seemed interested in the project and willing to be interviewed and help with the logistics of Lae. Being abandoned by him made me reflect on the importance of long-term ethnographic relations. Nobody in Goroka would have left me stranded like that.

Distribution

During the distribution phase of its global journey, thousands of people come into contact with the coffee bean. For coffee from Maimafu village and other rural localities in Papua New Guinea, once the coffee leaves Goroka it becomes harder to track the connections that move it along.[13] Scholars who analyze the labor that moves coffee once it leaves the hands of growers seem to be divided between those who valorize production as the engine for the global economy and the site of social reproduction and those who focus on consumption as part of a larger pattern of circulation and subjectivity. These two sets of scholars continually critique each other: Marxists and neo-Marxists in anthropology and cultural geography, who have focused on agricultural production, critique the "consumption" turn within the social sciences; and scholars writing about consumption critique the fixation on production in some anthropological analyses of circulation. Yet both groups have failed to demonstrate that production and consumption are only two-thirds of the story of circulation. Even scholars who have called into question the categorizing of peoples into "producers" and "consumers" and the reliance on assumptions about how the categories do and do not overlap have failed to add nuance to their discussions of circulation and its selves with a focus on distribution (Ettlinger 2004).

Why has distribution not been examined more thoroughly in anthropology or cultural geography? One answer is that it is not a glamorous portion of the commodity journey. Distribution takes place on trucks, ships, and planes. Its sites of social life are factories, offices, warehouses, and loading docks, locations that may not be difficult to access but are difficult places in which to conduct participant observation or interviews, and places that exclude outsiders because of health and safety regulations. Another answer is that some of the actors engaged in distribution are hard to approach and hesitant to spend enough time with anthropologists to allow for proper ethnography. Coffee traders in New York, for example, work at a staggering pace and in extremely high-energy and high-stress conditions; they cannot afford to have an anthropologist asking them thousands of questions about coffee and markets. Stevedores, as another example, work long hours on ships, spending many months at sea. The last thing they want to do when they are not working is spend time talking about work.

Another answer to the question of why there is a lack of focus on distribution is that distribution expands the ethnographic field of vision to staggering arenas. If one covered all aspects of the distribution of a commodity, the ethnographer would behave much like a journalist—having an interview with a dockworker, having an interview with the CEO of a large coffee company, touring a factory, or having a focus group with a team of stevedores. This type of sweeping examination is reportage, not the deep, long-term ethnographic engagement that many ethnographers find crucial for understanding the social lives connected to things. The following pages are based on journalistic methods using interviews and focus groups. Yet although it sheds light on distribution, it does not fully capture the lived experiences of the people who move coffee along its way from Papua New Guinea to its elsewheres.[14]

In 2004 Papua New Guinea exported 1.05 million bags of coffee with export earnings of 283.7 million Kina (Coffee Industry Corporation 2005, iii). Because of declines in the plantation sector's production and the inability of growers in rural and remote areas to get their coffee to markets, exports

TABLE 3 World supply, demand, and prices for coffee, 1999–2004 (in millions of bags)

	1999	2000	2001	2002	2003	2004
World production	114.5	112.3	109.3	122.0	103.1	112.7
Consumption by producers	24.6	25.9	26.8	27.3	27.9	28.6
Consumption by importers	65.8	64.3	65.6	64.5	67.3	68.0
Consumption by nonmembers of the International Coffee Organization	14.5	14.6	16.2	17.1	17.0	17.0
World consumption	103.9	102.8	108.6	108.9	112.2	113.6
Consumer stocks	12.0	17.2	19.5	19.5	21.3	21.5
Prices (in cents per lb.)	85.72	64.25	45.60	47.74	51.91	62.15

Source: Coffee Industry Corporation 2005, 5.

totaled 9.5 percent less than in 2003 (iii). In 2004 four large exporters controlled 66 percent of the crop in Papua New Guinea, with eleven smaller exporters controlling the remaining 44 percent (1). Globally there were 112.7 million bags of coffee produced in 2004–5, with inventories or stocks of coffee of about 21.5 million bags held in consuming countries that year. That year people consumed about 113.6 million bags of coffee, with consumption in the United States growing by 2.3 percent and in Japan by 6.8 percent between 2003 and 2004 (7).

The first stop for coffee from Goroka when it arrives in Lae is with companies that bulk the various deliveries. Bulking companies clean and sort the coffee after it arrives from Goroka and put it into containers. They are retained by the buyers, but the sellers pay for their services. Of all the coffee exported from the country, 85 percent is bulked directly into containers while 15 percent is bulked in bags that are then loaded into containers. A container holds 360 bags of coffee, or 21.6 tons. Bags weigh 60 kilograms when coming from Papua New Guinea, and for the most part coffees that are to be sold as organic, fair-trade, or single-origin are bulked in these bags, while other nonspecialty coffees are bulked directly into

TABLE 4 Estimates of world coffee production (in thousands of bags) by the International Coffee Organization (ICO), U.S. Department of Agriculture (USDA), and Neumann Kaffee Gruppe (NKG), 2003–2004 and 2004–2005

	2003–2004	2003–2004	2003–2004	2004–2005	2004–2005	2004–2005
	ICO	USDA	NKG	ICO	USDA	NKG
North America	16,498	17,469	17,090	16,389	17,211	15,460
South America	44,165	47,698	49,320	53,686	58,028	57,560
Africa	15,195	14,441	14,000	15,264	14,776	14,940
Asia and Pacific	24,833	29,898	29,090	27,334	29,005	29,470
Papua New Guinea	1,147	1,147	1,160	1,200	1,025	1,160
Total	100,691	109,506	109,500	112,673	119,020	117,430

Source: Coffee Industry Corporation 2005, 7.

containers. The coffee can be bulked in either standard containers or ventilated coffee containers. The containers are made of corrugated sheet steel, with the inner floor made of wood or some other material that will yield to changes in weight and pressure. Standard containers are lined with plastic fabric that suspends the coffee away from the steel during shipping. Most companies fill 12 containers a day, with 20,000 tons a year as the goal; currently most of them move about 15,000 tons a year. The containers are kept at about 10–20° C during shipping. Coffee containers, either the standard or the ventilated ones, which have openings along the floor and the roof—little holes that were punched into the steel—are stored below deck so that the temperatures can be controlled. Ships go through temperature extremes, passing from the tropical climes of New Guinea to winter in northern Europe during some of the voyages. Coffee risks moisture damage while on ships, so it must be checked for condensation in the container during the voyage, and it must be unloaded quickly if the temperature in the port of destination is significantly lower than the temperature that the coffee maintains during the voyage (about 18–20° C). Containers of coffee need to be unpacked within twenty-four to forty-eight hours of the ship's unloading. Shippers must also pay attention to the humidity in the ship, as green coffee beans are not completely dry but still retain about 10 percent moisture content.

The next actors to engage with the coffee are the people who run the

Coffee on the port in Lae

port and run the shipping industry regulation in Papua New Guinea. The Papua New Guinea Harbors Board is based in a smallish office in Port Moresby. There it manages, monitors, and enforces regulations for the entire shipping industry in the country. The ports handle about 90 percent of the import and export for the country, and as one of the longtime employees said, "The ports are the primary place of interface and exchange for the country." While the government owns the ports and regulates them, the port managers run the everyday operations of the two major ports, Lae and Port Moresby.

In Lae about eighty people at the port work for the Harbors Board in security, in maintenance, as marine pilots, and as administrative staff. In order to export something a shipping agent must apply to the port manager to pre-receive cargo in a port—for space in the wharf. If approved, the agent can move the cargo into the wharf, where it stays until it is moved to ships by stevedore companies. These companies are usually owned in part by shipping agencies. Three major stevedore companies in Lae handle almost all the coffee. About twenty people work on each cargo ship and about six hundred work at the port in Lae. Before the coffee is loaded onto the ships, it must be inspected.

Companies like Intertek and Caleb Brett also provide coffee-loading inspection in Papua New Guinea. These companies sample and analyze the beans for quality and for moisture content, broken beans, sour beans, bean size, and foreign material in the beans. They supervise loading and discharge and inspect the vessel holds and containers before and after coffee is loaded into them. They check the conditions of the bags and the bulked containers before and after fumigation and they monitor the fumigation process. Green bean is fumigated in Papua New Guinea with methyl bromide (MeBr), an odorless and colorless gas that is classified as a Class 1 ozone-depleting substance. Its use is being phased out in the United States as of 1 January 2005, although there are some exceptions, including quarantine and pre-shipment of agricultural commodities where there are thought to be no technologically or economically feasible alternatives to fumigation. Once these checks are made, the coffee can be loaded onto the ships, where the buyers then assume responsibility for it and all associated costs.

The *Papuan Chief v133*, the *Pacific Falcon v48*, the *S. Magellan*, the *Aotearoa Chief v67*, the *Chekiang v77*, the ANL *Lokoda*, and the *Folyebank* SP181 all leave Lae with cargos headed to places like Hamburg, Brisbane, Auckland, Sydney, Los Angeles, Yokohama, and points between. On 4 November 2004 these seven ships left Lae carrying coffee from the exporters Kongo, VFP, Nama, Kundu, Arabicas, NGHCE, Monpi, and Goroka Coffee Roasters. Much of the coffee on these ships was bulked on 27 October 2004 and had been waiting at the port for its journey off the island to begin. Some of the coffee that left Lae was on board a ship for a few days (the time between Lae and Sydney), some for thirty to sixty days (the typical travel time to Europe or the United States—for example, it takes forty-five days to get from Lae to Hamburg via Singapore and the Suez Canal). The coffee that left Lae on 4 November 2004 ended its journey at Balzac Coffee in Germany, Merlo Coffee in Australia, Coffee @ in the United Kingdom, various small shops that buy from Vornus Trading in the United States, and VOLCAFE, a global coffee giant in Hamburg.

7 | INTERNATIONAL COFFEE

In this chapter I track coffee from Maimafu village as it moves away from Papua New Guinea, and the lives of people there, into the lives of people in Germany, the UK, Australia, and the United States. I do this in three ways. First, I describe three of the coffee importers that buy coffee from three of the companies in Goroka that buy coffee from Maimafu. All these importers have ties to the colonial coffee industry in Papua New Guinea. I focus on the stories and images that they attach to the coffee so that it will come to have value in the global marketplace. Second, I describe two coffee shops in London and one shop each in Hamburg, Sydney, and Brisbane, focusing on the patrons of the shops and how they understand where the coffee that they buy comes from. Finally, I describe how college students living in New York City do and do not incorporate the messages of coffee advertisements and marketing campaigns into their understandings of coffee and its producers.

Adding Value Internationally

Hamburg is astonishingly green for such a large city, the second-largest in Germany and the ninth-largest in the European Union. In the north of Germany, on the Elbe and Alster Rivers and close to the North Sea, it has been a center of maritime trade for hundreds of years (Verg and Verg 2007). The port of Hamburg is the largest in Germany and the third-largest in Europe, handling about half of Germany's imports and exports. In 2007 the port handled 9.8 million containers (Van Marle 2008). The port itself is enormous, with gigantic ships docking there daily. Constructed where the Elbe River naturally flowed out toward the sea, the port consists of numerous human-made canals. Some of these canals are so small that only a tiny pleasure craft can navigate them, while some are large enough for the biggest container ships in the world.

Today, as with many old industrial sites in cities worldwide, areas of the port have been redeveloped. The redevelopment in Hamburg, "Hafen City," has been built on the reclaimed land that was once the site of docks and warehouses. The canals that border Hafen City are lined with warehouses built in the 1880s and refurbished in the 1990s. Today many of the buildings are showrooms for textiles from Afghanistan and Pakistan. The richly colored designs hang on the brick, evoking images of port cities worldwide and ancient global connections of trade. As you move down the main street, Am Sandtokai, you begin to smell coffee. The businesses on the street are grouped according to commodity, and right next to the Middle Eastern and South Asian textiles are coffee companies and buildings full of recently imported green beans waiting for shipment across Germany and throughout Europe.

Historically the port was a tax-free zone: no taxes were paid until the commodities went across the second of two canals lining the port.[1] This meant that people could import their commodities, sell them from their warehouses between the canals, and ship them back out on boats before any tax was assessed. The canals themselves were built so that coffee, tea, and spices could be brought directly to the warehouses on boats. Some of the companies in these refurbished warehouses today have been there and in business since the late 1700s. Today Hamburg is the largest coffee and tea port in the world. In 1996 about eleven million 60-kilogram bags of coffee came into Hamburg (Korner 1997). Eight million of these bags were imports, meaning that they would have stayed in Germany and gone to importers and roasters there. The other three million bags were re-exports that were to be shipped overland to other European countries.

In Hamburg there are trade houses that own the coffee and then sell it, and there are agents that never own the coffee but simply move it between buyers and sellers. Trade houses take on more risks than agents. A trade house has to finance about $54,000 per container for between sixty and ninety days, depending on how long the coffee is in its hands—from the

Container ship at the Port of Hamburg

moment it is Free On Board to the moment it goes over the rail of other ships or into trucks when it has been sold to roasters. There are three major coffee trade houses in Hamburg: the Neumann Kaffee Grup, the Hamburg Coffee Company, and VOLCAFE, and all are on Am Sandtorkai.

Steffen Maiburg works for one of these trade houses and has an office in a beautiful, refurbished turn-of-the-century warehouse. Steffen, who says he has "coffee in the blood," was about fifty when I first met him and looked exactly like the rock singer Sting. His family began trading coffee in 1922, and all the males in his family since then have "gone into coffee": "For decades we worked for ourselves, but now it makes more sense to work for the larger trade houses; it has become easier." Many of the traders who work for the large companies have old family connections to coffee. These men—and they are all men—usually spend several years after their formal schooling working in one of the "origin countries" at a company owned by a large trade house, or a company historically connected to the trade houses. For example, several of the traders I spoke with in Hamburg worked for ANGCO and lived in Papua New Guinea in the 1980s. After studying business or commerce at university they spent five to ten years living "in country" and "getting a feel for the business at origin." For Steffen, who lived and worked in Goroka, Papua New Guinea exists in his memories of the place, in his ongoing social relationships with people "in coffee" in the country, and in the background of his relations with the many other countries whose coffee he sells.

The traders in Hamburg must work to sell the coffee from Papua New Guinea in a market that demands commensurable coffees. By "commensurable coffees" I mean coffees that can easily fill existing purchase orders demanding particular qualities in the beans. For example, one of the largest coffee companies in the world has a set amount of high-altitude, volcanic-soil, arabica coffee that must be acquired to meet the consumption demand for its most popular blend. The company's buyers do not care if this coffee comes from Papua New Guinea, Kenya, Burundi, or Costa Rica, or any other country that produces "other milds," the category on the New York world indicator list that includes coffee from Papua New Guinea; they simply want to meet the formula for the blend. Because of the climate, altitude, and soil, coffees in this category have "good acidity in the cup," while also being "chocolaty, nutty, and fruity in the cup." Steffen's job is to acquire coffee from any place in the world that meets the needs of the buyers. If the buyers usually use Kenyan beans and he falls short of those beans, he must work to make an alternative bean seem commensurable with the Kenyan beans so that the buyers will buy them. With these coffee traders in Hamburg, Papua New Guinea coffee loses its distinction of being modern, written onto it by rural villagers, and its distinction of being a national commodity, written onto it by urban dwellers. The coffee becomes defined and valued by other qualities and distinctions that are crafted by the traders.

Producing distinct coffees is important because the global coffee market is plagued by overproduction. Worldwide there is more coffee grown yearly than there is coffee bought yearly. Because of this, traders with special connections to particular regions must work to first make that region's coffee seem ecologically commensurable with other similar coffees and then work to distinguish the coffee from the pool of commensurable coffees. For example, once Steffen Maiburg discursively produces coffee from Papua New Guinea as interchangeable with coffee from other "origins" (which he must do in case he cannot get enough coffee from Papua

New Guinea to meet all of his contracts for high-altitude, volcanic-soil coffee), he then must work to distinguish it from the other coffees. Because he knows that the fantasy images of Papua New Guinea work, even though he knows them to be just that—fantasy—he draws upon them anyway.

Steffen says that the ways he distinguishes the coffee depend on the market he is working with. One afternoon, while having lunch at an outdoor wine festival, he told me, "U.S. consumers want fairytale coffee; they want to feel socially connected to the coffee producers and feel like they are knowing the world by buying it." In contrast, "Germans just want a blended coffee that is designed for a delicate palate." He continued, "I do not wish to offend you, but we have more refined tastes. We know our wine, like the bottle now, we know our food, and we know our coffee. You Americans, you are slowly becoming more refined but your market differs from ours."

Because of this, when dealing with buyers from the United States, Steffen discusses the growing conditions of the coffee, the remote locations from which it must be transported, the "primitive" villages in which it is grown, and the like. He has pictures of the yearly "Goroka Show" in his office and many on his computer. This "cultural festival" brings together dancers and performers from across the Highlands on Independence Day each year. During the show people dress in "traditional costume" and perform "traditional dances." Steffen uses images from the show to demonstrate to buyers from the United Sates how "traditional" the growers in Papua New Guinea are. Steffen knows that the images are misleading: that many of the people dancing at the show are teachers, accountants, and the like, and that many of the villagers performing in the show, even those without modern jobs, never dress at any other time in the year as they do during the show. Yet he also knows how these images work to convince buyers from the United States that coffee from Papua New Guinea has a more interesting story than coffee from "some boring place in Latin America." For the German market Steffen uses his knowledge of coffee production in Papua New Guinea to distinguish the coffee after having made it commensurable ecologically. He talks to buyers about the process of fermentation undertaken by smallholder growers in Papua New Guinea, and describes the "fruity flavor" that one gets from the coffee because the fermentation period is longer in places where transportation from village to town is problematic. He also distinguishes the level of acidity in smallholder-grown coffee from that of plantation-grown coffee. So he uses his intimate knowledge of both the national palate and the conditions of production to distinguish the coffee. But other traders in other cities work to distinguish Papua New Guinea coffee in slightly different ways.

London feels like a city that is too big and old and complicated to describe. It is gigantic, sprawling out from its city center on the north bank of the River Thames and sprawling back in time, as a site of commerce and congregation, for two thousand years. For me it becomes describable in terms of its neighborhoods, and during the month I was there conducting research for this book I spent most of my time in two of those neighborhoods: the City of London, the small and ancient area that was the first core of the city, and Covent Garden.

When you walk in off the busy street near the Thames to the offices of a small trading company in the City of London the first thing you see is a photograph of a bare-breasted woman from Papua New Guinea picking coffee. She is from the Highlands, and stares not at the camera but at the coffee tree she is harvesting. She is a strange mix of lurid and benign, here in a modest, yet modern, office building in a central part of London. There are also various Papua New Guinea artifacts spread around the offices, like masks from the Sepik River region and shields from the Asmat peoples. The images and objects offer a kind of authenticity and credibility for those who know nothing about Papua New Guinea. It is as though the exoticism of the bare female breast and the otherworldly faces on the masks is meant to transfer an exoticism to the coffee. My first reaction upon walking into this office was one of concern. I assumed that Papua New Guinea would be discussed by traders in this company from a stereotypical perspective. Then I noticed that several of the people working in the office seemed to be from Papua New Guinea, and later I found out that they were.

Andrew Chesterfield runs the small company and sensed my concern over the images. He is extraordinarily intuitive, funny, and extremely knowledgeable about coffee in general and Papua New Guinea coffee in particular. One of the first things he said to me, when he saw the look on my face as I observed the bare-breasted women in the photographs around his office, was: "PNG coffee is a unique product but . . . we add value when we couple the coffee with these images."

Andrew's father started the company in 1969 and Andrew began his life in coffee in 1984, when he moved to Papua New Guinea to work for ANGCO. He was nineteen years old when he lived in Goroka and remembers it fondly: "Goroka in the 1980s . . . for a single man, it was a dream!"

Andrew, like all the other traders I worked with who lived in Goroka in the 1980s, speaks of living and working there in the ANGCO heyday as almost paradisiacal. They all had a rich social life, with golf, parties, trips to the seashore on weekends, and a large group of close friends. They paint a picture of the post-colony in the last days after independence and before the Bougainville revolution, when the income from the Bougainville mine was withdrawn from the national coffers, crippling the new country's infrastructure. Andrew said: "In the 1980s and very early 1990s the Kina was strong and there were only two real exporters. Business was booming. We [at ANGCO] gave a good, fair price to growers and we made sure that there was a good product. Today, it is harder. The Kina is weak and the infrastructure failures make it hard for exporters to meet their contracts. You work hard to keep them in business but it is getting increasingly difficult. The product is uneven these days too." He adds, "This is a hard business, but I stay in the business because it is exciting, it changes on a daily basis. I get to know the producers—the growers—and the exporters: it is a part of my job. And I travel from producer to producer and talk to them and it reminds me that coffee is more than a commodity, it is a way of life."

When Andrew talks about Papua New Guinea coffee today he does so with a mix of nostalgia and regret:

> It used to be known as a great coffee—good for both blending and specialty—but now it is so inconsistent that it is not thought of highly . . . It is a unique product but the inconsistency hurts it so we have to find ways to make it valuable above and beyond the inconsistency. To make people feel like when we have it they should buy it up immediately. . . . The images we create, the exotic images, that is value adding. If the coffee is good then it is good and the images can make it worth more, but if the coffee is bad, then the images are not going to make a difference at all. But with Papua New Guinea coffee, the images work to add that little bit of value. . . . With Papua New Guinea here in the UK, there have been so many TV documentaries of late. This has really increased the profile of the country here and we are seeing people want to connect to that image from the documentaries by buying the coffee.

As a commodity, coffee has a given monetary value at a given time depending on its grade and supply and demand. By infusing some sort of salient semiotic into it the traders can force the value of the coffee to increase—it is worth more in the marketplace because of the images attached to it. When they make the coffee reek of the primitive and poverty, the value seems to go higher than when they simply overlay images of growers trying to take part in a global system of capital and commerce. Andrew remarks:

> People often drink coffee, particular coffee, to stop poverty. We can use that to sell certain coffees. For example, we talk about Brazilians as "industrial" and disassociate it from growers, in part because we don't handle much Brazilian. We tell people, "If you really want to help growers, you will buy coffee from X origin, where coffee is local." But we find that we can make coffee from Papua New Guinea even more desirable because of these images of feathered warriors and the images like the ones of the walls here. . . . We bring Papua New Guinea into being, for the majority of people who buy our coffee. We know the place and the people who grow it there. We know the industry, and that it is an "industry" and not some painted warriors in a forest, but we have to sell the coffee to the roasters, and sometimes it is those painted warriors, and the stories about them, who seal the deal.

There is one story about coffee from Papua New Guinea that I have heard told by exporters, importers, marketers, and roasters. It connects coffee from its point of production to the coffee on specialty store shelves and infuses it with images of savage natives living on the edge of the modern. The story goes like this:[2]

> During the heyday of the coffee export company ANGCO, fighting broke out in the rural parts of the Western Highlands. There was a "tribal war" going on near Hagen (or in Banz or Chimbu, depending on the storyteller). During the first few months of the "tribal war," ANGCO was able to get trucks in to buy coffee, but the "warriors" were beginning to "attack" the trucks and rob the drivers. Back in Goroka at the ANGCO office, a group of intrepid "coffee men" put their heads together and came up with a plan. They would continue to send the trucks into the area to collect the coffee but they would fly the payment, the cash, by helicopter into the area. This way the trucks could safely move the coffee out of the area with no threats to the drivers.
>
> ANGCO sent word to the warring villagers that they were not going to send money on the truck but rather "by the sky." So everyone gathered around the truck when it came. They made their transactions with the

ANGCO agent in the truck and then he made a radio call. Soon afterwards they heard the sound of a helicopter and soon after that it came into view. The crowd looked to the sky just as the door opened and the ANGCO agent in the helicopter threw out a bag of money (the payment for the coffee). The bag caught the wind and burst open, and thousands and thousands of Kina whipped in the wind across the Highlands. The warriors brandished their spears to the sky and everyone scrambled to gather the fallen cash. Back at the ANGCO headquarters in Goroka, the intrepid coffee men knew that they had a problem. The money that had been expelled from the helicopter had not got to the ANGCO agent on the ground, because the bag broke. They were therefore not able to pay the growers who had actually sold them coffee. They knew they would have to revise their plan for the next drop. Several weeks later the whole scene played out again: the truck arrived, the coffee deal was transacted, the helicopter was called, and the warriors and villagers waited. When the helicopter arrived in view this time, the ANGCO agent opened the door and threw out a block of ice cream around which the payment for the money was taped. The cash-wrapped ice cream block flew to the ground to be collected by the ANGCO agent from the truck, and all the growers were paid with cash and a bite of tasty ice cream, which they, living in such a remote place, had never seen before.

I heard this story in London, Hamburg, Brisbane, and Sydney and at a specialty coffee convention in Charlotte, North Carolina. One of the storytellers, a man who uses the story to move the Papua New Guinea coffee that he buys, said, "Sitting in a train station in October in London and knowing what you are drinking came from a place so remote that the money had to be dropped there by an airplane. That is a different kind of feeling." However, when I asked another importer, based in Brisbane, about the story, he said, "What a load of bull."

Brisbane is the capital of Queensland, the northeastern-most state in Australia, and the third-largest city in Australia. Like Hamburg and London, it is situated along a river. The Brisbane River winds through the city, creating a watery road for boats and ferries, and separating the downtown shopping and business section of the city from the urban redevelopment zone of South Bank and the funky art zone of New Farm. Brisbane is an old city by Australian standards, but it only started to become an international city after the Commonwealth Games were held there in 1982. Trevor Bruce,

Man from Goroka watching traditional dance at the yearly celebration of national independence in Goroka

the coffee importer I spent the most time with in Brisbane, said of the games: "They really showed the world what we have here and they showed people here, who were not very worldly, what it would be like to develop the city as an international business center and tourism destination." He said this one afternoon as we sat at a bar in South Bank, an arts and recreation area that lines a bend in the river, and shops, bars, restaurants, galleries, and hotels.

Trevor Bruce was in his early forties when I interviewed him for this book, but I have known him since he was in his mid-thirties. I first met him in Goroka when I was conducting research for my PhD in the late 1990s. He is handsome and engaging, with a wonderful sense of humor and a love for rough sports and the out-of-doors. Trevor got his start in coffee with ANGCO. He lived in the country for a while, but once he got married and had children he felt that it was not a place to "raise children" and that his wife would not be safe there, so he moved to Brisbane. After his move he continued to work with one of the small coffee factories that exported coffee from Goroka to various companies in Australia. His work continually took him back and forth between Brisbane and Goroka, making him the only one of the importers I interviewed who traveled regularly to Papua New Guinea.

Trevor and I met numerous times over a few months in Brisbane, and at each meeting we talked about how he sold the coffee from Papua New Guinea and how uncomfortable he felt about the images he was encouraged to use in selling it. Trevor has been to many coffee marketing seminars that focused on specialty coffee, and has read much of the industry marketing literature, so he understands that the best way to increase the value of the coffee he was selling was to graft a set of images onto it. Since he works exclusively with coffee from Papua New Guinea, he does not have to do the work of creating images of other coffees and other places: he focuses only on the one "origin": "This origin marketing, when it is based on the quality of the coffee, is easy. I just talk about the acidity in the cup, the fruity flavor, and the ease with which the coffee blends and lifts other lower quality coffees. . . . What I don't like is having to paint a picture of Papua New Guinea that is not true."

Trevor's worry surrounds the images that he knows help to sell coffee, things like "feathers and painted faces and dancing," and the fact that "those ideas about Papua New Guinea cover up what is really happening there." As someone who moves to and from Goroka often, Trevor articulates the same sorts of critiques of infrastructure and public works as the members of the Goroka coffee community: "If I tell a buyer about some native tradition, that means that I don't tell him about the miracle of getting the coffee from Goroka to Lae, given how shocking the roads are." Nor does the image of the primitive he must paint allow him to "tell buyers about the women and men who make that industry possible. The people that growers would be lost without." Even with this hesitation, Trevor must create these images to compete in the marketplace. While he continues to sell coffee from Papua New Guinea the way he likes to sell it to his older customers, emphasizing the quality and ecological suitability of the beans, he must engage in fantasy production to bring new roasters and shops to his company.

Steffen Maiburg, Andrew Chesterfield, and Trevor Bruce are only three of the eight importers I interviewed for this book. All the other importers, also male, told similar stories: about having lived and worked in Papua New Guinea (or having a parent who had done so), about having long ties to the country and its coffee community, and about having to create particular images to sell their coffee in today's market. I chose to write about Steffen,

Andrew, and Trevor because I spent the most time with them and because I felt that their comments exemplified so many of the issues about image making in the contemporary coffee world. All of the men that I spent time with expressed some unease about the contemporary images they must craft to sell their coffee. They all know that the images are just fantasies. While Trevor expressed his unease in the strongest way, all those whom I interviewed talk to their exporter counterparts in Papua New Guinea regularly, understand the complex nature of social life in the country today, and know they are telling their customers stories that are less than true. Yet they all understand that to find a place in today's market, these stories must be told.

One of the most common conversations I had with the importers was a conversation about how the image making shifted. Uniformly, they said that before the early 1990s they sold coffee based on stories about its taste, its ecological characteristics (the quality of soil it was grown in and its altitude and climate of growth), and its possibility for fulfilling a particular niche in a blend. In the early 1990s they all noticed a shift in the way their buyers wanted to understand the coffees they were buying and the ways the marketing literature suggested that they sell the coffee. What is compelling is that in almost every instance this conversation happened before we talked about the decline of the ICO, the deregulation of the market, and the growth of third-party certification systems. In other words, the importers identified the emergence of images forced by neoliberalization without my having asked them about the neoliberalization of the market at all. I will return to this issue in chapter 8, but it is clear from the interviews that the shift in image making began at the same time as the deregulation of the market. It is also clear that the other trend that began in the early 1990s was the growth of small specialty coffee shops worldwide.

Locations of Consumption

Coffee shops and coffeehouses have been part of the European and American public sphere for a very long time (Habermas [1969] 1989; Sennett 1992; Warner 2002). They, like restaurants, are places with "a particular combination of style and type of food, social milieu and social function" (Mennell 1985, 136). Today coffee shops are ubiquitous in urban areas and serve varied social functions. Over the past five years I have followed coffee that was grown in the Eastern Highlands Province of Papua New Guinea to destinations in several metropolitan areas. While I visited numerous coffee shops and conducted extended participant observation and interviews, I will discuss five shops in Australia, England, and Germany that serve as examples of the five primary types of shop. While my research also took me to the United States, the data collected on coffee consumption there will be presented at the end of this chapter.

The coffee shops that I visited are designed around particular aesthetics of desire and sense. Each shop has a certain feel to it that is meant to evoke individuality, feelings of connections to coffee producers, fashionable hipster lifestyles, modern urban lifestyles, and food and beverage connoisseur lifestyles. The shops attempt, like all businesses that sell luxuries, to create new consumers and draw in people who may have shopped at other sites. They do this through various techniques, including the "opening up" of the "imagination and emotion to desire."[3] The actual design of the shops, the use of glass, fixtures, and light and the inclusion or exclusion of everyday objects such as newspapers, computers, books, and the like, work to create particular atmospheres of consumption (see Leach 1993, 39–70). These atmospheres of consumption infuse the coffee beans with a kind of veneer of meaning that connects the beans to the ways the consumers imagine themselves. In the shops, consumption becomes a form of communication in terms of sending and receiving messages (Appadurai 1986, 31).

Many small coffee shops roast their own coffee today, or they take pride in and articulate to their customers the roasting process used elsewhere to bring them exceptional coffee. Roasting has a rich history that is beyond the scope of this book, but it is important to understand a bit about the process, as it is a key step in coffee's journey from production to consumption.

In the late 1800s coffee roasting was no longer done in people's homes and individual coffee-selling establishments where coffee had always been roasted, and it became an industrial process (Schapira, Schapira, and Schapira 1982, 51). As demand for coffee grew in urban areas, coffee roasting became an industry in itself. Green bean coffee can be stored for long periods, years if need be, but roasted coffee has a relatively short life. With a concentrated market, large batches of coffee were roasted, since they could be distributed quickly in urban areas. The two means that developed to handle quantity and what was then thought of as quality (sameness in flavor) were mechanization and automation. The first modern coffee roaster was invented by Jabez Burns in 1864. In 1935 a more efficient process was invented by which heat was applied in great quantity (more bean surface gets more heat) and the temperature halved (Schapira,

Schapira, and Schapira 1982, 52). Industrial roasting today uses this method and Burns's basic machinery. In the 1870s major coffee companies began urging people to buy pre-roasted coffee (54) and from the early 1900s to the mid-1980s most consumers in the United States expected industrial roasting. Industrial roasting, like all Fordist technology, increased profits and cut costs. It created a uniform product and was highly mechanized.

Historically roasting has been a part of distribution. It was an invisible part of the process that consumers did not think about. Today discussions about roasting have been reintroduced into the specialty coffee industry because consumers are willing to pay more if they believe that their coffee has been specially roasted. This is exemplified by small shops where the coffee is roasted in front of the consumers.

Roasting coffee, the process of applying heat in a controlled way to the green beans, changes beans both physically and chemically. Physically the beans shrink in weight and gain in volume and go from a greenish color to a variety of rich, brown colors. They shrink in weight because all of the moisture is expelled during roasting, and they gain in volume because gases are produced inside the beans during roasting. Chemically the water, oil, proteins, caffeine, chlorogenic acid, trigonelline, tannin, caffetannin, caffeic acid, starches, sugars, and vitamins in the beans change with heat.

Roasting takes place in several steps. The first step dries the green beans until they are yellow and have a smell reminiscent of toasted popcorn kernels. The second step begins when the beans become light-brownish and have doubled in size but lost about 5 percent of their weight. This occurs when they are at about 200° C. Next the coffee beans become medium brown, as their weight continues to decrease and the heat rises to about 220° C. A chemical process called pyrolysis begins, and CO_2 is released from the bean at this stage. Then when the coffee reaches about 230° C this chemical process occurs again: the coffee becomes dark brown and begins to take on an oily sheen and texture. Roasters usually stop the coffee after the second pyrolysis and dump the beans into a metal box that can be cooled with cold air or cold water (Schapira, Schapira, and Schapira 1982).

As the coffee heats from about 150° to 200° the sugars in the beans begin to caramelize and all the moisture is expelled from the beans. Caramelized sugars are less sweet than uncaramelized ones, and dark-roasted coffee is dark because of the caramelized sugars and the carbonization that come with higher heat and longer periods at higher heat. Therefore darker roasts are less sweet than lighter roasts. During this entire process the coffee has

Coffee roasting in
Brisbane, Australia

to be kept moving so that the beans do not burn or roast unevenly. If coffee
is roasted too long or at very high temperatures it has a "thin," "burned,"
"industrial," "harsh," "bland" flavor. Most roasters have a rotating area or
drum above the heat source where air blows the coffee and the maximum
heat is usually about 250°.

One coffee shop I spent time in is located in the Covent Garden section
of London. The first thing you notice when you walk in is the smell of
coffee roasting. This is an altogether different smell from that of coffee
brewing. It is a smoky, dusky smell, and when big roasting machines are
used the smell can be overpowering. The smell in this little shop is, however, sensual enough to infuse the space but not overwhelm the senses. The
shop is tiny: a counter, a display of roasted beans from all over the world, a
minute shelf with pastry and sweets, and about seven seats at tables on a
little raised floor behind the counter. The walls are covered in dark wooden
planks, and walking into the shop feels like stepping into a wooden box.

The planks are the color of old wine barrels, with an uneven finish and a rustic look. Downstairs a roasting machine occupies the entire length and width of the shop. The machine is gleaming copper, and as you peer down the stairs from the shop floor you can catch a glint of it. The diminutive space is silent, aside from the quiet voices of patrons and the rustling of newspapers and book pages.

The shop sells coffee to "people from the neighborhood" and "people on their way home from work," according to the head roaster: "We cater to people who know and enjoy very high quality coffee." She remarks repeatedly that her shop is known "throughout London" for its roasts and for the quality of the coffee. The way the employees roast, and the way they talk about their roasting, adds value to the coffee. Their roasting technique incorporates a unique "artisan" form of labor that they argue is unlike that of "corporate roasters." The shop offers seminars on roasting techniques and printed materials about roasting for customers. The store is selling the beans and the idea that its roasting practices make the beans more valuable and desirable than other beans.

The Covent Garden shop sits on a street in a fashionable neighborhood that boasts small, expensive clothing stores, several sleek bars, one extremely popular pub, and only one chain retail store, the apothecary Kiehl's. The neighborhood has old, winding streets and is lined by small buildings with shops on the ground level and apartments on the upper levels. The people who populated the neighborhood when I was there for one month in 2004 were young, well dressed, and almost exclusively of European descent. Many of them tended to congregate on sunny afternoons on the steps to the small monument (the Dial) in the center of a traffic roundabout.[4] The roundabout sits equidistant between the old pub (built in the 1800s) and a bar fronted by smoky glass and flying a rainbow flag. The patrons of both establishments shared the Dial, creating a social mix between patrons who might not have otherwise have so readily mingled but who nonetheless all live in and frequent the shops in the neighborhood. Those whom I talked to over the course of many afternoons on the Dial were people working in banking and finance, lawyers, fashion and retail executives, young mothers staying at home with children, and otherwise solidly urban, middle-class professionals. This population frequents the little coffee shop.

The coffee shop patrons are buying distinction, individuality, and insider or specialist knowledge. Several patrons told me that they shop there even though the coffee is rather expensive, because the coffee is of a "higher quality" than what they might have got in a chain coffee shop or at the Tesco supermarket.[5] The patrons experienced and assumed this "higher quality" because of the "individual attention" given to each roast and the "knowledge" that the staff had about coffee beans, "where coffee comes from," and roasting. One young mother told me she patronized the shop because of its "expertise" and likened shopping there to being a discerning shopper for things like "housewares and linens." She said she could taste the "quality" of the coffee and expressed her enjoyment of the process of buying it. She, and many other consumers I spoke with, liked learning about the different roasts, "source countries," and "qualities" of the coffee (meaning the taste of the coffee). Each liked "learning about" and "becoming more of an expert" on coffee. One man who by his own description "entertains at home a lot" said that this allowed for a more effective and enjoyable "presentation" of the coffee when it was served in the home. Another woman told me that she liked to be able to "talk about the origins" of the coffee with her guests: "Here you learn about the growers and the origin countries and you come to understand coffee."

The Covent Garden shop focuses on "consumer education" by organizing events for customers. These events are grouped around culture and ecology themes. An "in store cupping" event focused on the ecology of coffee-growing regions and highlighted soil quality, altitude, and climate as the three key ingredients in "good coffee." The event's speaker also highlighted the biological diversity that one finds in many coffee-growing regions and connected small-scale coffee farming with biodiversity conservation and economic development: "Growers make a good living and the vast ecological diversity in the tropics is preserved by their farming techniques." She described the kinds of animals one might find in a coffee grove and the "fact" that coffee groves serve as "biological corridors" for "all manner of biodiversity!"

The shop tries to "educate" consumers about the lives of coffee growers, according to the shop manager. She says that she and her staff are "knowledgeable" about the "conditions that growers live in" and are "happy to help educate" customers. In addition to oral education, the shop provides handwritten descriptions of the lives of farmers and pamphlets with stories about how coffee improves the lives of impoverished growers. Much of the coffee sold in this shop is certified coffee, and the certification is a major selling point. The manager says, "Our customers understand that certification means better growing conditions, better ecology, and better coffee. It is a win-win. They get better coffee and growers get premium prices."

Most of the coffee shop patrons whom I talked with at this shop do buy the certified coffees. They all expressed a slight concern about the lives of the growers and the ecological conditions of production, but more often than not their major concern was about their own health. One young man said to me, "It is great that the coffee, I mean the organic kind, is better for the planet, but what interests me in organics is the health implications for me and my wife." This sentiment sums up what most people articulated about certifications. People seem pleased to have done something that may have a positive social or ecological effect, but much more concerned with their own health and well-being.

The second shop I spent time in while in London is in a formerly industrial part of town. The streets are wide, busy with traffic, and lined with old warehouses and big, cavernous buildings. The coffee shop is large and open, with a gigantic front window that looks out onto a busy street. The counters gleam in brushed steel, the light fixtures are modern and "funky," in bright colors and unusual shapes, there is a row of computers against one wall and an enormous magazine rack against the other, and the music is loud. There is a disheveled hipster feel to the place that is at once welcoming and mildly intimidating. The patrons of the coffee shop at the Dial would feel wildly out of place here. Here the patrons are young, ranging from late teens to mid-thirties, and many of them have bicycle helmets and skateboards. They are a pierced and tattooed crowd with lots of faux-hawk haircuts and interesting glasses. The majority are of English descent, but there are also a good number of students whose parents are immigrants from Africa, South Asia, and the Middle East.

The shop is owned by a man about my age, mid-thirties at the time, who grew up "in a pub," where his father was the bartender and general manager. He says that he had "service" in his blood but that after years of working in pubs he wanted to spend less time around "a bunch of drunks." Since his early childhood he had been fascinated by the island of New Guinea, and in his reading about Papua New Guinea he came across several stories about coffee production. He thought he might be able to turn his pub experience and his fantasy about New Guinea into a business, so he opened his first shop. In the summer of 2004 he owned three shops and was looking to open one more in the fall. The shop owner is a cool guy: tall, balding, and charismatic, with striking features. He embodies a sort of punk-rock aesthetic signaling to people of my generation that he listened to the Clash with an older sibling in the 1970s and then partook of the new wave phase of the 1980s, with Hüsker Dü and Fugazi thrown into the mix. He describes his shops as a "third place": "Your first place is home, your second is your office, and you need a third place. A place that is not home, not work, but that is comfortable and that expresses things you enjoy, that you connect to." He says that he puts his shops in "edgy, gentrifying, urban neighborhoods" because that is where people do not have "third spaces," and that his shop is a hybrid of a pub, a club, and a restaurant (he serves smoothies, light-toasted sandwiches, and juices in addition to coffee). One night each week he has an "open mic night" at which local performers play acoustic music, work on comedy routines, and tell stories. "Depending on what is brought in that is good," he has periodic art openings and exhibits. The space has computers but also serves as a wi-fi hotspot, and many of the patrons bring laptops and sit for hours in the comfortable chairs and on big, plush sofas. The shop sells its own blend of coffee, and the majority of the blend is from Papua New Guinea. There is no outward attempt at "education" in the shop, and the sort of "value adding" and "value creation" surrounding roasting, quality, and distinction through elite knowledge that happens in the Covent Garden shop do not take place here.

The patrons of this coffee shop frequent it because of its location and atmosphere. During the day most of the people in the shop are people who work in the neighborhood, which is an emerging hub of the Internet-related businesses, fashion-related businesses, and new media outlets, and they use the shop as an extension of their offices. People have meetings at the shop and take morning and afternoon coffee breaks there. In the late afternoon and early evening the composition of the crowd shifts to include students, people who live in the neighborhood (the gentrifying warehouse dwellers), and people who come from other areas of London to visit friends.

About six months before beginning my fieldwork, a Starbucks opened diagonally across the street from this shop, and most of the patrons I interviewed talked about how the "locally owned" shop had a sense of distinction. Many of the patrons felt as if the "mass-produced American coffee" at Starbucks was of a lesser quality than the coffee at the shop, and that by choosing it over Starbucks they were showing their knowledge about coffee quality. Some felt that their choice indicated an allegiance to "local business" and "noncorporate" business. One man said, "The people who work here know you and they don't just see you as another *venti* cup."

Another said, "Coming here keeps my money in the neighborhood and hopefully keeps it from becoming an American shopping mall." The patrons distinguish themselves from others by their choice to buy their coffee here and not elsewhere. They see their consumption as helping "to build community" in the "emerging neighborhood."

The patrons in this shop also enjoy its "edgy" feel. They appreciate the musical aesthetic and find that they feel an enlarged sense of being "in the know" from spending time in the shop. One woman said, "[The owner] really keeps his finger on things. He edits new culture, in a way. You know when you come here he will have the newest things." This sentiment of "newness" and the expression of a desire to be on the "cutting edge" but being too busy to track that edge oneself was prevalent among coffee consumers in the shop.

The owner produces all of the shop's fantasy formations around origins. He is very much present in the day-to-day lives of his shops, and many of the regular patrons know him. When one talks to him, the talk inevitably turns to New Guinea. I sought him out because he buys coffee from one of the exporters I know in Papua New Guinea. This exporter is a dear friend and knows me quite well. Upon hearing that I was to spend a month in London, he said to me, "You have to meet X: talking to him is like talking to the British, male version of you." He said this because he knew of my own long-standing fantasies about Papua New Guinea. In a paper I wrote in 1995:

> I became an anthropologist because of Papua New Guinea. For a child living in Georgia, there was no place that seemed farther away or more exotic than the island of New Guinea. I imagined New Guinea as an Edenic paradise that I could explore the way intrepid women characters had explored the generic "Africa" of Tarzan movies. Turner Broadcasting System (TBS) began in Atlanta, and one of Turner's first broadcasting moves was to buy the rights to all the old Tarzan films. TBS showed these films every Sunday morning, and I would watch them, rapt by their exotic Orientalist presentations of nature, culture and the "other." Somehow, I dreamed those movies into my vision of New Guinea. My grandmother taught me to read as a young child by using the National Geographic Magazine, and I imagine us reading the March 1972 edition, which has a story about headhunters of remotest New Guinea (Kirk 1972). I often wonder, because I got my own subscription when I was in

first grade, if I pored over an article by Gillian Gillison (1977) about the Gimi, imagining myself as Gillison or, more likely, as her young daughter of whom there are two photographs in the magazine. (West 2005a, 271)

Meeting the owner of the London coffee shop was indeed like looking into a strange mirror of myself. He and I have very similar backgrounds and both of us, when we were children, used the fantasy of New Guinea to escape urban childhoods. At the time we first met, he had never, despite being rather wealthy because of the success of his coffee shops, been to Papua New Guinea. But more than any person I have ever met, he spoke about the wonders of the country with such an engaging passion that it was hard not to get caught up in his fantasy. He spoke eloquently about its linguistic diversity. He knew all the recent discoveries of new species. Finally, he spoke passionately about the "pure traditional culture" that one can find there. He wove a picture of social and ecological diversity that was compelling. Importantly, he wove this picture for any patron who would listen to him.

The fantasy that the shop owner engaged in was one that sees difference and authenticity as enduring and that values them above the idea that western ways should permeate places and peoples outside the West. This fantasy is grounded in a failure to understand that the social lives of people in Papua New Guinea, and places like it, have shifted and transformed radically over the past few hundred years. It is also grounded in a sort of narrative of what Vincent Crapanzano has called "the beyond" (Crapanzano 2003, 14). "The beyond" is "an imagined frontier . . . a place that always turns on our images, ideas, and dreams, but that is also always destroyed by them. The beyond can never be found. Once it is constructed, it is immediately displaced; one can spend their whole life looking for it, and will never find what they are looking for" (West 2006, 3).

For both the coffee shop owner and me (before decades of anthropology), the beyond we are looking for is one where capitalist alienation does not exist and where everything "alternative" is not immediately taken up by capital and incorporated into it as a way to sell things. In chapter 1 of this book I discussed how contemporary advertising incorporates music, art, poetry, and other cultural forms as a strategy for selling products. Using alternative cultural forms or images that have captured the imagination of markets that are hard to reach is a well-known strategy for advertisers and marketers (Goldman 1994, 2001). For the coffee shop owner, his shops are

Man from Goroka in traditional costume at the yearly celebration of national independence in Goroka

Taking a break from the yearly celebration of national independence in Goroka

Traditional costume in Germany

an attempt to create a space where art, music, and poetry that are not funded by large companies and that are under the radar of most people have a place. They are, in his words, "an attempt to create a space for the truly alternative. Alternative people and alternative art."

It seems to me that both the coffee shop owner and I (before I spent my life working there) saw Papua New Guinea as the ultimate alternative to capital and its various forms of alienation. Before I began to learn about Papua New Guinea in earnest in graduate school, I imagined a land of happy natives who lived lightly on the land and outside the social ravages of capitalist production. When I met the coffee shop owner, he still believed this to be the case. This is most certainly, like images of poverty and savagery, one of the images used by contemporary marketers to add distinction to coffee from Papua New Guinea.

The coffee shop where I spent time in Hamburg is two blocks from the Rathaus. It is a part of a company that has thirty-one shops in Hamburg, Berlin, Hanover, Lübeck, and Cologne. The chain has a Starbucks business model and aesthetic, with multiple identical shops, but it has excellent coffee. The Rathaus shop seats about forty-five people inside and about eighteen outside. It has modern fixtures and a clean, polished look. Coffee, coffee-related beverages (such as cocoa, tea, and flavored, coffee-based drinks), and coffee-related items such as coffeemakers, cups, and presses are sold. Coffee from Papua New Guinea, Kenya, Brazil, Ethiopia, and Guatemala are featured, but the bestseller is the house blend. The staff members, all university students on the days that I spent time there, were enthusiastic about both the shop and the coffee. The prices are similar to those in an American chain coffee shop (see table 5), and the majority of patrons are people who work in the area and come in regularly. One staff member told me, "We are the best not-sitting-down coffee in town!"[6]

I spent a month in Hamburg and frequented the shop when I was there. The patrons whom I talked to mentioned the convenience of being able to get "good coffee" of diverse origins on the way to work. One man said, "Before now I had not had coffee from one country. We prefer blended coffee—a bit from here, a bit from there—we have a more sophisticated taste than the English or you Americans. But now it is nice to try coffee from Papua New Guinea, or Ethiopia and weigh them against themselves." This comparison of origins was reflected in many of my conversations with patrons. The coffee in this shop, because of how different origin countries are highlighted, leads customers to relational ways of thinking. They weigh

TABLE 5 Coffee prices at shop in Hamburg (in Euros)

	Short	Tall	Grande
Caffe latte, Cappuccino	2.20	2.50	2.75
Espresso	1.45	1.95	
House coffee	1.35	1.65	1.95

Source: Data collected by author between 1 September 2004 and 1 August 2005.

the taste of one origin against another and relate the places to each other. One woman told me how she chooses origin when she is buying bulk coffee from the shop: "I think about what news I have heard recently and what place seems to need more help with development. Then I buy." Another patron said, "You asked about coffee from Papua New Guinea. They are so poor so I buy their coffee."

The German customers had a relational way of thinking about both "origins" and "poverty." Numerous interviewees compared the things they knew about the political economy of various countries before they bought their coffee. One older man said to me, "I am new to drinking coffee from one place. Now that I can buy coffee from Kenya or Costa Rica or New Guinea, I think about what I have heard in the news of late while I am making my decisions about buying." Another patron said, "I try and buy from the places that I know need money, the poor people." Finally, an older woman said to me, "I am a historian and I like to buy from the countries that have a connection to Germany. It seems our duty, given our colonial history."

At the shops in London and Hamburg I asked patrons specifically about Papua New Guinea. I asked about images that people have of the place, geography, and, given British and German involvement, history. In London only one person out of about seventy-five whom I talked with in the shops had deep knowledge of British colonial history in Papua New Guinea. But in Hamburg the majority of shop patrons knew about the German history on the island. They also, unlike the Londoners who focused on poverty, had particular primitivist images of New Guinea natives. Of the twelve interviews I did at the shop in Hamburg, eight people used the phrase "Stone Age." This phrase was not used once in London. Ten people used the phrase "primitive" in Hamburg while only five (out of seventy-five) used it in London. In the British shops the patrons also saw Papua New

Guinea through a lens of nature. They discussed the plants, the birds, the "biological diversity," and their notion that cultivating coffee might contribute to conservation there. In the German shop the patrons saw Papua New Guinea through a lens of culture. They discussed the health and welfare of the people, the imagined "primitive conditions" there, and the "rapid" movement from "living like prehistoric times" to the present.

One of the coffee shops that I spent time at in Sydney is in the northern suburbs of the city. The neighborhood is residential, and most of its residents work in the city center and commute by bus, train, car, or bicycle. The houses in the area are very expensive, in part because of spectacular views of the Harbor Bridge and the Opera House, and in part because of the ease of the commute to downtown Sydney. The residents of the area, who are all of European descent, are professionals, mostly married couples, and mostly have two working incomes in the household.[7]

The shop is on a corner where four streets intersect, which contributes to its operating as the focal point of the neighborhood. It has a small shopfront that looks as if it might once have housed a pharmacy. The building is old, and the shop's décor mimics an old-time soda fountain aesthetic. The store smells like roasted coffee beans, and there are rows and rows of beans—dark, rich, and oily—in wooden barrels lined with jute coffee bags against one wall. These beans come from all over the world and are carefully labeled with handwritten cards reading Kona, Blue Mountain, New Guinea Peaberry, High Altitude Costa Rican, and the like. There is a smoky mirror behind the counter, a wall of old, dark wooden bookshelves filled with old books, and several old, wooden card catalogue filing cabinets behind the counter. In these cabinets are hundreds of cards with blends listed on them. When a new patron comes in, the owner or one of the employees sits down with her and talks about what sort of coffee she enjoys. The owner said to me, "Then, over the course of a time period, we define a blend that can be their signature household blend. We keep the blend-cards on file so that when they come in we can make their signature blend while they wait."

In addition to selling this bulk "signature blend" coffee, the shop sells single-origin coffee by the kilogram (although the owner says that he discourages people from buying single-origin alone because he wants to "educate their palates") and brewed coffee drinks. All the patrons I talked to were people who frequent the shop for both a "cuppa" and to buy coffee in bulk. They all seemed extremely enthusiastic about their "signature blends." One man who was about fifty said, "It is like wine. You become an expert and you know what you like. Once you get that down, you have a house blend, a house specialty, that when you have guests they know it is yours and yours alone." Many of the customers brought up the uniqueness they felt when they were "entertaining" and brought out their "signature blend" at the end of the meal. One woman said, "It was just so fun the first time we did it; no one had ever heard of such a thing."

The owner of the shop argued that this individuation was the "next step in retail businesses": "People are tired of being one of the crowd. They want to stand out, and this is one way that they can assert their individuality ... Many younger Australians, people in their thirties and forties in the early 1990s, associated coffee with their parents. They thought of it as freeze-dried and less than desirable. That has all changed now. We really have a wonderful coffee history here. We have so many people whose grand-parents were from Italy and Greece and Europe and they all drank beautiful coffee, but in the 1950s that freeze-dried coffee became what people drank on an everyday basis. So their grandparents had developed palates and their parents did not. Now people want to develop their own. They want to understand the coffee and to enjoy it like fine wine." The comparison between wine and coffee was often made. People talked about how they had grown up "going to pubs" and at some point realized that they enjoyed wine more than beer. One man said, "Now I still have a few beers here and again but at home, for entertaining, we serve wine and coffee."

The shop in Sydney was the first shop at which people talked about development aid to Papua New Guinea. Of the thirty-three patrons I inter-viewed at the shop, twelve brought up the "huge," "shocking," and "incred-ible" amount of aid money that they perceived as going to Papua New Guinea from Australia. One man in his mid-thirties said, "We send up billions of dollars and they can't get organized. They just steal it all." A woman in her mid-twenties told me that she was "terrified" of what was going to happen with "HIV rates" in Papua New Guinea, and that "even with the AusAid packages going up" she predicted a "health crisis the likes of which we have not even seen in Africa." The general sentiment was one of disillusionment with the government of Papua New Guinea for "squan-dering," "stealing," and "misusing" the money sent "up there" by Australia. There was, however, little knowledge of how the government was actually doing any of these things. A man in his fifties said, when I asked him what the government "squandered" the aid money on, "probably liquor and

whores like most politicians." But that was the extent of his analysis. Another woman in her mid-fifties said, "They just can't manage money yet. If
they hadn't gotten independence so soon, they would have learned ac-
countancy. But, at the end of the day, they are just not capable of running a country." The people I interviewed in Sydney often expressed this
sentiment—that Papua New Guineans lack the skills to manage things. The
most telling comment was made by a man in his mid-forties: "I don't know
how to say it, but, it is just that they are, well, primitive. They just aren't
developed like we are. They have not gotten there yet."

These comments show that although the patrons had some sense of the
financial connections between Papua New Guinea and Australia, they did
not have any idea of how the aid money was actually spent. Australia
currently spends about $400 million AU (roughly $328 million U.S.) a year
on aid to the country. Yet a recent report shows that over half of that money
was actually spent on Australian consultants (Fox et al. 2010).[8] The sense
that Papua New Guineans are stealing and squandering money from Australia is fueled by images of Papua New Guinea as a savage, untamed place.

One of the coffee shops I spent time at in Brisbane is owned by a
medium-sized roaster that has developed a brand used in hundreds of
restaurants and coffee shops around Australia. The company has been in
business in Queensland since 1958, and its flagship coffee shop is at its main
roasting facility in Fortitude Valley, the recently gentrified shopping district northeast of the city's main business district. There the company sells
coffee in bulk to the public, cups of coffee to passersby, and coffee-related
equipment to both the public and shop owners. I enjoyed the best cup of
coffee I've ever had at this shop. The company began to open other free-
standing coffee bars in 1992 and now has an active chain of them around
the country. The shop I spent time in is also the headquarters for the
import part of the business—it is large enough to serve as an importer and
therefore does not need to go through one of the importers I mentioned
earlier—so there are people around the shop who blur the line between
distribution and consumption.

In addition to cups of coffee they sell "origin beans" from Papua New
Guinea, Nicaragua, Colombia, Kenya, Indonesia, and Costa Rica. They
actively brand locations by giving them names, such as "New Guinea Gold"
and "Santos Brazil," and having product information cards and sheets available that detail the growing conditions, qualities of the coffee, supply chain
for the coffee, and other facts. They also have signature blends like "Arriba

Merlo Coffee, Brisbane, Australia

Arriba," which according to the card that accompanies bags of it "is literally translated as 'up up.' . . . This beautifully rounded South American blend combines the finest beans from Colombia, Nicaragua and Costa Rica. Each cup of Arriba Arriba delivers soft, medium body with a smooth aftertaste. A magnificent breakfast coffee."

The shop itself is bustling. There is a large amount of foot traffic by its front doors, and the windows are big and open so that passersby can see the gleaming copper roaster on the ground floor. The shop is in a converted warehouse, in a newly gentrified part of Brisbane that has individually owned clothing shops, shoe shops, posh eateries, new clubs, and well-worn pubs. The passersby are a mix of people exploring the neighborhood, locals, and tourists. The shop smells like brewed coffee, and the interaction between the different parts of the business—the roaster, the import offices, the baristas, and the coffee-hardware sales center—adds to the bustling atmosphere of the shop. Restaurant and coffee shop owners who are there to do business with the company mix with the tourists and neighborhood moms who stop in after they walk their children to the nearby school.

The shop and the company make mention in their public relations material that they are the "chain from grower to consumer" and make sure

TABLE 6 Coffee prices at shop in Brisbane (in Australian dollars)

	200 grams	400 grams	500 grams	800 grams	1 kilogram	3 kilograms
Espresso	8	15	16	26.50	27.50	75
Blends	8	15	16	26.50	27.50	75
Private	8.50	16	17	28.50	29.50	81
Decaf	9	18	19	30.50	31.50	86

Source: Data collected by author between 1 September 2004 and 1 August 2005.

that the "grower is compensated fairly." The employee whom I spent the most time with talked about this repeatedly. He lived for many years in Papua New Guinea, and many of the other buyers there also lived in "origin countries." He said, "We know the people we buy from. We trust them. We trust them to get us the best coffee and to pay fair wages to growers." This shop was also the only one that I spent time in that made extensive mention of Fair Trade and Organic-Certified coffee (see table 6).

How do American consumers hear the stories about people who grow coffee that is crafted by importers, roasters, and coffee shop owners? What do they learn from these stories? How do they understand places like Papua New Guinea as they are related to coffee? And how do they define themselves through consumption? If specialty coffee is indeed re-embedding political action and social relationships into economic choice, what does this re-embedding look like in terms of consumers?

The marketing of specialty coffee has taken place in numerous ways. One of the most powerful market forces today, according to the marketing seminar at the conference of the Specialty Coffee Association of America (SCAA) discussed in chapter 2, is the Internet. Mr. Nebraska, the marketing seminar leader, told us that people "research products on the Internet" and that this is the perfect place to "tell your story." Dean's Beans, the company discussed in the same chapter, took that advice and used a blog to craft a particular fantasy of Papua New Guinea through storytelling. This story, if we take seriously what Mr. Nebraska told us, should appeal to and help to craft the consumer consciousness of people born between 1983 and 2000, the "millennials."[9] Millennials are of particular interest to me, because I spend most of my working life with them as a university professor.

Because I wanted to see how these fantasy narratives about coffee and production were consumed by my students, over the course of one semester my student research assistants and I conducted one hundred interviews with people born between 1983 and 1989.[10] All the people interviewed were undergraduate students attending one of the colleges associated with Columbia University.[11] The interviews were concerned with people's knowledge of coffee production, distribution, and consumption and in particular with their ideas about the stories associated with certain kinds of specialty coffees.[12] Below I summarize the data collected and show quite clearly that the students we interviewed do not fit the consumer image produced by Mr. Nebraska.

First, what did these millennials know about Papua New Guinea? Ten people knew exactly where it was and gave us specifics like "sixty kilometers north of Australia" and "the eastern half of the island of New Guinea." Thirty-five interviewees knew that it was in the southern Pacific. They gave us answers like "near Australia in the Pacific Ocean," "sort of near the Philippines and Indonesia but closest to Oceania," and "near Malaysia and Indonesia." Ten people told us that Papua New Guinea was in Africa. Eleven told us something else incorrect, like "South America," "near Brazil," "close to India but not near China," and "in the Middle East but not near Iraq." Six interviewees freely admitted that they had no idea where Papua New Guinea was, while six refused to answer the question, instead saying things like, "the fuck I know," "fuck off," and "I refuse to answer that on the grounds that I incriminate my shitty knowledge of geography." So about 45 percent of our interviewees had an idea of where the country was but only about 10 percent had a good grasp of the geography of the region.

Next, what did millennials know about Papua New Guinea coffees? Forty-eight people interviewed had no idea that Papua New Guinea produced coffee. Thirty knew that Papua New Guinea produced coffee, and of those thirty, eighteen could tell us something about what they thought coffee production was like there. They said things like "People live in villages and grow coffee," "I think indigenous people grow it there," and "Yeah, its huge there, small farms all over the country." The remaining twenty-two people had a vague idea that Papua New Guinea produced coffee, saying things like, "Yeah, I kind of know it does" and "I've seen it in Starbucks." Of these twenty-two, nine people mentioned Indonesian coffee, saying things like, "Well, I know it is near Indonesia and they grow coffee so I assume they grow it there also." So 48 percent of the people interviewed had no idea that Papua New Guineans produced coffee at all.

In terms of consumption, nineteen of the people interviewed always drank fair-trade coffee, fifty-one never drank it, and thirty said that they drank it sometimes. Eighteen people always drank organic coffee, fifty-two never drank it, twenty sometimes drank it, and ten said they did not know how often they drank it. Of the twenty people who said they always drank fair-trade coffee, all mentioned "producers" and "labor" and about half mentioned either "ethical" or "fair" uses of their money as consumers. Of the eighteen people who always drank organic coffee, not one mentioned the health of workers or the earth's ecosystems but all mentioned their own health (but see below, some people do understand that the organic designation has to do with the health of the ecosystem). All the people who said that they sometimes drank fair-trade and organic coffee said that they did not seek it out but if given a choice preferred to drink it. Of the fifty people who never drank fair-trade coffee and were asked why not, twenty said they did not know what it was, eighteen said it was more "expensive" or "costs more," eight gave no specific reason, and four gave other responses ("is brewed in self-righteousness," "reminds me too much of poor people," "tastes like peasants," and is "left wing"). Of the fifty-two people who never drank organic coffee thirty-five said that it was more "expensive" or "costs more," fifteen said that it had never occurred to them to look for it in stores or shops, and two said "too fucking hippy" and "too liberal." So less than 20 percent of the people interviewed actively sought out and consumed fair-trade or organic coffees and over 50 percent of the interviewees never drank it. The rest of them drank it if it was convenient.

We also interviewed people about their level of knowledge concerning fair-trade-certified and organic-certified coffee and categorized responses as "understands," "has a good general idea," "has a vague idea," "has no idea," and "has the wrong idea." A response coded as "understands" had to include a mention of certification, but this does not necessarily mean that the respondent understood the process of certification. Of the one hundred people interviewed, eight fully understood what certification meant and entailed, eight vaguely understood it, nineteen wrongly thought that it was a process of ensuring quality by the FDA and the USDA, and sixty-five had no idea what it was. Of the sixteen people who either understood or vaguely understood the process, not one knew that growers must pay to have their coffee certified.

Fourteen people understood what fair-trade coffee was, twenty-three had a good general idea about what it was, twenty-five had a vague idea, twenty-seven had no idea, and eleven had the wrong idea. We coded answers as "understanding" if the respondent could convey to us that fair trade was a system intended to give producers a better wage for their labor and through which labor was regulated by external bodies of some sort.[13]

Answers were coded as "a good general idea" if the interviewees were able to link the term "fair trade" with at least five of the following goals: a living wage, a minimum price, long-term relationships, monitoring, certification, small farms, cooperatives, credit to farmers, cutting out middlemen, sustainable development, and fair labor practices. They did not have to use the specific terms but only mention the ideas behind them. For "vague idea" they had to mention three of the goals.

For organic-certified coffee we coded the answers as "understanding" if the respondents could convey to us that the coffee was grown without pesticides or fertilizers and that the process was intended to promote the health of the planet, workers, and consumers. Only six people fell into this category, while ten would have done so if we had eliminated comments about the health of the planet and workers as criteria. Seventeen people, all of whom mentioned that organic means an absence of pesticides and fertilizers, had a good general understanding of what organic meant. Thirty-five had a vague idea, mentioning that the organic label had something to do with how and where coffee was grown, twenty-three people had no idea, and nine had the wrong idea.

The first question during our interviews was "What are the different kinds of coffees?," and we were all surprised by the answers we got. Overwhelmingly people confused their kinds of specialty coffees. For example, one nineteen-year-old male said, "dark roast, light roast, fair-trade, hazelnut, decaf, French vanilla, mocha, Colombian, and Guatemalan," a twenty-year-old female said, "Origin, I mean the place they were grown, Organic, and flavored." Another nineteen-year-old female said, "Colombian, chocolate-hazelnut, Ecuadorian, American, Maxwell House." These answers were typical: 58 percent of the informants mentioned a type of flavored coffee, like "hazelnut," 45 percent mentioned a process, like "dark roast" or "decaffeinated"; 40 percent mentioned a form of coffee-shop production, like "espresso," "latte," or "cappuccino." The majority of people, 78 percent, mentioned a Latin American country when answering this question (Brazil, Colombia, and Guatemala were mentioned most often); 15 percent mentioned Africa; 6 percent mentioned countries within Africa

(Ethiopia, Kenya, Tanzania, Uganda, and Rwanda); 4 percent mentioned Indonesia.

The response with the highest score (85 percent of the interviews), given to the question "Who grows coffee?" was "poor farmers," whom 35 percent of respondents characterized as "impoverished," 22 percent as "minorities," and 18 percent as laboring under "slave" labor conditions. One respondent said: "The stereotypical image is of a South American working the fields—these aren't rich people. Depends on what conditions they're in—some of the farmers are abused, but others have gotten deals with artisan coffee makers who want to show off how much they've made from coffee." Another reported that "people with mustaches" and "people who tried to grow cocaine and got in trouble" grew coffee. While 38 percent of the answers included both "farmers" and some permutation of "businesses" or "corporations," the answers overwhelmingly reflected an image of poor people living in the tropics on the edge of the modern. Other descriptors used when students talked about these farmers were, "men," "brown people," "poor fuckers," "downtrodden men and women," "tropical people," "people in Africa and places like that," and "donkey-riding farmers."

The deregulated coffee market was supposed to be fairer and more flexible, but it has resulted in the lowest coffee prices in the history of the market. Growers in places like Papua New Guinea are cast into fantasy images of ecologically noble savages and pure, guileless economic primitives, so that people will see their coffee as a scarce resource and pay higher prices for it. Coffee consumers and potential consumers born between 1983 and 2000, a market segment with the largest ratio of disposable income to total income, are also cast into a fantasy image: that of wide-eyed, well-meaning, ecologically and socially noble actors who wish to change the world through their consumption practices.

But at least for the millennials, the Internet-based marketing of specialty coffees through narratives has not created consumers who can recall the narratives. Nor has it created consumers, at least the ones we interviewed, who wish to express their politics through consumption. The students we interviewed know almost nothing about specialty coffee, Papua New Guinea, or how the millions of poor people who grow coffee around the world have been adversely affected by neoliberalization. They most certainly do not seem to view consuming coffee as a political strategy meant to counter the ravages of neoliberal economic change. But they do overwhelmingly have the image of a poor farmer in their heads when they think about coffee. Their fantasy farmers are poor, brown, downtrodden, rural, and underdeveloped. These students had absolutely no sense of the sort of multi-classed coffee industry that exists in Papua New Guinea or the other nations where coffee is grown. They have internalized the virtual images of producers that they have been given, and the structural poverty afflicting many farmers becomes something to make a joke about.[14]

Today the constant cultural appropriation of alternative forms of music, clothing, and art by advertisers and marketers has created a cynicism on the part of some consumers. With the millennials discussed above we see a sarcasm about poverty that is troubling. Poverty adds value to coffee for many of the adults I interviewed in Hamburg, London, Sydney, and Brisbane, but the younger consumers seem to see poverty as something to be verbally played with and cast off as irrelevant.

Drinking coffee is a sensuous experience. When we consume coffee we smell it, taste it, and feel it as it flows down our throats. Although it is not necessarily connected to erotic desire, we can use Purnima Mankekar's notion of the "commodity affect" to theorize the sensorial experiences that are tied to coffee (Mankekar 2004, 408). For Mankekar, who is clearly drawing on the work of Wolfgang Haug, the "commodity affect" is "a range of emotions evoked and constructed by the desire for commodities" (408; see also Haug 1986). This range of emotions includes the desire to obtain the object, the desire to consume it, and the desire to display it, as well as the desire to look at or gaze upon objects even if they are not to be acquired. It also includes the sensual connection that people feel to others when they interact with the object. Using ethnographic examples from her work in India, Mankekar extends Haug's arguments about desire and erotics and shows that "commodities and their representations created a visual field that enabled forms of imaginative travel" (408). She argues that people use commodities and the stories told to sell them as vehicles for travel outside of themselves and as ways to imagine other lives and the lives of others. For Mankekar commodities create a sort of "third time space" (Marcus 1998).[15]

For Mankekar's Indians the "commodity affect" was always intertwined with erotics, yearning, and pleasure (Mankekar 2004, 409). The pleasure derived from consuming commodities (both literally and visually) was "bittersweet," because everyone knew that the images being conjured of life's possibilities through the commodities would never be realized (411).

University student from Papua New Guinea watching dancers in traditional costume at the yearly independence celebration in Goroka

The longing and pleasure derived from commodities allow people to travel imaginatively while at the same time reminding them of their own, often enviable, social and economic position. And these commodities are not only part of imaginative yearnings. Debra Curtis argues that the actual consumption of commodities, as it is related to these fantasies, "becomes some of the means by which individuals construct their own lives" (Curtis 2004, 105). These constructions of self include the self-fashioning of particular scripts that people tell themselves and others about themselves and others.

In the places where I conducted the research for this chapter, the commodity affect of the erotics of commodities are played out nicely, in just the way that Haug, Mankekar, and Curtis would expect them to be (Curtis 2004; Haug 1986; Mankekar 2004). However, there are two other kinds of affect at play. The first is what I would call the "therapeutics of commodities." Consumers feel dislocated from the global poverty and environmental change that they see regularly through the media, and they use commodities to seemingly connect to the people who they assume are bearing the brunt of poverty and environmental destruction. Consumers in

Germany, the UK, and Australia use this sort of buying to offset the guilt of their consumptive life style. It is a psychological corrective to modernity. It is emotional work. With this work consumers feel that they can both help to show the worth of the lifestyles they perceive as being lost to modernity, and contribute to the sustaining of those lifestyles. They also feel that they are connecting in some way to the plight of the global poor. Thus both guilt and poverty come to add value to particular kinds of coffee. They become grafted onto the coffee, overtaking use value, and creating a sort of skewed value of ethics.

The second kind of commodity affect is the phenomenon of "exotics through commodities." This is similar to the notion of travel that we see in Mankekar's work, since people use coffee to think about other places and fantasize about them. But it is different insofar as the sites of imaginative travel are always cast as exotic and full of a pristine nature and culture. In the mid-1990s a set of papers showed how "exotic" and "ethnic" images were used to sell commodities by adding value to them and how these images were incorporated into the individual identities of consumers (Crang 1996; May 1996; Smith 1996; Usherwood 1997). Leslie and Reimer refer to the images that are created in marketing as "geographic lores" (1999, 413). Coffee narratives create both geographic lores and fantasies of the primitive and authentic. They remove consumers from their day-to-day lives, if only for a few seconds, and allow them to fantasize about eleswheres and other ways of being-in-the-world. But these other ways of being-in-the-world are fantastic and have been produced by marketers specifically because they appeal to the consumers. They are hollow images, hollow geographies, and hollow ecologies.

8 | CONCLUSION

Coffee is a commodity that has, in its production, distribution, and consumption, shaped people's social and sensorial worlds for a very long time. In the Eastern Highlands of Papua New Guinea women carry 60-kilogram bags of green beans up and down the high mountains to airstrips. Over the years this bends their backs, flattens their feet, and crushes their ankles. Kobe, whom I called grandmother, once told me that coffee had made her old. She contrasted the strong body of her youth with the fragile body of her later years, and told me stories about walking all the way to Goroka with her parents to sell their coffee when she was a girl. Kobe's mother's brother's son, Ebule, whom I called grandfather, told me about the first coffee buyer to come to Maimafu when he was a boy, and how he had marveled at his shiny shoes. Later, he said, when he went to Goroka as a young man, he bought shiny shoes with money he had made from his own coffee sales. Kobe's and Ebule's life histories were interwoven with the growth of coffee production in the Gimi-speaking world. Today the commodity is the way that their children and grandchildren make a living.

Goroka came into being as a town and regional center in the 1940s and 1950s because of coffee. Today the whole city smells of drying and roasting coffee from the beginning of May until the end of November, and the smell literally permeates every aspect of Highland life. During the Goroka Show, the national cultural festival held yearly in September on Independence Day (and one of the few times when people still dress up in elaborate traditional costumes), several booths are dedicated to coffee and its production and marketing. Coffee growers from across the Highlands come to watch the show and enjoy the costumes and dancing. Against a backdrop of head-dresses, feathers, drumming, and spears, they discuss agricultural techniques and changes in the industry with factory owners, exporters, and visiting importers.

The contemporary mix of Papua New Guineans and expatriates who make up the coffee industry in Goroka today are the descendants of the women and men who built the town in the 1940s and 1950s. Their lives and bodies have also been made by coffee. The women who sort coffee at the factories in Goroka have hands that are soft to the touch, unlike other hard-working Highlands women, because of the oils from the beans that they meticulously check for defects. The men who carry coffee from planes to trucks to factories have hard bodies that are, by the time they are old, exhausted from labor. The men who work in the coffee industry as machinists, mechanics, security guards, and drivers, and the women who work as secretaries, cleaners, and receptionists, put aside the ritual and social business of their families and communities during the coffee season. They focus on their waged labor and its social relationships and not the social relations of village life.

In Lae, a city that largely revolves around the port which moves commodities like coffee out of the country, the people who work for shipping companies, bulking companies, and the harbors office change their daily work schedules beginning in May, when the huge trucks full of coffee come barreling down the Highlands Highway toward them. More ships come to the port, and the town picks up because of them. There are also more strangers in and around the port and town during the coffee season. This makes a place that is already difficult in terms of safety and security even more difficult.

At the port in Hamburg that same smell as in Goroka travels on the wind and whips around the old buildings, mingling with the smells of fuel and smoke from the port. There stevedores from all over the world have bent backs that they got from the lifting and machinery work of moving coffee and other commodities on and off ships. Coffee merchants work year-round, but their home lives suffer during the months when enormous amounts of coffee come to them from numerous "origin countries" simultaneously.

In coffee shops all over the world, the scent of roasting beans wafts around wood-paneled walls and glass and steel architecture, and out into streets, avenues, and boulevards. People pop into shops for a quick espresso or leisurely cappuccino, or to spend the afternoon drinking coffee, talking to friends, and working on their computers. They find what some coffee shop owners call "third spaces" in these shops. These are places where life happens outside the home or office.

In the preceding chapters I have tried to ethnographically represent some of the social lives and relations of coffee from and in Papua New Guinea. I have tried to pump life into the flat view of the industry that is produced by marketers when they make virtual producers and virtual consumers and use them to populate a false narrative of political ecology. The social world of Papua New Guinean coffee is messy and thick and complex. It is, in a word, rich. That richness is hollowed out and made flat and empty by third-party certification and marketing strategies that rely on images of primitivity and poverty to create value.

Certification

Certification is a growing audit culture that at first appears as though it can be all things to all people.[1] First and foremost, it acts as a way of getting a market share by means of storytelling that is meant to add value to the commodity. From the point of view of activists, it is viewed as a way to do a good thing for people and the environment, and from the point of view of marketers, roasters, and exporters it is a way to make more money. At one seminar at the conference of the Specialty Coffee Association that I discussed in chapter 2, an advocate of certification and a key player in the growth of the market said, "Consumers and companies, through their purchasing decisions, can make a difference in the way that coffee is farmed. For companies, working toward certification educates and empowers producers—being a part of this process gives us an edge over our competition." During a seminar on the certification "movement" various certifying bodies (Organic, Bird-Friendly, Fair Trade, Rainforest Alliance, and Utz Kaphe) made various arguments that can be summed up in terms of alleged farmer benefit, community benefit, and brand benefit.

Farms and farmers are assumed to enjoy "improved market access," "increased efficiency," "reduced dependency on expensive chemicals," "increased productivity," and "improved worker satisfaction and retention rates, lower turnover, more reliable labor pool," and they are thought to become "more educated about their businesses." Communities are assumed to benefit through "increased environmental awareness," "heightened education about how to run farms like businesses," "community clean up," "return of seasonal labor yearly," and "pride in business as a community endeavor." Coffee companies or "brands" benefit from "reduced risks from health and labor issues," "reduced criticism from advocacy groups," "increased compliance with and surpassing of pending government regulations," "a competitive advantage as more consumers seek out sustainable produced products," and "heightened positions in terms of corporate responsibility." The seminar leader ended with the following statement: "I've seen the heartfelt enthusiasm about certification and the great pride across the faces of these certified farmers. They want to produce a good product, and this process of certification allows for a better, more stable, uniform, and predictable product and reduced costs to your brand. The coffee also contributes to a sustainable future. Everyone wins." Over the course of the meeting of the Specialty Coffee Association it became clear that the discussion of "sustainability" was as much about sustaining a market for the coffee as it was about social, cultural, or biological sustainability. This is the case with most environmentally focused components of neoliberal economics (West 2006; West and Carrier 2004).

In their attempt to "combat the injustices of global capitalism by promoting the principles of democratic organization; no child labor; recognized trade unions for workers; and environmental sustainability" (Fridell 2003, 3), third-party regulatory systems export liberal morality and assume that coffee producers' ethics are the same as "ours"(Carrier 2010). While some scholars argue that certification "represents the founding of a nascent international moral economy which unites producers and consumers to demand greater social and ecological justice" (Fridell 2003, 3) and that the goal of the fair-trade movement specifically is the forging of a long-term social relationship between growers, sellers, and consumers, the only "moral economy" forged is one derived from liberal social ideology and driven by a neoliberal economic agenda (see Hughes 2001b).

Some sympathetic scholars and activists cast certification processes in opposition to what they see as the larger "unfair" global coffee economy— an economy that they characterize as driven by the Green Revolution use of chemical inputs, decline in forests and shade trees in coffee-growing areas, exploitation of the laboring poor, and a variety of negative ecological and social effects. This characterization of the wider industry is repeated over and over again in both coffee-related media and scholarly papers. The narrative that seemingly emerges from this is a political ecology narrative (Bryant and Goodman 2004). But it is an empty political ecology, one that has been sanitized to make it into a commodity.

In chapter 1 I argued that political ecology is a sophisticated analysis of accumulation by dispossession that takes into account semiotics, governmentality, and the state when asking questions about environmental change and uneven development. Marx saw the privatization of labor, land, and natural resources as the pivotal point in primitive accumulation, and David Harvey argues that privatization, financialization, the management and manipulation of crises, and state redistributions guide neoliberal accumulation by dispossession today. Harvey, drawing heavily on his student Neil Smith, connects accumulation by dispossession to uneven geographic development: "Access to cheaper inputs is, therefore, just as important as access to widening markets in keeping profitable opportunities open. The implication is that non-capitalist territories should be forced open not only to trade (which could be helpful) but also to permit capital to invest in profitable ventures using cheaper labour power, raw materials, low-cost land, and the like. The general thrust of any capitalist logic of power is not that territories should be held back from capitalist development, but that they should be continuously opened up" (Harvey 2005, 139). Neoliberalization has reopened the globe to accumulation by dispossession through deregulation and structural adjustment programs. Therefore capitalist accumulation by dispossession as a neoliberal strategy allows capital to address and stabilize the ever-present threat of over-accumulation, since accumulation by dispossession makes land, labor, and natural resources less expensive and allows more profit (Harvey 2005). This process of accumulation takes from people situated in one geographical area and gives to people situated in a different one, thereby producing both wealth and capital (for capitalists) and poverty and environmental degradation (for workers). The very process that gave rise to third-party certification is the object of the real study of political ecology, and the real narrative of political ecology is one whereby we cannot use capitalism to fix the problems of accumulation by dispossession and uneven development, because capitalism must give rise to these states of the world in order to thrive and grow.

While many argue that certification is a challenge to the imperatives of the market and thereby a challenge to capitalism as usual, in reality it is the ultimate in contemporary capitalism, because it puts the burden of social and political structural change on the backs of individuals—both consumers, who are expected to "change the world" through their buying habits, and producers, who are expected to join collectives that donate a portion of their income to infrastructure projects that in the past would have been paid for by states (e.g., roads, sewers, schools, parks, and hospitals).

Today, each form of certification meets a particular market niche, and the multiple forms of certification do not compete with each other.[2] This transition—from certification as something that stood in for the decline of the international coffee agreement to a form of branding that meets certain niche markets created by coffee marketers in the first place (see Roseberry 1996)—was predicted by Renard (1999, 490). With these niche markets ideas about the "quality" of the coffee, the "authenticity" of the origins, the ecological conditions in which the coffee was grown, and the circumstances of the growers emerge as key to the marketing of the beans (Renard 1999, 490). And yet many of the important figures in the circulation of coffee are cast aside as "middlemen." In fact, the majority of people in the industry within Papua New Guinea, aside from the rural producers, are considered "middlemen."

The business model behind certified coffee is based on an assumption that western consumers will increase what they are willing to spend on coffee if that coffee provides a direct connection to individual producers. To this end, coffee businesses that move certified coffees spend considerable time and resources to tell (and create) stories about individual producers to accompany the coffee being sold. Like westerners urged through charitable appeals to "adopt" a child in Africa or Latin America, coffee consumers are encouraged to travel along with the coffee company as it introduces them to the impoverished coffee growers being aided by their largess, benefiting because the consumers are willing to spend a few extra cents a day on coffee. In this story, however, the faux social connection that end-use consumers are supposed to develop with those who grow their coffee come at the expense of the real social relationships that exist between coffee growers, buyers, exporters, importers, and roasters.

In the certification narrative all of the so-called middlemen are painted as villains whose presence not only obscures consumers' direct relationship to the grower but is the source of the growers' poverty and exploitation. This demonizing of the middlemen allows inhabitants of the global North to imagine that they can end poverty in the global South with a minimum of pain, since it is not they but the middlemen who are the source of massive economic inequality. Organic certification promises to help save endangered species and ecosystems without requiring consumers in the global North to acknowledge the decades of overconsumption for which they are responsible or to radically alter their way of life.

From the perspective of Gimi involved in growing coffee, the exchange relationships they have with the coffee buyers who come to their village, and the people working in the business in Goroka, Lae, Hamburg, Sydney, and London, are important social relationships that have developed over time and through numerous transactions. These relationships are seen as expanding the growers' social networks and have been productively drawn upon to expand the social world that they feel they inhabit. Even among many of the expatriates in the coffee industry in Papua New Guinea there is a recognition that the business relationships of the coffee business are accompanied by social obligations. These social networks and relationships are reproduced throughout the coffee industry in the Highlands among the numerous people employed in the industry. Given that these relationships represent one of the most successful and sustained examples of how Papua New Guineans have been able to obtain wealth for important economic and social needs without radically altering existing social and cultural practices, the tendency to paint people in the industry as exploitative middlemen is as dangerous as it is inaccurate.

In addition, all certified coffees compete directly with "unfair" coffees—the ones grown by the poorest of the poor, the people who do not have access to certification. While the certification movement portrays itself as competing against "big coffee" and multinational corporations, in reality it competes with non-certified coffees and the people who grow them. Even advocates of fair trade see this: "The very survival of fair trade depends on the abilities of fair traders to steal market shares from traditional producers by winning consumer loyalties" (Fridell 2003, 4).

Certification also engenders a postmodern form of production that is born from a post-Fordist global market but recreates the uniformity of Fordism. This is a new postmodern uniformity. Coffee production has become restandardized by certification insofar as production in Papua New Guinea must mirror production in other parts of the world if the coffee there is to be certified. This standardization is discursively produced by marketers and by people working in certification as benefiting farmers, and while it might mean a little more money for farmers, it most certainly means a more standard and thus more salable product. Standardization in production makes the coffee more uniform and uniformity makes the coffee more easily commensurable with all other world coffee, and this is what marketers desire. Standardization is an attempt to create a culture-free agriculture, and the things that make production in many parts of the world unique and difficult for western buyers to grapple with or understand are done away with through certification and "standards."

Images and Value

Neoliberalism fetishizes the market by turning it into something that seems to work on its own apart from human social practices. Since the decline of the ICO the argument has been that if left alone and unregulated the market will produce consumer and producer behaviors that bring about environmental stability and social equity. It will do this by re-embedding the economic choice of what coffee one buys in social relations that enable consumers and producers to understand each other and form connections across vast physical distances and economic disparities. Consumers are meant to understand producers and thus make ecologically and socially progressive buying decisions. But all of this is built on a set of fictions. The consumers and producers in this story are all made up—they are produced, crafted, and constructed by the likes of Mr. Nebraska and the purveyors of Dean's Beans (whom we met in chapter 2). But these fantasy figures that populate the specialty coffee media and marketing world are not simply benign images used to sell coffee; they are careful productions that have material consequences.

The consumers fashioned by Mr. Nebraska's seminar, the producers fashioned by Dean's Beans blog, the Papua New Guineans who make up the vast coffee industry in their country, and the consumers in Brisbane, Hamburg, London, New York, and Sydney seem to have little in common. But they are all brought together as individuals by the contemporary neoliberal coffee market. They are targeted as individuals because that is what neoliberalization does; it focuses on individual producers and consumers as the loci of intervention and disallows regulation and intervention at other scales. All marketed forms of "ethical consumption" make individuals seem and feel responsible for both the conditions of production and the ecological and social justice consequences of these conditions of production. Based on this logic, governments, regulatory bodies, and the organizations behind the forced structural adjustment programs of the 1980s—programs that resulted in drastic economic changes, to the disadvantage of coffee farmers worldwide—are all let off the hook, freed of responsibility for the problems, contradictions, and negative effects inherent in the global capitalist system and particularly apparent today in the wake of neoliberalization.

In an essay that clearly shows the contradictory nature of labels and certifications as both a form of neoliberalization and a corrective to neoliberalization, Julie Guthman argues that "neoliberal valuation rests on the presumption that the market will assign high prices to scarce resources" (Guthman 2007, 470). Organic, fair-trade, and origin labeling and certification supposedly add value to coffee because they guarantee that in an unfair world the product in question was produced in socially and ecologically sustainable ways. Value seemingly accrues to the coffee because the monitoring systems guarantee sustainable production, and sustainable production is scarce. The entire system of labeling is built on the assumption that most coffee production is unethical and unsustainable but that specialty coffees, because of certification and labeling, are not. Here sustainable production, by which I mean production in socially and environmentally equitable conditions, is the scarce resource.

The stories told about coffee production by neoliberal marketing campaigns bring that scarce resource to the consumers. They package and market fair labor as something unique and scarce. These stories also do something else: they bundle together a set of images of Papua New Guinea as remote, biodiverse, primitive, and impoverished, and market them as scarce. They use poverty, which was itself aggravated by the processes of neoliberalism, to create a scarce resource that is meant to add value to the coffee. Poverty, as a necessary prerequisite to specialty coffee, becomes unique and valued in this skewed system of value creation. Poverty is disembedded from its structural causes and conflated with primitivism.

Socially and environmentally equitable conditions of production, poverty, and primitivity are then the scarce resources that add value to specialty coffees. Two issues emerge. First, there is an inherent tension between equitable conditions of production and poverty: if we increase one, the other should decrease. With truly equitable production, poverty will be ameliorated, and the value that poverty adds to the coffees will cease to exist. It therefore behooves companies like Dean's Beans to articulate poverty even when that poverty may not be the entire story, as with the coffee industry in Papua New Guinea. Certainly people who grow coffee in Papua New Guinea are poor by global economic measures, but they own their own land and thereby the means of production. Because of this they are in a structural position radically different from that of people in many other parts of the world. Although they have been pushed into a kind of new remoteness by neoliberalization, they have not suffered the worst of these reforms in terms of alienation from their land. In addition, the narratives that stereotype the entire coffee industry in Papua New Guinea in terms of poverty erase the lives of the thousands of people who work in middle-class jobs in the industry. By articulating coffee production through a fantasy vision of Papua New Guinea, neoliberal marketing misrepresents those whom it purports to help.

The second issue is that a condition in which fair labor and good environmental standards have become scarce and thereby valued should be unacceptable to people with truly progressive politics. Otherwise everyone else, people without access to sustainable systems of production, is written off as undeserving of our political attention. We must remember that all production should be made equitable, not just production that can add exchange value when marketed to a particular set of consumers. In other words, consumers are asked to make, through their economic choices, "regulatory decisions about ecological and public health risk, working conditions, and remuneration, and even what sort of producers of what commodities should be favored in the world market" (Guthman 2007, 472). They are made to feel that this is all they can do to redress inequality and that they are allowed to forget about all the people who do not have access to certification and labeling. The majority of the impoverished coffee farmers on the planet become someone else's problem and are disconnected from the lives of consumers. Consumers are meant to feel connected to the poor people who produce coffee sustainably, and are allowed to turn their backs on the much larger world of people who do not.

Mass consumer consumption is predicated on the creation of desires, and the development of exchange value by unrealistic hope that a given good will fill some need. This perceived value does not stem from anything inherent in the sensual nature of the commodity itself but from projections created by advertising, marketing, and consumer culture. Thus consumers are used to purchasing goods whose qualities, features, or usefulness do not meet expectations. What is innovative about fair-trade marketing is that the promised value (fair production practices and good environmental standards) is external to the commodity and that the consumer has no way of knowing whether this value has been received or not—even after the product has been purchased and consumed—other than by reference to the very marketing narratives that promised satisfaction in the first place.

During his presentation Mr. Nebraska expressed the belief that a generation's consumer choices were formed by its history and its social and political background. Whether that is true or not, the way that consumer culture shapes political and social choices and actions is far more dangerous. In her book *A Consumer's Republic*, Lizabeth Cohen showed that the atomized nature of consumer culture and the creation of consumer identities ultimately comes to supplant people's identities as political actors (Cohen 2003). In the case of fair-trade marketing this is the very point. The danger of fair-trade marketing is that people's desire for greater social justice is co-opted and satisfied by a narrative like the one presented by Dean's Beans. Because the professed value of fair-trade products is by definition outside the commodity itself, the consumer is in no position to learn to what extent the narrative departs from the real lives of the coffee producers.

The stories encouraged by Mr. Nebraska and told by coffee companies that market certified coffees are a new form of product endorsement. Primitive poverty adds value to specialty coffee, as does sustainable production. Poor, primitive people, instead of famous, wealthy people, increase this value again with their endorsement. In the past people bought a box of cereal with Michael Jordan on the front because they wanted to "be like Mike"—talented, successful, and rich. The "endorsement" from the primitive validates a set of relationships as good, ethical, and fair. If Jordan's endorsement sells by creating a desire to be better than one really is, the endorsement from the primitive sells by telling consumers that they are good just as they are, and that through their consumption choices they have an ethical and meaningful relationship with the economic have-nots of the world.

The great trick of specialty coffee marketing by distributors is that it highlights the global economic inequality created by the capitalist system from which they and their customers benefit, while at the same time cabining the extent to which consumers should be concerned about such injustices. (For example, "bad exploitative capitalism only gave people pennies for their backbreaking labor, but now, thanks to certification, those people get four times as many pennies for their backbreaking labor.") The production of the primitive as so backward and impoverished that even a pittance would effect a vast improvement allows marketers and consumers to absolve themselves (and capitalism as a whole) at no significant cost. If one accepts the narratives about how awful things used to be, then even the insignificant bonus of third-party certified coffees (the specialty coffees) is seen as a disproportionately good deal.

The depiction of Papua New Guinean coffee producers as primitive performs a double movement. On the one hand, it lowers expectations of what producers are entitled to receive, even under a "fair trade." Since they are constantly portrayed as so poor and primitive, it seems that any money they make is a vast improvement over their prior-to-capital lives. More importantly, the depiction reconfigures the political and economic disparity between third-world producers and first-world consumers in the world capitalist system as a cultural difference, perhaps even a biological difference. It naturalizes the disparities of wealth not by denying them but by valorizing them. The political and economic disparities are hidden, but like Poe's purloined letter, they are hidden in plain sight.

That the "millennial" students we met in chapter 7 do not really think about the plight of the have-nots, and that they take for granted that coffee is produced by people at the very bottom of the economic scale, shows what a small impact certification is having on people's consciousness about the exploitative nature of coffee production (in the sense that producers are alienated from almost all of the value they produce). On the other hand, to the extent that people are concerned about this inequality, they are told that certification helps to alleviate some of the worst effects of this exploitation, even if consumers are not quite sure how. This supposed embedding of the political and social into capitalist consumption may make for a good cup of coffee, but it makes for lukewarm political action. Ironically, the message of the endorsement of the primitive is not to create a desire among nascent socially conscientious consumers to demand greater social justice but to be satisfied in the knowledge that they have done their part to improve the world. This maneuver only works because the image of the primitive does what it always does: it tells us that the Other is so different from us that receiving a quadrupling of our pennies is "fair" compensation for hundreds of hours of backbreaking labor. Obviously consumers would not do similar work for that amount of money, but the producers are different, and they should be happy with what they get because the market has done the best it can.

Compressions of Time and Space

In the June 2010 issue of *Vogue* the magazine's resident food critic, Jeffrey Steingarten, tells his readers that "the time has come to rethink coffee" (Steingarten 2010, 177). On his "quest for the perfect cup," Steingarten has traveled down the road of coffee consumption numerous times (see Steingarten 1996, 2002). He tells us that today the key to the perfect cup of coffee is an understanding of how coffee is brewed (the process by which coffeemakers of all kinds move water through and around ground coffee) and of where the coffee beans come from ("not which geographic region or country but which hillside"; Steingarten 2010, 177). However, in the entirety of the article Steingarten focuses on brewing methods and machines, and never mentions origins again. Similarly, the 9–15 December issue of *Time Out New York* has "The City's Best Coffee" as its cover story (Rothman 2010, 10–14). The story focuses entirely on processes of brewing as "rituals" that are varied, complicated, and create the taste and value in a cup of coffee. These processes require particular forms of equipment like a siphon, an aeropress, or a cold brew extraction chamber. Third-party certification and origin are not mentioned in terms of coffee quality at all. It seems that coffee, and its connoisseurship, is transforming right before our eyes. While the late 1990s and 2000s may have been focused on origins and certification as a way to add value to coffee, with the attendant fantasy images of growers and their lives attached to the beans as a form of value adding, it seems that the next decade will be the decade of coffee accoutrements.

Throughout this book I have shown the process by which fantasies about culture and nature get grafted onto coffee beans and people's understandings of the lives of smallholder producers in Papua New Guinea. I have shown how and why these fantasies are created and how and why people create them. I have also shown how and why the images are false. I have shown that people know they are producing these images, that they know why they are producing them, and that they know these images do not reflect reality. People do not, however, understand what these images do in the long term. In the much-cited words of Foucault: "People know what they do; frequently they know why they do what they do; but what they don't know is what what they do does" (Dreyfus and Rabinow 1982, 187).

In chapter 1 I argued that images and fantasies, when grafted onto commodities, are extraordinarily powerful. The images come to stand in for reality and then become reality. The images transform the world in ways that attempt to make the real conform to the image (Carrier and Miller 1998). I also argued that once these images, or signs, are attached to commodities, they become part of the system by which material objects are turned over and moved into and out of fashion at an astounding velocity. Contemporary capitalism has drastically reduced the turnover time for commodities and fashions (Harvey 1989, 156). By this logic, Papua New Guinea, having been transformed into a brand through single-origin marketing, may soon be abandoned because of the rapid turnover of meanings that is part and parcel of contemporary capitalism.

The growth of fair-trade, organic, and other seemingly socially responsible certifications can be read as a process of deriving sign-value within a system of advertise-differentiation fixation. These labels circulate and allow people to experience things and images vicariously. Because in the contemporary world we have access to things and images from the entire globe, "it is now possible to experience the world's geography vicariously, as a simulacrum. The interweaving of simulacra in daily life brings together different worlds (of commodities) in the same space and time. But it does so in such a way as to conceal almost perfectly any trace of origin, of the labour processes that produced them, or of the social relations implicated in their production" (Harvey 1989, 300).

It is important to remember the double nature of the commodity fetish when thinking through this literature with regard to coffee. First, the commodity fetish seems to have value because of some quality inherent to it. In reality that value is derived from the labor that went into it—we just forget about the people who made the commodity. Second, we forget that the value of the commodity fetish also derives from its place in a hierarchy of value, according to which one commodity is measured against another commodity, and things are seen as equivalent or not. And we forget that it is people that make that hierarchy of value—we decide that one pound of coffee from Starbucks is more valuable than one pound of coffee from the corner deli, and we physically add the labor that does this work through advertising (Willis 1991) and consumption (Callon, Méadel, and Rabeharisoa 2002). We forget about the work that goes into producing the hierarchy of value. In the contemporary commodity fetish, labor is abstracted in these two ways through the forgetting about production at both the material and ideological-sign levels and through the forgetting about the labor that goes into creating hierarchies of value. This dual nature of the commodity fetish is similar to Georg Lukács's notion of the objective and subjective nature of the commodity fetish (Lukács 1971, 85–87).

Coffee has come to hold particular meanings that are arbitrary, but as a sign, coffee signifies something not inseparable from the object itself. Advertising makes and remakes the connections between signifiers and the signified and the conventions that allow us to connect them. One of the contradictions of seemingly "political" consumption is that the same force that drives it, namely advertising, is a main contributor to the force driving liberalism and individualism (Carrier 2010). One of the goals of early advertising was to make clear that homemade products paled in comparison to mass-produced products (Leach 1993). From the 1960s to the 1990s we were made to feel as if we could differentiate ourselves through products and consumption, that we could become individuals through our commodity choices (Miller 1997). Yet now, with the advertising that surrounds fair-trade, organic, and other seemingly socially and politically responsible forms of value adding, we are made to feel as if our consumption unites us with a larger community of sentiment. "Social conscience" has become no more than a socially acceptable and valorized meaning attached to commodity-objects (Baudrillard 1981, 148). Coffee is the commodity, poor workers living on the edge of the modern are the sign, and the two no longer exist alone but in a nonseparable form. A possible danger of the melding of images is that as coffee capitalists need new ways to differentiate their coffee from other coffee, the growers as sign-value will be forced into a sort of semiotic obsolescence in which they are no longer seen as adding value to the commodity. When this happens what happens to the real producers?

Susan Willis argues that the "throwaways of commodity consumption," the actual packaging of commodities, "may well offer the most fruitful way into the (commodity) culture as a whole" (Willis 1991, 3). The package attracts our attention, it alerts us to the content and use-value of the object it envelops, and it cues our sign-reading sensibility to the appearance of value that resides in the package. The package signals purity and security. We know—because it is packaged—that our commodity is clean and untainted. Packaging also "acts to separate the consumer from the realization of use value" and creates a sense of anticipation with regard to the commodity (3–7). After purchase, we wait to experience our safe and clean commodity. Our desire is met and fed by the aesthetic of waiting and anticipating the use-value, the bodily experience of having the object, while still desiring and waiting for it (5–7).

We anticipate the commodity's use-value: we think about how delicious our bottle of wine might be, and how the delicious wine will make dinner with our spouse more rich and lively; or we think about how nice we will look in our new jeans, and how looking good will lead to intriguing social interactions at a party. But somewhere deep down we know that the use-value will not fulfill our desire (Haug 1986). Indeed, it is no longer use-value that we desire, but rather the use-value as it is combined with the "appearance of value" (16–18). The appearance of value is the socially produced value that gives us the expectation of being valorized by the commodity will and made to be more than we really are. It is not the wine's use-value that we think will make our marriage better, or the use-value of our new jeans that we think will make going to parties easier, but rather the appearance of value that has come to be connected to the commodities.

Today use-value is never fully realized; the purchase will never meet the advertised promise of the commodity, and as soon as we have it our antici-pation and the pleasure that derives from it begin to decline (Willis 1991, 6). With coffee marketing, if the use-value is never fully realized then the marketing can become more and more elaborate. For example, in the 1980s we first saw single-origin marketing that tied the appearance of value to specific places and fantasies of worldly travel. Then the appearance of value was elaborated to include vague references to people who grew coffee, as in the television commercials for Colombian coffee that featured the fictional character Juan Valdez. Then the appearance was elaborated again to in-clude images of people growing and picking coffee. Then we saw the stories of growers and pickers hyper-elaborated, to the point where they came to confer the appearance of value to certified coffees. Today we see growers, origins, and certification superseded, as Jeffrey Steingarten and Jordana Rothman tell us that the key to a good cup of coffee is the object used to brew or produce it (Rothman 2010; Steingarten 2010).

Neoliberalization, Poverty, and the Problem of Culture
This all sets the stage for several troubling things. First, when fantasy im-ages of "primitive" "natives" imbued with "authentic" "culture" are melded with fantasy images of "natives" trapped in an overly simplistic version of "poverty," the two sets of images become fused in the global imaginary. "Indigenousness," "native" status, and "culture" thus become linked in peo-

ple's minds as the root of poverty and come to be seen as a justification for accumulation by dispossession. People seem too primitive to manage their own lands and therefore need state agents and others to do it for them. Throughout this book I have shown that some contemporary neoliberal marketers create this dual image of Papua New Guinea through the stories they tell about its coffee. With their marketing they portray Papua New Guineans as both primitive, and therefore possessing authentic culture, and impoverished. By conflating primitivity and poverty, these marketers make it seem as if poverty is inherent in the people because of their primitivity and not the result of structural inequality and global capital.

A key part of my argument about the image of the impoverished primitive is that it allows people to disregard the structural causes of poverty in Papua New Guinea and places like it. The meaning of "structural causes" lies in the difference between a Durkheimian view of poverty (poverty is a mistake made by people and a problem of society born of individuals: people don't work hard enough and because of that they are poor) and a Marxist view of poverty (poverty is a result of a capitalist system that causes unemployment and dispossession). This erasure of structural causes is intimately connected to dispossession by accumulation and uneven development.

When people are allowed or even encouraged to forget that the inequality we see today has structural causes, and attribute poverty to some problem inherent in a particular "culture," they open the door to arguments that blame "culture" for poverty and propose to radically alter people's lives so that they can achieve "development." For example, the neoliberal economists Helen Hughes and Francis Fukuyama have both argued that the lack of economic development in Papua New Guinea today results from culture and social practice (see Fukuyama 2007; Gosarevski, Hughes, and Windybank 2004). Their argument goes like this: Papua New Guinea is rich in natural resources, so it should, by extension, have a rich population. Sadly, however, "the problem is that the country's resources are inefficiently exploited and badly distributed, as a result of a highly dysfunctional political system" (Fukuyama 2007, 2). This is the result of a "lack of fit" between formal, European-derived, institutions and the "underlying society" or culture (3, 9). Culture, as a barrier to economic development, is exemplified by indigenous land ownership or tenure, which is enshrined in the country's constitution. Gosarevski, Hughes, and Windybank argue that "the security provided by communal land ownership in subsistence agriculture has been taken from its historical context to justify the barriers it creates to savings, investment, and productivity" (Gosarevski, Hughes, and Windybank 2004, 136). This process can be corrected by creating individual property rights which will allow suppressed entrepreneurs to develop their own land (141). The result will be fewer people with their own land but more jobs, income, and a higher productivity of export commodities.

Culture is also exemplified by the Big Man system, which according to Gosarevski, Hughes, and Windybank is outdated and perverted, leads to corruption, laziness, and mismanagement, and should be replaced with the rule of law and a system of individual rights. Then "harder working men and women will become wealthier than others" and will "be free to save without having the product of their labor stolen by those who do not want to work but are happy to rely on others for food and cash" (136). Additionally, "the extreme ethnolinguistic fragmentation" in Papua New Guinea "is obviously the root cause of the failure to generate strong collective action at a national level" (Fukuyama 2007, 9). However, "the acid of modernization that has dissolved traditional social structures and driven millions of people from countryside to cities or abroad in much of Latin America and Africa is much less evident in PNG" (9). Papua New Guinea, it would seem, is on the cusp of development, with the native holding one foot in the past and one in the future, and it is simply the culture that is keeping the native in poverty.

This native is the same native in the chronotopic fantasies that I discussed in chapter 2, and the mythic chronotope—that fantasy about the relationship between primitive and civilized people that is born in primitivist travel narratives, that endures in contemporary writing about Papua New Guinea, and that is presented to consumers in coffee marketing— drives the arguments that these economists make. However, it is not simply that they make these arguments. It is that they have an effect on the world. Their arguments precipitate a particular kind of agency, an agency that is built on chronotopic fantasy.

The end of this part of the story is this: neoliberalization created a market climate in which traders and others had to begin to infuse coffee from Papua New Guinea with fantasy images of poverty and cultural primitivity so that they could compete in the global coffee market, and thus provide jobs and income for thousands of people in Papua New Guinea. These images are now being used to justify the further neoliberalization of Papua New Guinea, amid racist claims that the global capitalist system has been unable to provide for people equitably only because the culture of Papua New Guinea is aberrant.

A final thing troubles me about the images attached to coffee from Papua New Guinea and thus Papua New Guineans. Today fantasy natives sell coffee, but what happens when they are no longer fashionable? What happens when consumers get tired of hearing about people from the global South? What happens when most coffee consumers, like the millennials discussed in chapter 7, become flippant and cynical about the very real plight of poor farmers across the planet? I do not know how we can work toward global social and environmental equity when people come to see the lives of my friends in Papua New Guinea as being out of fashion. By using images of growers to sell coffee beans in the contemporary, speeded-up world of capital, neoliberal marketing sets the stage for the moment when the lives of poor people across the planet become unfashionable and thereby unthinkable. Where will we be then?

NOTES

Chapter 1: The World of Coffee from Papua New Guinea

1. An international border bisects New Guinea, the third-largest island in the world. The western half of the island is a colony of Indonesia known as West Papua. The eastern half of the island is the nation-state of Papua New Guinea. In this book New Guinea refers to the island as a whole and Papua New Guinea to only the eastern half of the island, the independent nation-state of Papua New Guinea. The island of New Guinea is located in Oceania, a region which includes American Samoa, the Cook Islands, the Federated States of Micronesia, Fiji, Hawai'i, New Zealand, Norfolk Island, Papua New Guinea, Pitcairn Island, Rapa Nui, Samoa, the Solomon Islands, Tokelau, Tonga, Tuvalu, Vanuatu, and Wallis and Futuna, and which has traditionally been divided into three subregions: Melanesia, Micronesia, and Polynesia. These subregions are made up of hundreds of islands and include numerous nations, states, and protectorates. New Guinea is in Melanesia.

2. In studying commodity production, distribution, and consumption, contemporary readers often seem to desire narratives with good guys and bad guys. As with economic development (Mosse 2005) and environmental conservation (West 2006), many people want easy answers to complex questions. Much of the often-read popular literature on coffee provides these good and bad actors and easy answers. Careful ethnography shows that people and their roles in the trade of any global commodity are complicated and messy and deserve more nuanced analysis (Tsing 2004).

3. There is evidence that coffee seeds were exported for cultivation from Ethiopia to Yemen as early as 800 BCE (see Um 2009), and many

scholars see coffee as one of the most important global commodities (Paige 1997; Roseberry 1996; Topik and Wells 1998).

4. *Coffea robusta* and *Coffea arabica* make up the majority of the world's coffee crop, but two other species are grown on a small scale: *Coffea liberica* and *Coffea dewevrei*.

5. See http://www.ico.org/mission.asp for up-to-date coffee production statistics.

6. *Coffea arabica* is self-pollinating while *Coffea robusta* depends on cross-pollination.

7. What most of us see when we buy coffee is a roasted coffee bean. That bean begins its life as a coffee cherry—a bright red, berry-like fruit consisting of a pulpy external coating or skin (the exocarp) that covers a fruit (the mesocarp) containing two seeds. The seeds are enveloped in a sticky layer of parenchyma that protects them, along with a thin, waxy cover (the endocarp) and an even thinner membrane (the silver skin or spermoderm). These seeds are what become "coffee beans."

8. Coffee, like tea and many spices, is a unique commodity in that it is agriculturally produced but has no nutritional value. It contains no fat, no sugar, no cholesterol, no carbohydrates, no sodium, and no protein—only nutritionally inconsequential traces of thiamin, niacin, folate, phosphorus, magnesium, and manganese. Coffee is, however, full of caffeine—an alkaloid (an organic compound found in many plants and fungi) that has stimulant and diuretic properties (aside from caffeine, other popular alkaloids include nicotine and cocaine; more useful ones include morphine and quinine). The amount of caffeine found in one 6-ounce cup of coffee, about 100 milligrams, is enough to stimulate the human brain's cortex to educe feelings of alertness, heightened coordination, and increased concentration. Coffee can also cause nervousness, irregular heartbeat, stomach upset, headaches, and trembling. It has been tied to the growth of benign cysts in women's breasts, heart disease, and some birth defects as well as pancreatic, ovarian, kidney, and bladder cancers. Coffee stimulates adrenal glands and slows the brain's absorption of adenosine, a chemical that evokes a feeling of calmness. It is a drug (Edwards 1992; Haertzen, Kocher, and Miyasato 1983), though a legal one that most people consider a pleasant addition to their daily routine. Coffee is a luxury commodity— no one needs to ingest it for sustenance.

9. Thanks to Molly Doane for our collaborations around coffee and circulation. Our discussions gave rise to my understanding of the industry today as a post-Fordist industry.

10. In Papua New Guinea both types of commercially significant coffee (*Coffea arabica* and *Coffea robusta*) are grown, though the majority of the crop is Arabica. Arabica grows best at altitudes over 1,000 meters (but can be grown effectively anywhere between 700 meters and 2,050 meters), has a stronger, fuller flavor than other species, and accounts for about 75 percent of the world's coffee. Robusta is grown in low altitudes, below 600 meters. The beans are smaller, with a higher water content and more caffeine than arabica beans.

11. All direct quotations, unless otherwise noted, are from ethnographic interviews

and participant observation that I carried out between 1997 and 2010 in Papua New Guinea, Australia, England, Germany, and the United States.

12. Raggiana Birds of Paradise are stunning large birds. The male is about 34 centimeters long, with orange-maroon-brown feathers on its body, a bright yellow crown, and a deep, almost iridescent green throat. The adult male has a yellow band on his throat, a pair of long, black tail wires, and a set of ornamental plumes on the back end that are displayed to females during mating. These plumes are long, flowing, and deep red. Although some members of the family Birds of Paradise (*Paradisaeidae*) are found in Indonesia, northeastern Australia, and New Guinea, Raggiana Birds of Paradise are found only on the island of New Guinea. These birds are iconic and meaning-filled animals (Swadling 1996; see also Kirsch 2006; West 2006).

13. "Single-origin" coffee is coffee with a single geographical origin. Historically most coffee marketed in the Europe, the United States, Australia, and Japan was blended coffee, made up of beans with multiple geographical origins. The term "single-origin" can indicate a national origin (e.g., New Guinea coffee) or a specific plantation or farm origin (e.g., Perosa roast).

14. The best way to access the work done by the Summer Institute of Linguistics (SIL) is through its website, www.ethnologue.com (http://www.ethnologue.com/show _country.asp?name=PG).

15. Although explorers reached the island of New Guinea many years ago, in the 1930s gold prospectors walked across the Highlands and "found" a million people whom the colonial administration did not know existed. This discovery made the papers around the world and began to shape the global imagination of the island and its people (see Chinnery 1934).

16. See most recently the *New York Times* on 25 October 2010.

17. The best estimates for the number of people in Papua New Guinea who live in households where cash income is earned through coffee production are from the early to mid-1990s. That estimate is 1.7 million people, or about 53 percent of the country's rural population (Allen, Bourke, and McGregor 2009, 306). The numbers presented here are based on ethnographic interviews with members of the coffee industry and on numbers collected by coffee export companies, by colleagues working in agriculture in Papua New Guinea, and by the Coffee Industry Corporation of Papua New Guinea and presented in various reports and papers. Estimates of the number of households involved in the industry range from 270,000 to 397,000.

18. See Allen, Bourke, and McGregor (2009, 313), for a nice analysis of the relationship between the seasonality of coffee production and retail sales of other commodities in the Highlands.

19. Coffee production and its profits also link people in Papua New Guinea to other kinds of commodities. For example, New Zealand and Australian meat traders argue that one of the reasons that they initially targeted Papua New Guinea for

the export of the lamb and mutton scraps known locally as "lamb flaps" was the affluence in the Highlands from coffee production (Gewertz and Errington 2007, 499).

20. Papua New Guinea has a gross domestic product of about $5.3 billion per year, with about 38 percent of that from agriculture, including, in order of importance in 2005, coffee, cocoa, coconuts, palm oil, timber, tea, and vanilla. From 1990 to 1995 Papua New Guinea's rural villagers made about 200 million Kina per year from the sale of agricultural products. Arabica coffee provided 33 percent of all income from agriculture, with a return of about 47 Kina per person per year, while robust coffee provided about 1 percent of all agricultural income, with a return of about 9 Kina per person per year (Allen, Bourke, and McGregor 2009, 285).

21. From 1997 to 2004 coffee production made up the bulk of the labor-related income in and around Maimafu village, with a small amount of additional cash derived from working with a conservation organization within the bounds of the Crater Mountain Wildlife Management Area (West 2006). In 2004 men from Maimafu began mining for gold in alluvial gold mines to the northeast of Maimafu, and today these mines generate about half as much cash as the village's coffee production.

22. Estimates of the exact number of hectares under smallholder cultivation vary. One estimate is that in 1999 there were 70,000 hectares under cultivation, with 57,000 hectares worked by smallholders. However, based on average yield production data, others estimate that there are currently between 70,000 and 85,000 hectares cultivated by smallholders alone (Allen, Bourke, and McGregor 2009, 309).

23. Both hand-turned pulped coffee and hand-pulped coffee are almost always given a low grade. There are multiple systems for grading the quality of coffee, and all coffee beans everywhere in the world are given a grade based on shape, uniformity, size, color, horniness (the ability to be peeled with a knife, like a horn), smoothness, gloss, number of defective beans, foreign matter in the beans, and smell. There are flat beans, which came from a cherry, peaberries, from a cherry that had only one bean (thus the beans are not flat), and Maragogype beans, which are very large. Beans should be green to deep green in color; blue-green beans with a yellow tint are old. Beans are expected to be very hard and smooth, with a shiny glossy sheen. Finally, batches of beans should not contain stems, insects, stones, or bits of earth.

   In Papua New Guinea the grades are AA/A (usually plantation coffees that have big, uniform blue-green beans with few defects), X (usually from smaller plantations, with more defects), Y (smallholder-grown, with beans of mixed size, a green-grey color, and many defects), PSC X (smallholder-grown coffee that falls between X grade and Y grade), and finally T (the rest of the coffee). This system of grading affects the price of coffee; we will return to it in chapter 2.

24. The coffee brought to Goroka from Maimafu usually has a high moisture content, and the weight loss upon drying can be over 30 percent. At times a taint develops when the coffee has been stored improperly or villagers have had to wait a long time for a plane to retrieve the coffee. It is only upon rare occasions that this coffee can

be included in fair trade or fair trade–organic blends because of the taint. More often than not this coffee is blended with other "Y" grade coffees.

25. Freight costs are calculated to include gas prices, operation costs, and profit for the church- and missionary-owned air companies that fly coffee out of rural villages.

26. Coffee bags hold approximately 60 kilograms of coffee each.

27. Gold, copper, and oil account for 77 percent of the total value of exports from Papua New Guinea, while agriculture exports account for about 17 percent (Allen, Bourke, and McGregor 2009, 292).

28. About 60 percent of the coffee goes to Germany, 20 percent to Australia, 6 percent to the United Kingdom, 5 percent to the United States, and 2 percent to New Zealand, with the rest going to other destinations.

29. CIC, a self-financing corporation, was formed in 1991 by the Coffee Industry Corporation (Statutory Powers and Functions) Act, which merged the Coffee Industry Board (the institution formed in 1964 to oversee the industry), the Coffee Research Institute (formed in 1982 to oversee research in the country), and the Coffee Development Agency (formed in 1987 to conduct agricultural extension). It was restructured in 2003 in an attempt to make it more cost-effective and efficient. Its creation was the result of lobbying by the large coffee export firms, who wanted to protect their share of the market in the face of the decline of the International Coffee Agreement (ICA) in 1989 and the general mood of privatization in the late 1980s and early 1990s (MacWilliam 1993).

30. People in the Eastern Highlands rarely know the anthropologically accepted name for their sociolinguistic group—e.g., Gimi, Fore, Siane, Bena Bena, or Alekano (Gahuka)—but "wontok" or "one language" is a form of identification and recognition.

31. Anthropologists are of course not the only scholars to theorize objects as commodities and their power in social production and reproduction (Bourdieu 1984; Fiske 1989; Hebdige 1979; Lichtenberg 1998; Simmel [1904] 1971; Slater 1997; Veblen [1899] 1958). But anthropology has contributed greatly to our understandings of how value (Crump 1981; Gell 1998; Keane 1997; Parry and Bloch 1989; Sahlins 1994; Weiner 1992), desire (Appadurai 1986; Campbell 1994; Douglas and Isherwood 1979; Friedman 1991; Kopytoff 1986), and objects (Gell 1998; Miller 1987; Munn 1971) are connected by production, circulation, and consumption.

Anthropologists have approached production and consumption practices ethnographically in Africa (Burke 1996; Comaroff and Comaroff 2000, 2002; Weiss 1996a); the Americas (Orlove 1997; Price 1986; Weismantel 1989; Wilk 1989, 1994, 1995); East Asia (Bestor 2004; Creighton 1998; Davis 2000; Gruber 1999; Tobin 1992; Yan 1997); South Asia (Cohn 1989; Gell 1986; Liechty 2003); and Oceania (Foster 1995, 2002, 2008; Gewertz and Errington 1999, 2010; Kahn 2000; Kaplan 2007). Scholars from anthropology, geography, and sociology have also approached consumption topically, with focuses on families and kinship (Belk 1993; Carrier 1993; Clarke 2001; Miller 1988), the social lives of producers and consumers (Burke 1996; Gewertz and Errington 1996, Ivy 1995; Miller 1997; Weiss 1996a; Wilk 1994), shopping or provisioning (Carrier 1994; Miller 1998; O'Dougherty 2002), globalization and marketing (Fine and Leopold 1993; Foster 1995; Miller 1998a), media and new media (Abu-Lughod 1995; Ginsburg, Abu-Lughod, and Larkin 2002; Miller and Slater 2000), and overconsumption and debt (Frank 1999; Manning 2000; O'Dougherty 2002; Schor 2000). The fields of consumption studies within the social sciences have also generated various theoretical approaches that have been exported to other areas of analysis (Appadurai 1986, 1990, 1996; Baudrillard 1981; Douglas and Isherwood 1979; Fine and Lepold 1993; Foster 2002; Friedman 1991; Kopytoff 1986; Miller 1987, 1994; Rutz and Orlove 1989; Schneider 1978).

32. Some scholars argue that this work is inherently multidisciplinary (Slater 1997, 2), while others argue that the study of food is inherently post-disciplinary (Cook, Crang, and Thorpe 2004).

33. Scholars follow things like beef (Stassart and Whatmore 2003), fish (Bestor 2005; Mansfield 2003a, 2003b); tomatoes, broccoli, and beans (Barndt 2002; Fischer and Benson 2006; Freidberg 2004, 2005; Roe 2006); tortillas (Gabel and Boller 2003; Jaffee, Kloppenburg, and Monroy 2004; Lind and Barham, 2004); fresh fruit (Cook, Crang, and Thorpe 2004; Mather and Mackenzie 2006; Sheller 2005; Shreck 2002, 2005); hot pepper sauces (Cook and Harrison 2003; Cook, Harrison, et al. 2006); and tamales (Long and Villareal 1998).

34. For example, some scholars focus on the interface between buyers and sellers (Arce and Marsden 1993; Crewe 1994; Crewe and Davenport 1992; Crewe and Forster 1993; Hughes 1999; Marsden and Wrigley 1995; Shackleton 1996; Wrigley 1992; Wrigley and Lowe 1996), some on retailers and retail relationships (Crewe and Forster 1993; Ducatel and Blomley 1990), and some on power shifts from suppliers to others along the chain (Crew and Davenport 1992; Gereffi, Korzeniewicz, and Korzeniewicz 1994; Wrigley 1992).

35. Friedman 1982; see also Phillips 2006 for an excellent review of this literature.

36. For example, one might focus on grocery stores as sites that can tell us about food choice, gender, and how choice affects social life and subjectivity (Miller 1998a), or on fashion-related retail stores to tell us about gender, commodities, and globalization (McRobbie 1997).

37. The first anthropologist to use a food to tell us about globalization and the history of capitalism was Sidney Mintz, who wrote one of the first far-reaching anthropological studies of how an agricultural product, sugar, became a commodity that transformed social lives around the world (1985). Mintz considered sugar the epitome of the historical processes of colonialism and the transformation of a foodstuff into a global commodity: something material that we can use to understand social relations between people and between societies, and a consumable item that helped to fuel industrial development and thus the growth of global capitalism (1985, 214). He reveals the various ways in which meanings become attached to commodities depending upon social factors and historic contexts (121). Additionally, he shows that agricultural commodities can mark status, move people to new social positions, indicate wealth, and decline in value as more and more

people have access to them, and that people innovate with commodities as they become part of daily life (150); he argues that sugar, tobacco, and tea were the first global commodities that were used to convey difference and status and that by being consumed actually worked to transform people's notions of themselves.

Sugar, and people's desires for it, transformed political, social, economic, and military relations, people's diets and thus their health, agrarian life in tropical colonies and the relations between colonies and urban centers, and conditions of labor, leading to labor innovations, new forms of labor, and new schedules for production (Mintz 1985, 181). Its production, distribution, and consumption altered bureaucratic life, mercantile life, agricultural life, and industrial life on heretofore unprecedented scales while at the same time radically transforming the day-to-day lives of slaves, workers, farmers, and others, and this in turn forced a reconsideration of the very philosophy behind colonial relations among colonies and metropolis (185). Like sugar, coffee is an agricultural product that has been transforming the world for hundreds of years.

38. Noel Castree has written cogently about the history of neoliberalism. I draw this tripartite focus on philosophy, discourse, and practice in part from his work (see Castree 2005, 2008a, 2008b, 2010).

39. Geographers, by focusing on "sites," and sociologists, by focusing on "sectors," have worked to de-culture commodity chains (see Leslie and Reimer 1999; Mort and Thompson 1994). This tendency has been theoretically productive insofar as it has allowed for radically different commodity chains to be analyzed and compared in terms of transnational structures, yet it has in many ways erased the lived experience of people all along the commodity chains. Cook, Crang, and Thorpe (2004, 660) call for more ethnographic analysis of commodity flows and in particular, following Miller (2001a), they argue for more "participant observation" combined with historical research and other forms of qualitative and quantitative analysis.

Chapter 2: Neoliberal Coffee

1. The cut flower industry in Kenya provides an example of an agricultural sector that has been forced to "reregulate" because of international media pressure—a case where voluntary regulation was not so voluntary. Hughes (2001a) examines the growth of the Kenyan Flower Council, an industry governing council made up of representatives from the production and consumption (at the level of buyers and importers) ends of the global commodity chain as well as members of the administrative staff of the council. The council, because of international pressure, now audits the producers to check for standards of production set by buyers (e.g., supermarket chains in Europe and the UK). Hughes argues that these audits are "performative" and that they tend toward a form of governmentality insofar as they work to structure certain behaviors on the production side of the industry. If behaviors are not laid out clearly in the industry "code of conduct"—again, a code that is dictated by the consumption side of the commodity chain—they not only fall outside the audit system but are basically ignored (Hughes 2001a). Hughes

shows that auditing of any kind becomes a self-perpetuating process, making more and more paperwork, checklists, and codes of bureaucratic conduct. However, as it does so, auditing loses sight of real needs and substitutes a checklist mentality.

2. http://www.deansbeans.com/coffee/deans_zine.html?blogid=829, first accessed for this book on 13 November 2006, accessed again on 1 November 2010.

3. It is an unsettling example to be sure, one that locates Papua New Guinea in a morass of colonial nostalgia, the self-aggrandizing travel narrative bravado of white exploration, inaccurate information (e.g., the description of middlemen and the claim that cooperatives would "increase the farmer's income fourfold"), and outright falsehoods (e.g., references to anacondas and uncontacted tribes, which do not exist in Papua New Guinea, and the absurd claim that the writer was the "first coffee buyer" to enter places in the Western and Eastern Highlands).

4. http://www.youtube.com/watch?v=OHWt2w7Pp6U, last accessed on 26 September 2010.

5. A search in LexisNexis shows that between 1970 and 1979 there were no articles in popular magazines or major newspapers linking coffee and environmental sustainability. Articles began to appear in the 1980s (77 in newspapers, 12 in magazines) and then steadily increased in number in the 1990s (802 in newspapers, 187 in magazines), between 2000 and 2001 (422 in newspapers, 154 in magazines), and between 2005 and 2006 (over 1,000 in newspapers, 402 in magazines).

6. There are a few exceptions. Tanzania, Kenya, and Ethiopia have not deregulated but have rather kept a public auction system, and Colombia has not deregulated at all (Oxfam 2001, 8).

7. Interestingly, Ponte (2002b) shows how changes in the market regulation for coffee in East Africa have led to a decline in the quality of coffee exported from Kenya, Tanzania, and Uganda. As the market has been restructured there in the wake of the decline of the ICA, the actors involved have changed, as have the forms of "assessment, monitoring and valuation of quality parameters" for the commodity (250).

8. Roseberry (1996, 767) also shows that just as the specialty market was emerging, several technological and commercial changes helped it along: the containerization revolution in shipping, which cut the transit time between producing and consuming countries; changing relations between roasters, traders, and bankers, who were less willing to finance huge amounts of coffee but more willing to finance small amounts that could be moved quickly; and the development of valve packaging, which made it possible for beans to stay fresher for longer.

9. This is not new. Roseberry shows how "coffee men" worked to create virtual consumers in their publications and marketing strategies in the 1980s as they began to envision a more segmented market (1996, 765).

10. http://www.deansbeans.com/coffee/people_centered.html, accessed for this book on 13 November 2006.

11. Where Stasch's tourists diverge with conservation activists and practitioners is in their imaginings of the gendered nature of the political world of their primitives. They want masculine primitives who express self and political order "through

personalities rather than formal institutions" (2006, 4). The imaginary primitive of conservation-minded actors in Papua New Guinea is not gender-specific. While hunting, which is a male activity, is often singled out as a particular threat to biological diversity, the threats in general can be made by men, women, and children. All rural peoples, as they move from indigenous and primitive to modern, can be of danger to the biophysical world. What Stasch's work shows is that in the western tourist imaginary of the New Guinea native the native is often male.

12. Although Roseberry (1996, 766) predicted that particular attributes of both coffee and the people who grow it would be used to add value to coffee for the specialty market, I don't think he could have predicted that poverty would add value in this way.

Chapter 3: Historic Coffee

1. Scholars have written extensively about colonialism in the Pacific (see Thomas 1994), New Guinea's colonial history (Dorney 1990; McPherson 2001), the particulars of exploration in the New Guinea Highlands (Gammage 1998; Willis 1969), and the colonial history of coffee on the island (Cartledge 1978; MacWilliam 1993, 2009; Sinclair 1995).

2. Scott MacWilliam (1993, 1997, 2008, 2009) has written the most comprehensive and critical analysis of the colonial and postcolonial coffee industry in Papua New Guinea. He highlights the role of smallholder producers in the development of the industry in the country and argues that most other scholars have underestimated their role in the industry. James Sinclair (1995) has written an account of the history of coffee production in Papua New Guinea from the point of view of expatriate planters. His history incorporates personal accounts, profiles of individual personalities, and an explanation of colonial policy and procedure and its tension with individual experiences. Ben Finney (1973, 1987) describes and analyzes the role of indigenous business people and plantation owners in the development of the national coffee industry. Ian Cartledge (1978) provides a history of the industry focused on marketing, trade and tariff boards, and the various international coffee agreements that have enveloped the coffee industry in Papua New Guinea. Finally, Ila Temu (1991, 1995) analyzes the history of supply and demand for coffee from Papua New Guinea in a series of economic analyses of price policy in the country. Robin Hide has produced a bibliography concerned with coffee production in the Eastern Highlands (2001).

3. In the late 1920s Lutheran missionaries were the first Europeans to journey into the Highlands, but it is four brothers from Australia, Michael "Mick" Leahy, Pat Leahy, Jim Leahy, and Dan "Sir Danny" Leahy, along with Jim Taylor and Michael "Mick" Dwyer, who are credited with having "discovered" much of what is now the Eastern Highlands, Chimbu, and the Western Highlands in the early 1930s. Mick Leahy and Mick Dwyer were first lured to the island in 1930 by the discovery of gold in 1926, and Mick Leahy is credited with the "first contact" of many thousands of people in the valleys and mountains of the Highlands. He documented a good number of his

contacts with 16 mm film and 35 mm still photographs. These images can be seen in the film *First Contact* and in Leahy's published diary, *Explorations into Highlands New Guinea*. Leahy and Dwyer walked from Lae to the Eastern Highlands through the Markham and Ramu valleys and then veered south down the Purari River in 1930 and 1931.

4. Simbu and Chimbu are both names for the same province in Papua New Guinea. During the colonial period it was called Chimbu, and much of the anthropological writing about the place and the people uses this name. Today the province is called Simbu to better reflect local spellings and pronunciation—Simbu is the Melanesian spelling of the English word Chimbu.

5. Much of the information about Greathead presented here is taken from interviews with people who knew him, reports he wrote that are in the hands of family members and members of the coffee community in and around Goroka, and accounts of his work in publications by Downs (1986), Leahy (1994), and Sinclair (1995). See also Report no. 23, George Greathead's report "Crime in Mount Hagen," from the papers of Paul Quinlivan, Crown prosecutor, chief Crown prosecutor, assistant secretary for law, senior magistrate for PNG, and finally coordinator of magisterial studies, University of Papua New Guinea. Quinlivan's reports can be accessed at http://www.pngaa.net/Articles/Paul_Quinlivan/articles_Quinli vanP_index.htm.

6. Sinclair (1995, 78) recounts Nell Greathead's memory of her husband's journey. I have also read an unpublished account of the journey by Greathead that is in the possession of his son Brian Greathead.

7. George Greathead retired from service in 1952 and became a coffee farmer, just as Jim Taylor had done and just as Ian Downs, Greathead's successor as district officer, would eventually do. Greathead came to New Guinea seeking adventure and fell in love with the area and the life he could have there. Aside from brief trips home to Queensland, he stayed on the island until he died. He and his wife, Mrs. Nell Greathead, raised six children in a house on a small plantation up the highway from Goroka. George Greathead died in 1969; his son Brian, who was only sixteen at the time, dropped out of school and took over the family's plantation.

8. Although the war began in 1939, New Guinea became a part of it in 1942.

9. At that time Goroka was known as Humeleveka by the indigenous residents of the valley. It was during the period between the war and about 1950 that the name Goroka began to be used by both colonial officials and the indigenous people (Read 1965).

10. In addition to the local casualties suffered from these attacks, the indigenous people in the Goroka Valley suffered wartime diseases (Finney 1973, 27). Soldiers carried dysentery from the coasts, and thousands of people died.

11. Across the Highlands there was an assumption of corporate identity by the administration. It was assumed that since residents of villages lived close to each other, some sort of social alliance or bond would keep them together and allow them to work together. This was not, and is not currently, the case. People may live a

twenty-minute walk away from a rival clan today because the village was given a road by the administration, or because an airstrip was built. The peace that is found between clans is often short-lived or fragile.

12. In other parts of what is now Papua New Guinea colonial officials and missions introduced cricket and soccer as substitutes for fighting, and these sports were played to the rules governing warfare, raiding, and the like (Barker 2001, 367).

13. Goroka had begun to grow as a regional center after 1947 and took on the look of a country town when Les Gillies, a builder from New South Wales, began flying prefabricated houses to the country. After the war he had his workmen cut prefabricated sections of houses into parts small enough to fit into an aircraft, and since an airstrip had been built in Goroka during the war, they could then be flown to the town (Les Gillies, personal communication, August 2001).

14. It is important to note that although it is extremely difficult to write in non-ethnographically specific ways about Highlanders, because of the vast ethnolinguistic diversity in the region, some generalizations help to explain how exchange and money came together in the early 1950s to create a thriving coffee economy in which indigenous people produced more coffee than settler colonists did.

15. Traditionally men built prestige by engaging in exchange (both individual and ceremonial), oration, and ritual practice, by amassing pigs, and by developing skill in fighting. Prestige meant that a man had the power to make and influence decisions for groups of people and serve as a leader (see Finney 1973; Langness 1999; Meggitt 1965; Read 1965). But prestige was always in flux, and men had to work persistently at maintaining what is called "big man" status.

16. In some of the published literature on the development of the coffee industry there is a fixation on this "settler class" and its role in the development of the coffee sector (Sinclair 1995). MacWilliam (1993, 2008, 2009) argues that this fixation is unfounded and that it obscures the role of smallholder producers in the development of the industry.

17. Downs's career began with the Royal Australian Navy in 1929, when he entered the Royal Australian Naval College as a midshipman. In 1935 he joined the New Guinea administration as a patrol officer and in 1938 was a member of the famous Hagen-Sepik patrol. After his wartime service he returned to his job as a patrol officer and moved up through the ranks during the late 1940s and early 1950s. After four years of service as district commissioner in Goroka (1952–56) he retired, became a coffee planter, and entered politics. From 1957 until 1968 he held various elected positions in the government, serving as president of the Highlands Farmers and Settlers Association from 1957 to 1968 and as the chairman of the Coffee Marketing Board, precursor to the Coffee Industry Corporation, in 1964. He moved to Australia in 1971 and published three books about New Guinea. He died in 2004.

18. There is not enough room to discuss some of the issues that arose during this period. Cartledge (1978) examines the means by which the colonial government created markets for the coffee through negotiations with Australia, Sinclair (1995) tells the history of individual white planters and their families, and Finney (1968,

1973, 1987) tells the stories of individual indigenous planters and their families. Many of the people whom Sinclair and Finney write about are represented in this work through their current-day analysis of the coffee industry, as I interviewed as many of the people they wrote about as I could find.

19. In what follows, much of the information that I present is based on my interviews with people who were in Goroka in the 1960s and 1970s. When the information is drawn from a published source I indicate it; when it is not, I will not name the interviewee, as everyone interviewed was promised anonymity.

20. See West 2006 for a lengthy discussion of this phenomenon today.

21. By the time of independence (16 September 1975) about 70 percent of the coffee in the country was produced by smallholders, with the remaining 30 percent produced on white-owned estates or plantations (Cartledge 1978, 281).

22. See especially the chapter by Rickey Mitio in Walter 1981. See also Sinclair 1995, chapter 25.

23. When the Somare government lost to the government of Julius Chan in 1980, the Scheme was curtailed (Walter 1980, 1981).

24. Finney (1973, 70) argues that Highlanders had been reinvesting this since cash had been introduced. In the late 1940s they had immediately bought steel axes, knives, and shovels as capital investments. Finney gives numerous examples of individual Goroka men who used the cash that they made as capital, and many of these men are still the leaders of the Goroka coffee industry. These early businessmen bought licenses to open trade stores, trucks that they would drive to rural areas to collect coffee, and commercial vehicles like buses (69–73). In addition, once outsiders realized that Gorokans wanted to invest their cash, opportunities such as livestock operations, restaurants, and coffee production facilities emerged, and people pooled and invested their capital (74). Finney explains that this investment had two important functions. First, it enabled people to provide services to their clans and villages with things like trade stores and trucks, thus facilitating access to other needed things, as well as to other places. Second, Finney argues that these investments were a way to gain prestige and become a big man (80).

25. See Goodman 2008 for the clearest review of the events resulting in the "global coffee crisis."

26. See Denoon 2000 for a comprehensive history of the mine.

27. The reforms included "administrative reforms to the provincial government system (1997), private sector wage liberalisation (1992), public sector reforms (1999), currency float (1995), corporatisation as a prelude to privatisation (1990), investment deregulation (1990), trade policy reform (1990), tax and tariff reforms (1999), political party and electoral reforms (2001), financial sector reform (2001), and forestry reform (2000)" (Kavanamur et al. 2004, 9).

28. One of the state services hollowed out by structural reform was the law and order sector (see Pitts 2002). The result was a rapid decline in law and order in the country after 1990.

Chapter 4: Village Coffee

1. This story, "They're Circling for Me," can be accessed at http://www.adventist review.org/2002-1520/news2.html (last accessed for this book 26 October 2010).

2. Yet with heavy pesticide use, shade-grown coffee areas can be as destructive as other forms of agriculture (MacVean 1997).

3. Although some of these maintenance techniques involve introduced species, they are indigenous because people worked them out themselves: they are the result of local trial and error, not extension work (Bourke 1997, 1).

4. *Casuarina oligodon* is indigenous to the island of New Guinea, with "self-sown" seedlings most common along waterways, including streams and rivers (Bourke 1997, 7). The tree seems to colonize areas that have been deforested for natural reasons—floods and landslides—as well as areas where roads have been cut or there have been other human disturbances (7).

5. There are 45,868 people in the whole of the Lufa District. According to the Coffee Industry Corporation of Papua New Guinea they are all considered smallholder coffee farmers.

6. The Maimafu airstrip is used by all the mission groups that run aviation companies and services during their pilot-testing phase. The pilots must successfully land in Maimafu before being cleared to fly in the country.

7. Campbell recounts that by 1964, across the census divisions that make up the Lufa District there were at least 129 acres of coffee that produced about 64 tonnes of coffee (Campbell 1964–65, 6). (A patrol post established at Lufa in 1954–55 was part of the Goroka Subdistrict.) Donne states that by 1966 there were 16,098 trees (some producing, some not) in the Labogai and Unavi census divisions (Donne 1965–66, appendix A). And Foran recounts that by 1968 within Unavi alone there were 370 growers, with 32,962 mature trees and 14,924 immature trees (Foran 1967–68, appendix H). By the 1970s the reports detail production information, and the vast quantity of coffee produced is one of the reasons that patrol officers urged their superiors to build a road into Lufa, which is the location of the patrol station for the district.

8. See West 2006 for a book-length discussion of the environmental conservation and economic development projects associated with the Crater Mountain Wildlife Management Area.

9. In Maimafu people tithe to the Seventh-Day Adventist church.

10. I have worked on and around Gimi lands and with Unavisa Gimi speakers since 1997.

11. These substances include fluids contributed during conception, food contributed during nurture, and blood from ritual events. The substances that come into play here, once connected to the person, can be separated from her and then exchanged with others but retain aspects of the person who made them or began their circulation.

12. Here I use "surroundings" instead of "environment" or "nature" because Gimi have no notion of "nature" (Gillison 1980) or "environment" (West 2005b, 2006).

13. Here, as in all of my work, I draw on the ethnography of Gillian Gillison, who worked with Gimi-speaking people in the 1970s and early 1980s (twenty months in 1973–74, six months in 1975, and three to four months during academic summers from 1976 to 1985; Gillison 1993, xiii). When I cite Gillison, unless I specifically write something along the lines of "Gillian Gillison's informants told her," I am citing her because her observations and data reflect the same observations that I made and data that I collected. There is almost complete continuity between her data and mine.

14. *Kora* = domestic, blood, ancestral.

15. See Gillison 1993, 39–45, for a detailed discussion of garden planning.

16. Ideally, after a woman has had five children she can then begin to give food she has cultivated to her husband.

17. *Ano* = mother; also water that comes from the body but is not blood (sweat, skin oil, urine, semen, liquid from death). *Bak* = song.

18. Each male clan has a bird of paradise that is closely associated with it. The birds are (literally) the same as the sacred and secret flute of the clan about which the woman is not supposed to know (see Gillison 1993; West 2006).

19. All tubers have noses, anuses, shapes, and skins and grow to resemble the women who nurtured them (see Gillison 1993, 196).

20. Gillian Gillison (1993, 199) recounts a similar story, but in the version she collected it is a man who does the dreaming and planting. Elsewhere (West 2006, chapter 3) I have written about the forgetting of gender in the Gimi stories. Usually the forgetting is tied to mythological characters that are female—so, for example, stories that Gillison collected with female animal characters were recounted to me as all male tales. Conversely, stories that I collected about plants were almost always full of female characters doing the action, while the same ones were full of males when Gillison collected them.

21. Finch (1992) has argued that there is a negative side effect of coffee cultivation: across the Eastern Highlands people have used the best land and sites closest to villages for coffee gardens, making food gardens increasingly distant from villages. Among Gimi, who have always had small kitchen gardens near settlements and large grocery store gardens a day's or half a day's walk from settlements, this is not the case. Some coffee groves are equally interspersed with kitchen gardens near hamlets, while others are located between settlements and the grocery store gardens.

22. Women constantly maintain stocks of seedlings for both coffee and other cultivars.

23. Some anthropologists of the highlands have tended to see women's complaints as grousing about men and men's business. For example, arguments by Rappaport (1984) that mating ritual cycles are hurried along by women's complaints concerning pigs and their gardens give the impression that complaining women change men's behavior and influence social decisions, and that women derive political

power from complaint. In Maimafu women's complaints are much more than simple grousing about men's behavior. They yield some power to women. The women's complaints are detailed examinations of the gendered politics of labor, as they are meant to be.

Chapter 5: Relational Coffee

1. People are extremely uncomfortable talking about how much coffee they have sold in any given year. This information is private, and people attempt to keep it from their extended families and from other people in the village. The idea of amassing wealth is something that individuals very much want to do, but they do not under any circumstances want others to know about this wealth. I have collected data on coffee production by family since 1998, but the best data in Maimafu to date were collected by Coffee Connections in 2002, when the company paid for an organic certifier to visit the village and certify the groves. During this visit people were honest about the number of trees they had and the amounts of coffee they sold, because giving these numbers was required for gaining this certification. They are, however, not perfect, as they do not reflect those few people who did not want their groves certified or those who were absent from the village at the time of certification.

2. See West 2006, chapter 3, for a lengthy discussion of local narratives about the construction of the airstrip.

3. In Papua New Guinea the Mission Aviation Fellowship's main office is in Mount Hagen, with branch offices in twelve other towns and villages—urban centers such as Lae and Madang and rural places such as Telefomin and Kawito that happen to be staging grounds for gold-mining operations. MAF currently employs twenty-nine expatriates and ninety-three Papua New Guineans, and has six Cessna 206s, three DHC6 Twin Otters, two GA8 Airvans, one Cessna 208, and one Cessna 172 in Papua New Guinea. In 2005 the fleet flew 7,263 hours in Papua New Guinea and transported 55,258 passengers (Mission Aviation Fellowship 2005, 6). Each year they fly approximately 800 tonnes of coffee from rural villages to urban markets. They have been flying in the country since 1951.

4. Information about MAF was gathered during interviews with staff, managers, and pilots in Goroka in June 2003 and August–November 2004.

5. http://www.maf.org.au, accessed several times over the course of 2004–6 and accessed for these quotations on 20 October 2006.

6. On average MAF Papua New Guinea evacuates five hundred people for severe medical emergencies yearly. This does not include people injured in "tribal fighting," as the organization will not transport anyone injured in "traditional squabbles," according to employees in the Goroka office.

7. Information about Adventist Aviation Services in Papua New Guinea is from interviews conducted with pilots and employees between August and November 2004.

8. http://www.flyawa.org/index.php, accessed numerous times between 2000 and 2006, accessed for these quotations on 20 October 2006.

9. One of the last times I saw Pastor Les Anderson alive was when he flew into Maimafu in a terrible storm to collect a pregnant woman who was bleeding uncontrollably. Sadly, she lost the baby, but she survived because Pastor Les got her to the hospital in time.

10. Attiks ended up in Maimafu because Kevin, a man from Maimafu, grew tired of waiting for buyers to come to his village a few years ago. He walked from Maimafu to Goroka and spent time getting to know many of the men like Thomas in the industry. Finally, after a few weeks in town, Kevin selected Thomas as a possible buyer to come to Maimafu. They talked, and since then Thomas has been sending buyers. Kevin chose Thomas because he is a Seventh-Day Adventist who seemed "fair and honest."

11. In terms of this acidity, Papua New Guinea coffee is similar to Kenyan and Costa Rican coffees and coffee from Burundi. In coffee industry language, all fall into the category "other milds."

Chapter 6: National Coffee

1. The anthropologist Kenneth E. Read (1965, 10–12) writes so beautifully of his arrival in Goroka in 1950 that any attempt to describe a flight into the town pales in comparison. He writes, "But the quality of the light was the most remarkable ingredient of all. It was difficult to tell where it came from. Every feather of the landscape seemed to be its own source of brightness, possessed of such dazzling clarity that I could not trust my judgment to the usual yardstick of reality" (11). It would not be possible to better describe flying into the Goroka Valley.

2. The overlap between the coffee industry and the membership of the Goroka Golf Club today mirrors the historic relationship between the two institutions.

3. Papua New Guinea Coffee Exports is owned by VOLCAFE; New Guinea Highlands Coffee Export is a member of the Neumann Kaffe Gruppe, which operates with its own profit center. Niugini Coffee Tea and Spice is a publicly traded company listed on the Australian Stock Exchange (Coffee Industry Corporation 2005, 17).

4. Fair Trade is counted under "organic" here.

5. The factory has had three overseas owners, but its architect and initial owner has remained as a manager, a condition of sale each time the factory has changed hands.

6. People "load" their coffee bags with all sorts of objects to get more money for a sack of coffee. The most common materials are dirt, rocks, and gravel, but one acquaintance who buys coffee at the five-mile market outside of Goroka said he has recovered ancient museum-quality stone tools, books, and other interesting objects in the bags. He said that growers "are very creative."

7. The association was extremely active throughout the 1950s, 1960s, and 1970s. It was well represented at meetings between Hasluck and settlers in 1955, after he directed the freeze on land allocations, and it was central to the discussions at the meeting in Goroka in 1959 regarding Australia and coffee marketing (Sinclair 1995, 233). Select indigenous farmers were invited to join the association in 1959. Its members were

deeply involved in discussions surrounding the International Coffee Agreement in 1962 and in the review of coffee import duties by the Australian Tariff board in 1964 (278). The association was firmly opposed to expanded plantings by indigenous people and new settlers, and although there is no direct evidence that it influenced the decision to end agricultural extension, its involvement seems likely. Finally, the association was resolutely opposed to independence (*Highlands Quarterly Bulletin* 1960a, 1960b, 1962, 1965, 1968, 1971).

8. I should mention here that Goroka has several social venues (the Aero Club, the Goroka Yacht Club, the Lahini Club, the Goroka Golf Club, the Bird of Paradise Hotel, a Chinese restaurant, the Embassy club, and the Odyssey club) that are frequented by middle-class and upper-class residents of the town. The Areo Club, the Goroka Yacht Club, the Lahini Club, and the Goroka Golf Club are all for members only, and the fees preclude membership by most working residents of Goroka. The restaurant at the Bird of Paradise Hotel and the Chinese restaurant also have prices that are too high for most working residents of the town. The Bird of Paradise also has three bars: one downstairs which is rather formal, one upstairs attached to a bistro which is quite informal, and a third upstairs, the Gillies Club, which is a private pay-membership club. The Embassy club and the Odyssey club are dance and music clubs frequented by a younger crowd that is mostly Papua New Guinean but includes some younger expatriates.

   Although my biologist friends regard many of the other clubs frequented by expatriates as racist, the Bird of Paradise, which will allow biologists to enter its front doors wearing baseball hats and generally sloppy clothing including that worn to do fieldwork, has on numerous occasions denied entrance to my friends from Maimafu because their clothing has been "too dirty." In addition, in 2003 my friend Bill Kusiomo was denied entrance because he was wearing a baseball hat, while I, also wearing a baseball hat, waited for him upstairs. In addition, although the uniformed staff in the bistro restaurant at the hotel wear no shoes (as part of their uniform, which is meant to evoke nostalgia for the colonial era), my friends from Maimafu have also been turned away because they do not have shoes.

9. It is worth noting that in terms of long-term commitments to Papua New Guinea, the coffee industry expatriates have deeper ties to the country than any of the other expatriates I have met, including aid workers, embassy workers, extractive industry workers, and volunteers. While they may well not invest all their profits back into the country, they do invest some of them back into their businesses. They also live in Papua New Guinea long-term and contribute to local economies and the national economy.

10. I disagree with Madu's argument that British colonialism was not primarily fueled by a desire for extractive industry: a large literature in history and anthropology argues that this was one of the main goals of indirect rule, and that the infrastructure established by the British (train networks, etc.) was set up to facilitate the process of extraction. I am merely reporting Madu's ideas about colonialism.

11. This is a particularly interesting comparison to Rhodesian "culture" in Zimbabwe

in light of the current push by Mugabe for indigenization there and the simultaneous debate over nationality in the country (thanks to Colin Felsman for this insight).

12. Twisties are a sort of savory snack food.

13. When coffee cherries are on the trees, the villagers who own the trees own the cherries. Beyond that stage, ownership gets more complicated. Some coffee is sent from the village by airplane, and the seller (the villager) pays for the transportation of the coffee from the village to the Goroka airport. Once the coffee is at the Goroka airport, the buyer (the factory owner, processor, or exporter) bears the cost of transportation from the airport to the factory. In this case the villager owns the coffee until it lands in Goroka, where its ownership is transferred to the buyer. In other cases the coffee leaves a village in a truck; then the buyer bears all cost of transportation from the seller's premises to the factory (that is, the coffee is EX Works: the buyer bears all costs of transportation from the seller's premises until the moment the merchandise goes over the rail of the ship). Then, when the original buyer sells the coffee to a secondary buyer, the original buyers become sellers. Secondary buyers can be large companies like VOLCAFE, Maxwell House, and Starbucks, or small companies like Monipi Coffee, Coffee Connections, and Kongo Coffee. People living in Australia, Germany, the UK, and the United States make many of these transactions, in which the secondary buyers enter the picture. These people and companies never own the coffee themselves but rather connect sellers (the people who own the coffee when it is in Goroka) with overseas buyers (the people who will own the coffee when it leaves Papua New Guinea). Because of the geographic complexity of these trades, this part of coffee circulation is difficult to track.

Although all coffee is sold before it leaves Goroka, the coffee business is FOB (free on board: the seller is responsible for costs up to the moment the merchandise goes over the rail of the ship) and C&F / CIF (cost and freight / cost insurance and freight: the seller is responsible for costs to bring goods to a named destination, and the buyer's responsibility for costs commences at the ship's rail), so the seller pays for all transportation and insurance between Goroka until the moment the coffee goes onto the ships in Lae. These costs include trucking between Goroka and Lae, security for the trucks, and insurance for the trucks and coffee. Even when the coffee is on the wharf in Lae, the seller still has responsibility for it. This includes its storage while in Lae, the costs of bulking if coffee must be bulked with other coffees to fit into a container, the costs of security while the coffee is in Lae, the costs of transporting the coffee while it is on the wharf, and the costs of getting the coffee ready for the ships and then onto the ships.

When the coffee goes over the rail of a ship the ownership changes yet again. At this point coffee is FOB, so the seller in Goroka no longer has any financial responsibility for it. The buyer becomes responsible for insuring it and paying for its transportation. The seller still has responsibility for its quality, however, in that if the quality is poor once the coffee reaches its destination the seller will be blamed.

At the international port, once the coffee is loaded off the ship it is owned by the international buyer, whose goal is to sell it to roasters and local distributors.

14. I found overwhelming the sheer number of people involved in the distribution sector for coffee. Because Papua New Guinea is a small country where contacts are easy to make, I found the distribution sector challenging but still intellectually apprehensible, insofar as I could grasp the number of people connected to moving the coffee and see how their lives were touched by it. This was not so when I got to Hamburg and London. These two cities have thousands of workers on docks and in shipping offices and the like who move the commodity once it reaches their ports. They are supplemented by a huge number of office workers, couriers, cleaning staff, and others who are connected to the movement of coffee.

Chapter 7: International Coffee

1. The port was first made a tax-free zone in 1189 (Verg and Verg 2007, 26).
2. So many people recounted this story to me that what I offer here is a compilation of numerous versions. I set it aside from the main text so as to remind the reader that it is a story.
3. Emily Fogg Mead, Margaret Mead's mother, quoted in Leach 1993, 37.
4. I was in London during a heat wave, so this congregation may not be the norm. During the time I was there, in the late spring and early summer, it rarely rained and the city experienced record highs.
5. Typical prices at the shop were £4.70 for 250 grams, £8 for 500 grams, £16 for 1 kilogram, and £42 for 3 kilograms (data collected by author between 1 September 2004 and 1 August 2005).
6. All of my interviews in Germany were done in English. Each time I began in German, I was laughed at by the interviewee because of my poor German, and then accepted the suggestion that we do the interview in English. I translated documents in German with helpful suggestions from Andrew Bickford. All translation mistakes are mine alone.
7. The owner of the coffee shop, who has lived in the neighborhood for twenty years, provided this information to me.
8. http://www.abc.net.au/news/stories/2010/05/25/2908239.htm?section=justin.
9. In terms of how respondents defined themselves generationally only three people we interviewed defined themselves as "millennials," but 52 percent described themselves as being at the "tail end" of "generation X" or in "the generation behind" it, with 40 percent referring to "generation Y" at some point during the interview; 34 percent said they were the children of "Baby boomers"; 10 percent mentioned the 9/11 attacks, but no one mentioned the Oklahoma City bombing, President Clinton's affair with Monica Lewinsky, or the Columbine shootings (the events that Mr. Nebraska used to mark the generation), while only 4 percent mentioned "global," "globalized," or "globalization" (the main focus of the generation according to Mr. Nebraska). Only 3 percent used the word "community" and only 10 percent talked about social and ecological change or justice; 27 percent mentioned that they use

alcohol, despite Mr. Nebraska's assertion that virtually all respondents were "tee-totalers," and 12 percent mentioned openness toward sexuality (e.g., "We are not shocked by homosexuality or not clearly defined sexuality"); 30 percent said that they believed their generation to be a specific target of the media and that they were under more pressure to consume than other generations; 14 percent mentioned that their generation had a sense of "entitlement" or a "spoiled" nature.

Interestingly, 73 percent of the interviewees mentioned technology when asked to describe their generation; 66 percent mentioned the Internet; 35 percent mentioned speed of communication (e.g., "people over the age of twenty-five just don't understand the instantaneous nature of communication"); 20 percent mentioned Facebook or My Space; 25 percent mentioned television; and 10 percent mentioned cell phones. Over half mentioned the Internet as a source of information for consumer goods.

10. The campus interview sample presented here is not characteristic of most of the consumers of Dean's Beans coffees. Dean's Beans is part of a small group within the specialty coffee industry called "cooperative coffees," and its markets are in unusually progressive communities (Amherst, Ann Arbor, Berkeley, Madison) where there is a high awareness of social issues, fair trade, and organics. But this is a very small niche market.

11. Columbia is an interesting site for this survey because it was one of the sites of an attempt by the SCAA in the 1980s to invest $1.6 million in building the market for specialty coffees (Roseberry 1996, 767). The SCAA sponsored a coffeehouse on campus that was dedicated to specialty roasts and blends.

12. We limited the age range to people who would be classified by marketers as "millennials." We further limited the range to the ages of eighteen to twenty-four, because we did not want to engage with interviewing a "special class" of people, as we would have had to if we had interviewed people under eighteen. We did not interview a random sample of students; rather, the student interviewers and I determined interviewees during observation periods at eight coffee-related establishments in or around Morningside Heights. These establishments included a Starbucks, the coffee shop area of a student dining hall, the college café, an old, élite coffee house near campus, a new, non-chain coffee shop on Broadway, and a new "funky" one near campus. We wanted to include a range of types of shops and price ranges. We only interviewed people who identified themselves as coffee drinkers.

Seventeen people initially interviewed had taken the course Interpretation of Culture, our introduction to cultural anthropology, with me. Because all of these students would have heard "endlessly" (interview, 12 October 2006) about Papua New Guinea during the course, we replaced their interviews with seventeen others.

13. During analysis we used the following definitions as guides, only counting people as understanding if they gave us these answers in, of course, their own words: "Fair Trade is a trading partnership, based on dialogue, transparency and respect, that seeks greater equity in international trade. It contributes to sustainable development by offering better trading conditions to, and securing the rights of, margin-

alized producers and workers—especially in the South. Fair Trade organizations (backed by consumers) are engaged actively in supporting producers, awareness raising and in campaigning for changes in the rules and practice of conventional international trade. Fair Trade's strategic intent is to deliberately to work with marginalized producers and workers in order to help them move from a position of vulnerability to security and economic self-sufficiency, to empower producers and workers as stakeholders in their own organizations, to actively to play a wider role in the global arena to achieve greater equity in international trade" (http://www.fairtrade.net/faq_links.html?&no_cache=1, first accessed by West on 1 August 2006).

"Fair trade coffee is coffee that is traded by bypassing the coffee trader and therefore giving the producer (and buyer) higher profits. Fair Trade does not necessarily mean that the extra money trickles down to the people who harvest the coffee. TransFair USA is an independent 3rd party certification that ensures that: Coffee importers agree to purchase from the small farmers included in the International Fair Trade Coffee Register. Farmers are guaranteed a minimum 'fair trade price' of $1.26/pound FOB for their coffee. If world price rises above this floor price, farmers will be paid a small ($0.05/pound) premium above market price. Coffee importers provide a certain amount of credit to farmers against future sales, helping farmers stay out of debt to local coffee 'coyotes' or middlemen. Importers and roasters agree to develop direct, long-term trade relationships with producer groups, thereby cutting out middlemen and bringing greater commercial stability to an extremely unstable market" (http://www.coffeeresearch.org/politics/fairtrade.htm, first accessed by West on 1 August 2006).

14. There are very few studies of consumer feelings about certified coffees. Loureiro and Lotade (2005) examined consumer responses to fair trade, organic, and shade-grown coffee and how consumers "value" certain coffees over others. They surveyed 284 adults in Colorado at supermarkets between 10:00 a.m. and 6:00 p.m., and their results are interesting. They found that over half these consumers were willing to spend more money if they felt that the coffee was creating a better future for the environment and for people living in less developed parts of the world (132). Their results also show that for their sample, people are willing to pay about 21.64 cents more per pound for fair trade certified coffee (134). The authors argue that this willingness to pay may be tied to survey participants' concerns over working conditions in developing countries (135). They also found that young to middle-aged women with high incomes were more likely to show sensitivity toward environmental and social issues, and thus pay more for coffee, while older consumers were unwilling to pay more for coffee even if they were sympathetic to these issues.

15. George Marcus (1998) describes how anthropological fieldwork both elucidates the connections people feel to elsewhere and creates the possibility of elsewhere for the people with whom we work. The anthropologists' very presence makes a perhaps inarticulable "elsewhere" present for the subject / informant / participant / "other." A sort of complicity-affinity arises between anthropologists and their infor-

mants, and it "arises from their mutual curiosity and anxiety about their relationship to a third" (122). This "third time space" is what constitutes the "affinity" or bond between the two and what makes the relationship work.

Chapter 8: Conclusion

1. The growth rate for the certified coffee market is five times that of the market for conventional coffee, and "sustainability" and certification are now objectives for mainstream market leaders like Wal-Mart and Nestlé. But even with the economic incentive for certification, the market for coffee is still 90 percent conventional, 3 percent inferior (for blending only), 2 percent certified, and 5 percent specialty (flavored, and coffee-based beverages such as canned coffee). In terms of certification specifically, even though about 6 percent of the world's coffee is certified, the world market for certified coffee is only 2 percent. This means that 4 percent of the certified coffee is sold as something else.

2. In today's world of certification fair trade holds the largest market share, with organics holding the second-largest. New forms of certification such as Rainforest Alliance, Bird-Friendly, and Best Practices are smaller but growing. These certifications are increasingly valuable in and of themselves as brands.

REFERENCES

Abouharb, Rodwan, and David L. Cingranelli. 2007. *Human Rights and Structural Adjustment*. Cambridge: Cambridge University Press.

Abu-Lughod, Lila. 1995. "The Objects of Soap Opera: Egyptian Television and the Cultural Politics of Modernity." *Worlds Apart*, ed. D. Miller. London: Routledge.

Allen, Matthew R., Michael Bourke, and Andrew McGregor. 2009. "Cash Income from Agriculture (Part 5)." *Food and Agriculture in Papua New Guinea*, ed. R. Michael Bourke and Tracy Harwood, 283–424. Canberra: Australian National University E Press.

Alsever, Jennifer. 2006. "Fair Prices for Farmers: Simple Idea, Complex Reality." *New York Times*, 19 March, 5.

Anderson, Benedict R. 1991. *Imagined Communities: Reflections on the Origin and Spread of Nationalism*. London: Verso.

Appadurai, Arjun. 1986. "Introduction: Commodities and the Politics of Value." *The Social Life of Things: Commodities in Cultural Perspective*. Cambridge: Cambridge University Press.

———, ed. 1986. *The Social Life of Things: Commodities in Cultural Perspective*. Cambridge: Cambridge University Press.

———. 1988. "Putting Hierarchy in Its Place." *Cultural Anthropology* 3, 16–20.

———. 1990. "Disjuncture and Difference in the Global Cultural Economy." *Public Culture* 2, no. 2, 1–24.

———. 1996. *Modernity at Large: Cultural Dimensions of Globalization*. Minneapolis: University of Minnesota Press.

Arce, A., and T. K. Marsden. 1993. "The Social Construction of International Food: A New Research Agenda." *Economic Geography* 69, 293–312.

Armbrecht, Inge, Leonardo Rivera, and Ivette Perfecto. 2005. "Reduced

Diversity and Complexity in the Leaf-Litter Ant Assemblage of Colombian Coffee Plantations." *Conservation Biology* 19, no. 3, 897–907.

Babb, Sarah. 2005. "The Social Consequences of Structural Adjustment: Recent Evidence and Current Debates." *Annual Review of Sociology* 31, no. 1, 199–222.

Babbar, Liana I., and Donald Zak. 1994. "Nitrogen Cycling in Coffee Agroecosystems: Net N Mineralization and Nitrification in the Presence and Absence of Shade Trees." *Agriculture, Ecosystems, and Environment* 48, 107–13.

Bacon, C. 2004. "Confronting the Coffee Crisis: Can Fair Trade, Organic, and Specialty Coffees Reduce Small-Scale Farmer Vulnerability in Northern Nicaragua?" *World Development* 33, no. 3, 497–511.

Bacon, C., V. E. Mendez, M. E. Flores Gomez, et al. 2008. "Are Sustainable Coffee Certifications Enough to Secure Farmer Livelihoods? The Millennium Development Goals and Nicaragua's Fair Trade Cooperatives." *Globalizations* 5, no. 2, 259–74.

Bacon, Christopher M., V. Ernesto Mendez, Stephen R. Gliessman, et al., eds. 2008. *Confronting the Coffee Crisis: Fair Trade, Sustainable Livelihoods and Ecosystems in Mexico and Central America.* Cambridge: MIT Press.

Bakhtin, M. M. 1981. *The Dialogic Imagination: Four Essays,* trans. Caryl Emerson and Michael Holquist. Austin: University of Texas Press.

Barker, John. 2001. "Dangerous Objects: Changing Indigenous Perceptions of Material Culture in a Papua New Guinea Society." *Pacific Science* 55, no. 4, 359–75.

Barndt, D. 2002. *Tangles Routes: Women, Work and Globalization on the Tomato Trail.* London: Rowman and Littlefield.

Bashkow, Ira. 2006. *The Meaning of Whitemen.* Chicago: University of Chicago Press.

Baudrillard, Jean. 1970. *La société de consommation: Ses mythes, ses structures.* Paris: Gallimard. Engl. trans. London: Sage, 1998.

——. 1981. *Simulacra and Simulation,* trans. S. F. Glaser. Ann Arbor: University of Michigan Press.

——. 1983. *Simulations,* trans. P. Foss, P. Patton, and P. Beitchman. New York: Semiotext(e).

——. 1988. "Simulacra and Simulations." *Jean Baudrillard: Selected Writings,* ed. Mark Poster. Stanford: Stanford University Press.

——. 1993. *Symbolic Exchange and Death,* trans. I. H. Grant. London: Sage.

Belk, R. 1993. "Materialism and the Making of the Modern American Christmas." *Unwrapping Christmas,* ed. Daniel Miller. Oxford: Oxford University Press.

Benjamin, Walter. 1968. *Illuminations.* New York: Harcourt, Brace and World.

Bestor, Theodore C. 2001. "Supply-Side Sushi: Commodity, Market, and the Global City." *American Anthropologist* 103, no. 1, 76–95.

——. 2004. *Tsukiji: The Fish Market at the Center of the World.* Berkeley: University of California Press.

——. 2005. "How Sushi Went Global." *The Cultural Politics of Food and Eating: A Reader,* ed. J. Watson and M. Caldwell. Oxford: Blackwell.

Biersack, Aletta. 1995. "Heterosexual Meanings: Society, Economy, and Gender among Ipilis." *Papuan Borderlands: Huli, Duna, and Ipili Perspectives on the Papua New Guinea Highlands*, ed. Aletta Biersack. Ann Arbor: University of Michigan Press.

——. 1999. "The Mount Kare Python and His Gold: Totemism and Ecology in the Papua New Guinea Highlands." *American Anthropologist* 101, 68–87.

Blaikie, Piers. 1985. *The Political Economy of Soil Erosion in Developing Countries*. New York: Longman.

Blaikie, P. M., and H. C. Brookfield. 1987. *Land Degradation and Society*. London: Methuen.

Blowfield, M. 1999. "Ethical Trade: A Review of Developments and Issues." *Third World Quarterly* 20, 753–70.

Bourdieu, Pierre. 1984. *Distinction: A Social Critique of the Judgment of Taste*. Cambridge: Harvard University Press.

Bourke, Robert Michael. 1986. "Village Coffee in the Eastern Highlands of Papua New Guinea." *Journal of Pacific History* 21, 1–2, 100–103.

——. 1989. "Food, Coffee and Casuarina: An Agroforestry System from the Papua New Guinea Highlands." *Nair* PKR, *Agroforestry Systems in the Tropics*. Dordrecht: Kluwer Academic.

——. 1997. "Management of Fallow Species Composition with Tree Planting." Papua New Guinea Series: Resource Management in Asia-Pacific Working Paper no. 5. Resource Management in Asia-Pacific Project, Division of Pacific and Asian History, Research School for Pacific and Asian Studies, Australian National University.

Bradley, Phillip. 2008. *The Battle for Wau: New Guinea's Frontline, 1942–1943*. Melbourne: Cambridge University Press.

Brannstrom, Christian. 2001. "Producing Possession: Labour, Law and Land on a Brazilian Agricultural Frontier, 1920–1945." *Political Geography* 20, 859–83.

Bray, B. D., J. L. Plaza Sanchez, and E. C. Murphy. 2002. "Social Dimensions of Organic Coffee Production in Mexico: Lessons for Eco-labeling Initiatives." *Society and Natural Resources* 15, no. 6, 429–46.

Brockington, Dan. 2009. *Celebrity and the Environment: Fame, Wealth and Power in Conservation*. London: Zed.

Brosius, J. P. 1997. "Endangered Forest, Endangered People: Environmentalist Representations of Indigenous Knowledge." *Human Ecology* 25, 47–69.

——. 1999a. "Analyses and Interventions: Anthropological Engagements with Environmentalism." *Current Anthropology* 40, no. 3, 277–309.

——. 1999b. "Green Dots, Pink Hearts: Displacing Politics from the Malaysian Rain Forest." *American Anthropologist* 101, 36–57.

Browne, A., et al. 2000. "Organic Production and Ethical Trade: Definition, Practice and Links." *Food Policy* 25, 69–89.

Bryant R. L., and S. Bailey. 1997. *Third World Political Ecology*. London. Routledge.

Bryant, Raymond L., and Michael K. Goodman. 2004. "Consuming Narratives: The Political Ecology of 'Alternative' Consumption." *Transactions of the Institute of British Geographers* 29, no. 3, 344–66.

Buck-Morss, Susan. 1992. "Aesthetics and Anaesthetics: Walter Benjamin's Artwork Essay Reconsidered." *October* 62 (autumn 1992), 3–41.

Burke, Timothy. 1996. *Lifebuoy Men, Lux Women: Commodification, Consumption, and Cleanliness in Modern Zimbabwe.* Durham: Duke University Press.

Callon, Michel, C. Méadel, and V. Rabeharisoa. 2002. "The Economy of Qualities." *Economy and Society* 31, no. 2, 194–217.

Cambranes, J. C. 1985. *Coffee and Peasants: The Origins of the Modern Plantation Economy in Guatemala, 1853–1897.* Monografias no. 10. Stockholm: Institute of Latin American Studies.

Campbell, Colin. 1994. "Capitalism, Consumption and the Problem of Motives." *Consumption and Identity*, ed. J. Friedman. Chur: Harwood Academic.

Campbell, C. T. 1964–65. "Yagaria Census Division and Part Labogai Census Division." *Lufa* 2. Unpublished report, Department of District and Native Affairs, Australian Administration.

Carrier, James G. 1993. "The Rituals of Christmas Giving." *Unwrapping Christmas*, ed. Daniel Miller. Oxford: Clarendon.

——. 1994. *Gifts and Commodities: Exchange and Western Capitalism since 1700.* London: Routledge.

——. 1995. "Maussian Occidentialism: Gift and Commodity Systems." *Occidentalism: Images of the West*, ed. J. Carrier, 84–108. Oxford: Clarendon.

——. 1998a. "Abstraction in Western Economic Practice." *New Political Economy*, ed. James G. Carrier and Daniel Miller. New York: Berg.

——. 1998b. Introduction. *Virtualism: A New Political Economy.* Oxford: Berg.

——. 1998c. "Property and Social Relations in Melanesian Anthropology." *Property Relations: Renewing the Anthropological Tradition*, ed. C. M. Hann, 85–103. Cambridge: Cambridge University Press.

——. 2010. "Protecting the Environment the Natural Way: Ethical Consumption and Commodity Fetishism." *Antipode* 42, no. 3, 672–89.

Carrier, James, and D. Miller. 1998. *Virtualism: A New Political Economy.* New York: Berg.

Carson, Rachel. 1962. *Silent Spring.* Greenwich: Fawcett.

Cartledge, Ian. 1978. "A History of the Coffee Industry in Papua New Guinea." Prepared for the Papua New Guinea Marketing Board (Coffee Industry Board).

Castree, Noel. 2005. "The Epistemology of Particulars." *Geoforum* 36, no. 4, 541–44.

——. 2008a. "Neoliberalising Nature: The Logics of Deregulation and Reregulation." *Environment and Planning A* 40, no. 1, 131–52.

——. 2008b. "Neoliberalising Nature: Processes, Outcomes and Effects." *Environment and Planning A* 40, no. 1, 153–73.

——. 2010. "Neoliberalism and the Biophysical Environment: A Synthesis and Evaluation of the Research." *Environment and Society* 1, no. 1, 1–30.

Central Highlands District. 1947–48. Annual Reports, Papua New Guinea National Archives.

——. 1950–51. Annual Reports, Papua New Guinea National Archives.

Chinnery, E. W. P. 1934. "The Amazing Discovery of a New People." *New York Times*, 16 September, 4–5.

Clarke, A. 2001. "The Aesthetics of Social Aspiration." *Home Possessions: Material Culture behind Closed Doors*, ed. D. Miller. Oxford: Berg.

Clifford, M. N., and K. C. Willson, eds. 1985. *Coffee: Botany, Biochemistry and Production of Beans and Beverage*. London: Croom Helm.

Coffee Industry Corporation. 2005. Coffee Report no. 63, with contributions by Charles Dambui, Kessy Kufinale, Rose Kulua, Moses Alu, and Mick Wheeler. Goroka: Coffee Industry Corporation Ltd. of Papua New Guinea.

Cohen, L. 2003. *A Consumer's Republic: The Politics of Mass Consumption in Postwar America*. New York: Vintage.

Cohn, Bernard. 1989. "Cloth, Clothes and Colonialism: India in the Nineteenth Century." *Cloth and Human Experience*, ed. A. Weiner and J. Schneider. Washington: Smithsonian Institution Press.

Comaroff, Jean, and John Comaroff. 1997. *Of Revelation and Revolution: The Dialectics of Modernity on a South African Frontier*, vol. 2. Chicago: University of Chicago Press.

——. 1999. "Occult Economies and the Violence of Abstraction: Notes from the South African Postcolony." *American Ethnologist* 26, no. 3, 279–301.

——. 2000. "Millennial Capitalism: First Thoughts on a Second Coming." *Public Culture* 12, no. 2, 291–343.

——. 2002. "Alien-Nation: Zombies, Immigrants, and Millennial Capitalism." *South Atlantic Quarterly* 101, no. 4, 779–805.

——. 2009. *Ethnicity, Inc.* Chicago: University of Chicago Press.

Conklin, Beth A., and Laura R. Graham. 1995. "The Shifting Middle Ground: Amazonian Indians and Eco-politics." *American Anthropologist* 97, no. 4, 695–710.

Conroy, M. 2001. "Can Advocacy-Led Certification Systems Transform Global Corporate Practices? Evidence and Some Theory." Working Paper no. DPE-01-07, Political Economy Research Institute, Amherst, Mass.

Cook, Ian. 2006. "Geographies of Food: Following." *Progress in Human Geography* 30, no. 5, 655–66.

Cook, I., and P. Crang. 1996. "The World on a Plate: Culinary Culture, Displacement and Geographical Knowledges." *Journal of Material Culture* 1, no. 2, 131–53.

Cook, I., P. Crang, and M. Thorpe. 1998. "Biographies and Geographies: Consumer Understandings of the Origins of Foods." *British Food Journal* 100, no. 3, 162–67.

——. 2004. "Tropics of Consumption: Getting with the Fetish of 'Exotic' Fruit?" *Geographies of Commodities*, ed. A. Hughes and S. Reimer. London: Routledge.

Cook, I., and M. Harrison. 2003. "Cross over Food: Rematerialising Postcolonial Geographies." *Transactions of the Institute of British Geographers* 28, no. 3, 296–317.

Cook, I., M. Harrison, et al. 2006. "Follow the Thing: West Indian Hot Pepper Sauce." *Space and Culture* 10, no. 3, 40–63.

Crang, P. 1996. "Displacement, Consumption and Identity." *Environment and Planning A* 28, 47–67.

Crapanzano, Vincent. 2003. *Imaginative Horizons: An Essay in Literary-Philosophical Anthropology*. Chicago: University of Chicago Press.

Creighton, Millie. 1998. "Something More: Japanese Department Store's Marketing of a Meaningful Human Life." *Asian Department Stores*, ed. Kerrie MacPherson. Richmond: Curzon.

Crewe, L. 1994. "Consuming Landscapes: Designing Desire in the Nottingham Lace Market." *East Midland Geographer* 17, 22–27.

——. 2003. "Geographies of Retailing and Consumption: Markets in Motion." *Progress in Human Geography* 27, 352–62.

Crewe, L., and E. Davenport. 1992. "The Puppet Show: Changing Buyer-Supplier Relationships within Clothing Retailing." *Transactions, Institute of British Geographers* 17, 183–97.

Crewe, L., and Z. Forster. 1993. "A Canute Policy Fighting Economics? Local Economic Policy in an Industrial District: The Case of Nottingham's Lace Market." *Policy and Politics* 21, 275–88.

Crump, Thomas. 1981. *The Phenomenon of Money*. London: Routledge.

Cruz-Angon, Andrew, and Russel Greenberg. 2005. "Are Epiphytes Important for Birds in Coffee Plantations? An Experimental Assessment." *Journal of Applied Ecology* 42, 150–59.

Curtis, Debra. 2004. "Commodities and Sexual Subjectivities." *Cultural Anthropology* 19, no. 1, 95–121.

Darwin, Steven P. 1976. "The Subfamilial, Tribal and Subtribal Nomenclature of the Rubiaceae." *Taxon* 25, nos. 5–6, 595–610.

——. 1996. *Home Coffee Roasting: Romance and Revival*. New York: St. Martin's Griffin.

Davis, Deborah. 2000. *The Consumer Revolution in Urban China*. Berkeley: University of California Press.

Debord, Guy. (1967) 1995. *La société du spectacle*. New York: Zone.

de Certeau, Michel. 1984. *The Practice of Everyday Life*. Berkeley: University of California Press.

Denham, T. P., J. Golson, and P. J. Hughes. 2003. "Reading Early Agriculture at Kuk (Phases 1–3), Wahgi Valley, Papua New Guinea: The Wetland Agriculture Features." *Proceedings of the Prehistoric Society* 70, 259–97.

Denoon, Donald. 2000. *Getting under the Skin: The Bougainville Copper Agreement and the Creation of the Panguna Mine*. Melbourne: Melbourne University Press, 2000.

Department of External Territories, Australia. 1968. "Investing in Papua and New Guinea." Department of External Territories and issued under the authority of the Minister for External Territories, the Hon. C. E. Barnes, M.P. Canberra.

Doane, Molly. 2010. "Relationship Coffees: Structure and Agency in the Fair Trade System." *Fair Trade and Social Justice*, ed. Sarah Lyon and Mark Moberg. New York: New York University Press.

Donald, P. F. 2004. "Biodiversity Impacts of Some Agricultural Commodity Production Systems." *Conservation Biology* 18, no. 1, 17–38.

Donne, R. W. S. 1965–66. "Report on Unave and Labogai Census Divisions." *Lufa* 12. Unpublished report, Department of District and Native Affairs, Australian Administration.

Dorney, Sean. 1990. *Papua New Guinea: People, Politics and History since 1975*. Milson's Point, N.S.W.: Random House Australia.

Dorsey, Bryan. 1999. "Agricultural Intensification, Diversification, and Commercial Production among Smallholder Coffee Growers in Central Kenya." *Economic Geography* 75, no. 2, 178–295.

Douglas, Mary, and Baron Isherwood. 1979. *The World of Goods: Towards an Anthropology of Consumption*. New York: Basic Books.

Downs, Ian. 1980. "The Australian trusteeship Papua New Guinea, 1945–1975." Canberra: Australian Government Publishing Service.

———. 1986. *The Last Mountain: A Life in Papua New Guinea*. Brisbane: University of Queensland Press.

Dreyfus, Hubert, and Paul Rabinow. 1982. *Michel Foucault, beyond Structuralism and Hermeneutics*. Chicago: University of Chicago Press.

Ducatel, K., and N. Blomley. 1990. "Rethinking Retail Capital." *International Journal of Urban and Regional Research* 14, 207–27.

du Gay, P., et al. 1997. *Doing Cultural Studies: The Story of the Sony Walkman*. London: Sage, in association with the Open University.

Duncan, James. 2002. "Embodying Colonialism: Domination and Resistance in Nineteenth-Century Ceylonese Coffee Plantations." *Journal of Historical Geography* 28, no. 3, 317–38.

Easterly, William. 2000. "The Effect of IMF and World Bank Programs on Poverty." Washington: World Bank.

———. 2007. "Are Aid Agencies Improving?" *Economic Policy* 22, no. 52, 633–78.

Edwards, Bonnie. 1992. *America's Favorite Drug: Coffee and Your Health*. New York: Odonian.

Elek, Andrew. 1991. "Structural Adjustment in Papua New Guinea, 1989–1990." Discussion paper no. 47. Port Moresby: Institute of National Affairs.

Errington, Frederick, and Deborah Gewertz. 1995. *Articulating Change in the "Last Unknown."* Boulder: Westview.

———. 2001. "On the Generification of Culture: From Blow Fish to Melanesian." *Journal of the Royal Anthropological Institute*, n.s. 7, 509–25.

———. 2004. *Yali's Question: Sugar, Culture, and History*. Chicago: University of Chicago Press.

Escobar, A. 1996. "Constructing Nature" *Liberation Ecologies: Environment, Development, Social Movements*, ed. R. Peet and M. Watts, 46–68. London. Routledge.

———. 1999. "After Nature: Steps to an Anti-essentialist Political Ecology." *Current Anthropology* 40, no. 1, 1–30.

Ettlinger. N. 2004. "Towards a Critical Theory of Untidy Geographies: The Spatiality of Emotions in Consumption and Production." *Feminist Economics* 10, 21–54.

Ferguson, James. 2010. "The Uses of Neoliberalism." *Antipode* 42, no. 1, 166–84.

Filer, Colin. 2010. "Inter-disciplinary Perspectives on Society and Environment in Papua New Guinea." Manuscript, submitted to Environmental Conservation.

——. 2011. "Interdisciplinary Perspectives on Historical Ecology and Environmental Policy in Papua New Guinea." *Environmental Conservation* 38, 256–69.

Finch, John. 1992. "Women Work Harder Than Men." *Cultural Survival Quarterly* 16, no. 4.

Fine, B., and E. Leopold. 1993. *The World of Consumption.* London: Routledge.

Finney, Ben R. 1968. "Bigfellow Man Belong Business in New Guinea." *Ethnology* 7, 394–410.

——. 1973. *Big-Men and Business: Entrepreneurship and Economic Growth in the New Guinea Highlands.* Honolulu: University Press of Hawaii.

——. 1987. *Business Development in the Highlands of Papua New Guinea.* Honolulu: Pacific Islands Development Program.

Fischer, E., and P. Benson. 2006. *Broccoli and Desire: Global Connections and Maya Struggles in Postwar Guatemala.* Stanford: Stanford University Press.

Fiske, John. 1989. *Understanding Popular Culture.* London: Routledge.

Fitzpatrick, Peter, 1980. *Law and State in Papua New Guinea.* London: Academic.

Foran, S. P. 1967–68. "Unavi and Labogai Census Divisions." *Lufa* 9 (1967–68). Department of District and Native Affairs, Australian Administration. Unpublished report.

Foster, Robert J. 1995. "Print Advertisement and Nation Making in Metropolitan Papua New Guinea." *Nation Making: Emergent Identities in Postcolonial Melanesia,* ed. Robert J. Foster. Ann Arbor: University of Michigan Press.

——. 2002. *Materializing the Nation: Commodities, Consumption and Media in Papua New Guinea.* Bloomington: Indiana University Press.

——. 2008. *Coca-Globalization: Following Soft Drinks from New York to New Guinea.* Palgrave Macmillan.

Fox, J. C., et al. 2010. "Assessment of Aboveground Carbon in Primary and Selectively-Harvested Tropical Forest in Papua New Guinea." *Biotropica* 42, 410–19.

Frank, Robert H. 1999. *Luxury Fever: Why Money Fails to Satisfy in an Era of Excess.* New York: Free Press.

Freidberg, S. 2004. "The Ethical Complex of Corporate Food Power." *Environment and Planning D: Society and Space* 22, 513–31.

——. 2005. "French Beans for the Masses: A Modern Historical Geography of Food in Burkina Faso." *The Cultural Politics of Food and Eating: A Reader,* ed. J. Watson and M. Caldwell. Oxford: Blackwell.

Fridell, Gavin. 2003. "Fair Trade and the International Moral Economy: Within and against the Market." CERLAC Working Paper Series, York University.

Friedman, Jonathan. 1982. " 'Capital' Imperialism and Exploitation in the Ancient World-Systems." *History and Underdevelopment,* ed. L. Blusse, H. L. Wesseling, and

G. D. Winius. Leiden: Center for the History of European Expansion, Leiden University.

——. 1991. "Consuming Desires: Strategies of Selfhood and Appropriation." *Cultural Anthropology* 6, 154–64.

Friedman, M. 1962. *Capitalism and Freedom*. Chicago: University of Chicago Press.

Fukuyama, Francis. 2007. "Governance Reform in Papua New Guinea." Unpublished paper, available at www.sals-jhu.edu.

Gabel, T., and G. Boller. 2003. "A Preliminary Look at the Globalization of the Tortilla in Mexico." *Advances in Consumer Research* 30, 135–41.

Gailey, Harry A. 2004. *MacArthur's Victory: The War In New Guinea, 1943–1944*. New York: Random House.

Gammage, Bill. 1998. *The Sky Travellers: Journeys in New Guinea, 1938–1939*. Carlton South: Melbourne University Press.

Gell, Alfred. 1986. "Newcomers to the World of Goods: Consumption among the Muria Gonds." *The Social Life of Things*, ed. A. Appadurai. Cambridge: Cambridge University Press.

——. 1998. *Art and Agency*. Oxford: Oxford University Press.

George, Susan. 1990. *A Fate Worse Than Debt*. New York: Penguin.

Gereffi, G., R. Garcia-Johnson, and E. Sasser. 2001. "The NGO-Industrial Complex." *Foreign Policy* 125, 56–65.

Gereffi, Gary, and M. Korzeniewicz, eds. 1994. *Commodity Chains and Global Capitalism*. Westport, Conn.: Praeger.

Gereffi, G., M. Korzeniewicz, and R. Korzeniewicz. 1994. "Introduction: Global Commodity Chains." *Commodity Chains and Global Capitalism*, ed. G. Gereffi, M. Korzeniewicz, and R. Korzeniewicz, 1–14. Westport, Conn.: Greenwood.

Gewertz, Deborah, and Frederick Errington. 1996. "On PepsiCo and Piety in a Papua New Guinea 'Modernity.'" *American Ethnologist* 23, no. 3, 476–93.

——. 1999. *Emerging Class in Papua New Guinea: The Telling of Difference*. New York: Cambridge University Press.

——. 2007. "The Alimentary Forms of the Global Life: The Pacific Island Trade in Lamb and Mutton Flaps." *American Anthropologist* 109, no. 3, 496–508.

——. 2010. *Cheap Meat: The Global Omnivore's Dilemma in the Pacific Islands*. Berkeley: University of California Press.

Gillison, Andrew N., et al. 2004. "Impact of Cropping Methods on Biodiversity in Coffee Agroecosystems in Sumatra, Indonesia." *Ecology and Society* 9, no. 2, 7.

Gillison, Gillian. 1977. "Fertility Rites and Sorcery in a New Guinea Village." *National Geographic*, July, 124–46.

——. 1980. "Images of Nature in Gimi Thought." *Nature, Culture and Gender*, ed. Carol MacCormack and Marilyn Strathern. Cambridge: Cambridge University Press.

——. 1993. *Between Culture and Fantasy: A New Guinea Highlands Mythology*. Chicago: University of Chicago Press.

Ginsburg, F., L. Abu-Lughod, and B. Larkin. 2002. *Media Worlds: Anthropology on New Terrain*. Berkeley: University of California Press.

Glick, Leonard B. 1963. "Foundations of a Primitive Medical System: The Gimi of the New Guinea Highlands." PhD diss., University of Pennsylvania.

Goldman, Robert. 1994. "Contradictions in a Political Economy of Sign Value." *Current Perspectives in Social Theory* 14, 183–211.

Goldman, Robert, and Stephen Papson. 1998. *Nike Culture: The Sign of the Swoosh.* London: Sage.

Goodman, David. 2008. "The International Coffee Crisis: A Review of the Issues." *Confronting the Coffee Crisis: Fair Trade, Sustainable Livelihoods and Ecosystems in Mexico and Central America,* ed. Christopher M. Bacon, V. Ernesto Mendez, Stephen R. Gliessman, et al., 4–25. Cambridge: MIT Press.

Goodman, M. K. 2004. "Reading Fair Trade: Political Ecological Imaginary and the Moral Economy of Fair Trade Foods." *Political Geography* 23, 891–915.

Gosarevski, Steven, Helen Hughes, and Susan Windybank. 2004. "Is Papua New Guinea Viable?" *Pacific Economic Bulletin* 19, no. 1.

Goss, J. 2004. "Geography of Consumption, 1." *Progress in Human Geography* 28, 369–80.

Greathead, George. 1947. "Crime in Mount Hagen." Available at http://www.pngaa.net/Library/Quinlivan23.html.

"The Greening of Giving." 1993. *Economist,* 25 December, 53.

Gruber, Ruth. 1999. "The Consumer Co-op in Japan: Building Democratic Alternatives to State-Led Capitalism." *Consumers against Capitalism? Consumer Cooperation in Europe, North America, and Japan,* ed. E. Furlough and C. Strikwerda. Lanham, Md.: Rowman and Littlefield.

Guthman, J. 2003. "Fast Food / Organic Food: Reflexive Tastes and the Making of 'Yuppie Chow.'" *Social and Cultural Geography* 4, no. 1, 43–56.

——. 2004. "The 'Organic Commodity' and Other Anomalies in the Politics of Consumption." *Geographies of Commodity Chains,* ed. A. Hughes and S. Reimer. London: Routledge.

——. 2007. "The Polanyian Way? Voluntary Food Labels as Neoliberal Governance." *Antipode* 39, no. 3, 456–78.

Habermas, Jürgen. (1969) 1989. *The Structural Transformation of the Public Sphere: An Inquiry into a Category of Bourgeois Society,* trans. Thomas Burger. Cambridge: MIT Press.

Haertzen, C. A., T. R. Kocher, and K. Miyasato. 1983. "Reinforcements from the First Drug Experience Can Predict Later Drug Habits and/or Addiction: Results with Coffee, Cigarettes, Alcohol, Barbiturates, Minor and Major Tranquilizers, Stimulants, Marijuana, Hallucinogens, Heroin, Opiates and Cocaine." *Drug and Alcohol Dependency* 11, no. 2, 147–65.

Halvaksz, Jamon. 2003. "Singing about the Land among the Biangai." *Oceania* 7, no. 3, 153–69.

——. 2006a. "Becoming 'Local Tourists': Travel, Landscapes and Identity in Papua New Guinea." *Tourist Studies* 6, no. 2, 99–117.

——. 2006b. "Cannibalistic Imaginaries: Mining the Natural and Social Body in

Papua New Guinea." *Contemporary Pacific: A Journal of Contemporary Island Affairs* 18, no. 2, 335–59 [special issue: Melanesian Mining Modernities, ed. M. Macintyre and P. West].

——. 2007a. "Cannabis and Fantasies of Development: Revaluing Relations through Land in Rural Papua New Guinea." *Australian Journal of Anthropology* (forthcoming).

——. 2007b. "Whose Mine Closure? Appearances, Temporality and Mineral Extraction." *Journal of the Royal Anthropological Institute* (forthcoming).

Hannerz, Ulf. 1992. *Cultural Complexity: Studies in the Social Organization of Meaning.* New York: Columbia University Press.

Haraway, Donna. 1997. *Modest Witness @ Second Millennium: Female Man© Meets OncoMouse™.* New York: Routledge.

Harvey, David. 1989. *The Condition of Postmodernity.* London: Blackwell.

——. 1990. *The Condition of Postmodernity: An Enquiry into the Origins of Cultural Change.* Cambridge: Blackwell.

——. 1996. *Justice, Nature and the Geography of Difference.* Cambridge: Blackwell.

——. 2005. *The New Imperialism.* New York: Oxford University Press.

——. 2006a. *A Brief History of Neoliberalism.* Oxford: Oxford University Press.

——. 2006b. *The Limits to Capital.* New York: Verso.

——. 2007. "Neoliberalism as Creative Destruction." *Annals of the American Academy of Political and Social Science* 610, 22–44.

Hasluck, P. 1976. *A Time for Building: Australia Administration in Papua and New Guinea.* Melbourne: Melbourne University Press.

Haug, Wolfgang F. 1986. *Critique of Commodity Aesthetics: Appearance, Sexuality, and Advertising in Capitalist Society.* Minneapolis: University of Minnesota Press.

Hawksley, Charles. 2005. "Creating Hegemony: Colonialism, the Social Contract and State Legitimacy in Papua New Guinea." Paper presented at the conference "Hegemony: Explorations into Consensus, Coercion and Culture," during the panel "Class and Consensus," University of Wollongong, Australia, 14–15 February.

——. 2007. "Constructing Hegemony: Colonial Rule and Colonial Legitimacy in the Eastern Highlands of Papua New Guinea." *Rethinking Marxism* 19, no. 2, 195–207.

Hearst, Louise. 1932. "Coffee Industry of Central America." *Economic Geography* 8, no. 1, 53–66.

Heath, Joseph, and Andrew Potter. 2004. *Nation of Rebels: Why Counterculture Became Consumer Culture.* New York: Harper Collins.

Hebdige, Dick. 1979. *Subcultures and the Meaning of Style.* London: Methuen.

Hide, Robin, 2001. *A Partial Bibliography of Coffee in Eastern Highland Province, Papua New Guinea.* Canberra: Australian National University.

Hietz, Peter. 2005. "Conservation of Vascular Epiphyte Diversity in Mexican Coffee Plantation." *Conservation Biology* 19, no. 2, 391–99.

Highlands Quarterly Bulletin. 1960a. Vol. 1, no. 1. Sydney: Sydney and Melbourne Publishing.

——. 1960b. Vol. 1, no. 3. Sydney: Sydney and Melbourne Publishing.

——. 1962. Vol. 3, no. 2. Sydney: Sydney and Melbourne Publishing.

——. 1965. Vol. 6, no. 3. Sydney: Sydney and Melbourne Publishing.

——. 1968. Vol. 9, no. 2. Sydney: Sydney and Melbourne Publishing.

——. 1971. Vol. 12, no. 2. Sydney: Sydney and Melbourne Publishing.

Hobson, K. 2002. "Competing Discourses of Sustainable Consumption: Does the 'Rationalization of Lifestyles' Make Sense?" *Environmental Politics* 11, 95–120.

——. 2003a. "Consumption, Environmental Sustainability and Human Geography in Australia: A Missing Research Agenda?" *Australian Geographical Studies* 41, 148–55.

——. 2003b. "Thinking Habits into Action: The Role of Knowledge and Process in Questioning Household Consumption Practices." *Local Environment* 8, 95–112.

Holloway, Thomas. 1980. *Immigrants on the Land: Coffee and Society in São Paulo, 1886–1934.* Chapel Hill: University of North Carolina Press.

Holt, Flora Lu. 2005. "The Catch-22 of Conservation: Indigenous Peoples, Biologists and Culture Change." *Human Ecology* 33, no. 2, 199–215.

Hopkins, T. K., and I. Wallerstein. 1986. "Commodity Chains and the World Economy prior to 1800." *Review* 10, no. 1, 157–70.

Hoy, Harry E. 1938. "Blue Mountain Coffee in Jamaica." *Economic Geography* 14, no. 4, 409–12.

Hughes, A. 1999. "Constructing Competitive Spaces: On the Corporate Practice of British Retailer-Supplier Relationships." *Environment and Planning A* 31, 819–39.

——. 2001a. "Global Commodity Networks, Ethical Trade and Governmentality: Organizing Business Responsibility in the Kenyan Cut Flower Industry." *Transactions of the Institute of British Geographers* 26, 390–406.

——. 2001b. "Multi-stakeholder Approaches to Ethical Trade: Towards a Reorganization of UK Retailers' Global Supply Chains?" *Journal of Economic Geography* 1, 421–37.

Hull, Jennifer Bingham. 1999. "Can Coffee Drinkers Save the Rain Forest?" *Atlantic Monthly*, August, 19–21.

IBRD (International Bank for Reconstruction and Development). 1965. *The Economic Development of the Territory of Papua and New Guinea: Report of a Mission Organized by the International Bank for Reconstruction and Development at the Request of the Government of the Commonwealth of Australia.* Baltimore: Johns Hopkins University Press.

Igoe, James. 2010a. "The Spectacle of Nature in the Global Economy of Appearances: Anthropological Engagements with the Spectacular Mediations of Transnational Conservation." *Critique of Anthropology* 30, no. 4.

——. 2010b. "A Spectacular Eco-tour around the Historic Bloc: Theorizing the Current Convergence of Conservation and Capitalism," ed. J. Igoe, K Neves, and D. Brockington. *Antipode* 42, no. 3, 486–512.

Illy, A., and R. Viani. 1995. *Espresso Coffee: The Chemistry of Quality.* San Diego: Academic.

Ingold, Tim. 2000. *The Perception of the Environment: Essays on Livelihood, Dwelling and Skill.* New York: Routledge.

Ivy, Marilyn. 1995. *Discourses of the Vanishing: Modernity, Phantasm, Japan.* Chicago: University of Chicago Press.

Jacka, Jerry. 2001. "Coca Cola and *Kolo*: Land, Ancestors, and Development." *Anthropology Today* 17, no. 4, 3–8.

———. 2002. "Cults and Christianity among the Enga and Ipili." *Oceania* 72, no. 3, 196–214.

———. 2003. "God, Gold, and the Ground: Place-Based Political Ecology in a New Guinea Borderland." PhD diss., University of Oregon.

———. 2005a. "Emplacement and Millennial Expectations in an Era of Development and Globalization: Heaven and the Appeal of Christianity for the Ipili." *American Anthropologist* 107, no. 4, 643–53.

———. 2005b. " 'Our Skins Are Weak': Ipili Modernity and the Demise of Discipline." *Embodying Modernity and Postmodernity: Ritual, Praxis, and Social Change in Melanesia*, ed. S. Bamford. Durham: Carolina Academic.

———. 2006. "Whitemen, the Ipili, and the City of Gold: A History of the Politics of Race and Development in Highlands New Guinea." *Ethnohistory* 53, no. 4.

Jaffee, Daniel. 2007. *Brewing Justice: Fair Trade Coffee, Sustainability, and Survival.* Berkeley: University of California Press.

Jaffee, D., J. Kloppenburg, and M. Monroy. 2004. "Bringing the 'Moral Charge' Home: Fair Trade within the North and within the South." *Rural Sociology* 69, no. 2, 169–96.

Jimenez, M. 1995. "From Plantation to Cup": Coffee and Capitalism in the United States, 1830–1930." *Coffee, Society, and Power in Latin America*, ed. W. Roseberry et al. Baltimore: Johns Hopkins University Press.

Jonasson, Olof. 1933. "Natural Conditions for Coffee Culture." *Economic Geography* 9, no. 4, 356–67.

Jukes, Joseph Beete. 1847. *Narrative of the Surveying Voyage of H.M.S. Fly, Commanded by Captain F. P. Blackwood, R.N., in Torres Strait, New Guinea, and Other Islands of the Eastern Archipelago, during the Years 1842–1846.* London: T. and W. Boone.

Kahn, Miriam. 2000. "Tahiti Intertwined: Ancestral Land, Tourist Postcard, and Nuclear Test Site." *American Anthropologist* 102, no. 1, 6–24.

Kaplan, Martha. 2007. "Fijian Water in Fiji and New York: Local Politics and a Global Commodity." *Cultural Anthropology* 22, no. 4, 685–706.

Katz, Cindi. 1998. "Whose Nature, Whose Culture? Private Productions of Space and the 'Preservation' of Nature." *Remaking Reality: Nature at the Millennium*, ed. Bruce Braun and Noel Castree. London: Routledge.

Kavanamur, David, et al. 2004. *Understanding Reform in Papua New Guinea: An Analytical Evaluation.* Port Moresby: Institute of National Affairs Port Moresby, Papua New Guinea.

Keane, Webb. 1997. *Signs of Recognition: Powers and Hazards of Representation in an Indonesian Society.* Berkeley: University of California Press.

Keck, Verena. 2005. *Social Discord and Bodily Disorders: Healing among the Yupno of Papua New Guinea.* Durham: Carolina Academic.

Keesing, R. 1989. "Creating the Past." *Contemporary Pacific* 1, nos. 1–2, 19–42.

Kirk, Malcolm. 1972. "Head-hunters in Today's World: The Asmat of New Guinea." *National Geographic* 141, 377–409.

Kirsch, Stuart. 2006. *Reverse Anthropology: Indigenous Analysis of Social and Environmental Relations in New Guinea.* Stanford: Stanford University Press.

Klein, A. M., et al. 2003. "Pollination of Coffea Canephora in Relation to Local and Regional Agroforestry Management." *Journal of Applied Ecology* 40, 837–45.

Knauft, Bruce. 1993. *South Coast New Guinea Cultures: History, Comparison, Dialectic.* Cambridge: Cambridge University Press.

———. 1999. *From Primitive to Post Colonial in Melanesia and Anthropology.* Ann Arbor: University of Michigan Press.

———. 2002. *Exchanging the Past: A Rainforest World of Before and After.* Chicago: University of Chicago Press.

Kopytoff, Igor. 1986. "The Cultural Biography of Things: Commoditization as Process." *The Social Life of Things: Commodities in Cultural Perspective,* ed. Arjun Appadurai. Cambridge: Cambridge University Press.

Korner, Manfred. 1997. "Hamburg: Germany's Largest Tea and Coffee Port." *Tea and Coffee Trade Journal,* November.

Langness, L. L. 1999. *Men and "Woman" in New Guinea.* Novato, Calif.: Chandler and Sharp.

Larson, Bruce L. 2003. "Eco-labels for Credence Attributes: The Case of Shade-Grown Coffee." *Environment and Development Economics* 8, 529–47.

Leach, James. 1993. *Land of Desire: Merchants, Power, and the Rise of a New American Culture.* New York: Pantheon.

Leahy, M. J. 1994. *Explorations into Highland New Guinea, 1930–1935.* Bathurst, N.S.W.: Crawford House.

Lee, Martyn J. 1993. *Consumer Culture Reborn.* London: Routledge.

Lefebvre, Henri. 1991. *The Production of Space.* Oxford: Oxford University Press.

Leslie, Deborah, and Suzanne Reimer. 1999. "Spatializing Commodity Chains." *Progress in Human Geography* 23, no. 3, 401–20.

Lichtenberg, Judith. 1998. "Consuming because Others Consume." *The Ethics of Consumption: The Good Life, Justice, and Global Stewardship,* ed. D. Crocker and T. Linden. New York: Rowman and Littlefield.

Liechty, M. 2003. *Suitably Modern.* Princeton: Princeton University Press.

Lind, D., and E. Barham. 2004. "The Social Life of the Tortilla: Food, Cultural Politics and Contested Commodification." *Agriculture and Human Values* 21, 47–60.

Lindenbaum, Shirley. 2002. "Fore Narratives through Time." *Current Anthropology* 43, S63–S73.

Lipset, David M. 1997. *Mangrove Man: Dialogics of Culture in the Sepik Estuary (Papua New Guinea).* Cambridge: Cambridge University Press.

———. 2004. "Modernity without Romance? Masculinity and Desire in Courtship Stories Told by Young Papua New Guinean Men." *American Ethnologist* 31, 205–24.

——. 2007. "Women without Qualities: More Courtship Stories Told by Papua New Guinea Youth." *Ethnology* 46, 93–111.

——. 2011. "The Tides: Masculinity and Climate Change in Coastal Papua New Guinea." *Journal of the Royal Anthropological Institute* 17, 20–43.

LiPuma, Edward. 2000. *Encompassing Others: The Magic of Modernity in Melanesia.* Ann Arbor: University of Michigan Press.

Long, N., and M. Villareal. 1998. "Small Product, Big Issues: Value Contestations and Cultural Identities in Cross-border Commodity Networks." *Development and Change* 29, 725–50.

Loureiro, Maria L., and Justus Lotade. 2005. "Do Fair Trade and Eco-labels in Coffee Wake Up the Consumer Conscience?" *Ecological Economics* 53, 129–38.

Lukács, Georg. (1923) 1971. *History and Class Consciousness.* Cambridge: MIT Press.

Lyon, Sarah. 2010. "A Market of Our Own: Women's Livelihoods and Fair Trade Markets." *Fair Trade and Social Justice: Global Ethnographies,* ed. Sarah Lyon and Mark Moberg, 125–46. New York: New York University Press.

Lyon, Sarah, and Mark Moberg, eds. 2010. *Fair Trade and Social Justice.* New York: New York University Press.

MacVean, Charles. 1997. "Coffee Growing: Sun or Shade?" *Science,* new series 275 (5306), 1552.

MacWilliam, S. 1993. "The Politics of Privatisation: The Case of the Coffee Industry Corporation in Papua New Guinea." *Australian Journal of Political Science* 28, no. 3, 481–98.

——. 1997. Review of *The Money Tree: Coffee in Papua New Guinea. Journal of Pacific History* 32, no. 1, 129–31.

——. 2008. "Placing the Planters; European Settlers in Late Colonial Papua New Guinea." Unpublished manuscript.

——. 2009. "Development and Agriculture in Late Colonial Papua New Guinea." PhD diss., Australian National University.

Malkki, Liisa. 1997. "National Geographic: The Rooting of Peoples and the Territorialization of National Identity among Scholars and Refugees." *Culture, Power, Place. Explorations in Critical Anthropology,* ed. Akhil Gupta and James Ferguson, 52–74. Durham: Duke University Press.

Mankekar, Purnima. 2004. "Dangerous Desires: Television and Erotics in Late Twentieth Century India." *Journal of Asian Studies* 63, no. 2, 403–31.

Manning, Robert D. 2000. *Credit Card Nation: The Consequences of America's Addiction to Credit.* New York: Basic Books.

Mansfield, B. 2003a. "From Catfish to Organic Fish: Making Distinctions about Nature as Cultural Economic Practice." *Geoforum* 34, 329–42.

——. 2003b. " 'Imitation Crab' and the Material Culture of Commodity Production." *Social and Cultural Geographies* 10, 176–95.

Manuell, Naomi. 2003. "Green in Goroka: Naomi Manuell Provides a Child's-Eye View of White Society in Post-independence Papua New Guinea." *Meanjin,* 1 September.

Marcus, George. 1998. *Ethnography through Thick and Thin*. Princeton: Princeton University Press.

Marsden, T., and N. Wrigley. 1995. "Regulation, Retailing and Consumption." *Environment and Planning A* 27, 1899–1912.

Marx, Karl. (1867) 1975. *Capital*, vol. 1. New York: Penguin.

Mather, C., and C. Mackenzie. 2006. "The Body in Transnational Commodity Cultures: South Africa's Outspan 'Girls' Campaign." *Social and Cultural Geography* 7, no. 3, 403–20.

Mauss, Marcel. (1925) 1954. *The Gift: Forms and Functions of Exchange in Archaic Societies*. Glencoe, Ill.: Free Press.

May, J. 1996. "A Little Taste of Something More Exotic: Imaginative Geographies of Everyday Life." *Geography* 81, 57–64.

May, R. J. 1981. "The Artifact Industry: Maximizing Returns to Producers." Boroko, Papua New Guinea: Institute of Applied Social and Economic Development.

McArthur, J. R. 1953. "Report of Patrol to the Area between Goroka and Mount Karimui, December 28, 1952–February 11, 1953." Unpublished report, Department of District and Native Affairs, Australian Administration.

McBride, Sam, and Nancy McBride. 1973. *Gimi Anthropology Essentials*. Unpublished manuscript, Summer Institute of Linguistics, Anthropology Section, Ukarumpa, Papua New Guinea.

McPherson, Naomi M. 2001. *In Colonial New Guinea: Anthropological Perspectives*. Association of Social Anthropology in Oceania Monograph. Pittsburgh: University of Pittsburgh Press.

McRobbie. A. 1997. "Bridging the Gap: Feminism, Fashion and Consumption." *Feminist Review* 55, 73–89.

Meggitt, Mervyn J. 1965. *The Lineage System of the Mae-Enga of New Guinea*. London: Cohen and West.

———. 1971. "The Pattern of Leadership among the Mae-Enga of New Guinea." *Politics in New Guinea; Traditional and in the Context of Change, Some Anthropological Perspectives*. Nedlands: University of Western Australia Press.

Mennell, S. 1985. *All Manners of Food*. Oxford: Basil Blackwell.

Miller, Daniel. 1987. *Material Culture and Mass Consumption*. Oxford: B. Blackwell.

———. 1988. "Appropriating the State on the Council Estate." *Man* 23, 353–72.

———. 1994. *Modernity: An Ethnographic Approach: Dualism and Mass Consumption in Trinidad*. Oxford: Berg.

———, ed. 1995. *Acknowledging Consumption: A Review of New Studies*. London: Routledge.

———. 1997. *Capitalism: An Ethnographic Approach*. Oxford: Berg.

———. 1998a. *A Theory of Shopping*. Ithaca: Cornell University Press.

———. 1998b. "A Theory of Virtualism." In *Virtualism: A New Political Economy*. Oxford: Berg.

———, ed. 1998c. *Material Cultures*. Chicago: University of Chicago Press.

———. 2001a. *The Dialectics of Shopping*. Chicago: University of Chicago Press.

———. 2001b. *Home Possessions: Material Cultures behind Closed Doors*. Oxford: Berg.

———. 2001c. "The Poverty of Morality." *Journal of Consumer Culture* 1, 225–43.

Miller, Daniel, and D. Slater. 2000. *The Internet: An Ethnographic Approach*. Oxford: Berg.

Mintz, Sidney W. 1985. *Sweetness and Power: The Place of Sugar in Modern History*. New York: Penguin.

Mintz, Sidney W., and C. M. Du Bois. 2002. "The Anthropology of Food and Eating." *Annual Review of Anthropology* 31, 99–119.

Mission Aviation Fellowship. 2005. MAF: *Flying for Life: Annual Report*. Cairns, Australia: Mission Aviation Fellowship.

Mitchell, H. W. 1988. "Cultivation and Harvesting of the Arabica Coffee Tree." *Coffee: Agronomy*, ed. R. J. Clarke. New York: Elsevier Applied Science.

Moberg, Mark. 2010. "A New World? Neoliberalism and Fair Trade Farming in the Eastern Carribean." *Fair Trade and Social Justice: Global Ethnographies*, ed. Sarah Lyon and Mark Moberg, 47–71. New York: New York University Press.

Moberg, Mark, and Sarah Lyon. 2010. *Fair Trade and Social Justice: Global Ethnographies*. New York: New York University Press.

Moguel, Patricia, and Victor M. Toldeo. 2004. "Biodiversity Conservation in Traditional Coffee System of Mexico." *Conservation Biology* 18, no. 5 [literature review].

Morgan, Lewis Henry. 1868. *The American Beaver and His Works*. Philadelphia: J. B. Lippincott.

Mort, F., and P. Thompson. 1994. "Retailing, Commercial Culture and Masculinity in 1950s Britain: The Case of Montague Burton, the 'Taylor' of Taste." *History Workshop Journal* 38, 106–27.

Mosse. David. 2005. *Cultivating Development: An Ethnography of Aid Policy and Practice*. Ann Arbor: Pluto.

Munger, Edwin S. 1952. "African Coffee on Kilimanjaro: A Chagga Kihamba." *Economic Geography* 28, no. 2, 181–85.

Munn, N. 1971. "The Transformation of Subjects into Objects in Walbiri and Pitjantjatjara Myth." *Australian Aboriginal Anthropology*, ed. R. Berndt. Canberra: AIAS.

Muradian, Roland, and Wim Pelupessy. 2005. "Governing the Coffee Chain: the Role of Voluntary Regulatory Systems." *World Development* 33, no. 12, 2029–44.

Nava, M. 1992. *Changing Culture: Feminism, Youth, and Consumerism*. London: Sage.

Nevins, Joseph. 2003. "Restitution over Coffee: Truth, Reconciliation, and Environmental Violence in East Timor." *Political Geography* 22, 677–701.

O'Dougherty, Maureen. 2002. *Consumption Intensified: The Politics of Middle-Class Daily Life in Brazil*. Durham: Duke University Press.

Olschewski, Roland, et al. 2006. "Economic Evaluation of Pollination Services Comparing Coffee Landscapes in Ecuador and Indonesia." *Ecology and Society* 11, no. 1, 7.

Orlove, Benjamin S. 1997. *The Allure of the Foreign*. Ann Arbor: University of Michigan Press.

Ortner, Sherry B. 1998. "Generation X: Anthropology in a Media-Saturated World." *Cultural Anthropology* 13, no. 3, 414–40.

Oxfam. 2001. "The Coffee Market: A Background Study." Oxfam Division of International Commodity Research. Oliver Brown, Celine Charveriat, and Dominic Eagleton, contributing authors. Available at www.maketradefair.org/assets/english/ BackgroundStudyCoffeeMarket.pdf.

Paige, J. M. 1997. *Coffee and Power: Revolution and the Rise of Democracy in Central America*. Cambridge: Harvard University Press.

Palacio, Marco. 1980. *Coffee in Colombia, 1850–1970: An Economic, Social and Political History*. Cambridge: Cambridge University Press.

Parry, Jonathon, and Maurice Bloch. 1989. *Money and the Morality of Exchange*. Cambridge: Cambridge University Press.

Pascual, Aixa M. 2006. "Peace, Love and Coffee; Woodstock Coffeehouse Opens Third Store." *Atlanta Journal-Constitution*, 17 December, 18ZH.

Peet, Richard, and Michael Watts. 1996. *Liberation Ecologies: Environment, Development, Social Movements*. New York: Routledge.

Peluso, Nancy. 1995. "Whose Woods are These: Counter-mapping Forest Territories in Indonesia." *Antipode* 27, no. 4, 383–406.

Pendergrast, M. 1999. *Uncommon Grounds: The History of Coffee and How It Transformed Our World*. New York: Basic Books.

Pennypacker, Mindy. 1997. "Habitat-Saving Habit: Shaded Coffee Plantations Help Preserve Tropical Rainforests." *Sierra Journal* 82, no. 2.

Perfecto, Ivette, et al. 1996. "Shade Coffee: A Disappearing Refuge for Biodiversity." *Bioscience* 46, no. 8, 598–608.

Phillips, Lynne. 2006. "Food and Globalization." *Annual Review of Anthropology* 35, 37–57.

Philpott, Stacy M., and Thomas Dietsch. 2003. "Coffee and Conservation: A Global Context and the Value of Farmer Involvement (Comments)." *Conservation Biology* 17, no. 6, 1844–46.

Pigliasco, Guido Carlo. 2010. "We Branded Ourselves Long Ago: Intangible Cultural Property and Commodification of Fijian Firewalking." *Oceania* 80, 161–81.

Pineda, Eduardo, et al. 2005. "Frog, Bat, and Dung Beetle Diversity in the Cloud Forest and Coffee Agroecosystems of Vera Cruz, Mexico." *Conservation Biology* 19, no. 2, 400–410.

Pitts, Maxine. 2002. *Crime, Corruption, and Capacity in Papua New Guinea*. Canberra: Asia Pacific Press.

"PNG Coffee Is Healthy." 2005. *Post Courier*, 28 September.

Polanyi, K. 1958. *The Great Transformation*. Boston: Beacon.

Ponte, S. 2002a. "Brewing a Bitter Cup? Deregulation, Quality and the Re-organization of Coffee Marketing in East Africa." *Journal of Agrarian Change* 2, no. 2, 248–72.

——. 2002b. "The 'Latte Revolution'? Regulation, Markets and Consumption in the Global Coffee Chain." *World Development* 30, no. 7, 1099–1122.

Potvin, Catherine, et al. 2005. "Biodiversity and Modernization in Four Coffee-Producing Villages of Mexico." *Ecology and Society* 10, no. 1.

Price, S. 1986. *Co-wives and Calabashes*. Ann Arbor: University of Michigan Press.

Rangan, Haripriya. 1995. "Contested Boundaries: State Policies, Forest Classifications and Deforestation in the Garhwal Himalayas." *Antipode* 27, no. 4, 343–62.

Rappaport, Roy A. 1984. *Pigs for the Ancestors: Ritual in the Ecology of a New Guinea People*. New Haven: Yale University Press.

Rappole, John H., David I. King, and Jorge H. Vega Rivera. 2003. "Coffee and Conservation." *Conservation Biology* 17, no. 1, 334–36.

Raynolds, L. T. 2000. "Re-embedding Global Agriculture: The International Organic and Fair Trade Movements." *Agriculture and Human Values* 17, 297–309.

——. 2002. *Poverty Alleviation through Participation in Fair Trade Coffee Networks: Existing Research and Critical Issues*. Report for the Ford Foundation, Colorado State University, http://www.colostate.edu/Depts/Sociology/FairTrade ResearchGroup/doc/rayback.pdf.

Raynolds, L., et al. 2004. "Fair Trade Coffee: Building Producer Capacity via Global Networks." *Journal of International Development* 16, no. 8, 1109–21.

Raynolds, L., and D. Murray, eds. 2007. *Fair Trade: The Challenges of Transforming Globalization*. London: Routledge.

Read, Kenneth E. 1965. *The High Valley: An Autobiographical Account of Two Years Spent in the Central Highlands of New Guinea*. New York: Charles Scribner's Sons.

——. 1986. *Return to the High Valley*. Berkeley: University of California Press.

Renard, M. 1999. "The Interstices of Globalization: The Example of Fair Coffee." *Sociologia Ruralis* 39, 484–502.

Ricketts, Taylor H. 2004. "Tropical Forest Fragments Enhance Pollinator Activity in Nearby Coffee Crops." *Conservation Biology* 18, no. 5.

Robbins, Joel. 1995. "Dispossessing the Spirits: Christian Transformations of Desire and Ecology among the Urapmin of Papua New Guinea." *Ethnology* 34, no. 3, 211–24.

——. 2003. "Properties of Nature, Properties of Culture: Possession, Recognition, and the Substance of Politics in a Papua New Guinea Society." *Suomen Anthropologi* 1, no. 28, 9–28.

——. 2004. *Becoming Sinners: Christianity and Moral Torment in a Papua New Guinea Society*. Berkeley: University of California Press.

Roberts, Dina L., Robert J. Cooper, and Lisa J. Petit. 2000. "Use of Premontane Moist Forest and Shade Coffee Agroecosystems by Army Ants in Western Panama." *Conservation Biology* 14, no. 1, 192–99.

Rocheleau, Dianne, and Laurie Ross. 1995. "Trees as Tools, Trees as Text: Struggles over Resources in Zambrana Chacuey, Dominican Republic." *Antipode* 27, no. 4, 407–28.

Roe, E. 2006. "Material Connectivity, the Immaterial and the Aesthetic of Eating

Practices: An Argument for How Genetically Modified Foodstuff Becomes Inedible." *Environment and Planning A* 38, 465–81.

Roseberry, William. 1996. "The Rise of Yuppie Coffees and the Reimagination of Class in the United States." *American Anthropologist* 98, no. 4, 762–75.

Roseberry, W., L. Gudmundson, et al. 1995. *Coffee, Society, and Power in Latin America*. Baltimore: Johns Hopkins University Press.

Rothman, Jordana. 2010. "The Best Coffee in NYC." *Time Out New York*, 7 December, 10–14.

Roubik, David W. 2002. "The Value of Bees to the Coffee Harvest." *Nature* 417, no. 13.

Rutz, Henry, and Benjamin S. Orlove, eds. 1989. *The Social Economy of Consumption*. Lanham, Md.: University Press of America.

Sadasivam, Bharati. 1997. "The Impact of Structural Adjustment on Women: A Governance and Human Rights Agenda." *Human Rights Quarterly* 19, no. 3, 630–65.

Sahlins, Marshall. 1994. "Cosmologies of Capitalism: The Trans-Pacific Sector of 'the World System.'" *Culture, Power, History*, ed. N. Dirks et al. Princeton: Princeton University Press.

——. (1992) 2005. "The Economics of Develop-Man in the Pacific." *The Making of Global and Local Modernities in Melanesia: Humiliation, Transformation and the Nature of Cultural Change*, ed. J. Robbins and A. Wardlow. Aldershot, England: Ashgate.

Schapira, Karl, Joel Schapira, and David Schapira. 1982. *The Book of Coffee and Tea*, rev. edn. New York: St. Martin's.

Schivelbusch, W. 1993. *Tastes of Paradise: A Social History of Spices, Stimulants and Intoxicants*. New York: Vintage.

Schneider, Jane. 1978. "Peacocks and Penguins: The Political Economy of European Cloth and Colors." *American Ethnologist* 5, 413–47.

Schor, Juliet B. 2000. *The Overspent American: Upscaling, Downshifting and the New Consumer*. New York: Basic Books.

Scott, James. 1998. *Seeing like a State: How Certain Schemes to Improve the Human Condition Have Failed*. New Haven: Yale University Press.

Sennett, Richard. 1992. *The Fall of Public Man*. New York: W. W. Norton.

Sexton, Lorraine. 1986a. *Mothers of Money, Daughters of Coffee*. Ann Arbor: University of Michigan Research Press.

——. 1986b. "Mothers of Money, Daughters of Coffee: The Wok Meri Movement." *Studies in Cultural Anthropology* 10. Ann Arbor: University of Michigan Research Press.

Shackleton, R. 1996. "Retailer Internationalization: A Culturally Constructed Phenomenon." *Retailing, Consumption and Capital: Towards the New Retail Geography*, ed. N. Wrigley and M. Lowe. Harlow: Longman.

Sheller, M. 2005. "The Ethical Banana: Markets, Migrants and the Globalization of a Fruit." Paper presented to the STS visiting speaker series "Globalization in Practice: Science and Technology Studies (STS) Perspectives on the Every Day Life of Globalization." Said Business School, University of Oxford. Retrieved 14 February

2006 from www.sbs.ox.ac.uk/NR/rdonlyres/EE75C10F-5FAE-4B8C-8620-FB 353608F75B/953/MimiSheller.pdf.

Shreck, A. 2002. "Just Bananas? Fair Trade Banana Production in the Dominican Republic." *International Journal of Sociology of Agriculture and Food* 10, 13–23.

——. 2005. "Resistance, Redistribution and Power in the Fair Trade Banana Initiative." *Agriculture and Human Values* 22, 17–29.

Simmel, George. (1904) 1971. *On Individuality and Social Forms: Selected Writings.* Chicago: University of Chicago Press.

Sinclair, James. 1995. *The Money Tree.* Bathurst, N.S.W.: Crawford House.

Slater, Don. 1997. *Consumer Culture and Modernity.* Cambridge, England: Polity.

Smith, Julia. 2010. "Fair Trade and the Speciality Coffee Market: Growing Alliances, Shifting Rivalries." *Fair Trade and Social Justice: Global Ethnographies,* ed. Sarah Lyon and Mark Moberg, 28–47. New York: New York University Press.

Smith, Neil. 1991. *Uneven Development: Nature, Capital, and the Production of Space Ideas,* 2nd edn. Oxford: B. Blackwell.

——. 1996. "The Production of Nature." *Future Natural,* ed. George Robertson and Melinda Marsh. London: Routledge.

Soto-Pinto, Lorena, et al. 2000. "Shade Effect on Coffee Production at the Northern Tzeltal Zone of the State of Chiapas, Mexico." *Agriculture, Ecosystems and Environment* 80, 61–69.

Spark, Ceridwen. 2005. "Whites Out? Historicising the Relationship between Australia and Papua New Guinea." *Journal of Pacific History* 40, no. 2, 213–19.

Stasch, Rupert. 1996. "Killing as Reproductive Agency: Dugong, Pigs, and Humanity among the Kiwai, circa 1900." *Anthropos* 91, 359–79.

——. 2006. " 'The Sad Thing Is, Nothing Remains Unknown Forever': Contradictory Social Desires in 'Stone Age' Tourism and Journalism." Paper presented at the Society for Cultural Anthropology, Milwaukee, May 2006.

——. 2010. "Society of Others: Kinship and Mourning in a West Papuan Place." *Journal of Linguistic Anthropology* 20, no. 1, 248–50.

——. 2011. "Textual Iconicity and the Primitivist Cosmos: Chronotopes of Desire in Travel Writing about Korowai of West Papua." *Journal of Linguistic Anthropology* 21, no. 1, 1–21.

Stassart, P., and S. Whatmore. 2003. "Metabolizing Risk: Food Scares and the Un/Remaking of Belgian Beef." *Environment and Planning A* 35, 449–62.

Steingarten, Jeffrey. 1996. *The Man Who Ate Everything.* New York: Vintage.

——. 2010. "Brewed Awakening." *Vogue,* June, 177–79.

Stewart, R. G. 1992. *Coffee: The Political Economy of an Export Industry in Papua New Guinea.* Boulder: Westview.

Storey, John. 1993. *Cultural Theory and Popular Culture.* Athens: University of Georgia Press.

Strathern, Marilyn. 1988. *The Gender of the Gift: Problems with Women and Problems with Society in Melanesia.* Berkeley: University of California Press.

——. 1992. *After Nature: English Kinship in the Late Twentieth Century.* Cambridge: Cambridge University Press.

Strong, Thomas P. 2004. "Pikosa: Loss and Life in the Papua New Guinea Highlands." PhD diss., Princeton University.

Swadling, Pamela. 1996. *Plumes from Paradise*. Boroko: University of Papua New Guinea Press.

Taussig, Michael. 1980. *The Devil and Commodity Fetishism in South America*. Chapel Hill: University of North Carolina Press.

——. 1989. "History as Commodity in Some Recent American (Anthropological) Literature." *Critique of Anthropology* 9, no. 1, 7–23.

——. 1995. "The Sun Gives without Receiving: An Old Story." *Comparative Studies in Society and History* 37, no. 2, 368–98.

——. 2000. "The Beach (A Fantasy)." *Critical Inquiry* 26, no. 2, 248–78.

Temu, Ila. 1991. "An Economic Analysis of Coffee Development, Supply and Demand in Papua New Guinea." PhD diss., University of California, Davis.

——. 1995. "Price Policy Analysis: The Case of Coffee in Papua New Guinea." National Research Institute Paper no. 79, Boroko, Papua New Guinea.

Territory of Papua and New Guinea 1967. "Economic Development of Papua and New Guinea: A Report Prepared by Direction of His Honor, the Administrator of Papua and New Guinea, June 1967." Repr. of paper tabled in the House of Assembly, 9 June 1967.

Thomas, Nicholas. 1994. *Colonialism's Culture: Anthropology, Travel and Government*. Princeton: Princeton University Press.

Tobin, J. 1992. *Re-made in Japan*. New Haven: Yale University Press.

Topik, S., and A. Wells. 1998. *The Second Conquest of Latin America: Coffee, Henequen, and Oil during the Export Boom, 1850–1930*. Austin: University of Texas Press, Institute of Latin American Studies.

Tsing, Anna L. 2000. "Inside the Economy of Appearance." *Public Culture* 12, 115–44.

——. 2004. *Friction: An Ethnography of Global Connection*. Princeton: Princeton University Press.

Tuzin, Donald F. 1997. *The Cassowary's Revenge: The Life and Death of Masculinity in a New Guinea Society*. Chicago: University of Chicago Press.

Um, Nancy. 2009. *The Merchant Houses of Mocha: Trade and Architecture in an Indian Ocean Port*. Seattle: University of Washington Press.

Usherwood, B. 1997. "Transnational Publishing: The Case of Elle Decoration." *Buy This Book: Studies in Advertising and Consumption*, ed. M. Nava, A. Blake, I. MacRury, and B. Richards. London: Routledge.

Van Dongen, Irene S. 1961. "Coffee Trade, Coffee Regions, and Coffee Ports in Angola." *Economic Geography* 37, no. 4, 320–46.

Van Marle, Gavin. 2008. "Europe Terminals Stretched to Limit." *Lloyds List Daily Commercial News*, 31 January, 8–9.

Veblen, Thorstein. (1899) 1958. "The Theory of the Leisure Class: An Economic Study of Institutions." *The Portable Veblen*, ed. M. Lerner. New York: Viking.

Verg, Erich, and Martin Verg. 2007. *Das Abenteuer das Hamburg heißt*, 4th edn. Hamburg: Ellert & Richter.

von Hayek, F. 1960. *The Constitution of Liberty*. Chicago: University of Chicago Press.

Walter, Michael A. H. B., ed. 1980. *Cattle Ranches Are about People: Social Science Dimensions of a Commercial Feasibility Study*. Monograph no. 14. Institute of Applied Social and Economic Research, Boroko, Papua New Guinea.

——, ed. 1981. *What Do We Do about Plantations?* Monograph no. 15. Institute of Applied Social and Economic Research. Boroko, Papua New Guinea.

Wardlow, Holly. 1993. " 'Women Are Our Coffee': Historical Factors and Current Variables in Smallholder Coffee Production in Papua New Guinea." Unpublished paper, Emory University.

——. 2006. *Wayward Women: Sexuality and Agency in a New Guinea Society*. Berkeley: University of California Press.

Warner, Michael. 2002. *Publics and Counterpublics*. New York: Zone.

Watts, M., and J. McCarthy. 1997. "Nature as Artifice, Nature as Artifact: Development, Environment and Modernity in the Late Twentieth Century." *Geographies of Economies*, ed. R. Lee and J. Wills. London: Arnold.

Weiner, Annette. 1992. *Inalienable Possessions: The Paradox of Keeping while Giving*. Berkeley: University of California Press.

——. 1995. *The Lost Drum: The Myth of Sexuality in Papua New Guinea and Beyond*. Madison: University of Wisconsin Press.

Weismantel, 1989. "The Children Cry for Bread." *The Social Economy of Consumption*, ed. H. Rutz and B. Orlove. Lanham, Md.: University Press of America.

Weiss, Brad. 1996a. "Coffee Breaks and Coffee Connections: The Lived Experience of a Commodity in Tanzanian and European Worlds." *Cross-Cultural Consumption: Global Markets, Local Realities*, ed. D. Howes. London: Routledge.

——. 1996b. *The Making and Unmaking of the Haya Lived World*. Durham: Duke University Press.

West, Paige. 2001. "Environmental Non-governmental Organizations and the Nature of Ethnographic Inquiry." *Social Analysis* 45, no. 2, 55–77.

——. 2005a. "Holding the Story Forever: The Aesthetics of Ethnographic Labor." *Anthropological Forum* 15, no. 3, 267–75.

——. 2005b. "Translation, Value, and Space: Theorizing an Ethnographic and Engaged Environmental Anthropology." *American Anthropologist* 107, no. 4, 632–42.

——. 2006. *Conservation Is Our Government Now: The Politics of Ecology in Papua New Guinea*. Durham: Duke University Press.

West, Paige, and J. Carrier. 2004. "Ecotourism and Authenticity: Getting Away from It All?" *Current Anthropology* 45, no. 4, 483–91.

Wild, A. 2005. *Coffee: A Dark History*. New York: W. W. Norton.

Wilk, Richard. 1989. "Houses as Consumer Goods." *The Social Economy of Consumption*, ed. H. Rutz and B. Orlove. Lanham, Md.: University Press of America.

——. 1994. "Goods as a Dialogue about Development." *Consumption and Identity*, ed. J. Friedman. Chur: Harwood Academic.

———. 1995. "Learning to Be Local in Belize." *World Apart*, ed. D. Miller. London: Routledge.

Willis, Ian. 1969. "Who Was First? The First White Man into the New Guinea Highlands." *Journal of the Papua and New Guinea Society* 3, no. 1.

Willis, Susan. 1991. "Unwrapping Use Value." *A Primer for Daily Life*. New York: Routledge.

Wilson, Patrick C. 2010. "Fair Trade Craft Production and Indigenous Economies: Reflections on 'Acceptable' Indigeneities." *Fair Trade and Social Justice*, ed. Sarah Lyon and Mark Moberg. New York: New York University Press.

Wrigley G. 1988. *Coffee*. London: Longman.

Wrigley, N. 1992. "Antitrust Regulation and the Restructuring of Grocery Retailing in Britain and the USA." *Environment and Planning A* 24, 727–49.

Wrigley, N., and M. Lowe, eds. 1996. *Retailing, Consumption and Capital: Towards the New Retail Geography*. Harlow: Longman.

Yan, Yunxiang. 1997. "McDonalds in Beijing: The Localization of Americana." *Golden Arches East*, ed. J. Watson. Palo Alto: Stanford University Press.

INDEX

Adventist Aviation Services, 133–40
Adventist Review, 103–4
advertise-differentiation fixation, 250–55
aesthetics, marketing and, 25–26
Africa: decline of coffee quality in, 264 n. 8;
regulation of coffee production in, 264
n. 6
agricultural production: anthropological
research on, 18–26, 262 nn. 36–37;
deregulation and reregulation of, 263 n. 1;
ecological impact of, 105–9
Air Niugini, 97, 159
airstrip coffee, 8–9
air transport, 74–75, 86; in Maimafu, 131–
40; mission groups' use of, 104, 269 n. 6;
rural vs. urban life and, 153–55; social relations of growers and buyers and, 141–45
Aiyura Station, 75
ancestors, 126–29
Anderson, Les (Pastor Les), 101–4, 132, 272
n. 9
animals, 116–18, 126–29, 269 n. 11
anobak (chant), 118–19, 121–26
ant diversity, 107
anthropological research: on agricultural
production, 18–26, 262 nn. 36–37; on distribution, 194–99; on expatriates and
industry elites, 180–92; methodological
approaches to, 18–26, 277 n. 15; on millen-

nials' coffee consumption, 229–36, 275
n. 9, 276 nn. 10–13; research stereotypes
in, 61–65
"appearance of value," 24
Arabicas Ltd., 5–7
Atticks (coffee buyer), 136–40, 272 n. 10
auna (Gimi life forces), 117–18; coffee
cultivation vs., 121, 127–29
AusAid program, 226
Australia: certification teams from, 145;
coffee importers in, 209–12; coffee shops
in, 225–29; expatriates in New Guinea
from, 102, 183–92; indigenous coffee and,
91–96, 109–10; New Guinea coffee consumption in, 85–90, 92–93; Papua New
Guinea perceived in, 226–29; privatization initiatives in, 96–97; racial issues
in coffee production and settlers from,
173–80
Australian and New Guinea Coffee Company Marketing Proprietary Limited
(ANGCO): Australian coffee importers
and, 210–12; British coffee traders in,
206–8; certification standards and, 151;
coffee industry and, 161–62; creation of,
87–88; demise of, 97–100; German coffee
traders in, 203–4; myths about coffee
production and, 208–9; structural adjustment programs and, 99–100

coffee: anthropological research on, 21–26; botanical properties of, 2, 257 n. 3, 258 n. 4, 258 n. 10; chemical properties of, 258 n. 8; ecological impact of cultivation of, 106–9; German imports of, 201–12; Gimi cultural significance of, 120–26; industrial production and, 42–48; market share statistics for, 45; neoliberal market deregulation and, 27–32; production and sales figures for, 2, 9–10; quality grades for, 260 nn. 23–24; territorial development and, 90–96

Coffee Connections, 5–7, 193, 271 n. 1; certification standards and, 145–52

Coffee Industry Board (CIB), 97

Coffee Industry Corporation (CIC), 5, 97; certification standards and, 150–52; structure and activities of, 10, 261 n. 29

Coffee Marketing Board (CMB), 87

coffee production: census figures for, 269 n. 7; distribution and, 194–99; racial issues in, 173–80; small holders' dominance of, 7; statistics on, 132, 271 n. 1; suspicion in Maimafu toward, 147–52

Cohen, Lizabeth, 247

colonialism, 71–72, 265 n. 2; division of New Guinea and, 73–76; expatriates, industry elites, and, 180–92; in Goroka, 160–61; Highlands white settlements and, 79–85; Indian experiences with, 183–84, 189–92, 273 n. 10; pacification and land legibility programs under, 76–80, 267 n. 12; Plantation Redistribution Scheme and, 89–90; race, coffee production, and, 173–80; white-owned coffee plantations and, 91–96. See also expatriate culture

Colyer Watson Ltd., 86

commensurable coffees, 204

commodification: of commensurable coffees, 204–5; of local culture, 65; neoliberalism and, 27–32

commodity affect, 234–36

commodity chain: anthropological research on, 18–26, 263 n. 39; governance structures and, 48–49

commodity circuit: anthropological research and, 20–26; labeling initiatives and, 51–55; Papua New Guinea coffee industry and, 10, 48–55

commodity fetish, 250–55

commodity production: coffee in Gimi culture as, 128–29; ethnographic research and, 28–32, 257 n. 2, 261 n. 31, 262 n. 37; global capitalism and, 1–2; marital bonds defined by, 120–22

commodity societies, 114–15

Commonwealth Scientific and Industrial Research Organisation (CSIRO), 178

community structure: certification standards and, 240–44; coffee production and, 12

Conroy, M., 53–54

conservation initiatives: indigeneity stereotypes and, 60–65; Maimafu conservation-as-development projects, 110–11; suspicion in Maimafu toward, 147–48

Consumer's Republic, A (Cohen), 247

consumption patterns: compression of time and space and, 249; embedded social relations and, 55–59; of expatriates and industry elites, 187–92; for fair trade coffee, 277 n. 14; generational analysis of, 33–38; global capitalism and increase of, 26; locations of consumption and, 212–36; of millennial generation, 231; organic labeling preferences and, 54–55; perceived values and, 246–48; postwar decline in coffee consumption and, 43–44. See also ethical consumption

containerized shipping: coffee distribution and, 196–99; specialty coffee and growth of, 264 n. 9

cooperatives, 146–52

Cooperative Societies Act of 1985, 150–51

corporate coffee producers, 4

Costa Rica, 106–7

Crater Mountain Wildlife Management Area, 110–12

critical race theory, 177–80

cross-pollination, 106–9

culture: capitalist usurpation of, 25–26, 263

culture (*cont.*)
n. 39; of expatriates and industry elites, 180–92; generational analysis and, 34–38; locations of consumption and, 214–36; marketing and images of, 221–36; in Melanesia, 112–14; neoliberalism and, 252–55
currency exchanges, 142–43
Curtis, Debra, 235–36
Customs Tariff (Papua and New Guinea Preference) Act, 74

Dean's Beans, 39, 58–59, 64–66, 148, 229, 244–47, 276 n. 10
death, in Gimi culture, 116–18, 127–29
demand, in specialty coffee market, 47–48
deregulation, 44–46, 244–48; fantasy narratives and, 66–67; price volatility and, 233–36
developing countries: labeling initiatives in, 51–55; poverty alleviation in, 253–55
"developman" concept, 22
disembedding, 55–56
distribution of coffee: anthropological research on, 194–99, 275 n. 14; ownership of coffee and, 274 n. 13; production and, 192–94; roasting and, 214–36
Doane, Molly, 50, 258 n. 9
Downs, Ian, 79, 81–82, 163, 173, 267 n. 17
Dunatina trail (Goroka), 71
Durkheim, Émile, 253
Dwyer, Michael, 71, 265 n. 3

Eastern Highlands administrative unit, 78
ecological change, 106–9
economic choice, 55–59
economic development, 90–92
"Eight Aims" document, 95–96
embedded social relations, 55–59, 244–48
enterprise initiatives, 51–52
environmental sustainability: labeling initiatives and, 51–55; market sustainability and, 240–44; specialty coffee production and, 41–48, 264 n. 5
epiphyte diversity, 107–8

Errington, Frederick, 180–92
ethical consumption: class-related patterns of, 41; fantasy narratives and, 65–67; organic labeling initiatives and, 54–55; social embeddedness and, 55–59
ethnicity, 171–73
European planter enclaves, 81–85
exchange relationships: in Gimi culture, 243–44; Maimafu coffee production and, 109–10; personhood-based relations in, 84–85, 114–15; postwar cash economy and, 79–80, 83–85, 267 nn. 14–15
exotics through commodities, 236
expatriate culture: class and, 180–92, 273 n. 8; racial issues in coffee industry and, 102, 173–80; social obligations in, 243–44. *See also* colonialism
export commodities, 9–10, 259 n. 19, 261 nn. 27–28; coffee exporters' statistics, 164–65; coffee industry growth and, 87–89; distribution systems and, 195–99; indigenous coffee production and, 94–96
export prices, 15–18
extended family groups: bird of paradise and clan identity in, 270 n. 18; certification standards and cooperation from, 145–52; coffee harvesting and processing and, 124–26; differences in coffee production among, 122–26; dominance of coffee production in, 7–8, 109–12; women's reproductive horticultural labor and, 118–20, 127–29
external investment, 94–96

Faber Report, 95–96
factory owners: labor and staffing decisions by, 171–73, 272 n. 5; social relations of, 137–40, 166–68, 272 n. 5
Faden, Patrick, 192–94
fair trade coffee: certification for, 52–55, 145–52; consumption patterns for, 50, 277 n. 14; Gimi culture influenced by, 128–29; marketing of, 39–41, 228–29; market share for, 278 n. 2; millennials' knowledge of, 231–36, 275 n. 13; suspicion of certifica-

tion for, 148–52; voluntary regulatory systems and, 49
fallow species management, 108–9
family groups. *See* extended family groups
fantasy formation: about Papua New Guinea, 59, 220–21; coffee importers' role in, 204–12; commodity affect and, 234–36; growers' vs. consumers', 131–32; global capitalism and, 24–26; indigenous stereotyping and, 61–65; in millennials' knowledge of coffee production, 229–36; neoliberal economics and, 244–48; racial issues in coffee production and, 173–80; on rural vs. urban life, 152–55; in specialty coffee market, 56–59, 65–67, 218–19; time and space compressed in, 249–51; by U.S. coffee consumers, 229–36
Ferguson, James, 27
fermentation, 144–45
Fine, B., 20
Finney, Ben, 83–84, 95, 265 n. 2, 268 n. 24
first-party regulation, 49
Fitzpatrick, Peter, 186
Five-Mile market, 70–72, 137
flexible accumulation, 26
Folgers Coffee, 45
food industry and culture: anthropological research on, 18–26, 262 nn. 36–37; vertical production systems and, 45
Fordist industrial economy: coffee production and, 4; flexible accumulation and, 26; industrial coffee roasting and, 214; post-Fordist economy, 48, 243–44
forests, 117–18, 126–29
Foucault, Michel, 249
free on board (FOB) status, 202–3, 274 n. 13
Fukuyama, Francis, 253–54

Gahuka ethnic group, 138
gardens: in Gimi culture, 127–29; kitchen, 270 n. 21; Maimafu social relations and, 120–26
gas prices, 135–36
gendered divisions: coffee certification and, 53; in Goroka coffee production, 169–73;

237–38; in Maimafu coffee production, 124–26, 270 n. 20; in Melanesian culture, 112–14; neoliberalism and, 254–55; primitivist tourism and, 265 n. 12
Gender of the Gift, The (Strathern), 114
General Foods, 45
generational stereotyping: marketing and, 34–38, 57–59, 275 n. 9; neoliberal economics and, 247–48
Generation X, 33–38, 57–58
Germany: coffee cultivation in New Guinea by, 73–74; coffee imports in, 201–12; coffee shops in, 223–25, 275 n. 6; cultural images in, 222–23
Gewertz, Deborah, 180–92
gift systems: Gimi personhood and, 126–29; Melanesian personhood and, 114–15
Gillison, Gillian, 119, 269 n. 13, 270 n. 20
Gimi culture: anthropological characteristics of, 261 n. 30; coffee cultivation and, 29–32, 110–12, 237–38; fantasy images of, 67; patrilineal extended family groups in, 109–12; personhood in, 115–18, 126–29; religious and spiritual beliefs in, 102–4; social relations in coffee industry and, 141–45, 243–44; subjectivity in, 116–18; sweet potato cultivation in, 118–20
global coffee-trading corporations, 9, 45
global commodity ecumene: anthropological research and, 20–26; labeling initiatives and, 51–55; Papua New Guinea coffee industry and, 10, 48–55
globalization: certification process vs., 240–44; circulation of commodities and, 21–26; commodity production and, 1–2; impact in Papua New Guinea of, 13–14, 21–26, 131–32; indigenous cultures and, 22–26; marketing and images in, 24–26; sustainable special coffee production and, 41–48
global price stabilization, 4
gold mining, 74, 265 n. 3
Goroka, Papua New Guinea: air transport system in, 135–40, 157–61; coffee industry in, 69–70, 85–90, 156–57, 237–38, 266

Leahy, James "Jim," 71, 78, 81–82, 173, 265 n. 3
Leahy, Michael ("Mick"), 71, 265 n. 3
"legibility" of Highlands land, 76–80
Leopold, E., 20
Leslie, Deborah, 19–20, 236
Lipset, David, 64
locations of consumption: Australian coffee shops, 225–29; British coffee shops, 220–23; fantasy formation and, 212–36; German coffee shops, 223–25; as "third spaces," 239; U.S. coffee shops and, 229–36
Lufa district, 127–29, 141–45, 269 n. 5, 269 n. 7
Lukács, Georg, 251
Luxemburg, Rosa, 30

magical naturalism, 61
Maiburg, Steffen, 203–5, 211–12
Maimafu, Papua New Guinea: coffee production in, 6–8; colonial demarcation of, 77; cultural significance of coffee production in, 120–26; current coffee production in, 109–12; growers, buyers, and exporters in, 136–40, 144–45; middlemen in, 131–32; modernization in, 11–13; Seventh-Day Adventists in, 101–4, 269 n. 9; social networks in, 12; suspicion of certification standards in, 146–52; wages for coffee growers in, 16–17
Malkki, Liisa, 60–61
Mandated Territory of New Guinea, 73–75
Mankekar, Purnima, 234–36
Manuell, Naomi, 178–80
marketing: by coffee importers, 202–12; commodity fetishism and, 250–55; environmental sustainability as tool for, 240–44; fantasy formation and, 24–26, 56–59, 65–67, 218–19; generational stereotyping and, 34–38, 57–59; locations of consumption and, 213–36; narrative creation in, 39–41, 47–48; time and space compressed in, 249–51
marriage, 120–22
Marx, Karl, 18, 30, 241

Matton, Bruce, 184–87
Maxwell House, 4, 18; early market dominance of, 42–48; market share for, 45
McArthur, J. R., 77
media coverage, 148–52
medical emergencies, 135, 271 n. 6
Melanesian culture: expatriate and industry elite views of, 191–92; gender, knowledge, power, and change in, 112–14; globalization and, 22–26; growers, buyers, and exporters in, 140–45; Papua New Guinea coffee production and, 1–2; personhood in, 114–15
methyl bromide, 199
Mexico, 107–9
middlemen, 131–32, 242–44
mihi: coffee production vs., 120–26; ecological impact of, 106–9; as Gimi cultigen, 118–20, 126–29
millennials, 34–38, 229–36, 248, 275 n. 9, 276 nn. 10–12
Miller, Daniel, 56–57
mining, 98
Mintz, Sidney, 262 n. 37
miscarriages, 125–26
Mission Aviation Fellowship, 104, 132–40, 269 n. 6, 271 n. 3, 271 n. 6
modernity: coffee production as link to, 11–13, 111–12, 128–29; expatriates, industry elites, and, 188–92; racial issues in coffee industry and, 177–80; stereotypes of, 59–65
Monpi Coffee Company, 164
multiculturalism, 10–11
multiracialism, 10–11
Murphy, E. C., 52
Murray, George Hugh, 74

Nama Coffee Company, 164
Namdu, Madu, 183–84, 273 n. 10
narrated chronotope, 63–65
national identity: certification standards for coffee and, 148–52; coffee industry linked to, 12–13; social relations in coffee industry and, 141–45; in Zimbabwe, 274 n. 11

native coffee growers: ban in 1960s on, 85–86; certification standards and, 239–44; ownership and, 274 n. 13; Plantation Redistribution Scheme and, 89–90; postwar colonialism and, 76–85, 268 n. 24; stereotyping of, 175–80
native movements, 61
Native Plantations Ordinance, 74
Native Regulation Act of 1894, 74
Native Taxation Ordinance, 74
neoliberal capitalism: deregulation of coffee industry and, 46; embedded social relations and, 55–59; globalization and, 26–32; importers affected by, 212; market fetishization and, 244–48; Papua New Guinea coffee production and, 1–2; politics of, 65–67; poverty, culture, and, 252–55; specialty coffee market and, 56–59
Nestlé, 45, 278 n. 1
Neu Guinea Compagnie, 73–74
Neumann Kaffee Gruppe, 9, 203, 272 n. 3
New Guinea: colonial division of, 73–76; ecology and geography of, 105–7
New Guinea Coffee Agents Association, 85–87
New Guinea Company Ltd., 86
New Guinea Highlands Coffee Export, 164
Niugini Coffee Tea and Spice, 164, 272 n. 3
nongovernmental organizations (NGOs): global coffee deregulation and, 46–47, 264 n. 7; labeling and certification initiatives and, 52–55; Maimafu coffee growers' cooperation with, 110–12

On-ko, 45
organic coffee: certification for, 145–52, 243–44; labeling as marketing tool for, 50; marketing of, 39–41, 228–29; market share of, 278 n. 2; millennials' knowledge of, 231–36; voluntary regulation and, 49
origin marketing: in Australian coffee shops, 227–28; fantasy formation and, 220–36; importers' use of, 211–12
Orokaiva culture, 177–80
Ortner, Sherry B., 57–58

overproduction, 204–5
ownership, 274 n. 13

pacification, 75–80
Pacific Trading Company, 164
packaging, 251–52
Papua and New Guinea Union Party (Pangu Pati), 95
Papua New Guinea: as British Commonwealth member, 73–74; certification standards in, 145–52; chronotopic fantasies concerning, 64–65; coffee production in, 1–2, 5, 9–10, 33, 69–100, 109–12, 258 n. 10, 260 n. 22; development linked to coffee industry in, 21–26; duelling images of, 13, 15, 259 n. 15; economic reliance on coffee industry in, 7, 259 n. 17; economic statistics for, 260 n. 20; ethical consumption and, 58–59; exodus of coffee value from, 16–18; expatriates and industry elites in, 180–92; fantasy narratives concerning, 65–67; geography of, 257 n. 1; German coffee traders in, 203–5; independence of, 88–89; linguistic diversity in, 6; marketing narrative for, 39–41, 264 n. 3; millennials' knowledge of, 230–31, 275 n. 9, 276 nn. 10–12; mining in, 98; stone age stereotype of, 59–65; Structural Adjustment Loan Project in, 45–46; as trust territory, 90–96
Papua New Guinea Coffee Exports, 164, 272 n. 3
Papua New Guinea Harbors Board, 198–99
Papua New Guinea Institute of Biological Research, 105
parchment (dried coffee berries), 9, 12; Maimafu methods for, 124–26; quality variations and, 142–45, 168–69
partnerships, 83–85
patrilineal extended family groups. See extended family groups
people-centered development, 58–59
performance methods, 51–55
personhood: coffee production and changing concepts of, 128–29; exchange rela-

Rainforest Alliance, 18
Rainforest Stewardship Council, 53–54
Raynolds, L. T., 52–53
Read, Kenneth, 159–61, 272 n. 1
regional identity, 141–45
Reimer, Suzanne, 19–20, 236
relational thinking, 223–25
reproductive horticultural labor, 117–20, 127–29, 270 n. 16, 270 n. 23
Research and Conservation Foundation of Papua New Guinea (RCF), 110–12, 152–53
Rio Tinto, 98
road construction, 79
roasting, 213–36
Rockefeller, Michael, 64
Roseberry, William, 47

Sahlins, Marshall, 22
Samaiza, 45
Sara Lee multiproduct group, 45
Savarti, Ravi and Anu, 189–92
second-party regulation, 49
Second World War: coffee rationing in, 42–43; Japanese occupation of New Guinea in, 71–73, 75–76, 266 n. 10
Seventh-Day Adventist Aviation (SDAA), 132–40
Seventh-Day Adventists, 101–4, 109, 132–40, 269 n. 8
shade-grown coffee: ecological impact of, 106–9; history of, 52; in Maimafu coffee groves, 110–12; Maimafu cultivation of, 122–26; species biodiversity and, 106–9; voluntary regulation and, 49
shipping companies, 198–99, 274 n. 13; in Hamburg, 202–12
"signature blend coffee," 225–29
Silent Generation, 34–38
Sinclair, James, 265 n. 2
single-origin coffee, 6, 259 n. 13; Gimi culture influenced by, 128–29; Papua New Guinea shaped by, 23–26; use-value in marketing of, 252
Smith, Neal, 241
social relations, 12; cash economy and social

obligations in, 111–12; certification standards and, 146–52; of coffee growers, buyers, and exporters, 131–32, 136–45; of consumers and coffee growers, 242–44; in distribution of coffee, 194–99; of expatriates and industry elites, 180–92; in Gimi culture, 117, 126–29; in Goroka coffee industry, 161–64, 238–39; of Goroka women coffee sorters, 169–73; postwar economy of Papua Highlands and, 79–80, 267 n. 11; in public space, 159–60; single-origin coffee production and, 23–26; specialty coffee industry and, 29–32; value of coffee in, 128–29
soil fertility, 108–9, 269 n. 3
Somare, Michael, 95
South America, 107, 264 n. 6
space, in coffee marketing, 249–52
Spark, Ceridwen, 179–80
specialty coffee: marketing of, 229–36, 242–44; millennials' knowledge of, 229–36; roasting of, 214–17; suspicion of certification standards for, 148–52
Specialty Coffee Association, 33–34, 239
Specialty Coffee Association of America (SCAA), 47–48, 229–30, 276 n. 11
specialty coffees: chronotopic fantasies and marketing of, 64–65; claimed ecological benefits of, 108; embedded social relations and, 55–59; emergence of, 4; historical evolution of, 41–48; labor costs and, 17–18; marketing narrative for, 39–41, 264 n. 3; neoliberal market deregulation and, 27–32; targeted marketing of, 47–48; technology improvements and, 264 n. 9
Starbucks: certification standards and, 150–52; generational appeal of, 37; labor costs of coffee from, 16; local shops vs., 219–20; voluntary regulation at, 49
Stasch, Rupert, 61–64, 265 n. 12
Steingarten, Jeffrey, 249
stereotyping: in Australian images of Papua New Guinea, 226–29; generational, 34–38, 57–59; importers' use of, 202–12; of indigenous peoples, 59–65, 92–96, 221–

Paige West is an associate professor in the Department of
Anthropology at Barnard College, Columbia University.

Library of Congress Cataloging-in-Publication Data
West, Paige, 1969–
From modern production to imagined primitive : the social
world of coffee from Papua New Guinea / Paige West.
p. cm.
Includes bibliographical references and index.
ISBN 978-0-8223-5136-8 (cloth : alk. paper)
ISBN 978-0-8223-5150-4 (pbk. : alk. paper)
1. Coffee industry—Papua New Guinea. 2. Coffee—
Social aspects—Papua New Guinea. I. Title.
HD9199.P252W47 2012
338.1'737309953—dc23   2011027663